DAPHNE INTO LAUREL

DAPHNE INTO LAUREL

Translations of classical poetry
from Chaucer to the present

Richard Stoneman

Duckworth

TO MY PARENTS, KEN AND NAN

First published in 1982 by
Gerald Duckworth & Co. Ltd.
The Old Piano Factory
43 Gloucester Crescent, London NW1

ISBN 0 7156 1646 3 (cased)

British Library Cataloguing in Publication Data

Daphne into laurel: translations of classical poetry
   from Chaucer to the present.
   1. Classical poetry – Translations into English
   2. English poetry – Translations from classical
      languages
   I. Stoneman, Richard
   881'.008   PA3622

ISBN 0-7156-1646-3

Photoset by E. B. Photosetting Ltd
Woodend Avenue, Speke, Liverpool
and printed in Great Britain by
Redwood Burn Limited, Trowbridge, Wiltshire

Contents

Preface

> Some hold translations not unlike to be
> The wrong side of a Turkey tapestry.
>
> James Howell (1594-1666).

I hope that the translations in this book will persuade readers of the untruth of this and similar assessments of translation as a literary form. To quote the doyen of modern translators, Ezra Pound,

> to have gathered from the air a live tradition,
> Or from a fine old eye the unconquered flame,
> This is not vanity.

The metamorphosis of a poet through the inspired craftsmanship of a poet in another language may assist the original to a longer permanence even as the touch of Apollo turned the nymph Daphne to undying laurel.

It has not been easy to select from the vast number of translations in English; even to identify the range is a task beyond the resource of any single bibliography, of any period. I am nevertheless confident that I have not omitted any poet of major importance in the history of translation, and I have certainly included some unimportant ones who deserved a place for one or another work. A few egregiously bad writers have honour of a kind, but I have avoided the merely representative and mediocre. I have used a generous interpretation of 'translation' which has allowed me to include some of the famous imitations, and must claim indulgence if anyone wishes to use this book to construe classical authors.

There are the inevitable inconsistencies of presentation. I have arranged the selections as far as possible in order of the first publication by their authors, so that writers of the same generation and hence working in the same tradition appear together; some whose works were published posthumously appear at the point where their translations seem to have been written. I have generally preserved original spellings, except in the case of one or two seventeenth-century authors already well known in modern editions. I have normalised i/j and u/v in sixteenth-century texts, and capitalisation throughout.

My interest in the English translators of classical poetry was first stimulated by a class held in Oxford in 1975 by Peter Levi and Nicholas Richardson. I have owed much to the advice and assistance of friends, particularly Joanna Martindale (now Parker).

This book is dedicated to my parents.

R.S.

Acknowledgments

Richard Aldington: copyright Mme C. Guillaume for Richard Aldington 1914. Robert Bridges: Oxford University Press. Basil Bunting: copyright Basil Bunting 1978; Oxford University Press. Robert Fitzgerald: copyright Robert Fitzgerald 1974; Doubleday & Co., Inc. A. E. Housman: the Society of Authors and Holt, Rinehart & Winston, Publishers. Ted Hughes: copyright Ted Hughes 1969; Olwyn Hughes. Christopher Logue: copyright Christopher Logue 1980; Jonathan Cape Ltd. Robert Lowell: copyright Robert Lowell 1967, 1968, 1969, 1970, 1973; Faber & Faber Ltd and Straus & Giroux, Inc. Louis MacNeice: Faber & Faber Ltd. Gilbert Murray: George Allen & Unwin Ltd. Ezra Pound: copyright Ezra Pound 1926, 1934; Faber & Faber Ltd and New Directions. Edwin Arlington Robinson: Macmillan Publishing Co., Inc. C. H. Sisson: Carcanet Press Ltd. Arthur Symons: H. F. Read. F. A. Wright: Routledge & Kegan Paul Ltd. W. B. Yeats: copyright Macmillan Publishing Co., Inc. 1928, renewed 1956 by Georgie Yeats; Macmillan Publishing Co., Inc., M. B. Yeats and Macmillan London Ltd.

Introduction

Why Translation?

Why an anthology of translations? Translation has never received much acclamation as an art form, though it has in most languages been the source of major works of art – Livius Andronicus' *Odyssey*, Chapman's and Pope's Homers, the Homer of J. H. Voss, Goethe's *Westöstliche Divan*. The prejudice is perhaps a modern one, paradoxical in a period when, as now, there may well be more translators engaged on the reproduction of literary works than ever before.

Writers in the seventeenth century would have sensed the justice of the judgment that translation is simply a branch of rhetoric,[1] one of the means at one's disposal for the assembly and organisation of material. It can be a source of inspiration where the poet's own language and literature is lacunose, or when his own genius sleeps (as it was for Cowper, Shelley and Robert Lowell). Even in the Romantic Age, Novalis called the translator 'the poet of poetry' – an odd expression but recognising that translation is a recreation of a literary original as art is the recreation of a natural original. There is no need to look down on the translator.[2] Ezra Pound[3] went so far as to say that every great age of literature is preceded by a great age of translation. Longinus[4] pictures the imitator as one inspired by the Pythia, or as a young wrestler meeting a champion. Dryden quotes the image in the Preface to *Troilus and Cressida*, and it illustrates nicely the idea that translation is an exercise admirably suited to giving sinew to a writer. But a translation is not a mere ancilla or training ground for a writer's independent creation; many major poets have devoted a substantial part of their energies to translation: if that is not often recognised, it is partly the fault of editors who omit translations from collected works. The

---

1. E. Jacobsen, *Translation a Traditional Craft* [Works listed in the bibliography are cited by author and title only].
2. The remarks of Nadezhda Mandelstam, *Hope Against Hope* (1970; 1975), p. 85, do not seem to be borne out by the history of English translation: 'The process of doing a translation is the exact opposite of work on original verse . . . and ordinary translation is a cold and calculated act of versification in which certain aspects of the writing of poetry are imitated. Strange to say, in translation there is no pre-existing entity waiting to be expressed . . . A real poet should beware of translation – it may only prevent the birth of real poetry.'
3. In 'Elizabethan Classicists', *Selected Essays* (1954), p. 232.
4. *De Sublimitate* 13.2-4.

meeting of two poetic minds can be at least as interesting as the outpourings of a single one.

Every age needs its translations: the question is, What kind of translations? How is the linguistic and cultural transference to be effected? The austere view is that of, for example, St Jerome, Du Bellay, Robert Frost: that translation is in a strict sense impossible.

> What is translation? on a platter
> A poet's pale and glaring head,
> A parrot's speech, a monkey's chatter,
> And profanation of the dead.[5]

But that has not prevented poets from making the attempt on a favourite author. If the 'subject' of translation consists only of 'praxis' and no theory,[6] it is in the study of particular translations that we shall best understand the issues at stake.

And why translations of classical authors? Apart from the Christian religion, the classics have been the single most constant factor in European culture – indeed, they go back further than Christianity. To follow the response of English writers to classical literature is in an important way to trace the development of English culture itself. Translation is just one aspect of that response; it will, therefore, seem interesting to observe the different forms of that response at different times.

To stress the importance of this tradition is not to adhere to the Eliotean notion of the Classic, already present in Matthew Arnold, as a single immutable source of goodness and right thinking, analogous for Eliot at least to the Established Church. A more historical view is to regard as a classic a work of such resonance, such 'superabundance of significance', that it has something to give every age. And after Petrarch placed his ideal world in classical antiquity, for many centuries men looked to that world for a source of stability and attitude in changing fortunes and manners, and found it. It is perhaps the surest refutation of Eliot's position to observe that *what* they found was rarely the same from age to age, or, often, from poet to poet.

Why do people translate poetry? Some do it as a service to their contemporaries. Ben Jonson translated Horace's *Ars Poetica* because he thought its subject matter worth the attention of less learned contemporaries. The same applies of course to translations of the Bible. At its lowest, this is the justification for the merest crib or enlivened literal translation, like those of Richmond Lattimore. Goethe,[7] curiously, put Luther's translation of the Bible in this category.

Secondly, a translation can be seen as a service to the original work – perhaps not a very different thing, except that it puts rather more responsibility on the translator not to traduce the tone of his original. 'It is not an impertinence to try to translate great masters. It is a tribute that one pays.'[8]

5. Vladimir Nabokov, *On Translating Eugene Onegin* in *Poems and Problems* (1970).
6. G. Steiner, *After Babel*, p. 272.
7. Preface to the *West-östliche Divan*.
8. C. H. Sisson in *In the Trojan Ditch* (1974), p. 159.

Brower's[9] interesting discussion of 'Seven *Agamemnons*' gives the golden apple to Louis MacNeice for producing an *Agamemnon* which is as far as possible in contemporary poetic idiom and thus does not set up barriers between author and reader. Aeschylus was modern to his contemporaries.

The third purpose is perhaps the most interesting, and can be described as 'service to *poetry*'. This includes the great translations which add something to the literature of their own language by extending its range to a mid-space between (or above?) the literature of that language and that of the original. It should perhaps be allowed to include the great unreadable translations, like Hölderlin's versions of Sophocles and Pindar, which the author certainly saw as an attempt to penetrate to an original form of expression lying behind both Greek and German.[10] It is an achievement that can only be expected of one who is a poet in his own right.

Allied to these three purposes of translation are different ways of translating. They have never been better summed up than by Dryden in the Preface to *Ovid's Epistles* (1680).[11] He distinguishes (i) *Metaphrase* or literal translation, and gives as an example Ben Jonson's *Ars Poetica*. One might add George Sandys' translation of Ovid's *Metamorphoses*. (ii) *Paraphrase* 'where the author is kept in view by the translator, so as never to be lost, but his words are not so strictly followed as his sense, and that too is admitted to be amplified, but not altered. Such is Mr Waller's translation of Vergil's fourth *Aeneid*'. (iii) *Imitation*, which elaborates on the sense and may vary from its original as the variations do from a theme, or may bring the original up to date by contemporary allusions. Dryden cites Cowley's Pindar.

The second type he elaborates on in the Preface to the *Second Miscellany*. Though he claims to have reconsidered the matter after reading the Earl of Roscommon's *Essay upon Translated Verse*, his position does not seem to have changed. He describes this freer translation as 'drawing after the life', and later says of the translator that 'he must properly understand his author's tongue, and absolutely command his own, so that to be a thorough translator, he must be a thorough poet. Neither is it enough to give his author's sense, in good English, in poetical expressions, and in musical numbers. For, though all these are exceeding difficult to perform, there yet remains an harder task; and 'tis a secret of which few translators have sufficiently thought. I have already hinted a word or two concerning it; that is, the maintaining the character of an author, which distinguishes him from all others, and makes him appear that individual poet whom you would interpret'. The demand is that a translation should make you feel, as H. A. Mason says of Chapman's Homer,[12] that the author would himself have written this way if he were living in the period of the translator.[13]

9. In R. A. Brower (ed.) *On Translation*.
10. Cf. G. Steiner, *After Babel*, pp. 316ff.
11. The discussions of Goethe and Schleiermacher add little refinement to Dryden's categories. The ramifications of the basic positions are excellently traced by Louis Kelly, *The True Interpreter*.
12. *To Homer through Pope*, pp. 146f.
13. 'Fidelity is not literalism ... Fidelity is ethical, but also ... economic ... The translator-interpreter creates a condition of significant exchange.' G. Steiner, *After Babel*, p. 302.

The border between 'paraphrase' and imitation is rarely easy to define. I would put Samuel Johnson's *The Vanity of Human Wishes* in the second category. The modernisation of names is a triviality. The compression or expansion of particular passages is legitimate under Dryden's criteria. What gives pause is the suspicion that the *tone* of Juvenal has given place to a Johnsonian solemnity and Christianity. But if a classical (or any) tradition is to mean anything, it is in its reinterpretations that it is important. Imitations of this kind therefore find a place in this anthology.

The imitation proper is perhaps best exemplified by Swift, who frequently uses a Horatian (for example) *topos* as a starting point, and then writes a poem of similar sentiment but of his own invention. Indeed this is true of most of the lyric poetry of the early seventeenth century, as it was of Augustan poetry in Rome. Here above all, when translations appear side by side with imitations (e.g. in the *Miscellanies*) we sense the force of translation as one source of poetical 'invention'. The poem of classical sentiment but original expression is the mirror-image of the 'Johnsonian' imitation, and like a mirror-image would not exist without such translation or imitation.

After Ezra Pound, we must add to these the category of 'creative translation', which is perhaps no more than the doctrine of imitation applied with more regard to the inconcinnities of the two epochs brought face to face. Pound stresses the unfamiliar in Propertius, where Swift adapted his world to the tones of Horace. It may seem perverse to take *Homage to Sextus Propertius* as an exemplar of the classical tradition – but it both demonstrates the difficulty of escape from classical literature and represents a part of the single most significant upheaval which re-directed modern poetry.

It is time to trace the historical fate of these different approaches to translation in the course of English literature.

Translation in England

Twentieth-century literary cant generally deprecates the suggestion of influence. But in fact the history of English literature could almost be written in terms of the influence of the classics – at least until 1750. From the beginnings of modern English literature with Chaucer people have been translating and theorising about translation. Though some of the earliest translations (Alfred, Aelfric) are of medieval Latin works, and the Elizabethans for example found an almost equally important source of inspiration in Italian literature, it does not seriously distort the picture to concentrate on translations from classical literature (regarded as ending with Claudian and Ausonius, though it is impossible to avoid admitting the later poets of the *Greek Anthology*, since that work was received as a single entity).

The beginnings

The first classical authors to affect English literature are Vergil and Ovid. Ovid stands as an important influence behind Chaucer's *Legend of Good Women*

(1380-6), though there is little that we can call translation extending beyond a
few lines. Much of the Ovidian material comes through the intermediacy of
Boccaccio and other Italian writers. William Caxton's is the first English
translation of the *Aeneid* (1490). It is however only an indirect translation,
being 'englisht from the French *livre des Eneydes*'. Gavin Douglas said of the
version that it and its original were 'no more like than the devil and St Austin'.
But even at this date the principle of fidelity was being enunciated by, for
example, John Lydgate in his *Pilgrimage of the Life of Man*:

> I wyl translate hyt sothly as I kan,
> After the lettre, in ordre effectually.
> Thogh I not folwe the wordes by and by,
> I schal not faille teuching the substance.[14]

Caxton's own aim was to present to the public a 'Booke as me semed sholde be
moche requysyte to noble men to see as wel for the eloquence as the
historyes'.[15]

The spread of knowledge of the classics coincided naturally enough with the
spread of printing, which was also seminal in the dissemination of knowledge
of the Bible. Nevertheless, until the Elizabethan period most translations were
of works of edification – religion, history, and especially law – made at the
request of private patrons.[16] From the belief that the information in classical
writers is worth having follows naturally the tendency to use their works as
models of excellence. The prevalence of translations from classical literature
coincides with the increase in printed popular literature – chapbooks and the
like – and numerous writers were, like Thomas Churchyarde and Timothe
Kendall, authors of chapbooks and almanacks as well as translations from the
classics. The classical tradition is at the centre of the movement of literary
popularisation and popular literature in the fifteenth century, which
culminates in the literature of Elizabethan England, perhaps the greatest age
of translation in our history.[17]

The Elizabethans: the spirit of the age

A mere list of the classical translations which have retained their status as vital
works of English literature is enough to astound. Besides the verse translators
whom I shall be discussing there are North's Plutarch, Adlington's Apuleius,
Greenaway's Tacitus and the numerous translations of Philemon Holland.
Translations from the French and Italian were equally abundant: Florio's
Montaigne, Hoby's Castiglione, Harington's *Orlando Furioso*. Hoby gives
reasons for the importance attached to translation:

> Therefore the translation of Latin or Greeke authours, doeth not onely not
> hinder learning, but it furthereth it, yea it is learning it self, and a great stay to
> youth, . . . and a vertuous exercise for the unlatined to come by learning, and to

14. See F. R. Amos, *Early Theories of Translation*.
15. Preface; easily accessible in the one-volume Twickenham edition of Pope, pp. 438-46.
16. H. S. Bennett, *English Books and Readers 1475-1557*.
17. See above n. 3.

fill their minds with the morall vertues, and their body with civill condicions, that they may bothe talke freely in all company, live uprightly though there were no lawes, and be in a readinesse against all kinde of worldlye chaunces that happen, whiche is the profit that cometh of Philosophy.[18]

None the less translation began earlier on the continent than in England. Thomas Nashe writes

> But lest in this declamatory vein I should condemn all and commend none, I will propound to your learned imitation those men of import that have laboured with credit in this laudable kind of translation. In the forefront of whom I cannot but place that aged father Erasmus, that investest [sic] most of our Greek writers in the robes of the ancient Romans; in whose traces Philip Melancthon, Sadolet, Plantine, and many reverent Germans insisting, have re-edified the ruins of our decayed libraries, and marvellously enriched the Latin tongue with the expense of their toil. Not long after, their emulation being transported into England, every private scholar, William Turner,[19] and who not, began to vaunt their smattering of Latin in English impressions.[20]

Notably popular classical authors were Plutarch, Cicero, Ovid, Seneca and Vergil,[21] though in many cases the number was exceeded by the quantities of translations of the same authors into French or Italian. The first English translation of a Greek tragedy was the *Iphigeneia at Aulis* of Lady Lumley (probably soon after 1549; first printed in 1909). George Gascoigne's *Jocasta* (produced 1566) is a translation of Euripides' *Phoenissae* only at several removes.

But who were the translators? Thomas Phaër's work was addressed to 'the nobilitie, gentlemen and ladies, that studie not Latine'. He further justifies his undertaking by pointing out that the scholars, best qualified for the task, are the most reluctant to undertake it.

> Knowynge, that of such, as have greater knowledge, to set forth things more exactlye, should heare my plainness not overmuche discommended; they then, should be more provoked, wyth hope of the mervaylous fame, that their doings should deserve if they listed, to employe some paines, in attempting the like. Of the whych, as I knowe there is a great number (in both universities inespecially) so I would wyshe, that eyther they ceasing any longer, too envie knowledge to our Englyshe tongue, would staine the same, with better: or else, that thay woulde not disdaine to forde their favourable wordes, to suche, as expresse their good will in the same: although not so well as it might be, yet as their eloquence will permit them.[22]

It is characteristic of nearly all the translators of the period that they are not university men – rather, many of them are associated with the Inns of Court.

---

18. From the Dedication to *The Courtier*.
19. Cambridge scholar, d. 1568.
20. From the Preface to Greene's *Menaphon*.
21. See appendix II in R. R. Bolgar, *The Classical Heritage and its Beneficiaries*.
22. Preface to the *Aeneid*.

This is true not only of the translators of Ovid's erotica – deliberately cocking a snook at middle-class society[23] – but of Timothe Kendall, George Turbervile, Phaër himself, and Richard Stanyhurst; Thomas Churchyarde was a soldier of fortune, Jasper Heywood left All Souls to become a Jesuit, Thomas Drant was archdeacon of Lewes. The march of humanism took place for a long time in England outside the universities.

Though the evidence for hostility to the translators is considerable, stemming apparently not only from the universities but from the church,[24] and though the translators are loud in their defences of their undertakings, one must not overestimate the attacks of other literate men on their contemporaries' translations. Thomas Nashe in *A Generall Censure* takes a line most inconsistent with the passage quoted above:

> It is daily apparent to our domesticall eyes that there is none so forward to publish their imperfections, either in the trade of glose or translations, as those that are more unlearned than ignorance and lesse conceiving than infants.[25]

The most noteworthy object of translation in the Elizabethan age, because the one who least retained his popularity in later times, is Seneca. Seneca is also interesting because his appeal seems to have been, like broadsides, primarily popular: classical literature was not only for Phaër's gentlemen and ladies. Seneca's influence on English literature coincides with the development of that great popular art form, the drama. It would be over simple to suggest that it was the reading of Seneca that gave Elizabethan drama its impetus – rather, the Elizabethans found in Seneca something that they, however misguidedly, felt was akin to their own dramatic aims, and adopted therewith other aspects of the drama as well. T. S. Eliot,[26] discussing the importance of Seneca in the development of the tragedy of blood, suggests that our picture of the bloodiness of Seneca is in fact partly determined by his Elizabethan followers, and lays more stress on Seneca's influence on the development of diction and of 'thought' – the Stoic moralising and pointed wit which can still be detected in Shakespeare.

Be that as it may, most of the translations in *Seneca his Tenne Tragedies* (1581) emphasise or exaggerate the bombastic elements of Seneca –

And threatning thunders thumping thick do bounce out all the day[27]

– or recreate them in the most grotesque style of Elizabethan diction. Aside from this misprision of the tone of much of Seneca, the translations are close, though the translators feel themselves free to expand their material in the choruses. Though they sometimes write genuine poetry, their importance is chiefly as a document of literary history; and the importance of Seneca declines, never to re-emerge, when the more classical style of Jonson becomes the dramatic norm.

23. John Carey, *The Ovidian Love Elegy in England*.
24. Well documented by C. H. Conley, *The First English Translators of the Classics*, pp. 86ff.
25. pp. 314f. in G. G. Smith, *Elizabethan Critical Essays*, vol. I.
26. 'Seneca in Elizabethan Drama' in *Selected Essays* (1932), 65-105.
27. John Studley, *Hercules Oetaeus*, act II.

The same cannot be said of the other Elizabethan translations. Arthur Golding's translation of Ovid's *Metamorphoses* (1565 and 1567) remains one of the English classics, and Ezra Pound went so far as to call it 'the most beautiful poem in English'. Despite the obvious shortcomings of the fourteener, it lends itself to the smooth swift narrative of Ovid in a way that makes it difficult to stop reading. Contemporaries[28] described his style as 'thondryng', which underplays the sweetness and charm of his language. The picture is often far from Ovidian – there are too many knights and dames – but the poem remained the standard Ovid until the literal version of George Sandys (1626), and is worthy to be mentioned beside Chapman's Homer.

Most other translations of the period – the Ovids of George Turbervile, Thomas Churchyarde, the Vergilian versions of Abraham Fleming and Thomas Phaër, Chapman's *Iliad* and Drant's Horace, are in the same metre. Iambic has yet to establish itself as the metre of English verse.[29]

Vergil's *Aeneid* is probably the single most often translated work in this early period. The version of Thomas Phaër (1558-1584) received this accolade from William Webbe:[30] 'There is not one book among the twelve which will not yield you most excellent pleasure in conferring the translation with the copy and marking the gallant grace which our English speech affordeth.' Read aloud, Phaër's *Aeneid* has a characteristic Elizabethan music.

A year earlier had appeared the version of the *Aeneid* in iambic pentameters by the Earl of Surrey (1557). Though this often derives directly from the version of Gavin Douglas it not surprisingly gained wider currency. T. S. Eliot argues that it was the coincidence of the influence of Senecan diction with the development of the iambic pentameter that determined the course of English literature thereafter. Certainly the fourteener was doomed; but that the iambic took time to become established is evident from the confidence and lack of conscious eccentricity with which Richard Stanyhurst produced his translation of Books 1-4 of the *Aeneid* in 1582, written in English quantitative hexameters. Fortunately Stanyhurst's translation is in all ways an aberration – though without it we should have been deprived of some of the most unintentionally comic passages of English verse, which met with considerable indignation from contemporaries such as Thomas Nashe, who called his style 'low and ludicrous'.

All that Stanyhurst says of his metrical innovation is

> Thee meaner clarks wyl suppose, my travail in these heroical verses too carrye no great difficultie, in that yt lay in my choise, too make what word I would short or long, having no English writer beefore mee in this kind of poetrye with whose square I should leavel my syllables . . . But as for thee general facilitiee, this much I dare warrant yoong beginners, that when they shal have some firme footing in this kind of Poetrie, which by a little payneful exercise may bee purchast, they shal find as easy a veyne in thee English, as in thee Latin verses, yee and much more easye than in the English rythmes.[31]

---

28. 'T.B.' in lines prefixed to Studley's version of Seneca's *Agamemnon*.
29. See in general D. Attridge, *Well-weighed Syllables: Elizabethan Verse in Classical Metres*.
30. In G. G. Smith, *Elizabethan Critical Essays* vol. 1, p. 262.
31. Too my Lord of Dunsanye; p. 5 in E. Arber's edition (1880).

Debate on the proper forms for verse remained lively for some years. Gabriel Harvey put more energy into his apologia for English hexameters:

> [Homer and Vergil] accompted [the hexameter] the onely gallant trompet of brave, and heroicall acts: and I wis, the English is nothing too good to imitat the Greeke, or Latine, or other eloquent languages, that know the hexameter, as the soveraigne of verses, and the high controuler of rimes. If I never deserve anye better remembrance, let mee rather be epitaphed, The Inventor of the English Hexameter; whom learned M. Stanihurst imitated in his Virgill; and excellent Sir Philip Sidney disdained not to follow in his *Arcadia*, and elsewhere: then be chronicled, the greene maister of the Blacke Arte: or the founder of ugly oathes; or the father of misbegotten unfortunates: or the scrivener of crossbiters: or as one of his own sectaries termed him, the patriarch of shifters.[32]

In an earlier letter to Harvey Spenser writes of the laws of English hexameters laid down by Sidney, and Dyer, and of those prescribed by Drant.[33] If it took time for English poetry to settle into the iambic, part of the reason was the desire to learn from the classics; the nineteenth and twentieth centuries have seen a resurgence of metrical experiments both in translation and in original works which recalls the Elizabethan ferment, though the reasons for it are different.

Common to all the writers of this period is a predilection for classical works that *tell a story*, the narrative being the mainstay of popular literature. The same is true of Chapman's Homer, one of the great neglected works of English literature.[34] Homer is one of the very few Greek authors to find English translators in this period – other Greek writers were scarcely translated until the mid-seventeenth century. Besides Chapman, the most noteworthy is the *Ten Bookes of the Iliades* by Arthur Hall (1581), though this version was made from the French of Salel and not from the original.

The move from fourteeners in Chapman's *Iliad* to pentameter couplets in his *Odyssey* signifies the final victory of the iambic pentameter in English verse. Chapman is also explicit in the preface to the *Seven Bookes of the Iliad* on the principles of his translation. He does not aim at a literal version, but at recreating Homer as he would have written had he been an Elizabethan.

> The worth of a skilfull and worthy translator is to observe the sentences, figures, and formes of speech proposed in his author, his true sense and height, and to adorne them with figures and formes of oration fitted to the originall in the same tongue to which they are translated.

Similar sentiments appear in the verse preface, *To the Reader*, and in his *A Censure of the Poets*:

> Were those poets at this day alive,
> To see their books, that with us thus survive,
> They'd think, having neglected them so long,
> They had been written in the English tongue.

32. *Correspondence of Spenser and Harvey* (ed. A. B. Grosart), vol. 1 (1884), p. 181f. (first printed 1592).
33. Ibid., pp. 7f. and 9f.
34. See e.g. G. Lord, *Homeric Renaissance: The Odyssey of George Chapman*.

The Elizabethans: new directions

While Ovid's narrative poems and Epistles were popular through the Middle Ages and into the Renaissance, the erotic works remained long under a cloud. Sir Thomas Elyot admitted that 'good sentences' could be found even in 'his most wanton books', but this attitude gave scope to no more than florilegia like Wynkyn de Worde's *The Floures of Ovide de arte with their englysshe afore them* (1513). Perhaps the turning point was Chapman's *Banquet of Sense* whose elaborate and ingenious discourse would have stimulated interest in Ovid. Professor John Carey[35] traces a number of MS translations after 1595: the first printed version of one of the erotic works is Marlowe's *Amores* (?1590). It is also the first Ovidian translation in iambic pentameters and marks the beginning of the seventeenth-century florescence in which translation and imitation are both part of the same movement to re-appropriate and absorb classical models in a distinctively English style.

But Marlowe's rugged style does not entirely preserve Ovid's effortless fluency – and the tone often becomes vulgarised, or, alternatively, idyllised, in Marlowe's hands. This is not merely misconstruction of the original, or failure of historical perspective, as with Golding's knights and dames or the Elizabethan adoption of Seneca as a fellow; it represents a new freedom of attitude in which the author is not there to be 'served' and made available, but is to be used to broaden and enliven the range of what the poets themselves wished to write about. Even those works which to us read like a translation, like Francis Beaumont's wooden *Remedia Amoris*, in fact often diverge in directions the author himself wished to expand.[36]

Similarly Leonard Digges in his translation of Claudian's *Rape of Proserpine* (1617) felt himself free to vary his original with conceits in a 'metaphysical' style: the 'Mariti illecebras' of l. 35 become

> Redde lips, faire eyes, sweet lookes, soft cherishing,
> Confus'd embraces, limbes proportioning,
> To their proportion all strange delight,
> Two soules combin'd in one, which makes one white.
> Like yvie (twining) yvorie necks, that one,
> One body, which one common breath alone,
> Gives life unto: this one, and yet not one
> For (lovers) each hath a companion . . .[37]

The tendency is particularly marked in Thomas Drant's version of Horace's *Satires, Epistles and Ars Poetica* (1566 and 1567). He writes in his Preface:

> I have interefered (to remove his obscenity and sometimes to better his matter) much of mine own devising. I have pieced his reason, eked and mended his similitudes, mollified his hardness, prolonged his cortall kind of speeches, changed and much altered his words, but not his sentence, or at least (I dare say) his purpose.

35. Op. cit. above in n. 23.
36. Ibid., pp. 296-300.
37. See S. Musgrove, *Critical and Literary Changes in the Seventeenth Century* . . ., p. 162.

The matter is acceptable and even seen as useful, but Horace clearly had much to learn from the Elizabethan translator (though certainly not in the matter of style!) The moral is seen through Christian spectacles and the style altered accordingly.

The same Christian tendency is noticeable in Sir John Beaumont's interesting selection of works to translate, which includes Vergil's fourth *Eclogue* (the Messianic *Eclogue*), and Persius' *Satire* 2, which asserts that the gods prefer humble reverence to ostentation of wealth. The occasional Christian echo creeps into Golding too. But as the seventeenth century progresses the Christian element becomes increasingly attenuated. Indeed, in Cavalier writers a conscious paganism of attitude appears, in reaction against the ethics of Puritanism. It is time to turn to this period.

The seventeenth century

The number of translations of the classics in this century is overwhelming. By the Restoration, translation was nothing short of a craze, and hardly anyone of literary pretensions altogether denied himself the pleasure of translating one or two passages of ancient authors.

The preponderance of authors remains Latin until the mid-century, when Greek works, particularly short lyric, epigram and Anacreontic make their appearance in the works of Philip Ayres, Thomas Stanley and Robert Herrick. Longer works find translators later on, in Sir Edward Sherburne, John Ogilby and Abraham Cowley. Shorter forms are in general more popular in the early part of the century, perhaps not only because they were simpler to translate and more akin to the tendency towards short forms in original compositions, but because they could more readily be adapted and welded into new 'imitations'. The influence of Horace was central for many of the poets of the period.[38]

Ben Jonson is of course foremost among the Horatians. An educated, even learned man, his purpose in his translation of the *Ars Poetica* was to make available to his contemporaries precepts he felt to be of lasting value. His translations are in the main closely literal, as is usually the case with those of a learned man. One thinks of his contemporary John Selden's assertion that translation should serve as a commentary on a work.[39] Though there is an element of popularisation in the attempt, the chief beneficiaries will be those to whom the work is already familiar. Samuel Johnson complained of the excessively knotty style of Jonson's *Ars Poetica*:

> This absurd labour of construing into rhyme was countenanced by Johnson [sic] in his version of Horace; and whether it be that more men have learning than genius, or that the endeavours of that time were more directed towards knowledge than delight, the accuracy of Johnson found more imitators than the elegance of Fairfax.[40]

38. See the detailed examination by Joanna Martindale, *The Response to Horace in the Seventeenth Century*.
39. *Table Talk* s.v. Books, Authors.
40. *Idler* 69.

Far from popular, too, is the subtlety and complexity with which Jonson and some of his followers used the Horatian ode to structure their own writing and perceptions. Elizabethan translation has given place to coterie poetry.

The adaptation and imitation of classical models by Stuart writers is well exemplified by Sir Richard Fanshawe, who besides his translations of Guarini's *Il Pastor Fido* and Camoens's *Lusiads* made versions of numerous poems of Horace and of the fourth book of the *Aeneid*; his Horatianism, according to the testimony of his wife, extended into all spheres of his life and not into his writing alone.[41] Fanshawe's *Aeneid* translation is written in Spenserian stanzas, which lend themselves well to the reflective side of Vergil but do not assist in onward-moving action. The Horatian versions are written like those of Ashmore in a 'timeless' idiom, but Horace's imagery is converted to the characteristic seventeenth-century style, so that the result is not a pastiche, but a genuine assimilation of a distinct sensibility to new demands. Ben Jonson is an exception to this tendency, as he frequently imitates the Horatian concrete metaphor which other writers tone down; a notable example is the conclusion to the ode *To Himself*:

> Make not thyself a page,
> To that strumpet the stage,
> 　But sing high and aloof,
> Safe from the wolf's black jaw, and the dull ass's hoof.

Where Jonson modelled himself on Horace, others found more amusement in recasting Horatian themes and reflections in new forms. One of the most charming is the version of Horace, *Odes* 1.9 in Francis Davison's *Poetical Miscellany*, which consciously re-locates the dialogue of Horace and Lydia in a contemporary setting:

> *Lover*: Though Cloe, be lesse fayre, she is more kinde,
> 　　　　Her graceful dauncing so doth please mine eye,
> 　　　　And through mine eares her voyce so charmes my minde
> 　　　　That so deare she may live Ile willing die.
> *Lady*: Though Crispus cannot sing my praise in verse,
> 　　　　I love him for his skill in tilting showne,
> 　　　　And graceful managing of coursiers fierce:
> 　　　　That his deare life to save, Ile lose mine owne.

Where a translation comes so near to an imitation, it becomes very clear what it means to say that translation is simply one means of rhetorical *inventio*. Throughout the seventeenth century we find scarcely any conception of translation as having a historical function.[42] To be sure, a number of writers point out the impossibility of producing a really accurate translation: Leonard Digges, in the preface to *Gerardo, the Unfortunate Spaniard* (1622), writes that 'translations (as sayes a witty Spaniard) are, in respect of their originals, like the knottie wrong-side of Arras-hangings', an image which gained some

---

41. See the memoirs of Lady Fanshawe in *The Memoirs of Ann Lady Fanshawe and Anne Lady Halkett* (ed. J. Loftis; Oxford 1979).
42. J. Sutherland, *English Literature of the Late Seventeenth Century* (Oxford 1969), pp. 409f.

currency in the period;[43] but the objection is to the distortion of style rather than of content. Andrew Marvell is even more severe in his 'To Dr Witty':

> He is translations thief that addeth more,
> As much as he that taketh from the store
> Of the first author.[44]

It is characteristic of what is sometimes called the mid-century revolution in translation that precisely this literal fidelity is not prized, is indeed eschewed so long as the sense is retained and made accessible. Sir John Denham is usually seen, along with Edmund Waller and Abraham Cowley, as leading and exemplifying this movement or tendency.

> That servile path thou nobly dost decline
> Of tracing word by word, and line by line.
> Those are the labour'd births of slavish brains,
> Not the effects of poetry, but pains;
> Cheap vulgar arts, whose narrowness affords
> No flight for thoughts, but poorly sticks at words.
> A new and nobler way thou dost pursue
> To make translations and translators too.
> They but preserve the ashes, thou the flame,
> True to his sense, but truer to his fame.
> Fording his current, where thou find'st it low
> Let'st in thine own to make it rise and flow;
> Wisely restoring whatsoever grace
> It lost by change of time, or tongues, or place.
>
> (Sir John Denham on Fanshawe's translation of
> Guarini's *Pastor Fido*)

Cowley can be seen as the inventor of the formal 'imitation'. His versions of a poet who, he claimed, could not be translated literally, set a fashion for scores of imitations of 'Pindaric' style, mostly unsuccessful, as well as freer renderings of other poets – especially Horace – in the new style. Cowley's versions of Pindar were designed to introduce an author new to contemporary readers – and whom Cowley himself only came to read through being marooned a while in a place where there were no other books to hand![45] In this his imitations differ from those of the Augustan writers whose aim was to play variations on an already familiar author. So it is no surprise to find that Cowley looks backward as well as forward across the century, in maintaining the serious moral view of Horace which in his younger contemporaries gives place to a view of Horace as a cheery songster. While Cowley's *Essays* and Cotton's poems are written in a philosophical-Epicurean tradition, Horace's odes

---

43. Cf. James Howell, *Familiar Letters* 1.6: 'Some hold translations not unlike to be / The wrong side of a Turkey tapestry.'
44. It is curious that this remark, uncharacteristic for the period, is to be found, with that cited in n. 43, in the *Oxford Dictionary of Quotations*. The choice seems to show the prejudices of the compiler rather than a prevailing attitude of the seventeenth century. (The lines by Howell are omitted from the third edition of the august work.)
45. See Sprat's Life of Cowley in J. E. Spingarn, *Critical Essays of the Seventeen.h Century*, p. 131.

become now little more than jumping-off points for variations on a theme[46] – an attitude more suited to the increasing blandness of poetic diction.

The most extreme example of a free translation is Cotton's *Scarronides, or, le Virgile travesty* (1664), itself a translation of a burlesque of the *Aeneid* by Paul Scarron (1648), an example of a genre popular in France at the time. The systematic lowering of style produces an effect that is not amusing but merely tedious:

> At last they saw one Ilioneus,
> A Trojan very ceremonious;
> A youth of very fine condition;
> A very pretty rhetorician;
> One that could write, and read; and had
> Been bred at free-school from a lad,
> Thrust up to Dido in good fashion,
> And thus begins his fine oration.

I will spare the reader the oration.

At the same time there was no shortage of literal translations. As Dryden remarks in the preface to *Sylvae* (1685), the aim of a translator will be different if he is to make a version of an entire work and if he is merely to render one part which attracts him. So Sandys' Ovid or Creech's Lucretius are rightly closer to their originals in sense than Dryden's selections. The former, indeed, aimed to translate Ovid in the same number of lines as the original – no easy feat, and one which accounts for the almost unintelligible compression which sometimes characterises his style.

A similar literalness mars Hobbes' versions of the *Iliad* and *Odyssey*, the amusement of his old age after the supposed failure of his philosophical and political works. He seems deliberately to have aimed at (for he certainly achieved) a bald, prosaic and frequently bathetic style.

It is no surprise in an age when so much energy was being expended on translation, to find comparable energies directed into theorising on translation. This is a phenomenon characteristic not only of England, and extending to theorising on language in general.[47] Though the English theorists avoided getting embroiled in the linguistic perplexities surrounding translation, their desire to establish some principles was timely and certainly contributed to the establishment of a standard classic poetic diction. Both developments are associated with Dryden.

Dryden's careful and still not superseded treatment of styles of translation has already been discussed. His purification and refinement of English poetic diction was not, any more than his remarks on translation, due to an academic approach to letters like that of the Academie Française; rather it represents the achievement of a craftsman building on the experience of a century's writing to construct a uniquely flexible instrument to convey what he had to say. This achievement was made easier by the firm limits to what he did have to say; but compared with the regular beat of Marlowe's couplets, or the irregular and

46. J. Martindale, op. cit. above in n. 38, pp. 380f.
47. G. Steiner, *After Babel*, pp. 236ff.

much enjambed stiffness of Sandys', the bite of Dryden's couplet is that of a precision instrument, ideally suited to satire. There is a loss too in this precision; it is easy to write epigrams and to construct antitheses, the development of which reaches its culmination in Pope and is largely responsible for the distance of Pope's *Iliad* from its original. But Dryden wields his verse with inimitable force; and his technical excellence is due to his concentration on forms where the manner of saying was at least as important as the content: satire and translation.[48] Dryden in his translation of Vergil had the advantage of numerous predecessors to steer him away from technical error; that his achievement was nevertheless much more than a technical one is clear from the time that elapsed before a new attempt was made to translate the *Aeneid*.[49]

William Walsh had commended the ancients[50] for the sincerity and integrity of the passions they portray, in contrast to the 'surprising and glittering, but not tender' thoughts of the moderns. John Oldmixon prefaced his translation of Anacreon[51] by saying 'You will find nothing in this little volume, but what was the real sentiments of my heart at the time I writ it'. So translation and imitation were justified not only as technical exercises but as the way to discover a truth of feeling known to the ancients and since lost. This veneration of the ancients, where the poets of the first half of the century had treated them as equals, is the central strand in literary aspiration and polemic for the next century.

It is Dryden and his epigoni who represent for us the flowering of verse translation from 1680 to the turn of the century. The successive volumes of *Miscellanies* are composed at least half of translations or imitations as against original poems – and most of the latter are thoroughly classical in mould though modern in setting.

At the same time there is a notable rise in the popularity of Ovid against Horace who had set the keynote for the previous two generations. The vitality of the erotic poems clearly appealed to the authors of Restoration comedy: a translation of Ovid's *Epistles* by Dryden and others appeared in 1680, of the *Amores* by Dryden, Sedley, Creech and others in 1719, of the *Ars Amatoria* by Dryden, Yalden (anonymously) and Congreve followed by the *Remedia Amoris* by Nahum Tate and the *Medicamina Faciei* (anonymous) in 1725. The narrative ease of the *Metamorphoses* also lent itself to the new-found fluidity of expression: Sir Samuel Garth's Ovid of 1717 was a compilation of translations largely from the *Miscellanies*, with some new material to complete the work.[52] The vigour of Juvenal found a new response in Dryden, where before there had been only the wooden Holyday. Lucretius comes into his own, after labouring, despite his attraction for men like Bacon, Hobbes and Temple, under the hostility of men of piety. The partial translation of John Evelyn and the unpublished one of

---

48. Cf. R. Trickett, *The Honest Muse*, pp. 148f.
49. See L. Proudfoot, *Dryden's Aeneid and its Seventeenth Century Predecessors*.
50. Preface to *Letters and Poems*, 1692.
51. *Poems* . . . (1696) A6v.
52. The translators include Dryden, Addison, Eusden, Tate, Gay, Pope, Congreve, Croxall, Harvey, Rowe and others.

Lucy Hutchinson are succeeded by the complete and competent one of Creech
and the superb selections by Dryden. Dryden himself was most prolific of
translations in the years following 1690, though some had already appeared in
the *Miscellanies* for 1684 and 1685.

This resurgence of translation against satire was one skirmish in the Battle
of the Books occasioned by the publication in 1690 of Sir William Temple's
Essay upon the Ancient and Modern Learning and Bentley's riposte in the *Epistles of
Phalaris* (1697). Swift, the protégé of Temple, has immortalised the picture of
the sour Bentley with his bucket of ordure spitting venom at the true, the
beautiful and the good. In fact of course right was on Bentley's side. But Swift
portrays every conceivable figure of the contemporary world – from Dryden to
Descartes, Paracelsus to Hobbes, Polydore Virgil to Harvey – as on the side of
the moderns, with the opposition consisting of the great ancients and their
allies Vossius and Temple, engaged in fearful conflict.

Rachel Trickett demonstrates[53] how the turn from satire to translation
represents a cautious retreat, in the face of this kind of attack, from the dangers
of a public poetry to a quietist antiquarian competence. But even the poets
were not safe, at least from the attacks of Matthew Prior in his *Satire on the
Modern Translators*, whose subtitle, 'Odi imitatores servum pecus', showed that
even devotion to the ancients was far from beyond censure.

In the end the conservative attitude triumphed. The ancients retained their
place of honour, while Bentley had to wait a century to find a scholarly
successor in Richard Porson. Imitation became the norm, though satire,
making a virtue of necessity, absorbed the form of imitation while turning it
again to contemporary uses. This is where Pope stands: a culmination and yet
a beginning – a return to satire but a satire based on sincerity more than
invective. The tone of Pope's satire is again that of Horace, where Dryden's
model had been Juvenal. The poets of the Augustan age represent a new,
'civilised' version of the classical world, where the division of ancient and
modern is irrelevant.

The Augustan Age

This Augustan poise was not achieved in one step. The Augustan age is the age
par excellence of the translation as exercise of wit or as commentary,[54] where
the learned world is congruent with the educated world, and a poet can rely on
his readers' knowledge of the work he imitates.[55] But this generalisation, while

53. Op. cit. above in n. 48.
54. Cf. R. A. Brower, op. cit. above in n. 9, especially the essay by Douglas Knight.
55. R. A. Brower, *Pope: the Poetry of Allusion* (Oxford 1959). Joseph Trapp writes in his preface to
    his translation of Vergil's *Aeneid*: 'A work of this nature is to be regarded in two different views;
    both as a poem, and as a translated poem. In the one, all persons of good sense, and a true taste
    of poetry, are judges of it; though they are skilled in no language, but their own. In the other,
    those only are so, who besides the qualification just mentioned, are familiarly acquainted with
    the original. And it may well admit of a question, to which of these two species of readers a good
    translation is the more agreeable entertainment. The unlearned are affected like those, who see
    the picture of one whose character they admire, but whose person they never saw: the learned,
    like those, who see the picture of one whom they love, and admire; and with whom they are
    intimately acquainted.'

true of the works of Pope's maturity, the Imitations of Horace, takes less than full cognisance of the twenty or thirty years preceding the appearance of those masterworks.

The work of Pope's youth is his Homer; and the Odyssey also engaged the talents of Elijah Fenton and William Broome. Some remarks in the Preface to the *Iliad* are revealing:

> When we read Homer, we ought to reflect that we are reading the most ancient author in the heathen world; and those who consider him in this light, will double their pleasure in the perusal of him. Let them think they are growing acquainted with nations and people that are now no more; that they are stepping almost three thousand years back into the remotest antiquity, and entertaining themselves with a clear and surpassing vision of things no where else to be found, one only true mirror of that ancient world.

The justification for his translation is partly historical; he puts himself in the camp of the Ancients, of Mme Dacier whose prose translation of the Iliad (translated into English, three years before the inception of Pope's *Iliad*, by Broome, Ozell and Oldisworth (1714)) had aimed to reproduce the ancient author for the benefit of modern readers.[56] Yet Mme Dacier received Pope's *Iliad* with sarcasm: 'un homme capable de corriger Homère, sera capable de former des hommes.' Mme Dacier's own *Iliad* was unavoidably coloured by a Christian moralism, yet she recognised one aspect of Pope's Homer which has been a stumbling block to many later readers: its distance in tone from its original. If Pope's historical aim made this difference opaque to him, Chateaubriand was equally blind to the distortions of Mme Dacier's *Iliad* when he wrote (what ought to have been true): 'S'il fut jamais un siècle propre à fournir des traducteurs d'Homère, c'était sans doute celui-là, où non seulement l'esprit et le goût, mais encore le coeur, étaient antiques et où les moeurs de l'âge ne s'altéraient point en passant par l'âme de leurs interprètes.'[57] Coleridge censured the language above all of Pope's Homer as 'the main source of our pseudo-poetic diction'.[58] This very distance is symptomatic of Pope's inability merely to translate or reproduce. His *Iliad* is a modern poem: its theodicy, as much as that of Chapman, is a contemporary one.[59] Homer is both the 'recorder of an historic world now gone, and . . . maker of a poetic world that endures'.[60] The extensive display of learning in Pope's notes is largely directed towards the problem of how best to reproduce the *poetic* effect of Homer. In this way Pope subtly by-passes the *querelle des anciens et modernes*, and it is from here an easy step to his achievement in the *Imitations* where ancient Rome and modern London converge. It is significant that it is on these two poets that Pope expended his talents, in contrast to the flurry of Ovid in preceding years which could never be more than picturesque or amusing. Only Johnson and perhaps Addison equalled this seriousness.

56. See K. Simonsuuri, *Homer's Original Genius.*
57. In *La Génie du Christianisme.*
58. *Biographia Literaria*, ch. 2 (p. 22, n. 1 in the Everyman edition).
59. See M. Mack, *The Poems of Alexander Pope*, vol. 7, pp. ccxiff.; and on Chapman, G. Lord, op. cit. above in n. 34.
60. Mack, op. cit. above in n. 59, p. 1.

The real achievement of Pope was however partly obscured for
contemporaries by the very assurance with which the two worlds are
assimilated. It is scarcely any longer recognised at this period that the ancient
world differs from the modern; it is distant in time but not in ethos; a
satisfaction with the contemporary polity induces the sense that the ancient
world really resembled it closely. Translation is unnecessary – everyone can
read the original; indeed, hints are taken from one society and applied directly
to another conceived to be similar to it.

This view is very apparent in *Translation: A Poem* (1753) by Thomas
Francklin, Professor of Greek at Cambridge, much of which is occupied with
denigration of the poets of the previous generation.

> O'er Tibur's swan the muses wept in vain
> And mourn'd their bard by cruel Dunster slain.
> By Ogilby and Trapp great Maro fell,
> And Homer dy'd by Chapman and Ozell (line 13 ff.).

(The imagery is still that of the battle of the books.) But he is full of praise for
the 'fire'

> Such as in Pope's extensive genius shone
> And made immortal Homer all our own (16 f.),

and goes on

> Why cou'd not Congreve Afer's charms revive
> Or tender Hammond bid Tibullus live?
> Plautus had pleas'd in Vanbrugh's looser page,
> And Otway shou'd have trod the Graecian stage (169 ff.).

These last lines make it clear that it is not merely a work of assimilation that
Francklin has in mind; he conceives of the modern authors as actually like
enough to the ancients to convey them without falsity. A good translation is a
matter only of literary skill; Ogilby and the rest fail through ineptitude and not
through dissimilarity of aims or *mores*.

The same attitude is apparent in Lady Mary Wortley Montagu's *Verses
address'd to the Imitator of Horace* –

> Whilst on one side we see how Horace thought;
> And on the other, how he never wrote:
> Who can believe, who view the bad and good,
> That the dull copi'st better understood
> That spirit, he pretends to imitate,
> Than heretofore that Greek he did translate

– verses whose malice springs from .dislike of the author more than from
understanding of his literary intentions.

Francklin himself went on to translate Sophocles into English verse –
another demonstration that the learned and literary worlds are scarcely
divided at this period. What culture gained, scholarship lost; if classical
studies stagnated until the new recognition of the *strangeness* of the ancient
world fostered by the expeditions of the Society of Dilettanti and the studies of

Winckelmann, the classical tradition was at its most consciously vigorous – consciously, because for the first time since the rediscovery of the classics real alternatives seemed to be present.

But the educated world was still steeped in the ancients; and the poets were not just poets, or men of leisure, but from diverse walks of life. Johnson, Pope and Addison were professional men of letters; but a number of translators were professors – Francklin, and Trapp, Dryden's first successor as translator of Vergil (1718), and first Professor of Poetry at Oxford (1708-1717); or priests – Philip Francis, the eighteenth century's best translator of Horace, of whom Johnson said, 'The lyrical part of Horace never can be perfectly translated; so much of the excellence is in the numbers and expression. Francis has done it the best. I'll take his, five out of six, against them all',[60a] and Pitt, who translated Vergil; William Hamilton of Bangour was caught up in the Rebellion of the '45, and his versions of classical authors are diverse: most interesting is his imitation of Horace, *Epistles* 1. 18, where he strays far from his model to convey some very individual attitudes and reflections through a predominantly Horatian persona.

In this civilised poetry Horace is normally the predominant figure; but Martial's raillery at this time achieves a real popularity. One of the finest versions of Martial is an anonymous one of 1695, which was swiftly followed by numerous others, not merely the execrable Elphinston of whom Burns wrote

> O thou whom Poetry abhors,
> Whom Prose has turned out of doors,
> Heard'st thou that groan – proceed no further,
> 'Twas laurell'd Martial roaring murther

which nevertheless acquired the status of the classic translation, but the excellent William Hay, who transposed Martial with one blow into contemporary London.

Mark Akenside is another bridge between ancient and modern.[61] Steeped in Greek learning, and portrayed in Smollett's *Peregrine Pickle* as forever quoting Greek authors, his attainments as a physician were considerable and he composed a Hymn to Science. However, his lectures to the Royal College of Physicians in 1757 were on the rather unlikely topic of 'The Revival of Learning'. It is perhaps just because he felt no real gulf between the two worlds that actual translation in his works is confined to a passage in the *Hymn to the Naiads*.

In the midst of this civilised literary world one should not forget those who aimed to earn their living by their pens; translation was the standard diet of the needy writer (Thomas Cooke, the translator of Hesiod, is the best example, as his Hesiod provided more or less his sole source of income). The professional side of translation is nicely illustrated by an anecdote in one of Pope's letters[62] about the publisher Lintott, who

60a. Boswell, *Life* (Oxford edition), 2.269.
61. See J. Buxton, *The Grecian Taste*.
62. To the earl of Burlington, November 1716: *Correspondence* 1.371-5; cited from the *Oxford Book of Literary Anecdotes* (1975), no. 94.

bargained with Sewell for a new version of Lucretius to publish against Tonson's; agreeing to pay the author so many shillings at his producing so many lines. He made a great progress in a very short time, and I gave it to the corrector to compare with the Latin; but he went directly to Creech's translation, and found it the same word for word, all but the first page. Now, what d'ye think I did? I arrested the translator for a cheat; nay, I stopped the corrector's pay too, upon this proof that he had made use of Creech instead of the original.

Besides the vigour and confidence that inspired these large numbers of translators, there were also the first signs of a real *lack* of assurance in the writing of poetry. If Coleridge could blame Pope for 'our pseudo-poetic diction', T.S. Eliot chastised Akenside and his congeners for their inability to write as they felt, or to perceive how they felt: they wrote indeed 'under the shadow of Milton'.[63] He might equally have quoted the ludicrous misprision of Miltonic style by Elijah Fenton in his 'The eleventh book of Homer's Odyssey . . . in Milton's style':

> Meantime I firm abode, till the dear shade
> Had sip'd the sacred purple; then her son
> Instant she knew, and, wailing, thus began:
>   'My son! how reach'd you these Tartarean bounds,
> Corporeal? Many a river interfus'd,
> And gulphs unvoyageable, from access
> Debar each living wight; besides th' expanse
> Of ocean wide to sail. Are you from Troy,
> With your associate peers, but now return'd,
> Erroneous, from your wife and kingdom still?'

Less extreme, but in the same vein, is the conscious and artificial sublimity of Trapp's Vergil, too flat in style to allow more than a brief and exceptional quotation:

> Dark to futurity, and blind in fate
> Are mortal minds; indocile to observe
> Due measure, when elated with success.
> A time will come, when Turnus from his soul
> Shall wish young Pallas by his hand untouch'd;
> And hate those spoils, and that victorious day.
>
> (from *Aeneid* 10)

The fashion for writing poetry was, perhaps for the first time in a hundred and fifty years, producing really inept poetry. The effect coincides with the decline of poetry as a social grace and its redirection as a vehicle for personal considerations and expression. But before the full onset of Romanticism came the vitally important years of neo-classicism or, as John Buxton has recently and sensibly re-termed it, 'The Grecian Taste'.[64]

63. T. S. Eliot, 'Johnson's *London* and *The vanity of Human Wishes*'; reprinted in the Penguin *History of English Literature* vol. 4, pp. 271-7.
64. Op. cit. above in n. 61.

Neo-classicism and Romanticism

The Augustans' confidence in their understanding of ancient society could hardly long survive the rediscoveries of Herculaneum in 1739, of Pompeii in 1748, and of the temples of Paestum, or the works of Winckelmann of the mid-century which re-located the vision of the classical ideal in Greece and not in Rome.[65] 'Between the age of Pericles and the age of George III the Society of Dilettanti constructed its own amateur bridge.'[66] In 1751 it sent the young antiquaries Stuart and Revett to survey and report on the antiquities of Athens. By 1810 Lord Elgin was busy removing the Parthenon sculptures to London, and before that date two translations of Pausanias' itinerary of Greece had already appeared.[67] The rediscovery of Greece was under way, the romantic Hellenism of Byron and of Chateaubriand, who never travelled without his copy of Homer, was imminent.

The effects of this second Renaissance were more marked in Germany, which had largely avoided a literary Renaissance of the kind experienced in France, England and Italy. The Lutheran tradition had contained poetry and staved off the influence of Latin and Greek, despite a modicum of translations into German, at least from Latin. Reuchlin to be sure also translated part of the *Iliad* (1495), but it was never printed. But now the influence of Winckelmann brought Germany rapidly to the forefront both in scholarship and in the appreciation and literary assimilation of Greek culture. In 1781 the translation of Homer by Johann Heinrich Voss made the *Iliad* and *Odyssey* into German classics too. Goethe's and Schiller's enthusiasm for classical culture needs no illustration, and we have already referred to Goethe's theories on translation.[68] Goethe's attitude to Homer recalls that of Pope fifty years earlier: 'We now no longer saw in the Homeric poems a description of an exaggerated and artificial heroic age, but the truthful picture of society as it existed in remote antiquity, and tried to realise it for ourselves.'[69]

Whereas in Germany the revived interest in classical antiquity rapidly led to the development of an extremely fine and exacting scholarship (so that the aim of reconstructing the ancient world was brought much closer through archaeology than it ever had been by the work of Pope), in England the borderline between scholarship and literary culture still remained unclear. The differences in these simultaneous developments are illuminating. Gilbert West, the first Englishman to produce a notable translation of any quantity of Pindar, prefaced his version of Pindar and other poems (1749) with a lengthy and exhaustive disquisition on the Olympic Games.

Alexander Tytler, Lord Woodhouselee, in his work *The Principles of Translation* (1791), the first comprehensive treatise on translation (but nevertheless containing little that adds to the observations of Dryden), cites a number of versions of rather obscure Greek authors – dramatists fragmentarily preserved by Athenaeus – by Cumberland, which must have

65. See e.g. E. M. Butler, *The Tyranny of Greece over Germany* (Cambridge 1935).
66. William Gaunt, *Victorian Olympus* (1952 and 1975) p. 11.
67. By Uvedale Price (1780) and by Thomas Taylor the Platonist (1794).
68. Above, n. 11. See also H. Trevelyan, *Goethe and the Greeks* (reissued Cambridge 1981).
69. *Dichtung und Wahrheit* Pt. 3, bk. 3 (1771-3).

been made in a primarily archaeological spirit, to make little known work
accessible. Other translations from the Greek include the first English
Aeschylus by Robert Potter (1777), and the same author's Euripides.

Besides this awakening interest in Greek we find an increasing predilection
for the light-hearted side of classical literature. The trend begins with Smart's
jaunty Horace of 1767, and is continued by Smart's friend Bonnell Thornton,
who translated Plautus (completed by Richard Warner) and by George
Colman who translated Terence. Thornton was a founder member of the
'Nonsense Club', as was a more significant writer, William Cowper, who
likewise produced translations of several humorous poems including two of
Horace's best satires and the pseudo-Vergilian *Moretum*, or *Salad*. But Cowper
went on to greater things with his Homer, the major Greek translation of his
generation. Though it labours under a fair overlay of Miltonic diction, it has as
much vigour and nobility as any of the major translations – a remarkable
achievement for a work which he undertook as anodyne when 'in such distress
of mind as was hardly supportable'.[70] It remains one of the most readable of
Homeric versions.

However, Greek still seems to have been relatively little taught in schools, so
that the effects of the rediscovery of Greece were slow.[71] '[Plato] certainly wants
patronage these days, when philosophy sleeps and classical literature seems
destined to participate in its repose', wrote Thomas Love Peacock in 1818.[72]
In scholarship Porson remained a lone luminary blazing a trail through Greek
drama in the 1790s and later – and at the same time remaining, as did
succeeding generations, resolutely textual in his concerns, where German
scholars like Boeckh and Welcker were already learning from Winckelmann to
consider evidence from history, archaeology and art to explain the texts.

The early works of the English Romantic poets show them still essentially in
the Augustan tradition. Wordsworth began an imitation of Juvenal – but also
translated the ancient Athenian revolutionary Harmodius-song; Byron
translated Catullus, and remodelled (for the last time for over a century) the
Ars Poetica to fit contemporary concerns. The break comes with Shelley and his
circle.

Shelley's awakening interest in the classics, especially Greek, is signalled by
his translations from the Homeric hymns, Euripides' *Cyclops*, and the laments
of Bion for Adonis and of Moschus for Bion, which were made during the years
1818-1822.[73] They thus span the composition of *Prometheus Unbound* (1820), a
work heavily classical in its inspiration, and finding in the Aeschylean
Prometheus a foreshadowing of the revolutionary fire of Shelley's own work;
and of *Adonais*, whose direct descent from Bion's Adonis is unmistakable:

> I mourn Adonis dead – loveliest Adonis –
> Dead, dead Adonis – and the loves lament

becomes

70. *Correspondence* (ed. T. Wright; 1904), 2.393-4.
71. R. M. Ogilvie, *Latin and Greek*, pp. 74ff.
72. *Works* 8.203.
73. *Poems* (ed. T. Hutchinson; Oxford 1905 etc.), p. 680n.

> I weep for Adonais – he is dead!
> O weep for Adonais! though our tears
> Thaw not the frost which binds so dear a head!

The word 'head' is itself borrowed from the diction of Greek tragedy (e.g. Sophocles, *Antigone* 1); and the second stanza goes back to the tradition of Theocritus' first *Idyll*, Vergil's tenth *Eclogue*, and Milton's *Lycidas*.

Shelley's own poetry is steeped in the classics. Like Plato in his condemnation of literature, Shelley regarded translation as an activity at a third remove from reality, and analogous to 'the distillation of a violet in a crucible',[74] and in his prose translations was clearly more interested in the matter than the manner. He translated the *Symposium* of Plato because he found what it had to say of importance. His verse translations were composed, like Cowper's, as anodyne when he was unable to work at original poetry. At the same time, one is reminded of Keats' 'negative capability' by Shelley's chamaeleon-like skill at casting his talent in a new mould.

Once again the progressive and the classical act in concert. There is however nothing in English poetry of the period quite so startling as the Sophoclean and Pindaric versions of Friedrich Hölderlin. Hölderlin's versions represent a quite different conception of what a translation should be: they are deliberately as strange as possible, preserving Greek word order and full of mannered diction, the intention being to produce a virtual interlinear crib which at the same time has aesthetic status *because* it brings the reader (or hearer) directly, as far as is possible, in contact with the original work. The force of Hölderlin's writing is undeniable – and he has produced the only poetry in any language that succeeds in imitating Pindar[75] – but the recipe is a risky one. Though Walter Benjamin valued it highly, perhaps as a result of his own tendency to antiquarianism, English poets avoided these extremes of diction in favour of a more approachable, and, at this period, even colloquial style.

The age of neo-classicism can be identified with the floruits of Flaxman (who illustrated Potter's Aeschylus as well as Pope's Homer), of Akenside and Shelley. The last years of the period see the later works of Byron, by now far from the classical tradition, of his friends Thomas Moore and William Gifford, of Walter Savage Landor, John Hookham Frere and Thomas Campbell. It has been suggested[76] that the growing strength of Utilitarianism[77] did much, paradoxically, to foster the spirit of aestheticist withdrawal that characterises the works of Moore and Campbell. Landor too devoted much of his literary energy to the creation of an imaginary and highly idealised classical past. At the same time the poets of the period continue to make much of the comic works of ancient literature. This is particularly true of Frere's vivacious versions of Aristophanes, but humour is also a predominant characteristic of the poems of Moore and Landor as it was of Byron. Shelley extracted the full humour from the Homeric *Hymn to Hermes*, and Leigh Hunt's

74. In this paragraph I am much indebted to T. Webb, *The Violet in the Crucible.*
75. See in general M. B. Benn, *Hölderlin and Pindar* (The Hague 1962).
76. By R. G. Cox, in the Penguin *History of English Literature*, vol. 6, p. 199.
77. Jeremy Bentham's *Introduction to the Principles of Morals and Legislation* appeared in 1789.

versions of Theocritus 15, 'Vergil's' *Copa* and numerous epigrams show a rich
sense of the wit and humour of his authors. Gifford belongs perhaps to an
earlier age: his muscular translation of Juvenal has more of the spirit of the
Restoration than of the Regency. (Two other younger friends of Byron,
Hobhouse and Hodgson, also turned their hands to translating Juvenal.)[78]

1820 to 1919

Classical education and scholarship were slow to catch up with the lead given
by Porson and the archaeologists. Seminal for the nineteenth century is the
figure of Thomas Arnold, who already as an undergraduate in 1812[79] found
more in the prose of Plato and Thucydides than in classical poetry, and by the
mid-century had established a system of classical education which was
flourishing far more widely than in Rugby alone. The concentration on prose
writers meant that classical literature was seen as a preparation for public life
rather than a discipline of letters and of correctness of expression. John Keble,
in his prize essay *On Translation from Dead Languages*,[80] finds the justification of
translation chiefly in its *moral* benefit, to author and reader, though he also
admits the advantages for the perfection of one's own literary style.

Scholarship however remained philological – which had always been the
English forte – so that there was little interplay between the worlds of
scholarship and of education, of exactitude and of action. This is in sharp
contrast with the situation in Germany, where the great generation of Wolf,
Hermann and Welcker had put the understanding of the ancient world on a
new footing by the application of knowledge drawn from archaeology as well
as philology, and where links between scholars and public figures were direct.
Welcker corresponded all his life with Wilhelm von Humboldt, who besides
his public career and his linguistic scholarship translated Aeschylus and
Pindar. Perhaps in England only Gladstone corresponds to such a Ciceronian
model of the man of action as well as of letters.

Despite the rise of the novel, which took literary activity ever further away
from classical models, the spell of the ancients remained strong, for better or
worse, over the majority of poets. It is very noticeable that the greatest upsurge
in translation in the nineteenth century was in tragedy. Before 1822 there was
one translation of Aeschylus (Potter's); between 1822 and 1900 there were
sixty; there were 121 versions of Euripides in the course of the century. At the
same time there was a renewed enthusiasm for metrical experiment, such as
had not been seen since the days of Elizabeth.

Landor had already commented on the predilection of his contemporaries
for unusual metres:

> Porson was askt what he thought of hexameters written in English:
> 'Show me,' he said, 'any five in continuance true to the metre,
> Five where a dactyl has felt no long syllable punch'd thro' his midrif,

78. Leslie Marchand, *Byron: A Portrait* (1971), p. 47.
79. Ogilvie, op. cit. above in n. 53, p. 98.
80. *Oxford English Prize Essays* (Oxford 1830), 3.33.

Where not a trochee or pyrrhic has stood on one leg at the entrance
Like a grey fatherly crane keeping watch on the marsh at Cayster.
Zounds! how they hop, skip, and jump! Old Homer, uplifting his eyebrows,
Cries to the somnolent gods . . . 'O ye blessed who dwell on Olympos!
What have I done in old-age? have I ever complain'd of my blindness?
Ye in your wisdom may deem that a poet sings only the better
(Some little birds do) for *that*; but why are my ears to be batter'd
Flat to my head as a mole's or a fish's, if fishes have any?
Why do barbarians rush with a fury so headstrong against me?
Have they no poet at home they can safely and readily waylay?' . . .

Tennyson was vigorous in metrical experiment; Conington's *Aeneid* was in octosyllables, and Sir John Herschel's *Iliad* (1866) in hexameters; less happy experiments were those of Francis Newman, and of William Morris in his *Odyssey*.

Except in tragedy, we have to wait until the 1860s to see the flowering of Victorian translation. Matthew Arnold's lectures on translating Homer were delivered in 1861 (their target, Newman's *Iliad*, had appeared in 1856). In 1862 C. S. Calverley published his *Poems and Translations*, Plumptre's *Aeschylus* appeared in 1863, the Earl of Derby's *Iliad* in 1864. In 1865 Swinburne published his first classical drama, *Atalanta in Calydon*, and Conington's versions of Horace, Vergil and Homer appeared at intervals through the decade, provoking the ire of Mark Pattison who regarded translation as 'the laziest of all occupations with the classics'.[81] (What a contrast with the views of previous generations!) These years see too the floruit of the Victorian classicist painters G. F. Watts and Frederic Leighton.[82]

The lack of direction, uncertainty of touch and inadequacy of technique that ensued on the decline of Augustan standards and the turn to literature for its matter more than its manner, are very apparent in the grotesque productions of Francis Newman, as well as of William Sewell in the 1850s. Newman's comment on Horace's third Epode shows his inability to appreciate Horace: 'The terse diction and clever bombast of this piece may suggest, that if Horace had not been too lazy to execute his Satires in the same style, he might have produced a work far more truly classical than they.' Classicism is confused with mere panache and tidiness, and is denied to those works that above all had embodied the classical ideal of the previous century. Lionel Trilling[83] writes of Newman 'the style of Homer, simple, noble, centric and sane, stands as condemnation of the eccentric, verbose, petty mind of Newman, a liberal catchall for the catchwords of his day, the very type of the vices of contemporary thought.' Matthew Arnold himself is unwittingly symptomatic of the change. His requirements of a translator are rapidity, plainness, directness – quite unexceptionable – but in his fourth requirement he gives the game away. He demands nobility. Demanding nobility is like pursuing happiness or culture, an aim that Arnold, like Aristotle, believed it was

---

81. Mark Pattison, *Memoirs*, p. 251.
82. See William Gaunt, op. cit. above in n. 66.
83. Lionel Trilling, *Matthew Arnold* (2nd ed.; 1949), p. 178.

possible to pursue directly.[84] Pope would have recognised perhaps more readily that nobility is god-given in the soul, all men can offer is a technique. Where the eighteenth century had demanded correctness of diction, Arnold goes further and demands 'correctness' of soul. Instead of sincerity he requires authenticity,[85] and the search is doomed. The loss of 'sincerity', in Trilling's sense, surely has to do with the social upheavals of the French and Industrial Revolutions, after which men no longer had an allotted or inherited position in society, and the story of later thought is the search for the Utopia of culture.[86]

But if Arnold's tempting visions were doomed to remain at the end of the rainbow, his sure and articulate sense of literary style communicated itself, and set the tone, no doubt indirectly, for the translations of the 1860s – all characterised by considerable metrical competence, a desire to represent their authors honestly, without slavishness or travesty, and helped in this by an increased understanding of ancient Greek thought. Swinburne's classical dramas could sometimes be mistaken for translations, so convincingly ancient Greek are the thoughts they purvey, often through careful scholarship:

> [Phaedra to Hippolytus] Death is not like thee,
> Albeit men hold him worst of all the gods.
> For of all gods Death only loves not gifts,[87]
> Nor with burnt-offering nor blood-sacrifice
> Shalt thou do aught to get the grace of him . . .

Particularly notable is the new popularity of Theocritus in this century, which produced two fine versions – the partial one of Leigh Hunt and the complete one of C. S. Calverley. Tennyson was a great admirer of Theocritus and wrote of *Idyll* 13. 58-60,

> τρὶς μὲν ῞Υλαν ἄυσεν, ὅσον βαθὺς ἤρυγε λαιμός·
> τρὶς δ' ἄρ' ὁ παῖς ὑπάκουσεν, ἀραιὰ δ' ἵκετο φωνά
> ἐξ ὕδατος, παρεὼν δὲ μάλα σχεδὸν εἴδετο πόρρω

> [And thrice called 'Hylas' – ne'er came lustier roar
> From that deep chest. Thrice Hylas heard and tried
> To answer, but in tones you scarce might hear;
> The water made them distant though so near.]

'I should be glad to die if I had written anything equal to this.'[88] Calverley's version here hardly reproduces the music Tennyson found in the lines.

Some fine translations continued to appear through the 1870s – among them William Morris's *Aeneid* (1875), Browning's *Agamemnon* (1877) – and subsequently. The intimacy with classical authors of the eighteenth century has given place to a deliberate attempt at strangeness – either to reproduce the

---

84. Apparent in *Culture and Anarchy*, passim.
85. The opposition is that of Lionel Trilling, *Sincerity and Authenticity* (Oxford 1971).
86. Cf. Raymond Williams, *Culture and Society* (1958).
87. Aeschylus fr. *Niobe monos theōn gar thanatos ou dōrōn erā.* (Swinburne's note).
88. F. T. Palgrave, *Memoir*, vol. 2, p. 495.

Aeschylean strangeness, in Browning's case, or to recreate Vergil in terms of Pre-Raphaelite pseudo-medievalism (Morris). Another indication of the failure of touch. 'Browning was never more himself than when he was most trying to be Greek';[89] and it adds a dimension to Housman's deathless *Fragment of a Greek Tragedy* to realise how closely much of its diction resembles that of Browning's *Agamemnon*, which contains lines like

> Not well of thy midriff the rudder directing,

and sometimes actually borrows phrases directly from Browning. The direction taken by Morris was perhaps more disastrous; the work of his old age, the translation of the *Odyssey*, begins like this:

> Tell me, O Muse, of the Shifty, the man who wandered afar,
> After the Holy Burg, Troy-town, he had wasted with war . . .

As the 1890s merge into the Edwardian age, the impression does not diminish that

> Things fall apart; the centre cannot hold;
> Mere anarchy is loosed upon the world

of classical translation as well as all the rest. Homer may have been a continuing inspiration to young men as they went to be killed in Belgium[90] –

> Was it so hard, Achilles,
> So very hard to die?
> Thou knowest and I know not –
> So much the happier I . . .
>
> I will go back this morning
> From Imbros over the sea.
> Stand in the trench, Achilles,
> Flame-capped and shout for me[91]

– but the tendency was more to light Horace and versions of the *Ars Amatoria*. A noble exception was Gilbert Murray's translation of nearly the whole of Greek drama, translations which were astonishingly popular; but T. S. Eliot's strictures of 1920 can hardly be refuted (though one may disagree with his remedies):

> The Classics have, during the later part of the nineteenth century and up to the present moment, lost their place as a pillar of the social and political system – such as the Established Church still is. If they are to survive, to justify themselves as literature, as an element in the European Mind, as the foundation for the literature we hope to create, they are very badly in need of persons capable of expounding them. We need someone – not a member of the Church of Rome, and perhaps preferably not a member of the Church of England – to explain how vital a matter it is, if Aristotle may be said to have been a moral pilot of Europe, whether we shall or shall not drop that pilot. And we need a number of educated

89. R. A. Brower, *Seven Agamemnons* in op. cit. above in n. 9.
90. Ogilvie, op. cit. above in n. 71, p. 54.
91. Patrick Shaw-Stewart on the flyleaf of his copy of *A Shropshire Lad*.

poets who shall at least have opinions about Greek drama, and whether it is or is not of any use to us. And it must be said that Professor Gilbert Murray is not the man for this. Greek poetry will never have the slightest vitalising effect upon English poetry if it can only appear masquerading as a vulgar debasement of the eminently personal idiom of Swinburne. These are strong words to use against the most popular Hellenist of his time; but we must witness of Professor Murray ere we die that these things are not otherwise but thus.[92]

In the circumstances it is remarkable that T. S. Eliot never translated a line of classical poetry. And it is perhaps doubtful whether his austere vision of *What is a Classic?* (answer: Vergil) is or ever was adequate. No more satisfactory is the argument of Kermode[93] that we do not ask a classic to speak to us: we learn to listen to it. For there has to be a reason, when the study of the classics is no longer socially determined, why we should listen to these writers rather than to others. The answer has to be found in the material the work has to offer. The most convincing argument from translations of classic works is that offered by Schleiermacher:[94] the classic retains its own identity, but at the same time provides a superabundance of significance which is transmuted by the successful poet/translator so that the work becomes new as well. The jargon is rebarbative, but the importance laid on the merit of the translator sound. And in 1917, on the ruins of the old world, there appeared a translation of a classical author which took the opportunity offered by the dissociation of the classic from the Establishment, and gave the possibility of a new life to classical literature in an alien age.

Ezra Pound and after

In 1917 Ezra Pound published the *Homage to Sextus Propertius*. The reaction was immediate and violent.[95] Classical scholars were outraged at Pound's mistranslations and misunderstandings. Pound was ever cavalier in his treatment of material, but some of his howlers cannot have been other than tongue in cheek: not only the 'frigidaire patent' but the 'Welsh mines' too.[96] Pound was not trying to provide a version or crib of Propertius. Particularly revealing is a comparison of his two versions of Propertius 2.28c:

> Here let thy clemency, Persephone, hold firm . . .'
>
> (*Personae*)

and

> Persephone and Dis, Dis, have mercy upon her,
> There are enough women in hell . . .'
>
> (*Homage*)

92. 'Euripides and Professor Murray', *Selected Essays* (1932), pp. 60-1.
93. Frank Kermode, *The Classic* (1975), p. 43.
94. 'Methoden des übersetzens', *Werke* 3.2 (Berlin 1838), 207-45; e.g. in W. Störig, *Problem des Übersetzens*, pp. 38-70.
95. See J. P. Sullivan, *Ezra Pound and Sextus Propertius*.
96. 'Homage' 1 and 5 respectively. Cf. Gilbert Highet's parody of Pound, reproduced in *Parodies* (ed. D. Macdonald; 1960), pp. 227-9.

the first in a tone of fin de siècle melancholy, the second forceful, demanding attention to detail, and full of dry humour. *Homage to Sextus Propertius* brings us face to face with a more real poet than that of Pound's first translation, or that of Grainger (1759) or Elton (1895), or of any literal version. But Propertius lived long ago in a different world. Humour is the first thing to get overlaid in the geological layers of unfamiliarity. Pound has restored a character to Propertius, and resurrected him as a twentieth-century poet. The classic lived again, and yet it became new. This had always been the ideal characteristic of a translation – but how much easier for Sir John Denham or even Alexander Pope or Jasper Heywood, all able to rely on the familiar poetic style of their day as a cultural norm. In Pound's case the achievement is the greater as he, to a large extent alone, created the typical diction and verse forms of much twentieth-century poetry. The poetry of the Anglo-Saxon world is still a movement of fragments, but the unity it has results from the innovative diction of Pound. 'Pound freed us from the inert Arnoldian conception of a classic.'[97]

Of the followers of Pound it is difficult to say much – they have not acquired the rust of age, which, as Horace ironically observed, is what gives a writer a claim to respect based on endurance.

Pound wrote

> The thought of what America would be like
> If the classics had a wide circulation
> Troubles my sleep.

There is now a journal in America which is dedicated to the study of classical literature as a humanist pursuit: *Arion*. Conscious and conscientious humanism does little for scholarship, but it provides a platform where poets and others can air their translations of favourite authors. (Pindar has become particularly popular, no doubt in part because of the misconception that he has affinities with the Symbolist poets.)

In 1964 *Arion* ran a questionnaire, canvassing the views of thirty-four distinguished poets and scholars on the value of the classical tradition. The replies are worth reading. A keynote of all of them was the insistence that we do *not* need pedestrian verse translations by mere scholars, of the kind which make the nineteenth-century bibliographies so unwieldy, and most of which must be rejected as worthless.[98] W. H. Auden argued a need for cribs as well as re-creations; most contributors insisted that the most important thing was to write translations that are good poems.

'If we can get superb poems in modern language deriving from older poems in ancient languages – so much the better for us. What we do not want is bad writing (Lattimore) hiding behind efficiency in ancient languages,' wrote Christopher Logue. (Similar views came from Michael Benedikt and D. S. Carne-Ross.) This is far, we note, from the austere idea of the Classic to which we 'learn to listen'. With modern arrogance, it demands that the ancient poet fit himself to our needs, but in the best examples the characteristics of the

97. J. P. Sullivan, Ezra Pound as a Latin Translator', *Arion* 3 (1964), 3. 100-11.
98. John Conington omitted nearly all the nineteenth-century versions from his survey of translators of Vergil (*Quarterly Review* 110 (1961)').

original shine through. One might cite Robert Fitzgerald's *Homer*, in which the finest lines are often Fitzgerald's invention yet maintain a tone that seems entirely Homeric, or Ted Hughes's *Oedipus*, which by reducing syntax to a minimum transforms Seneca's rhetoric into twentieth-century surrealism and perhaps makes it easier to see what Seneca's first readers, or the Elizabethans, found in poetry that to us seems hopelessly overweight.

But besides that arrogance twentieth-century writers display a considerable receptivity and a quasi-anthropological readiness to understand other cultures, which manifests itself not only in the discipline of social anthropology but in the great range of translations now available from all literatures. In 1948 a yearly index of translations began to appear: the volumes run to 400 pages in 1948, to 1000 pages in 1971. This itself has made translation an attractive activity for poets, by no means confined to classics. One thinks of Pound himself, of Robert Lowell, Edwin Morgan, Paul Celan and any number of others. Several of the most important translations of this century have been in prose: E. V. Rieu's and T. E. Shaw's *Odysseys*, Robert Graves' *Golden Ass* — which is itself symptomatic of the relative status of verse in our time. The poetic translation has lost its centrality as a form.

C. H. Sisson describes the value of the exercise of translation for a poet in terms which recall T. S. Eliot's appreciation of Dryden's translations:

> as the inevitable facility comes, the conscious task becomes the rejection of whatever appears with the face of familiarity. The writing of poetry is, in a sense, the opposite of writing what one wants to write, and it is because of the embarrassing growth of the area of consciousness which writing, as indeed the other serious encounters of life, produces that one has recourse to the conscious manipulation of translation, as it were to distract one while the unwanted impulses free themselves under the provocation of another's thought.[99]

Translators in the twentieth century have been eclectic, but some trends are discernible. There is a predilection for the epigram or short elegy (Martial, Catullus, the Greek Anthology),[100] which of ancient forms corresponds most closely to the modern style of lyric poetry. Generally the poets in question are 'modernised', cast in the mould of the translator's contemporaries.

Again, the more violent works of ancient drama prove themselves popular. Wole Soyinka has adapted the *Bacchae*, Ted Hughes Seneca's *Oedipus*; in 1979 David Rudkin's *Hippolytus* was staged at Stratford, and the same year saw a television version of Aeschylus' *Oresteia*. And there are a number of major authors of whose work a significant part has been the production of excellent and interesting translations; I would select among these Louis MacNeice, Robert Lowell, Robert Fitzgerald, Robert Fagles, Christopher Logue, and Ted Hughes, besides the more functional translations of poets like Richmond Lattimore, C. Day Lewis, Patric Dickinson, Dudley Fitts and James Michie.

The business of classics is in recession, but translation goes on. Literature

99. C. H. Sisson in *In the Trojan Ditch* (1974), p. 13.
100. Translations by James Michie, C. H. Sisson, Frederic Raphael and Kenneth McLeish; Peter Jay, Robin Skelton, Kenneth Rexroth etc.

may be more important than scholarship; but with the discovery of papyri in the sands of Egypt, a greater quantity of ancient literature has been recovered in this century than at any time since the Renaissance. And if the translations currently appearing seem in any way to excel – Steiner regards this age as being as rich as that of Chapman and Turbervile, Surrey and Golding[101] – we may take comfort from the suggestion of Pound[102] that 'a great age of literature is perhaps always a great age of translation, or follows it', and await the work that, through its acquired skill in the art of imitation, will sum up and transform the world we live in, and be our own classic.

101. *Arion* 3 (1964) 4. 81ff.
102. See above, n. 3.

1. The Beginnings to Ben Jonson

GEOFFREY CHAUCER

(*c*. 1340-1400)

Chaucer's father was a merchant. Chaucer himself won the patronage of John of Gaunt, through which he entered the royal service and travelled to northern Italy. In 1382 he was appointed comptroller of customs; but in 1386 he was imprisoned in the Tower on account of his friendship with the Duke of Lancaster. In 1389, when the political situation eased, he was released, and the Canterbury Tales were published soon after. His other works are not securely dated; the *Legend of Good Women*, in which Ovidian and Italian influence is most apparent, may be from any time after 1369.

Though the main classical influence on Chaucer is Ovid, almost the only direct piece of translation to be found is that from Vergil's *Aeneid* below. Venus' clerke Ovyde was a figure reverenced in the Middle Ages second only to Vergil; the response of English poets to both was conditioned by the intermediaries of Boccaccio and Dante, both important influences on Chaucer. It is the heroic and rhetorical Ovid that moves the Ricardians, and gives the *Legend of Good Women* its structure: Chaucer seems not to have known the *Amores*, which were neglected if not frowned upon until the Elizabethan period.

Dido and Aeneas go hunting
(Vergil, *Aeneid* 4.129-50), from *The Legend of Good Women*

The dawenyng up-rist out of the se.
This amorous queene chargeth hire meyne
The nettes dresse, and speres brode and kene;
An huntyng wol this lusty freshe queene,
So priketh hire this newe joly wo.
To hors is al hir lusty folk ygo;
Into the court the houndes been ybrought;
And upon coursers, swift as any thought,
Hire yonge knyghtes hoven al aboute,
And of hire women ek an huge route.
Upon a thikke palfrey, paper-whit,
With sadel red, embrouded with delyt,
Of gold the barres up enbosede hye,

Sit Dido, al in gold and perre wrye;
And she as fair as is the bryghte morwe,
That heleth syke folk of nyghtes sorwe.
Upon a courser stertlynge as the fyr –
Men myghte turn him with a litel wyr –
Sit Eneas, lik Phebus to devyse,
So was he fressh arayed in his wyse.
The fomy brydel with the bit of gold
Governeth he, ryght as himself hath wold.
And forth this noble queen thus lat I ride
On huntynge, with this Troyan by hyre side.

GAVIN DOUGLAS

(*c.* 1474-1522)

Third son of the fifth earl of Angus, Douglas became Dean or Provost of St
Giles, Edinburgh, in 1501. Elevated to the See of Dunkeld in 1515, he was
imprisoned for a year on the charge of the unlicensed purchase of benefices at
Rome. The rest of his life was given up to ecclesiastical and secular politics.
The translation of the *Aeneid* appears to have been completed by 1513, and the
oldest MS dates from 1515; but the work was not published until 1553. Surrey,
who died in 1547, clearly knew Douglas' translation, as many passages of his
own are scarcely more than anglicisations of Douglas. His dialect and
orthography have proved a barrier, but the enthusiasm, if not the terms, of
Pound's encomium, indicate his merit: 'Better than the original, as Douglas
had heard the sea.'

(priest)

The death of Laocoon
(Vergil, *Aeneid* 2.199-229)

Betyd, the ilke tyde, a fer grettar woundir
And mair dreidful to catyvis be sik hunder,
Quhilk of Trojanys trublit mony onwarnyt breste.
As Laocon, that was Neptunys prest
And chosen by kavill onto that ilk office,
A fair gret bull offerit in sacrifyce
Solemnytly befor the haly alteir,
Throw the styl sey from Tenedos infeir,
Lo, twa gret lowpit edderis, with mony thraw,
Fast throu the flude towart the land gan draw.
My spreit abhorris this mater to declare:
Abufe the watir thar hals stude evermare,
With bludy crestis owtwith the wallis hie;
The remanent swam always under see,

With grysly bodeis linked mony fald;
The salt fame stowris from the fard thai hald.
Onto the grund thai glaid with glowand eyn
Stuffit ful of vennom, fyre and fellon teyn,
Wyth tongis quhislyng in that mowthis rede
Thai lyk the twynkland stangis in thar hed.
We fled away al bludeles for affeir,
Bot, wyth a braid, to Laocon infeir
Thai start atanys, and hys twa sonnys ying
First athir serpent lappyt lyke a ryng,
And, with thar cruell byt and stangis fell,
Of tendir membris tuke mony sary morcell.
Syne thai the prest invadit, baith twane,
Quhilk with hys wapynnys dyd hys byssy pane
His childryng forto helpen and reskew.
Bot thai about hym lowpit in wympillis threw
And twys cyrkyllit his myddil rownd about
And twys faldis that sprutlit skynnys but dowt
About his hals – bath nek and hede thai schent.
As he etlys thar hankis to have rent
Of with his handis, and thame away have draw,
Hys hed bendis and garlandis all war blaw
Ful of vennom and rank poyson atanys,
Quhilk infekkis the flesch, blude and banys.
And tharwith eik sa horribilly schowtis he,
His cryis dynnyt to the sternys on hie;
Lyke as a bull doith rummysing and rayr
Quhen he eschapis hurt from the altair,
And charris by the ax with his nek wight,
Gif on his forhed and dynt hyttis nocht rycht.
Syne thir twa serpentis hastely glaid away,
Onto the cheif tempil fled ar thai
Of stern Pallas to the hallowit place
And crap in under the feit of the goddes,
Hyd thame behynde the boys of hir bukleir.
Than trymlit thar mony stowt hart for feir,
The onkowth dreid into thar brestis crap.

The Death of Dido
(Vergil, *Aeneid* 4.688-705)

And scho agane, Dydo, the dedly queyn,
Pressyt fortil uplift hir hevy eyn,
Bot tharof falys; for the grysly wound
Deep in hir breist gapis wyde and onsound.
Thrys scho hir self raxit up to rys;
Thrys on hir elbok lenys; and als feill sys

Scho fallys bakwart in the bed agane.
With eyn rollyng, and twynkland up ful fane,
Assays scho to spy the hevynnys lyght,
Syne murmouris, quhen scho tharof gat a sycht.
Almychty Juno havand reuth, by this,
Of hir lang sorow and tarysum ded, I wys,
Hir mayd Irys from the hevyn hes send
The throwand sawle to lowys, and make ane end
Of al the juncturis and lethis of hir cors;
Becaus that nothir of fatis throu the fors
Nor yit by natural ded peryschit sche,
Bot fey in hasty furour emflambyt hie
Befor hir day had hir self spilt,
Or that Proserpyne the yallow haris gilt
From hir fortop byreft, or dubbyt hir hed
Onto the Stygian hellis flude of ded.
Tharfor dewy Iris throu the heavyn
With hir safron weyngis flaw ful evin,
Drawand, quhar scho went, forgane the son cleir,
A thousand cullouris of divers hewys seir,
And abufe Dydoys hed arest kan:
'I am commandyt,' said scho, 'and I man
Omdo this hayr, to Pluto consecrate,
And lowis this sawle out of this mortale stait.'
Thys sayand, with rycht hand hes scho hynt
The hair, and cuttis in twa, or that scho stynt;
And tharwithall the natural heyt outquent,
And, with a puft of aynd, the lyfe furthwent.

SIR THOMAS ELYOT

(*c*. 1490-1546)

Elyot commended translations of Ovid, despite the author's frivolity, on grounds of the 'good sentences' contained therein. His choice of this passage of Claudian is determined by its moral and civic appropriateness. It appears in the chapter of *The Governor* 'What things he that is elected or appointed to be a governor of a public weal ought to premeditate'. Of the lines Elyot writes that they are 'full of excellent wisdom . . . unto whose eloquence no translation in English may be equivalent'. He admits that he produced his version 'not without great study and difficulty, not observing the order as they stand, but the sentence belonging to my purpose.'

Precepts for a ruler
(Claudian, On the Fourth Consulship of Honorius 214-382, selected)
from *The Boke named the Governour* 2.1

Though that thy power stretcheth both far and large,
Through Inde the rich, set at the world's end,
And Mede with Araby be both under thy charge,
And also Seres that silk to us both send,
If fear thee trouble, and small things thee offend,
Corrupt desire thine heart hath once embraced,
Thou art in bondage, thine honour is defaced.

Thou shalt be deemed then worthy for to reign,
When of thyself thou winnest the mastery.
Evil custom bringeth virtue in disdain.
Licence superfluous persuadeth much folly;
In too much pleasure set not felicity,
If lust or anger do thy mind assail,
Subdue occasion, and thou shalt soon prevail.

What thou mayst do delight not for to know,
But rather what thing will become thee best;
Embrace thou virtue and keep thy courage low,
And think that alway measure is a feast.
Love well thy people, care also for the least,
And when thou studiest for thy commodity
Make them all partners of thy felicity.

Be not much moved with singular appetite,
Except it profit unto thy subjects all;
At thine example the people will delight,
Be it vice or virtue, with thee they rise or fall.
No laws avail, men turn as doth a ball;
For where the ruler in living is not stable,
Both law and counsel is turned into a fable.

HENRY HOWARD, EARL OF SURREY

(1517?-1547)

Henry Howard spent his life a courtier. In 1536 he was knighted, and sent to
Norwich, where among his pages was Thomas Churchyarde, the translator of
Ovid's *Tristia*. In 1545 he was committed to the Tower, along with his father,

on a charge of high treason, and beheaded in 1547. Anthony à Wood writes of him: 'He was a man of a very ripe wit, and educated with great learning; so that the eulogy afterwards given to his son Henry earl of Northampton, that he was the learnedst among the nobility, and the most noble among the learned, might have been as justly applied to him.' His translation of two books of the *Aeneid* is often closely modelled on that of Gavin Douglas, but shares with Surrey's other works the distinction of being among the earliest written in blank verse.

Mercury's journey to Carthage
(Vergil, *Aeneid* 4.238-64)

When Jove had said,
Then Mercury 'gan bend him to obey
His mighty father's will: and to his heels
His golden wings he knits, which him transport
With a light wind above the earth and seas.
And then with him his wand he took, whereby
He calls from hell pale ghosts; and other some
Thither also he sendeth comfortless:
Whereby he forceth sleeps, and then bereaves;
And mortal eyes he closeth up in death.
By power whereof he drives the winds away,
And passeth eke amid the troubled clouds,
Till in his flight he gan descry the top
And the steep flanks of rocky Atlas' hill,
That with his crown sustains the welkin up:
Whose head forgrown with pine, circled alway
With misty clouds, is beaten with wind and storm;
His shoulders spread with snow; and from his chin
The springs descend; his beard frozen with ice.
Here Mercury with equal shining wings
First touched; and with body headlong bet,
To the water then took he his descent:
Like to the fowl that endlong coasts and stronds
Swarming with fish, flies sweeping by the sea;
Cutting betwixt the winds and Libyan lands,
From his grandfather by the mother's side,
Cyllene's child so came, and then alight
Upon the houses with his winged feet;
Tofore the towers where he Aeneas saw
Foundations cast, arearing lodges new;
Girt with a sword of jasper, starry bright;
A shining 'parel, flamed with stately eye
Of Tyrian purple, hung his shoulders down,
The gift and work of wealthy Dido's hand,
Striped throughout with a thin thread of gold.

ANON.

'All worldly pleasures fade'
(Horace, *Odes* 4.7) from Tottel's *Miscellany*, 1557

The winter with his griefly stormes no lenger dare abyde,
The pleasant grasse, with lusty grene, the earth hath newly dyde.
The trees have leves, the bowes don spread, new changed is the yere.
The water brokes are cleane sanke down, the pleasant bankes apere.
The spring is come, the goodly nymphes now dance in every place
Thus hath the yere most pleasantly of late ychangde his face.
Hope for no immortalitie, for wealth will weare away,
As we may learne by every yere, yea howres of every day.
For Zepharus doth mollifye the colde and blustering windes:
The somers drought doth take away the spryng out of our minds.
And yet the somer cannot last, but once must step asyde,
The Autumn thinkes to kepe his place, but Autumn cannot bide.
For when he hath brought furth his fruits and stuft the barns with corn,
The winter eates and empties all, and thus is Autumn worne.
Then hory frostes possesse the place, the tempestes work much harm,
The rage of stormes done make al colde which somer had made so warm
Wherfore let no man put his trust in that, that will decay,
For slipper welth will not continue, pleasure will weare away.
For when that we have lost our lyfe, and lye under a stone,
What are we then, we are but earth, then is our pleasure gon.
No man can tell what god almight of every wight doth cast,
No man can say to day I live, till morne my life shall last.
For when thou shalt before thy judge stand to receive thy dome,
What sentence Minos doth pronounce that must of thee become.
Then shall not noble stock and blud redeme the from his handes,
Nor surged talke with eloquence shal lowse thee from his handes.
Nor yet thy lyfe uprightly lead, can help thee out of hell,
For who descendeth downe so depe, must there abyde and dwell.
Diana could not thence deliver chaste Hyppolitus,
Nor Theseus could not call to life his frende Periothous.

THOMAS DRANT

(? d. 1578)

Educated at St John's College, Cambridge, Drant followed a distinguished
ecclesiastical career which he completed as Archdeacon of Lewes. Like many
contemporaries he concerned himself with problems of quantitative metre,
though his translations from Horace are in ballad fourteeners. He seems to
have been as stern a moralist in the pulpit as in his Horace; besides Horace he
translated Jeremiah and Gregory Nazianzen.

The Stoic sage
(Horace, *Satires* 2.3. 18-48)

Damasip:
I sufferd shipwracke of my goodes,
    whilst I a merchant was.
And therefore now can spare an eye,
    the world to overvewe.
Then was I plunged in affaires,
    as they me drove and drew,
To know what vantage by exchang,
    to clippe, and washe my goulde,
By subtilties in mineralles,
    my state for to upholde.
By such lyke sort came I to have
    an ample wealthie share,
To purchase orchards for mine ease
    and bowers bright and fayre.
My witts so deepe soe sore to deale,
    such lucke to win, or save,
That me a Mercurialiste,
    to surname then they gave.
Horace:
I know it well and marvel much,
    if that be ridde and gone:
Except thou hast sum worse diseas
    whiche needes wyl rayne alone.
As Phisikes cure from head to brest,
    diseases can convey,
As by excesse of much madnes,
    dryve lythargie away.
Perchance you setting fraude apart,
    the mad mans part wil play.
Damasip:
Friend Horace, you are mad likewise,
    and so is every foole,
If Stoicke Stertein taught us once,
    true doctrine in his school.
Of whome, I learnde this trade of lyfe,
    no trewande in my lore,
He dubde me then a stoick Stage,
    and bad me morne no more.
Though al the worlde shoulde go to wracke,
    (for from a brydge I ment
All headlonge to have horlde my selfe
    so things against me wente.)
Approaching nygh, O do not so,
    friend Damasip (quod he)

What thirlinge throwes doth twitche thy harte?
    What shame confoundeth the?
The people cawle thee giddishe mad,
    Why, all the worlde is so:
If thou be mad, and thou alone
    be drounde: I lette the goe.
But what is madnes to defyne?
    Crysip that noble clarke,
Cals all fooles mad, and all whose mindes
    are duskde with errours darke.
This rule makes mad a noumberouse swarme
    of subjects and of kinges,
And none exemptes, save those in whome
    the well of wysdome springes . . .

THOMAS UNDERDOWNE

(fl. 1566-1587)

Best known for his translation of Heliodorus' prose romance, the *Aethiopica*, Underdowne also translated Ovid's *Invective against Ibis*. Though this work is now regarded as an exercise in the genre rather than a personal document, the seriousness with which Underdowne took its implications is evident from his Preface: 'There is not so hyghe an hill, but a man may clyme to the toppe thereof, not so longe a journey, but it may be gone at length, not so deepe a sea, but it may be sounded with leade, nor so stronge a castell, but it may be battered wyth shotte, not so hid a thinge, but it may be revealed by time, only the heart of man is unsearchable, so that in twenty yeres a man shall not finde the depth thereof. Wherefore in myne opinion he was a wyse man, that wylled us to eate many bushels of salte, with him whom we meaned to make our freend, whereby he meant nothing els, but by long continuance, to trye whether he whome we love, be meete to be our freende or not.'

A curse on an enemy
(Ovid, *Ibis* 107-26)

Let not the sun shine bright on thee,
    nor glistering moone by night;
And of thy eyes let glimsing starres,
    forsake the wicked sight.
Let not the fire graunt thee his heate,
    nor ayre humiditie:
Let neither earth nor yet the sea,
    free passage grant to thee.
That banyshed and poor thou mayst,
    straunge houses seeke in vaine:

That craving to, with trembling voyce
   small almes mayst obtaine,
That neither sownd of body, nor
   thy mynde in perfect plight:
This night be worse than passed day,
   and next day than this night.
That thou mayst still be pitifull,
   but pitied of none:
And that no man nor woman may
   for thy mischaunces mone.
And that thy teares may hatred move,
   thou judged worthy to:
On whom (though many mischiefes light)
   yet worthy many mo.
And that, that seldom comes to passe,
   I wishe thy whole estate:
All wonted favour for to want,
   and be replete with hate.
And that thou want no cause of death,
   but mayest be voyde of powre:
And that thy life be forste to flye,
   of death the wicked hour.
And that thy soule with troubles tost,
   constrayned stil to stay:
May leave thy very limmes at length,
   tormented with delay.
It shal be so, and Phoebus to,
   that this in force should stande:
Did give a signe, a dolfull byrde,
   did fly on my left hand.

THOMAS CHURCHYARDE

(*c.* 1520-1604)

Thomas Churchyarde was for a time in the service of the Earl of Surrey, but when Surrey died in 1546, 'the hopes of Churchyarde's rising higher were in a manner buried in his grave' (Anthony à Wood). He thereafter became a soldier of fortune, and later in life, through an unrequited love, 'he became much passionate and troubled in mind' (ibid.). He nevertheless found time for a good deal of writing, ranging from popular broadsides such as *Davy Dycar's Dream* (1552) to a descriptive poem on the monuments of Wales, *The Worthiness of Wales* (1587), and the *Legend of Shore's Wife* (his most famous work), as well as his translation of Ovid's *Tristia* and contributions to Tottel's *Miscellany*.

   There is no clear distinction between the popular (broadsides) and the literary in such an oeuvre; and when we read broadside ballads that are replete with classical allusion we realise on what a considerable common stock a writer of this generation was drawing, and how the rediscovery of classical literature went hand in hand with other literary activities.

Spring in Tomi
(Ovid, *Tristia* 3.12)

The fertile fields do florishe now, with flowers of sundry hewe,
And babling byrdes w' tongue untaught, do chaunt with notes so newe.
The swallow eke a mother vile her cruel deedes to hide,
Her neast by beames she maketh close, and builds by houses syde.
The growing graine in plowed fieldes, with furrowes lai'd unsene,
With slender spiere through tender earth apper'th with joyfull greene.
The vines also (whereas they be) their buds from branches lowe
Do now bringe out: in Scythia for, no vines at all do growe
And whereas lofty woods be set, the bowes do spread from tree
(For nere to coast of Geta land, no trees deserned bee)
Lo there this is the vacant time, for sport and pleasaunt playes,
And taulkinge tongues in judgment haules, do cease fro certaine dayes.
On hinneyghinge horse with armour light, they bravely now disport;
And some to ball, and some to toy, with mery minde resort.
The lusty youth anoynted long with thinne and sliding oyle,
Their weary limmes with water washe, and rest from former toyle.
Now triumphes are: with sounding voyce, the lookers on do crye,
From three fould stage the factions three, their favouring words let flie.
O foure times blest, and blessed more then number can make plaine:
That mayst the city free enjoy, and in the same remaine.
But I with snow with sunne consum'd O wretch do here approve,
And frozen sea the yse whereof no force might them remove.
No yce the same doth now congele, as wont it was to do,
Nor herdsmen way by Ister make to Sauromathia go.
Yet if by happe that any shippe arrive within this coast,
Or any stranger happe to be in Pontus haven at hoast,
In hast I seeke the shippemen out, and salvinge them before
Then they (unless it marveile be) from some nere joyninge land,
Do aunswer make: from nations farre, to sayle few tak'th in hand.
And seldom from Italia seas do any passage take,
Nor in these ports from haven so wide, no shippe his bydinge make.
But if that any come that speake the Latin or the Greeke,
Hee is for that more welcome much, such language do I seeke.
It lawfull is from mouth of sea, and from Propontus longe,
That men may saile with Northren winde these Scythian seas among.
Who so hee bee may happely make, some whispering rumour lowe,
Whereby a past occasion gev'th, more fame thereof to growe.
Then do I pray him make discourse of Caesars triumph brave,
And eke what vowes that duty driv'th the Latin Jove to have.

Or els if that Germania land, which still rebell'th in fielde,
With carefull minde at Captaines feete, al prostrate now do yelde.
Who doth (which would my selfe had seene) of these things haply tell,
I pray him use as welcome ghest, the house wherein I dwell
But well away is Nasoes house, now set on Scythia's ground?
Or shall to helpe my payne withall, a place therefore be found?
God graunt that Caesar may commaunde, not this my house to be,
But rather for a time a place, wherein to chastise me.

ARTHUR GOLDING

(1536?-1605?)

Golding may have been educated at Queens' College, Cambridge; 1549 finds
him in the service of Protector Somerset, and he seemed to have had the
acquaintance of Cecil, to whom his first translation, of Caesar's *Commentaries*
(1565), was dedicated. The first four books of his best remembered work,
Ovid's *Metamorphoses*, appeared in the same year; on the appearance of the
whole in 1567 Peend abandoned his own attempt at the same task. In 1577
appeared a translation of Seneca, *De Beneficiis*. Thereafter he turned his
attention to translations from Calvin, in harmony with his own puritan
outlook. He was a friend of Sir Philip Sidney, whose translation of De
Mornay's *Concerning the trewnesse of Christianity* he completed on Sidney's death.
His works are numerous but include next to no original poetry. Nashe praises
his 'industrious toyle' in the preface to Greene's Menaphon, and Shakespeare
paid him the compliment of using a passage of the description of Medea's
powers (below) in *The Tempest*.
    'Is there one of us so good at his Latin, and so ready in imagination that
Golding will not throw upon his mind shades and glamours inherent in the
original text which had for all that escaped him? . . . It is certain that 'we' have
forgotten our Ovid . . . since Golding went out of print.' (Ezra Pound, *Notes on
Elizabethan Classicists*).

Medea's sorcery
(Ovid, *Metamorphoses* 7. 197-293)

Ye Ayres and Windes: Ye Elves of Hilles, of Brookes, of Woods alone,
Of standing Lakes, and of the Night approche ye everychone.
Through helpe of whom (the crooked bankes much wondering at the
    thing)
I have compelled streames to run cleane backward to their spring.
By charmes I make the calme seas rough, & make the rough Seas plaine
And cover all the Skie with Cloudes, and chase them thence againe.
By charmes I raise and lay the windes, and burst the Vipers jawe:
And from the bowels of the Earth both stones and trees doe drawe.

Whole woods and Forestes I remove: I make the mountaines shake,
And even the Earth itselfe to grone and fearfully to quake.
I call up dead men from their graves: and Thee O lightsome Moone
I darken oft, though beaten brasse abate thy perill soone.
Our Sorcerie dimmes the Morning faire, and darkes the Sun at Noone.
The flaming breth of firie Bulles ye quenched for my sake.
And caused there unweeldie neckes the bended yoke to take.
Among the Earthbred brothers you a mortall war did set
And brought a sleepe the Dragon fell whose eyes were never shet.
By meanes whereof deceiving him that had the golden fleece
In charge to keepe, you sent it thence by Jason into Greece.
Now have I neede of herbes that can by vertue of their juce
To flowring prime of lustie youth old withered age reduce . . .

The medicine seething all the while a wallop in a pan
Of brasse, to spirt and leape aloft and gather froth began.
There boyled she the rootes, seedes, flowres, leaves, stalks & juce togither
Which from the feelds of Thessalie she late had gathered thither.
She cast in also precious stones fetcht from the furthest East,
And (which the ebbing Ocean washt) fine gravell from the West.
She put thereto the dew that fell upon a Monday night:
And flesh and fethers of a Witch a cursed odious wight
Which in the likenesse of an Owle abrode a nightes did flie,
And Infants in their cradels chaunge or sucke them that they die.
The singles also of a Wolfe which when he list could take
The shape of man, and when he list the same againe forsake.
And from the River Cyniphis which is in Lybie land
She had the fine sheere scaled filmes of watersnayles at hand.
And of an endlesselived hert the liver had she got.
To which she added of a Crowe that then had lived not
So little as nine hundred yeeres the head and Bill also.
Now when Medea had with these and with a thousand mo
Such other kinds of nemeless things bestead hir purpose through
For lengthening of the old man's life, she tooke a withered bough
Cut lately from an Olyf tree, and tumbling all togither
Did raise the bottom to the brim: and as she stirred hither
And thither with the withered sticke, behold it wexed greene.
Anon the leaves came budding out: and sodainly were seene
As many berries dangling downe as well the bough could beare.
And where the fire had from the pan the scumming cast, or where
The scalding drops did fall, the ground did springlike florish there,
And flowres with fodder fine and soft immediately arose.
Which when Medea did behold, with naked knife she goes
And cuttes the old man's throte: and letting all his old blud go,
Supplies it with the boyled juce: the which when Aeson tho
Had at his mouth or at his wound receyved in, his heare
As well of head as beard from gray to coleblacke turned were.

His leane, pale, hore, and withered corse grew fulsome, faire, and fresh:
His furrowed wrincles were fulfilde with yong and lustie flesh.
His limmes wert frolicke, vaine and lithe: at which he wondring much,
Remembred that at fortie yeares he was the same or such.
And as from dull unweeldsome age to youth he backwarde drew:
Even so a lively youthfull spright did in his hart renew.

Metamorphosis of the dead Memnon
(Ovid, *Metamorphoses* 13.600-22)

No sooner Jove had graunted dame Aurora hir desyre,
  But that the flame of Memnons corce that burned in the fyre
Did fall: and flaky rolles of smoke did dark the day, as when
A foggy mist streames upward from a River or a fen,
And suffreth not the Sonne to shyne within it. Blacke as cole
The cinder rose: and intoo one round lump assembling whole,
Grew grosse, and tooke bothe shape and hew. The fyre did lyfe it send,
The lightnesse of the substance self did wings unto it lend.
And at the first it flittred like a bird: and by and by
It flew a fethered bird in deede. And wyth that one gan fly
Innumerable mo of selfsame brood: whoo once or twyce
Did sore about the fyre, and made a piteous shreeking thryce.
The fowrth tyme in theyr flying round, themselves they all withdrew
In battels twayne, and feercely foorth of eyther syd one flew
Too fyght a combate. With theyr billes and hooked talants keene
And with theyr wings couragiously they wreakt theyr wrathfull teene.
And myndfull of the valeant man of whom they issued beene,
They neuer ceased jobbing eche uppon the others brest,
Untill they falling both downe dead with fyghting overprest,
Had offred up theyr bodyes as a worthy sacrifyse
Untoo theyr cousin Memnon whoo too ashes berned lyes.
Theis soddeine birds were named of the founder of theyr stocke:
For men doo call them Memnons birds. And every yeere a flocke
Repayre to Memnons tumb, where twoo doo in the foresayd wyse
In manner of a yeeremynd slea themselves in sacrifyse.
Thus where as others did lament that Dymants daughter barkt,
Aurora owne greef busyed her, that smally shee it markt
Which thing shee too this present tyme with piteous teares dooth shewe:
For through the universall world she sheadeth moysting dewe.

TIMOTHE KENDALL
(fl. 1577)

Kendall was educated at Eton and at Magdalen College, Oxford, whence he continued to Staples Inn. His *Floures of Epigrammes* were published in 1577. He was evidently acquainted with other poets and translators of the day, including Abraham Fleming, the translator of Vergil's *Eclogues* and *Georgics*, but otherwise nothing else is known of him.

Leander
(Martial, *Epigrams* 14.181)

What tyme Leander lustie ladde,
  his Ladie went to see:
When as with waltryng waves out worne,
  and wearied quight was he:
He saied: Now spight me not (ye seas)
  Leander spare to spill?
When I have seen my Ladie once,
  then droune me if you will.

Reason for marrying
(Martial, *Epigrams* 1.10)

Gemellus, Maronilla faine
  would have unto his wife:
He longs, he likes, he loves, he craves,
  with her to lead his life.
What? is she of such a beautie brave?
  naie none more foule maie be:
What then is in her to be likte
  or lovd? still cougheth she.

'Of the picture of kyng Craesus, translated out of the first book of Greke
Epigrams'
(*Greek Anthology* 9.145)

Thy picture Craesus kyng that didst
  for riches all excell:
Uncivill rude Diogines
  behelde beneth in hell.
And vewyng it aloofe, he laught
  as though his harte would breake:
At last (when he had laught his fill)
  he thus began to speake.
O foolishe Craesus, what availes
  now all thy paultrie pelfe?

Sith now thou poorer art, then poore
  Diogines hym self.
For what was myne I bare with me,
  when selie Craesus poore
Thou penilesse didst packe from hence,
  for all thy busy store.

JASPER HEYWOOD

(1535-1598)

Heywood was educated at Merton College, Oxford, and became a Fellow of All Souls. At this period he translated the *Troas* (1559), *Thyestes* (1561) and *Hercules Furens* (1561) of Seneca, but shortly afterwards was forced to resign his fellowship. He went to Rome and was admitted to the Society of Jesus, only returning to England in 1581, the year of publication of *Seneca his Tenne Tragedies,* which included his own three. He was soon arrested as a priest, and when the privy council failed to compel him to conform to the established church, he was imprisoned in the Tower, while five others tried with him were executed. After seventeen months he was sent into exile on pain of death if he should return, and died in 1597/8.

Calm after Storm
(Seneca, *Thyestes* 573-97)

Chorus:
Now are the threats of cruel sword laid down,
And now the rumour whists of battles sown,
  The noise of crooked trumpet silent lies,
And quiet peace returns to joyful town.
  So, when the waves of swelling surge arise,
While Corus' wind the Brutian seas doth smight,
  And Scylla sounds from hollow caves within,
And shipmen are with wafting waves affright,
  Charybdis casts that erst it had drunk in;
And Cyclops fierce his father yet doth dread,
  In Etna bank, that fervent is with heats,
Lest quenched be with waves that overshed
  The fire, that from eternal furnace beats;
And poor Laertes thinks his kingdoms all
  May drowned be, and Ithaca doth quake.
If once the force of winds begin to fall,
  The sea li'th down more mild than standing lake;
The deep, where ships so wide full dreadfull were
  To pass, with sails on either side outspread,
Now fall'n a-down, the lesser boat doth bear;

And leisure is, to view the fishes dead
Even there where late, with tempest beat upon,
The shaken Cyclads were with seas aghast.
No state endures. The pain and pleasure, one
To other yields; and joys be soonest past.

JOHN STUDLEY

(1545?-1590?)

Studley was one of the original scholars of Westminster School. He went on to Trinity College, Cambridge, where he became a fellow. But the college was at the time sharply divided on the religious question, and in 1573 Studley, who was a puritan, departed and may have crossed to the Low Countries, where Chetwood says that he died at the siege of Breda (1590). His share of *Seneca his Tenne Tragedies,* edited by Thomas Newton (1581), consisted of the *Medea, Agamemnon, Hippolytus* and *Hercules Oetaeus.*

Brightness falls from the air
(Seneca, *Hippolytus*, 761-78)

A brittle jewell beauty is on mortall men employde,
Thou gift that for a season short of mankinde arte enjoyde,
How soone alas with feathered foot hence dost thou fading slide?
The partching sommers vapour hoate in Vers most pleasant pride
So withers not the meadowes greene, (when as the scorching sunne)
In Tropick ligne of burning crab full hoate at noone doth runne
And on her shorter clowdy wheeles unhorseth soone the night.
With wanny leaves downe hang the heads of withred lillies whight,
The balmy bloomes and sprouting floure do leave the naked head,
As beauty bright whose radiant beames in corauld cheekes is spred,
Is dashed in the twincke of eye: no day as yet did passe,
In which not of his beauty reft some pearles person was.
For favour is a fleetyng thing: what wight of any wit
Will unto frail and fickle joy his confidence commit?
Take pleasure of it while thou mayst, for Tyme with stealing steps
Wil undermint, an howre past strayght in a worser leps:
Why flyest thou to the wilderness, to seeke thy succour there?
Thy beauty bydes not safer in the waylesse woodes than here.

SIR PHILIP SIDNEY

(1554-1586)

Educated at Christ Church, Oxford, Sidney spent his short life in the royal service, and died in battle at Zutphen while assisting the Dutch against Spain. His poetry dates from the years 1578-1582, though none of it was published in his lifetime. Aubrey speaks of him as a man 'whose fame will never die, whilst poetrie lives. [He] was the most accomplished cavalier of his time . . . a reviver of poetrie in those dark times.'

'Out of Catullus'
(Catullus 70)

Unto no body my woman saith she had rather a wife be
Than to my selfe; not though Jove grew a suter of hers.
These be her words, but a womans words to a love that is eager
In wind or water stream do require to be writ.

ARTHUR HALL

(1539-1605)

Born in Calais, Hall was brought up as a ward of Sir William Cecil. He entered Parliament, but was expelled following his violent quarrel with Melchisedech Mallory. Work on his Homer (which is based on the French version of Hugues Salel (1555)), began some time after 1556; he was encouraged by Roger Ascham and Jasper Heywood, but resumed work on it in earnest only after his expulsion in 1576. He later quarrelled also with Lady Sussex, and was imprisoned in the Tower (1588/9); the Homer was published soon after his release. In 1601 he was imprisoned again, this time for debt, and it is not known whether he was released before his death. See the biography by H. G. Wright, *Arthur Hall of Grantham* (1919).

The story of Bellerophon
(Homer, *Iliad* 6.144-202)

That time a King Proteus hight in Greece did sceptre holde,
Whose wealth was great, under whose raigne th' immortal Gods so would.
Bellerophon his tender yeares and youth with him he spends,
Who had his linage much in price: but there the king pretends
Gainst him, and to procure his death he after doth conspire:
Not willingly, but woode thereto by the wicked desire
Of Andia his wife, who then enflamde with whorish love,
Could finde no meanes to have hir will, nor yong mans fancie move:

No, though she sued earnestly, lamented, whinde, and howlde,
Wherefore in moode she turne to spite, when nothing gaine she could.
So that the vehement liking turnd to hate, yea, by and by,
One day she commes her husband to with countnance like to die,
And spake him thus: choose of these two and thinke to do the one,
Either to die thy selfe, or else, to slay Bellerophon.
Who gone about hath to assault thy honour, it to blot,
Meaning by force to ravish me, when as prevailed not
His fawning toyes and sewing tales, to end his foule desire.
Thus sets the trayterous tale the king with grief and wroth a fire,
Who straight doth thinke to be revengde, yet deemes not he it wel
Bycause he was one of his house, in house him there to quell.
He likes of treason in the case, to treason then he goes:
Malicious, false, and ful of guile he letters doth compose,
Which he unto his father in law king Rheon sends away
The Lycian prince to deal herein, he doth king Rheon pray
And that without returne of word he cause the bearer die.
When as Proteus thus had writ, the yong man presently
He sendeth forth, he takes his way, with gods his guides he goes,
In Lyce they cause him to arrive, where head of Xanthus flowes,
Which flood the province watereth: At his first lighting there
The prince receivde him curteously, with joy and joyly cheare.
Nine days throughout right brave they feast, the banquets were not bad,
Nine chosen beeves on th' alters layde, th' immortall Gods they had.
And all to welcome this new guest: And now when comth the tenth
The king then of Bellerophon to know the message menth:
And whether that he letters brought had from his son in law:
The packet false he toke the king, which having red, he saw
The treason and the deede devisde, he faines and holds him stil,
Minding the letters whole effect at ful for to fulfil,
And for to kil the messenger, his force yet wil he stay,
Against Chimere he him imploies that monster dire to slay,
The gastfulst thing that ere was seene: which beast ye Gods on hie,
To see revengde the hateful facts of humaine trecherie,
Had formde by nature of such shape, ful hidious and ful rare.
The head and breast right lion like, the midst the forme it bare
Of goate, behind like dragon broode, and more, from him there gone
Right terrible flames which forth he breathes. And yet Bellerophon
(Though fel he were as fel might be) the beast he doth assayle,
With favour of the Gods, and of his wil he doth not fayle.
For after wearie toyle, in fields the beaste he stoutly slue,
That done, the Solymes down he hacks, and quite them overthrew.
Report so goes, him much it pleasde the Solymes to have slaine,
And yet beside all this, the king commandeth him agayne
To try with maine an Amazon, but stil he was so steelde
With heart so good, as victor he dead left them in the field.
At length to make an end of him, a bushment doth provide

Of Lycians to set on him, harde by a mountain side.
But al in vaine, for no not one of all the packed craft
Did one returne unto their home, for murdered them he left.
Wherewith the king repents the guile, he stands amazed dum
And knoweth wel that from the Gods, the victorie did come,
Who knew him innocent, himself his deedes doth disalow,
With him for his own quiet he doth minde to keepe him now.
For his preferment him to give his daughter wife to bee
And halfe the whole of all his raigne, to joyne sure amitie.
The curteous virgin given him was, and for his place to dwel
The fertilst soyle, two sons he had of this fair damosel,
A daughter eke, Isander first, the next a warlike knight
Hippolochus, Laodomie his daughter fayre she hight,
Whom Jove did wish to have to friend: with brand of love did sweate
Divine Sarpedon in hir wombe, himself he left hir great
But after this it was not long, but that Bellerophon
Did lose the favour of the Gods and stirrde them every one:
He hates himself, he companie flyes, he corners eke doth seeke
He wanders up and down his grounds most mad and frantike like,
Therefore his fields are wandring calld . . .

RICHARD STANYHURST

(1574-1618)

Stanyhurst was born in Dublin, attended University College, Oxford, where he was a contemporary of William Adlington, the translator of Apuleius, and afterwards Furnival's and Lincoln's Inn. His literary output is large, including historical works on Ireland as well as his unique translation of Vergil.

'After that he professed Poetry, and many other fictions, he tooke upon him to translate Virgill, and stript him out of a velvet gowne, into a Fooles coate, out of a Latin Heroicall verse, into an English riffe raffe.' (Barnaby Rich). Thomas Nashe is equally eloquent: 'But fortune, the mistress of change, with a pitying compassion respecting master Stanihursts praise, would that Phaer should fall that hee might rise, whose heroicall poetrie, infired, I should say inspired, with an hexameter furie, recalled to life whatever hissed barbarisme hath bin buried this hundred yeare, and revived by his ragged quill such carterlie varietie as no hodge plowman in a countrie but would have held as the extremitie of clownerie' (*A Generall Censure*, in *Elizabethan Critical Essays* (ed. G. G. Smith), p. 315).

The Vergil is perhaps one of the most unintentionally comic works in English. His 'kitchen rhetoric' characterises his prose works as well. He defends himself rather unnecessarily against the charge of plagiarism from Phaër, and clearly had no doubts about the merits of his originality.

The prophecy of Helenus
(Vergil, *Aeneid* 3.441-62)

When ye in this passage too Cumas cittye shall enter,
And lake with rumbling forrest of sacred Auerna,
A braynsick prophetesse se ye shal, whom dungeon holdeth
In grounde deepe riueted, future haps and destenye chaunting.
But yeet al her prophecyes in greene leaues nicelye be scribled,
In theese slipprye leaues what sooth thee virgin averreth,
Shee frams in Poëtry: her verses in dungeon howsing,
They keepe rancks ordred, with aray first setled abyding:
But when on a suddeyn thee doors winds blastye doe batter,
And theese leaves greenish with whisking lightlye be scatterd,
Neaver dooth she laboure to revoke her flittered issue,
Or to place in cabban, theire floane lyms freshlye rejoyning.
Thus they fle, detesting thee lodge of giddye Sibylla:
Heere for a spirit linger, no good opportunitye scaping.
(Al thogh thee to seaward thy posting coompanye calleth,
And winds vaunce fully thy sayls with prosperus huffing)
Post to this prophetesse, let her help and sooth be required.
Shee wyl geeve notice to the streight of al Italye dwellers:
How thow wiselye travayls shalt shun, shalt manfulye suffer.
Theare she wyl enstruct thee, thy passadge fortunat ayding.
Theese be such od caveats, as I to the frendlye can utter.
Foorth: and with thy valor let Troian glorye be mounted.

The death of Dido
(Vergil, *Aeneid* 4.683-92)

Speedelye bringe me water, thee greene wound swiftlye toe souple;
And yf in her carcasse soom wind yeet softlye be breathing,
With lip I wil nurse yt: thus sayd shee climd toe the woodpile,
Claspt in her arms bracing thee panting murtheres haulf-quick,
With grunt wyde gasping: thee blackned gellyeblud, hardning,
Shee skums with napkins; shee would haue lifted her eyebal,
Feeble agayne weixing shee droups; thee deadlye push yrcks her.
Thrise she did endevoure, too mount and rest on her elbow;
Thrise to her bed sliding shee quayls, with whirligig eyesight
Up to the sky staring, with belling skrichcrye she roareth,
When she the desyred soonbeams with faynt eye received.

EDMUND SPENSER

(1552?-1599)

The major non-dramatic poet of the Elizabethan age was educated at the
Merchant Taylors school and at Pembroke Hall, Cambridge, where he

showed proficiency in Greek, Latin, French and Italian. From about 1578 he
was in the service of the Earl of Leicester, and moved in the circles of Sidney,
and of Dyer and Drant, in whose 'Areopagus' he participated in the
discussion, reflected for us in his correspondence with Gabriel Harvey, over
the use of classical metres in English verse. *The Faerie Queene* seems to have been
well in hand by 1579 when he published the *Shepherd's Calendar,* and was
published in 1590; it was followed in 1591 by the *Complaints,* which includes his
translation of Vergil's *Gnat,* a fine version of a slightly tedious poem. In his
later Hymns and Epithalamia the lessons of classical poetry have been
absorbed into his own lyric style.

Invocation of Venus
(Lucretius, *On the Nature of Things* 1.1-28) from *The Faerie Queene* 4.10

Great Venus! Queene of beautie and of grace,
The joy of gods and men, that under skie
Doest fayrest shine, and most adorne thy place;
That with thy smiling look doest peaifie
The raging seas, and makst the stormes to flie;
Thee, goddesse, thee the winds, the clouds doe feare,
And, when thou spredst thy mantle forth on hie,
The waters play, and pleasant lands appeare,
And heavens laugh, and al the world shows joyous cheare.

Then doth the daedale earth throw forth to thee
Out of her fruitfull lap aboundant flowres;
And then all living wights, soone as they see
The spring breake forth out of his lusty bowres,
They all doe learne to play the Paramours;
First doe the merry birds, thy prety pages,
Privily pricked out with thy lustfull powres,
Chirpe loud to thee out of their leavy cages,
And thee their mother call to coole their kindly rages.

Then doe the salvage beasts begin to play
Their pleasant friskes, and loath their wonted food:
Thy lyons rore; the tygres loudly bray;
The raging buls rebellow through the wood,
And breaking forth dare tempt the deepest flood
To come where thou doest draw them with desire.
So all things else, that nourish vitall blood,
Soone as with fury thou doest them inspire,
In generation seeke to quench their inward fire.

So all the world by thee at first was made,
And dayly yet thou doest the same repayre;
Ne ought on earth that merry is and glad,
Ne ought on earth that lovely is and fayre,

But thou the same for pleasure didst prepare:
Thou art the root of all that joyous is:
Great God of men and women, queen of th'ayre,
Mother of laughter, and welspring of blisse,
O graunt that of my love at last I may not misse!

THOMAS PHAËR

(1510?-1560)

Phaër was trained in both law and medicine, and among his early works there is a translation of *The Regiment of Life* (*Regimen Sanitatis Salerni*, a famous work already translated by Thomas Paynell, and later to be translated by Sir John Harington), to which he added some appendices in which he claimed to be the first to make medicine intelligible to Englishmen in their own tongue.

He might have claimed the same for his *Aeneid*, for only Gavin Douglas and the Earl of Surrey preceded him in the task; but he died when he had completed only nine books. The remaining books, plus the thirteenth of Maphaeus Vegius, were added by Thomas Twining and published in 1584. He earned a eulogistic epitaph from Barnabe Googe, and Arthur Hall compares his own Homer unfavourably with Phaër's Vergil.

Anchises to Aeneas in the underworld
(Vergil, *Aeneid* 6.724-51)

First heaven and earth, and of the seas the flittring feeldes and sines,
These glorious stars, this glittring globe of moone so bright that shines,
One lively soule there is, that feedes them all with breath of love,
One mind through all these members mixt this mighty masse doth move.
From thence mankinde, and beasts, and lives of fowles in aier that flies,
And all what marblefaced seas conteines of monstrous fries,
One chafing fier among them all there sits, and heavenly springes
Within their seedes, if bodies noisom them not backward bringes.
But lompe of liveles earth, and mortall members make them dull.
This causeth them, of lust, feare, griefe and joy, to be so full.
Nor closed so in darke, can they regarde their heavenly kinde,
For carcas foule of flesh, and dongeon vile of prison blinde.
Moreover, when their ende of life, and light them doth forsake:
Yet can they not their sinnes nor sorowes all (poore soules) ofshake.
Nor all contagions fleshly, from them voides, but must of neede
Much things congendred long, by wondrous meanes at last outspreed.
Therefore they plagued ben, and for their former fautes and sinnes
Their sondry paines they hide, some hie in ayer doth hang on pinnes.
Some fleeting ben in floods, and deepe in gulfes them selves they tier
Till sinnes away be washt, or clensed cleere with purging fier.

Eche one of us our penaunce here abides, than sent we bee
To Paradise at last, we few these fieldes of joy do see:
Till compass long of time, by perfit course, hath purged quight
Our former cloddrid spots, and simple sparkes of heavenly light.
Then all, when they a thousand yeeres that wheele have turned about,
To drinke of Lethee flood, by clusters great, God calls them out.
That these forgetting all their former lives, and former sin,
The mortall world afresh, in bodies new they may begin.

ANON.

The gifts of the Muses
(Theocritus, *Idyll* 16.58-109) from *Charites, or Hiero* in *Six Idillia* (Oxford 1588)

Immortal fame to mortal men, the Muses nine do give:
But dead men's wealth is spent and quite consumed of them that live.
But all one pain it is, to number waves upon the banks,
Whereof great store, the wind from sea doth blow to land in ranks;
Or for to wash a brick with water clear till it be white:
As for to move a man whom avarice doth once delight.
Therefore 'Adieu!' to such a one for me! and let him have
Huge silver heaps at will, and more and more still let him crave!
But I, Goodwill of Men, and Honour, will prefer before
A many mules of price, or many horses kept in store.
Therefore I ask, To whom shall I be welcome with my train
Of Muses nine? whose ways are hard, if Jove guides not the rein.

The heavens yet have not left to roll both months and years on reels;
And many horses yet shall turn about the chariot's wheels:
The man shall rise that shall have no need of me to set him out;
Doing such deeds of arms as Ajax, or Achilles stout,
Did in the fields of Simois, where Ilus' bones do rest.
And now the Carthaginians, inhabiting the west,
Who in the utmost end of Liby' dwell, in arms are prest:
And now the Syracuseans their spears do carry in the rest;
Whose left arms laden are with targets made of willow tree.
'Mongst whom King Hiero, the ancient worthies' match, I see
In armour shine; whose plume doth overshade his helmet bright.

O Jupiter, and thou Minerva fierce in fight,
And thou Proserpina (who, with thy mother, has renown
By Lysimelia streams, in Ephyra that wealthy town),
Out of our island drive our enemies, our bitter fate,
Along the Sardine sea! that death of friends they may relate

Unto their children and their wives! and that the towns opprest
By enemies, of th' old inhabitants may be possest!
That they may till the fields! and sheep upon the downs may bleat
By thousands infinite, and fat! and that the herds of neat
As to their stalls they go, may press the ling'ring traveller!
Let grounds be broken up for seed, what time the grasshopper
Watching the shepherds by their flocks, in boughs close singing lies!
And let the spiders spread their slender webs in armories;
So that of war, the very name may not be heard again!

But let the poets strive, king Hiero's glory for to strain
Beyond the Scythean sea; and far beyond those places where
Semiramis did build those stately walls, and rule did bear.
'Mongst whom, I will be one: for many other men beside,
Jove's daughters love; whose study still shall be, both far and wide,
Sicilian Arethusa, with the people, to advance;
And warlike Hiero. Ye Graces! (who keep resiance
In the Thessalian Mount Orchomenus; to Thebes of old
So hateful, though of you beloved) to stay I will be bold,
Where I am bid to come: and I with them will still remain,
That shall invite me to their house, with all my Muses' train.
Nor you, will I forsake! For what to men can lovely be
Without your company? The Graces always be with me!

CHRISTOPHER MARLOWE

(1564-1593)

Marlowe was a scholar of Corpus Christi College, Cambridge, where he probably made his translation of Ovid's *Amores*; he may also have translated Colluthus at this time, though the version is not extant. He may thereafter have served in the military for a while, or have entered directly on his dramatic career which made him illustrious even among his contemporaries. It was while escaping from the danger of being arrested on a charge of atheism that he was killed in a drunken brawl in Deptford. His Ovid was first published at 'Middleborough' (? Middleburg in Holland; n.d.), and then in *Epigrams and Elegies* of c. 1597; his Lucan was published in 1600 but it is not known when he made the translation.

Lament for a dead parrot
(Ovid, *Amores* 2.6)

The parrot, from east India to me sent,
Is dead; all fowls her exequies frequent!
Go, godly birds, striking your breasts bewail,
And with rough claws your tender cheeks assail.

For woeful hairs let piece-torn plumes abound,
For long shrilled trumpets let your notes resound.
Why, Philomel, dost Tereus' lewdness mourn?
All-wasting years have that complaint outworn.
Thy tunes let this rare bird's sad funeral borrow,
Itys is great, but ancient cause of sorrow.
All you whose pinions in the clear air soar,
But most, thou friendly turtle dove, deplore;
Full concord all your lives was you betwixt,
And to the end your constant faith stood fixed.
What Pylades did to Orestes prove,
Such to the parrot was the turtle dove.
But what availed this faith? her rarest hue?
Or voice that how to change the wild notes knew?
What helps it thou wert given to please my wench?
Birds' hapless glory, death thy life doth quench.
Thou with thy quills mightst make green emeralds dark,
And pass our scarlet of red saffron's mark;
No such voice-feigning bird was on the ground,
Thou spokest thy words so well with stammering sound.
Envy hath rapt thee, no fierce wars thou movedst,
Vain babbling speech and pleasant peace thou lovedst.
Behold how quails among their battles live,
Which do perchance old age unto them give.
A little filled thee, and for love of talk,
Thy mouth to taste of many meats did balk.
Nuts were thy food, and poppy caused thee sleep,
Pure water's moisture thirst away did keep.
The ravenous vulture lives, the puttock hovers
Around the air, the cadess rain discovers,
And crow survives arms-bearing Pallas' hate,
Whose life nine ages scarce bring out of date.
Dead is that speaking image of man's voice,
The parrot given me, the far world's best choice.
The greedy spirits take the best things first,
Supplying their void places with the worst.
Thersites did Protesilaus survive,
And Hector died, his brothers yet alive.
My wench's vow for thee what should I show,
Which stormy south winds into sea did blow?
The seventh day came, none following mightst thou see,
And the Fate's distaff empty stood to thee;
Yet words in thy benumbed palate rung:
'Farewell, Corinna', cried thy dying tongue.
Elysium hath a wood of holm-trees black,
Whose earth doth not perpetual green grass lack;
There good birds rest (if we believe things hidden)

Whence unclean fowls are said to be forbidden;
There harmless swans feed all abroad the river,
There lives the Phoenix one alone bird ever,
There Juno's bird displays his gorgeous feather,
And loving doves kiss eagerly together.
The parrot into wood received with these,
Turns all the goodly birds to what she please.
A grave her bones hides; on her corpse' great grave
The little stones these little verses have:
'This tomb approves I pleased my mistress well,
My mouth in speaking did all birds excel.'

Love in the afternoon
(Ovid, *Amores* 1.5)

In summer's heat, and mid-time of the day,
To rest my limbs upon a bed I lay;
One window shut, the other open stood,
Which gave such light as twinkles in a wood,
Like twilight glimpse at setting of the sun,
Or night being past, and day not yet begun.
Such light to shamefast maidens must be shown,
Where they may sport and seem to be unknown.
Then came Corinna in a long loose gown,
Her white neck hid with tresses hanging down,
Resembling fair Semiramis going to bed,
Or Lais of a thousand wooers sped.
I snatched her gown; being thin, the harm was small,
Yet strived she to be covered therewithal,
And striving thus as one that would be cast,
Betrayed herself, and yielded at the last.
Stark naked as she stood before mine eye,
Not one wen in her body could I spy.
What arms and shoulders did I touch and see,
How apt her breasts were to be pressed by me!
How smooth a belly under her waist saw I,
How large a leg, and what a lusty thigh!
To leave the rest, all liked me passing well;
I clinged her naked body, down she fell.
Judge you the rest: being tired she made me kiss;
Jove send me more such afternoons as this.

Portents of Civil War
(Lucan, *Pharsalia* 1.522-83)

Now evermore, lest some one hope might ease
The commons' jangling minds, apparent signs arose,
Strange sights appeared, the angry threat'ning gods

Filled both the earth and seas with prodigies;
Great store of strange and unknown stars were seen
Wandering about the north, and rings of fire
Fly in the air, and dreadful bearded stars,
And comets that presage the fall of kingdoms;
The flattering sky glittered in often flames,
And sundry fiery meteors blazed in heaven,
Now spear-like, long, now like a spreading torch;
Lightning in silence stole forth without clouds,
And from the northern climate snatching fire
Blasted the Capitol; the lesser stars,
Which wont to run their course through empty night,
At noonday mustered; Phoebe, having filled
Her meeting horns to match her brother's light,
Strook with th' earth's sudden shadow, waxed pale;
Titan himself throned in the midst of heaven
His burning chariot plunged in sable clouds,
And whelmed the world in darkness, making men
Despair of day, as did Thyestes' town,
Mycenae, Phoebus flying through the east.
Fierce Mulciber unbarred Aetna's gate,
Which flamed not on high, but headlong pitched
Her burning head on bending Hespery.
Coal-black Charybdis whirled a sea of blood;
Fierce mastiffs howled; the vestal fires went out;
The flame in Alba, consecrate to Jove,
Parted in twain, and with a double point
Rose like the Theban brothers' funeral fire;
The earth went off her hinges, and the Alps
Shook the old snow from off their trembling laps.
The ocean swelled as high as Spanish Calpe,
Or Atlas' head. Their saints and household gods
Sweat tears to show the travails of their city.
Crowns fell from holy statues, ominous birds
Defiled the day, and wild beasts were seen,
Leaving the woods, lodge in the streets of Rome.
Cattle were seen that muttered human speech;
Prodigious births with more and ugly joints
Than nature gives, whose sight appals the mother;
And dismal prophecies were spread abroad;
And they whom fierce Bellona's fury moves
To wound their arms, sing vengeance; Sibyl's priests,
Curling their bloody locks, howl dreadful things;
Souls quiet and appeased sighed from their graves;
Clashing of arms was heard; in untrod woods
Shrill voices shright, and ghosts encounter men.
Those that inhabited the suburb fields

Fled; foul Erinnys stalked about the walls,
Shaking her snaky hair and crooked pine
With flaming top, much like that hellish fiend
Which made the stern Lycurgus wound his thigh,
Or fierce Agave mad; or like Megaera
That scared Alcides, when by Juno's task
He had before looked Pluto in the face.
Trumpets were heard to sound; and with what noise
An armed battle joins, such and more strange
Black night brought forth in secret: Sulla's ghost
Was seen to walk, singing sad oracles;
And Marius' head above cold Tav'ron peering
(His grave broke open) did affright the boors.

GEORGE CHAPMAN

(1559?-1634)

Chapman's earliest works are plays, followed by his completion of Marlowe's
Hero and Leander. He turned to Homer in the 1590s, and his Seven Bookes of the
Iliad appeared in 1598, to be followed at intervals over the next two decades by
his other translations, concurrently with the rest of his dramatic output.
    In *To the Reader* in his *Iliads* he writes

> Whom shall we choose the glory of all wits . . .
> But Grecian Homer? . . .
>   since true virtue lovely is
> With her own beauties; all the suffrages
> Of others I omit; and would more fain
>   That Homer, for himself, should be belov'd
> Who every sort of love-worth did contain.

Chapman's aim is to reproduce Homer, not literally, but to make him seem a
contemporary (see Introduction, p. 9). So strong is the moulding Chapman
gives his author that the poem lends itself, quite as much as Pope's, to
interpretation as an original composition. The Odysseus of Chapman, an
admirer of Epictetus, is a Stoic hero, and where Chapman expands his original
it is often to draw a moral or make a religious point (see in general George de F.
Lord, *Homeric Renaissance: the Odyssey of George Chapman* (1956)).
    Despite the magnificence of the *Iliad*, it is an unwieldy work, and the later
Odyssey is Chapman's masterpiece. He also translated, besides Musaeus' *Hero
and Leander*, Hesiod, the *Homeric Hymns*, and the tenth satire of Juvenal.

Sarpedon encourages Glaucus
(Homer, *Iliad* 12.299-322)

As ye see a mountain-lion fare,
Long kept from prey, in forcing which, his high mind makes him dare

Assault upon the whole full fold, though guarded never so
With well-arm'd men, and eager dogs; away he will not go,
But venture on, and either snatch a prey, or be a prey;
So far'd divine Sarpedon's mind, resolv'd to force his way
Through all the fore-fights, and the wall; yet since he did not see
Others as great as he in name, as great in mind as he,
He spake to Glaucus: 'Glaucus, say, why are we honour'd more
Than other men of Lycia, in place; with greater store
Of meats and cups; with goodlier roofs; delightsome gardens; walks;
More lands and better; so much wealth, that court and country talks
Of us and our possessions, and ev'ry way we go,
Gaze on us as we were their Gods? This where we dwell is so;
The shores of Xanthus ring of this; and shall we not exceed
As much in merit as in noise? Come, be we great in deed
As well as look; shine not in gold, but in the flames of fight;
That so our neat-arm'd Lycians may say: 'See, these are right
Our kings, our rulers; they deserve to eat and drink the best;
These govern not ingloriously; these, thus exceed the rest,
Do more than they command to do.' O friend, if keeping back
Would keep back age from us, and death, and that we might not wrack
In this life's human sea at all, but that deferring now
We shunn'd death ever, nor would I half this vain valour show,
Nor glorify a folly so, to wish thee to advance;
But since we must go, though not here, and that besides the chance
Propos'd now, there are infinite fates of other sort in death,
Which, neither to be fled nor 'scap'd, a man must sink beneath,
Come, try we, if this sort be ours, and either render thus
Glory to others, or make them resign the like to us.

Achilles to Hector
(Homer, *Iliad* 22.261-72)

'Hector, thou only pestilence in all mortality
To my sere spirits, never set the point 'twixt thee and me
Any conditions; but as far as men and lions fly
All terms of cov'nant, lambs and wolves; in so far opposite state,
Impossible for love t' atone, stand we, till our souls satiate
The God of soldiers. Do not dream that our disjunction can
Endure condition. Therefore now, all worth that fits a man
Call to thee, all particular parts that fit a soldier,
And they all this include (besides the skill and spirit of war)
Hunger for slaughter, and a hate that eats thy heart to eat
Thy foe's heart. This stirs, this supplies in death the killing heat;
And all this need'st thou. No more flight. Pallas Athenia
Will quickly cast thee to my lance. Now, now together draw
All griefs for vengeance, both in me, and all my friends late dead
That bled thee, raging with thy lance.'

Priam's visit to Achilles
(Homer, *Iliad* 24.513-51, 596-620)

But now Aeacides
(Satiate at all parts with the ruth of their calamities)
Start up, and up he rais'd the king. His milk-white head and beard
With pity he beheld, and said: 'Poor man, thy mind is scar'd
With much affliction. How durst thy person thus alone
Venture on his sight, that hath slain so many a worthy son,
And so dear to thee? Thy old heart is made of iron. Sit,
And settle we our woes, though huge, for nothing profits it.
Cold mourning wastes but our lives' heats. The Gods have destinate
That wretched mortals must live sad; 'tis the Immortal State
Of Deity that lives secure. Two tuns of gifts there lie
In Jove's gate, one of good, one ill, that our mortality
Maintain, spoil, order; which when Jove doth mix to any man,
One while he frolics, one while mourns. If of his mournful can
A man drinks only, only wrongs he doth expose him to,
Sad hunger in th' abundant earth doth toss him to and fro,
Respected nor of Gods nor men. The mix'd cup Peleus drank
Ev'n from his birth; Heav'n blest his life; he liv'd not that could thank
The Gods for such rare benefits as set forth his estate.
He reign'd among the Myrmidons most rich, most fortunate,
And, though a mortal, had his bed deck'd with a deathless dame.
And yet, with all this good, one ill God mix'd, that takes all name
From all that goodness; his name now, whose preservation here
Men count the crown of their most good, not bless'd with pow'r to bear
One blossom but myself, and I shaken as soon as blown;
Nor shall I live to cheer his age, and give nutrition
To him that nourish'd me. Far off my rest is set in Troy,
To leave thee restless and thy seed; thyself that did enjoy,
As we have heard, a happy life; what Lesbos doth contain,
In times past being a bless'd man's seat, what the unmeasur'd main
Of Hellespontus, Phrygia, holds, are all said to adorn
Thy empire, wealth and sons enow; but, when the Gods did turn
Thy blest state to partake with bane, war and the bloods of men
Circled thy city, never clear. Sit down and suffer then;
Mourn not inevitable things; thy tears can spring no deeds
To help thee, nor recall thy son; impatience ever breeds
Ill upon ill, makes worst things worse, and therefore sit.' . . .

This said, he went, and what was done
Told Priam, saying: 'Father, now thy will's fit rites are paid,
Thy son is giv'n up; in the morn thine eyes shall see him laid
Deck'd in thy chariot on his bed; in mean space let us eat.
The rich-hair'd Niobe found thoughts that made her take her meat,
Though twelve dear children she saw slain, six daughters, six young sons.

The sons incens'd Apollo slew; the maids' confusions
Diana wrought, since Niobe her merits durst compare
With great Latona's, arguing that she did only bear
Two children, and herself had twelve; for which those only two
Slew all her twelve. Nine days they lay steep'd in their blood, her woe
Found no friend to afford them fire, Saturnius had turn'd
Humans to stones. The tenth day yet, the good Celestials burn'd
The trunks themselves, and Niobe, when she was tir'd with tears,
Fell to her food, and now with rocks and wild hills mix'd she bears
In Sipylus the Gods' wrath still, in that place where 'tis said
The Goddess Fairies use to dance about the fun'ral bed
Of Achelous, where, though turn'd with cold grief to a stone,
Heav'n gives her heat enough to feel what plague comparison
With his pow'rs made by earth deserves. Affect not then too far
Without grief, like a God, being a man, but for a man's life care,
And take fit food; thou shalt have time beside to mourn thy son;
He shall be tearful, thou being full; not here, but Ilion
Shall find thee weeping-rooms enow.'

Mercury visits Calypso
(Homer, *Odyssey* 5.50-75)

. . . he stoop'd Pieria, and thence
Glid through the air, and Neptune's confluence
Kiss'd as he flew, and check'd the waves as light
As any sea-mew in her fishing flight,
Her thick wings sousing in the savory seas.
Like her, he pass'd a world of wilderness;
But when the far-off isle he touch'd, he went
Up from the blue sea to the continent,
And reach'd the ample cavern of the Queen,
Whom he within found, without seldom seen.
A sun-like fire upon the hearth did flame,
The matter precious, and divine the frame,
Of cedar cleft and incense was the pile,
That breath'd an odour round about the isle.
Herself was seated in an inner room,
Whom sweetly sing he heard, and at her loom,
About a curious web, whose yarn she threw
In with a golden shittle. A grove grew
In endless spring about her cavern round,
With odorous cypress, pines, and poplars, crown'd,
Where hawks, sea-owls, and long-tongued bittours bred,
And other birds their shady pinions spread;
All fowls maritimal; none roosted there,
But those whose labours in the water were.
A vine did all the hollow cave embrace,

Still green, yet still ripe bunches gave it grace.
Four fountains, one against another, pour'd
Their silver streams; and meadows all enflower'd
With sweet balm-gentle, and blue-violets hid,
That deck'd the soft breasts of each fragrant mead.
Should anyone, though he immortal were,
Arrive and see the sacred objects there,
He would admire them, and be over-joy'd;
And so stood Hermes' ravish'd pow'rs employ'd.

The song of the Sirens
(Homer, *Odyssey* 12.184-91)

'Come here, thou worthy of a world of praise,
That dost so high the Grecian glory raise,
Ulysses! stay thy ship, and that song hear
That none pass'd ever but it bent his ear,
But left him ravish'd, and instructed more
By us, than any ever heard before.
For we know all things whatsoever were
In wide Troy labour'd; whatsoever there
The Grecians and the Trojans both sustain'd
By those high issues that the Gods ordain'd.
And whatsoever all the earth can show
T'inform a knowledge of desert, we know.'

ANON.

Invitation
(Martial, *Epigrams* 5.78) from a sixteenth-century MS

To supp alone if grievous bee,
At your own home, come fast with me:
Your stomach to prepare, you shall
Have lettice and strong leekes with all;
A piece of ling with eggs, and greene
Coleworts with oil, shall there be seene
In platter brown, new gathered
From the cold garden where 'twas bredd;
Pudding or sausage shall not faile,
And bacon redd, with beanes more pale.
If second course you do affect,
Dried latter-grapes you may expect;
The pleasant boasted Syrian peares;
And chestnuts which learn'd Naples bears,
Roasted i' th' embers, shall attend;
The wine your drinking will commend.

After which if you hungry grow
(As many cupps will make men doe),
Rich olives we will you allow,
Fresh gather'd from the Picene bough;
Or scalded lupines, or parch'd peas:
A slender supper, I confess,
But yet unforc'd; where you may bee
In your discourse and garb most free;
Nor tedious volumes forc'd to hear;
Nor wanton Spanish wenches there,
Wriggling with heat of lust, shall make
Their practised limbs all postures take:
The small pipe's notes shall then rebound,
But with no harsh unpleasing sound;
And the nice Claudia there shall bee,
Whom you would rather have than mee.

THOMAS CAMPION

(d. 1620)

Educated at Cambridge, Campion went on to Gray's inn, but from 1606 we find him practising as a physician (he treated Sir Thomas Monson when in the Tower accused of complicity in the murder of Sir Thomas Overbury). His poetic and musical talents came to the notice of the court, for which he composed songs for the death of Prince Henry in 1612, and a masque for the marriage of Princess Elizabeth the following year. His masques were noted for the importance they gave to the musical element – an element also prominent in his own poems, really songs.

'Harden now thy tyred hart'
(Catullus 8)

Harden now thy tyred hart, with more than flinty rage;
Ne'er let her false teares henceforth thy constant griefe asswage.
Once true happy dayes thou saw'st, when shee stood firme and kinde:
Both as one then liv'd, and held one eare, one tongue, one minde.
But now those bright houres be fled, and never may returne:
What then remaines, but her untruths to mourne?

Silly Traytresse, who shall now thy careless tresses trace?
Who thy pretty talke supply? whose eares thy musicke grace?
Who shall thy bright eyes admire? what lips triumph with thine?
Day by day who'll visit thee and say 'th'art onely mine'?
Such a time there was, God wot, but such shall never be:
Too oft I feare thou wilt remember me.

FRANCIS BEAUMONT

(1585?-1616)

Francis Beaumont is best remembered as the collaborator with John Fletcher in their considerable dramatic output, dating from 1605-1616. The *Salmacis and Hermaphroditus* was his first work, published in 1602.

How to dispel love-melancholy
(Ovid, *Remedia Amoris* 579-90, with additions)

Fly lovely walkes, and uncouth places sad,
They are the nurse of thoughts that make men mad;
Walk not too much where thy fond eye may see
The place where she did give love's rights to thee:
For even the place will tell thee of those joyes,
And turne thy kisses into sad annoies.
Frequent not woods and groves, nor sit and muse
With armes acrosse, as foolish lovers use:
For as thou sitt'st alone, thou soone shalt find
Thy mistris' face presented to thy mind,
As plainly to the troubled phantasie
As if she were in presence, and stood by.
This to eschew open thy doores all day,
Shun no man's speech that comes into thy way.
Admit all companies, and where there's none,
Then walke thou forth thy selfe, and seek out one;
When he is found, seeke more, laugh, drinke, and sing;
Rather than be alone, do any thing.
Or if thou be constrain'd to be alone,
Have not her picture for to gaze upon:
For that's the way, when thou art eas'd of paine,
To wound anew, and make thee sick againe.
Or if thou hast it, think the painter's skill
Flattered her face, and that she looks more ill;
And thinke as thou dost musing on it sit,
That she herselfe is counterfeit like it.
Or rather fly all things that are inclin'd
To bring one thought of her into thy mind.
View not her tokens, nor thinke on her words,
But take some book, whose learned wombe affords
Physic for soules, there search for some reliefe
To guile the time, and rid away thy griefe.
But if thy thoughts on her must needs be bent,
Thinke what a deale of precious time was spent
In quest of her; and that thy best of youth
Languish'd and died while she was void of truth.

Thinke but how ill she did deserve affection,
And yet how long she held thee in subjection,
Thinke how she changed, how ill it did become her,
And thinking so, leave love, and flie far from her.

BEN JONSON

(1572-1637)

Ben Jonson was educated at Westminster, and he acknowledged his tremendous debt to Camden, his teacher there. On leaving the school he apparently worked as a bricklayer, and spent some time on military service in the Low Countries. On his return he became a figure in the society of the Inns of Court, the home of the intellectual and literary coteries of the day. His first play, *Every Man in his Humour*, and even more its intellectual successor, *Every Man out of his Humour*, already mark Jonson's break with theatrical tradition by the role he gives himself of *corrector morum*, in which he may owe something to the influence of Nashe. His acerbic moralism prompted the attack in Marston's *Histriomastix*, to which he responded with *Poetaster* (1601). The further attack in Dekker's *Satiromastix* drove him to retire for a while from comedy, and he seems to have spent the next five years in study and the composition of epigrams, besides being the centre of the circle that met at the Mermaid Tavern. *Sejanus*, which reflects the new fashion for learning in the age of Bacon and Burton, was a failure; but at this time he gained the patronage of the court of James I and produced many of his Masques, as well as being friendly with the Haringtons and Sidneys. His major plays date from the succeeding years. In 1618 he walked to Scotland where he visited William Drummond of Hawthornden, and returned to England to academic honours. From 1634 he was in receipt of a pension, and the centre of the Tribe of Ben that met in the Apollo tavern. The Tribe includes many of the most distinguished names of seventeenth-century literature, and it is not exaggerating to say that the learning of Ben Jonson, combined with his thoughtful reinterpretation and modification of classical motifs, was the mainspring of the poetry of the first half of the century. His tomb bears the simple legend: 'O rare Ben Jonson!'

The stylistic mean
(Horace, *Ars Poetica* 24-37)

Most writers, noble sire, and either son,
Are, with the likeness of the truth, undone.
Myself for shortness labour; and I grow
Obscure. This, striving to run smooth, and flow,
Hath neither soul, nor sinews. Lofty he
Professing greatness, swells: that, low by lee

Creeps on the ground; too safe, too afraid of storm.
This, seeking in a various kind, to form
One thing prodigiously, paints in the woods
A dolphin, and a boar amidst the floods.
So, shunning faults, to greater faults doth lead,
When in a wrong, and artless way we tread.
The worst of statuaries, here about
The Aemelian school, in brass can fashion out
The nails, and ev'ry curled hair disclose;
But in the main work hapless: since he knows
Not to design the whole. Should I aspire
To form a work, I would no more desire
To be that smith; than live, marked one of those
With fair black eyes, and hair, and a wry nose.

The changes of language
(Horace, Ars Poetica 60-72)

As woods whose change appears
Still in their leaves, throughout the sliding years,
The first-born dying; so the aged state
Of words decay, and phrases born but late
Like tender buds shoot up, and freshly grow.
Ourselves, and all that's ours, to death we owe:
Whether the sea received into the shore,
That from the north, the navy safe doth store,
A kingly work; or that barren fen
Once rowable, but now doth nourish men
In neighbour towns, and feels the weighty plough;
Or the wild river, who hath changed now
His course so hurtful both to grain, and seeds,
Being taught a better way. All mortal deeds
Shall perish: so far off it is, the state,
Or grace of speech, should hope a lasting date.
Much phrase that is now dead, shall be revived;
And much shall die, that now is nobly lived,
If custom please; at whose disposing will
The power, and rule of speaking resteth still.

To Venus
(Horace, Odes 4.1)

Venus, again thou mov'st a war
Long intermitted, pray thee, pray thee, spare:
I am not such, as in the reign
Of the good Cynara I was: refrain,
Sour mother of sweet loves, forbear

To bend a man now, at his fiftieth year,
   Too stubborn for commands, so slack:
Go where youth's soft entreaties call thee back.
   More timely hie thee to the house,
With thy bright swans, of Paulus Maximus:
   There jest, and feast, make him thine host,
If a fit liver thou dost seek to toast;
   For he's both noble, lovely, young,
And for the troubled client files his tongue;
   Child of a hundred arts, and far
Will he display the ensigns of thy war.
   And when he smiling finds his grace
With thee 'bove all his rivals' gifts take place,
   He will thee a marble statue make
Beneath a sweetwood roof, near Alba lake:
   There shall thy dainty nostril take
In many a gum, and for thy soft ear's sake
   Shall verse be set to harp and lute,
And Phrygian hautboy, not with the flute.
   There twice a day in sacred lays,
The youths and tender maids shall sing thy praise:
   And in the Salian manner meet
Thrice 'bout thy altar with their ivory feet.
   Me now, nor wench, nor wanton boy,
Delights, nor credulous hope of mutual joy,
   Nor care I now healths to propound;
Or with fresh flowers to girt my temples round.
   But why, oh why, my Ligurine,
Flow my thin tears, down these pale cheeks of mine?
   Or why, my well-graced words among,
With an uncomely silence fails my tongue?
   Hard-hearted, I dream every night
I hold thee fast! But fled hence, with the light,
   Whether in Mars his field thou be,
Or Tiber's winding streams, I follow thee.

Dialogue of Horace and Lydia
(Horace, *Odes* 3.9)

Horace:
   Whilst, Lydia, I was loved of thee,
And ('bout thy ivory neck) no youth did fling
   His arms more acceptable free,
I thought me richer than the Persian king.

Lydia:
   Whilst Horace loved no mistress more,

Nor after Chloe did his Lydia sound;
  In name I went all name before,
The Roman Ilia was not more renowned.

Hor:
  Tis true, I am Thracian Chloe's, I,
Who sings so sweet, and with such cunning plays,
  As, for her, I'd not fear to die,
So Fate would give her life, and longer days.

Lyd:
  And I am mutually on fire
With gentle Calais, Thurine Orinth's son;
  For whom I doubly would expire,
So Fates would let the boy a long thread run.

Hor:
  But, say old love return should make,
And us disjoined force to her brazen yoke,
  That I bright Chloe off should shake;
And to left-Lydia, now the gate stood ope.

Lyd:
  Though he be fairer than a star;
Though lighter than the bark of any tree,
  And than rough Adria, angrier, far;
Yet would I wish to love, live, die with thee.

Ovid recites
(Ovid, *Amores* 1.15) from *Poetaster*

Envy, why twit'st thou me my time's spent ill,
And call'st my verse, fruits of an idle quill?
Or that, unlike the line from whence I sprung,
War's dusty honours I pursue not young?
Or that I study not the tedious laws,
And prostitute my voice in every cause?
Thy scope is mortal; mine eternal fame,
Which through the world shall ever chaunt my name.
Homer will live whilst Tenedos stands, and Ide,
Or, to the sea, fleet Simois doth slide:
And so shall Hesiod too, while vines do bear,
Or crooked sickles crop the ripen'd ear.
Callimachus, though in invention low,
Shall still be sung, since he in art doth flow.
No loss shall come to Sophocles' proud vein;
With sun and moon, Aratus shall remain.

While slaves be false, fathers hard, and bawds be whorish,
Whilst harlots flatter, shall Menander flourish.
Ennius, though rude, and Accius' high-rear'd strain,
A fresh applause in every age shall gain,
Of Varro's name, what ear shall not be told,
Of Jason's Argo and the fleece of gold?
Then shall Lucretius' lofty numbers die,
When earth and seas in fire and flame shall fry.
Tityrus, Tillage, Aenee shall be read,
Whilst Rome of all the conquered world is head!
Till Cupid's fires be out, and his bow broken,
Thy verses, neat Tibullus, shall be spoken.
Our Gallus shall be known from east to west;
So shall Lycoris, whom he now loves best.
The suffering plough-share or the flint may wear;
But heavenly Poesy no death can fear.
Kings shall give place to it, and kingly shows,
The banks o'er which gold-bearing Tagus flows.
Kneel hinds to trash: me let bright Phoebus swell
With cups full flowing from the Muses' well.
Frost-fearing myrtle shall impale my head,
And of sad lovers I be often read.
Envy the living, not the dead, doth bite!
For after death all men receive their right.
Then, when this body falls in funeral fire,
My name shall live, and my best part aspire.

Chaste lust
([Petronius], Anth. Lat. 1.2.700)

Doing, a filthy pleasure is, and short;
And done, we straight repent us of the sport:
Let us not then rush blindly on unto it,
Like lustful beasts, that only know to do it:
For lust will languish, and that heat decay,
But thus, thus, keeping endless holiday,
Let us together closely lie, and kiss,
There is no labour, nor no shame in this;
This hath pleased, doth please, and long will please; never
Can this decay, but is beginning ever.

A pleasant life
(Martial, *Epigrams* 10.47)

The things that make the happier life, are these,
Most pleasant Martial; substance got with ease,
Not laboured for, but left thee by thy sire;

A soil, not barren; a continual fire;
Never at law; seldom in office gowned;
A quiet mind; free powers; and body sound;
A wise simplicity; friends alike-stated;
Thy table without art, and easy-rated:
Thy night not drunken, but from cares laid waste;
No sour, or sullen bed-mate, yet a chaste;
Sleep, that will make the darkest hours swift-paced;
Will to be, what thou art; and nothing more:
Nor fear thy latest day, nor wish therefore.

2. The Seventeenth Century to Abraham Cowley

BARTEN HOLYDAY

(1593-1661)

Holyday was educated at Christ Church and became Archdeacon of Oxford in 1626. Though a royalist, and chaplain to King Charles I, he kept in sufficient favour with the Protectorate to retire to Iffley and live on his archdeaconry. His version of Persius was published in 1616, and a posthumous reissue of 1673 was accompanied by his translation of Juvenal.

William Gifford, in the preface to his own translation of Juvenal, writes of him: 'Of this ingenious man it is not easy to speak with too much respect. His learning, industry, judgment, and taste are every where conspicuous: nor is he without a very considerable portion of shrewdness to season his observations. His poetry indeed, or rather his ill-measured prose, is intolerable: no human patience can toil through a single page of it; but his notes, though inelegantly written, will always be consulted with pleasure.'

An anonymous translation of Horace's odes, published in 1652 and reissued in 1653 as the work of 'Unknown Muse', has been ascribed to Holyday by the British Library catalogue. This rests on a confusion. Anthony à Wood ascribed to Holyday a translation of Horace, which, he said, was indistinguishable from that of Sir Thomas Hawkins. There is a book of 1652 which contains a translation of Horace (by Hawkins) followed by Holyday's Persius, with an ambiguous title-page which led Wood to suppose both were by Holyday. Subsequent bibliographers, unable to find any identified translation of Horace by Holyday, have ascribed to him that of Unknown Muse. There is no reason to suppose that Holyday ever translated Horace (see W. J. Cameron, 'Brome's "Horace" 1666 and 1671', *Notes and Queries* 202 (1957), 70-1).

Domitian's councillors
(Juvenal, *Satires* 4.37-44, 81-98, 105-18)

When the last Flavius th' half-dead world did tear,
And Rome to bald-pate Nero crouch'd with fear,
'Fore Venus' shrine, Dorique Ancona's grace,

An Adriatick turbet of vast space
Plung'd in, choak'd up the net and stuck no less
Than those, which the Maeotick waves oppress,
Till thaw'd at the dull Pontick gates they throw
Them out, first with long cold made fat and slow . . .

Then came all pleasant Crispus, of a sweet
Temper and eloquence, and none more meet
To have advis'd him, that rul'd sea and land,
Might he but have condemned foul actions; and
Had not that plague of mankind loath'd to hear
Truth. But what's fiercer than a tyrant's eare?
With whom to talk of heat, cold, spring-show'rs, straight
(As if you'd in the weather search his fate)
Was death! Hee'd ne're then swim against the flood:
No man for truth durst spend words, much less blood.
Arm'd with these arts of proof, this man, in fears
And such a court, did live safe fourscore years!
Next came Acilius of the like great age;
His son too, whom the tyrants bloody rage
Mark't-out and seiz'd on. But meer prodigie
Long since, great age was in nobilitie. . .

Rubrius too, though of no noble race,
Went thither with as sad a heart and face.
He did a court-fault, which to name's no wit,
Yet, then the pathick that a satyre writ,
Was worse. Montanus came too, and his slow
Paunch; and Crispinus, who did rankly flow
With sweat of morning-ointments; they scarce wast
So much upon two fun'rals! Then did hast
Pompey more cruel: he could, with a fine
Whisper, cut throats. Fuscus did likewise joine
In speed and councel; on whose entrailes fed
The Dacian vultures. He to the wars was bred
In his brave marble summer-house. Then went
The shrewd Vejento, and Catullus bent
To bloody plots. He us'd to be enflam'd
With beauties, which he saw not, but heard nam'd;
A grand, conspicuous monster in these worst
Times, a blind, flatt'ring, cruel states-man, first
Brought from some bridge, fit still to beg, and throw
His flatt'ring kisses towards those, that go
By waggon down to Aricia.

LEONARD DIGGES

(1588-1635)

Born into a family of mathematicians – his father was respected by Tycho
Brahe – Digges was educated at University College, Oxford. Besides his
Claudian he translated a Spanish novel, *Gerardo, the Unfortunate Spaniard.*

Pluto begs Jupiter for a bride
(Claudian, *The Rape of Proserpine* 1.89 ff.)

Joves high-borne brood, Cylenian Mercurie:
Olde Atlas Nephew, common deity
To heaven and hell: thou, that hast passage free
Through both the Poles, and equall liberty;
Thou, that of all the gods both high and low,
The mysteries and strict commerce dost know:
Fly hence, with speedy wing cut through the winde,
To thy ungratefull Sire thus speake our minde.
What right hast thou, or what prioritie,
(Cruel'st of all thy brothers) over me?
Say, Fortune blind with an unequall hand,
(To me denying) gave thee heav'ns command?
Yet are these temples honour'd with a crowne,
As well as thine, nor can thy pride beat downe
Our glory; though we want the light, thou shalt
Percieve our strength, when I thy walls assault:
Think'st thou the Cyclop's handy-worke I feare;
Or those vaine claps that mocke the yeelding ayre?
Cast downe thy darts of thunder, let them strike
Affrighted mortals, we are farre unlike
To such; Know, Jupiter, I keepe my vowe,
And to revenge my griefes, am sure (though slowe)
Was't not enough? I then repined not
At Fates, that first to my accursed lot
Gave this third kingdome, and deprived quite,
(Though satisfied) I never sought for light:
Nor wisht bright Phoebus might descend so farre
As my sad palace, or the morning starre
Lighten these vaults; when unto thee the seav'n,
(That make Charles-wayne twinkle in spangled heav'n)
And millions more thy glorious state adorne:
Poore I, that all in darknesse sit forlorne
(Discomfortably mournfull) no glad sight
Enjoy, but waste in a perpetuall night,
Where are no comforts to the eye or eare,
Nothing but noyse, and notes of ghastly feare,

For what harmonious musick hath hells king?
Where ghosts keep howling time, whil'st scriech-owles sing:
Yet thou that see'st me bare of all reliefe,
(The more to aggravate my sullen griefe)
Forbidd'st me Nuptiall rites; thus Jove repines
At Pluto's wishes, when his Concubines
Are numberlesse; the Sea-god happier is,
(Though lesse in power then I) and hath more blisse,
That when the raging billowes he allayes,
Faire Amphitrite with her Neptune playes
And he (intangled in her soft embrace)
Forgets the use of his three-forked mace.
When thou in midst of Tytans scorching heate,
With labour of thy thunder-claps dost sweate
To coole the partch't earth, with moist drops of raine,
And (weary of thy toyle turn'st backe againe)
Incestuous Juno sits in longing state
With open lap her Lord to recreate:
Latona, Ceres, Themis: (each of which
Sufficient were) but all of these, enrich
Thee, with the name of father, and thy seate
Keepe still with hopefull successors repleate:
Thus thou, in lustfull ryot (varying)
Liv'st at thine ease, whil'st I (thy brother king)
In darkest dungeon (like a slave) am voyde
Of those delights, with which thou most art cloid:
And thus my prime of youth doth fade, and pride
Of issue, failes; (by wanting a lov'd Bride)
But come revenge, awake dull patience,
(Suffice long pardon for so just offence)
By all the shades of night, by all the Ghosts
That hover o'er blacke Styx, by all the hosts
Of dreadfull horror, mischiefe vengeance dire,
If Iupiter denie this last desire;
The walls of Tartarus shall open wide
(Thorough whose breach) the soules that there abide
(Condemn'd to endlesse ruth) shall sally out,
And hast thy downfall with confused rowt:
('Mongst whom) old Saturne once againe shall free
The golden age from her captivitie.

SIR THOMAS OVERBURY
(1581-1613)

The story of Overbury's life and death is bound up with that of his one-time friend Robert Carr, later Viscount Rochester. Rochester was angered when Overbury refused to connive at his plans to induce the Countess of Essex to divorce her husband for his benefit, and attempted to have Overbury dispatched to a diplomatic post abroad. Overbury however refused to go, with the result that he was eventually confined to the Tower, and subsequently poisoned in mysterious circumstances. Overbury had made use of his best-known poem 'A Wife' in the attempt to dissuade Rochester from marriage with his mistress; though it is not known when the translation of the *Remedia Amoris* was made – the first surviving edition is the posthumous one of 1620 – Overbury may well have found the arguments of Ovid useful in his attempts to persuade his erstwhile friend.

How to dispel passion
(Ovid, *Remedia Amoris* 543-6, 557-74, 579-92, compressed and altered)

He that from farre his mistress doth admire,
And dares not hope of his having desire:
His wound, a cure, uncurable will prove,
For what we thinke forbidden, most we love.
Distrust not then, till thou heare her reply,
'Who asketh faintly, teacheth to deny.'
If all these faile, this next will helpe impart,
And love of others to self-love convert.
 Since thoughts of love no longer us possesse,
Then while we live in health and happinesse,
Let him that is indebted thinke alone,
That while he thinkes his day drawes neerer on:
Whom a hard father from his will doth let,
Let him before him still his father set.
Let him which will a wife with nothing take,
Thinke from preferment she will keepe him backe:
None need this physicke of physitions borrow,
For none but hath some cause for feare or sorrow.
Let him that deeply loves and is forgone,
(Like an ill-doer) feare to be alone.
Use not to silent groves alone to shrinke,
Nothing love more upholdeth then to thinke:
Then will thy minde thy mistresse picture take,
For mem'ry all things past doth present make.
Then like Pigmalion we an image frame,
And fall in love devoutly with the same.
Therefore, then night, lesse dangerous is the day,
Because then, thoughts newborne, talk sends away.
Then shalt thou finde how much a friend is worth,
Into whose breast thou maist thy griefe poure forth.
Phillis alone frequented th' rivers side,
Clowded with shade of trees, till there she di'd.

GEORGE SANDYS

(1578-1614)

The translation of Ovid's *Metamorphoses* was completed in America, and was the first of his translations: others are versions of the Psalms and the Song of Solomon, and a translation of Grotius' Latin tragedy *Christ's Passion*. He also translated Book 1 of Vergil's *Aeneid*. His earlier writings are descriptions of his travels in the Near East. After his return from America he joined Lord Falkland's literary circle at Great Tew.

Sandys' aim is a close literal translation, and he in fact succeeded in rendering the *Metamorphoses* in the same number of lines as the original, with the not surprising result that his version is often too compressed to be easily intelligible. It was much admired by contemporaries – one refers to the 'sumptuous bravery of that rich attire' in which Ovid has appeared (in *Wits Recreations*, 1640). The *Metamorphoses* was first published in 1626, and went through five editions.

The flight of Icarus
(Ovid, *Metamorphoses* 8.183-235)

The Sea-impris'ned Daedalus, mean-while,
Weary of Creet, and of his long exile;
Toucht with his countries love, and place of birth,
Thus said: Though Minos bar both sea and earth;
Yet heaven is free. That course attempt I dare:
Held he the world, he could not hold the ayre.
This said; to arts unknowne he bends his wits,
And alters nature. Quils in order knits,
Beginning with the least: the longer still
The short succeeds; much like a rising hill.
Their rurall pipes, the shepheards long, agoe,
(Fram'd of unequall reeds) contrived so.
With threds the midst, with wax he joynes the ends:
And these, as naturall wings, a little bends.
Young Icarus stood by, who little thought
That with his death he playd; and smiling, caught
The feathers tossed by the wand'ring ayre:
Now chafes the yellow wax with busie care,
And interrupts his Sire. When his last hand
Had made all perfect: with new wings he fand
The ayre that bare him. Then instructs his sonne:
Be sure that in the middle course thou run.
Dank seas will clog the wings that lowly fly:
The Sun will burn them if thou soar'st too high.
'Twixt either keepe. Nor on Bootes gaze,
Nor Helice, nor stern Orions rayes:

But follow me. At once, he doth advise;
And unknown feathers to his shoulders tyes.
Amid his work and words the salt tears brake
From his dim eyes; with feare his fingers shake.
Then kist him, never to be kissed more:
And rais'd on lightsome feathers flies before;
His feare behinde: as birds through boundlesse sky
From ayrie nests produce their young to fly;
Exhorts to follow: taught his banefull skill;
Waves his owne wings, his sonnes observing still.
These, while some Angler, fishing with a Cane;
Or Shepheard, leaning on his staffe; or Swaine;
With wonder views: he thinks them Gods that glide
Through ayrie regions. Now on his left side
Leaves Juno's Samos, Delos, Paros white,
Lebynthos, and Calydna on the right,
Flowing with hony. When the boy, much took
With pleasure of his wings, his Guide forsook:
And ravisht with desire of heaven, aloft
Ascends. The odor-yeelding wax more soft
By the swift Sunnes vicinitie then grew:
Which late his feathers did together glew.
That thaw'd he shakes his armes, which now were bare,
And wanted wherewithall to gather ayre.
Then falling, Help O father, cries: the blew
Seas stopt his breath; from whom their name they drew.
His father, now no father, left alone,
Cry'd Icarus! where art thou? which way flowne?
What region, Icarus, doth thee containe?
Then spies his feathers floating on the maine.
He curst his arts; interres the corpse, that gave
The land a name, which gave his sonne a grave.

The Cave of Sleep
(Ovid, *Metamorphoses* 11.592-615)

Neere the Cimmerians lurks a Cave, in steep
And hollow hills; the Mansion of dull Sleep:
Not seen by Phoebus when he mounts the skies,
At height, nor stooping: gloomie mists arise
From humid earth, which still a twi-light make.
No crested fowles shrill crowings here awake
The cheerfull Morn: no barking Sentinell
Here guards; nor geese, who wakefull dogs excell.
Beasts tame, nor salvage; no wind-shaken boughs,
Nor strife of jarring tongues, with noyses rouse
Secured Ease. Yet from the rock a spring,

With streams of Lethe softly murmuring,
Perles on the pebbles, and invites Repose.
Before the entry pregnant Poppie grows,
With numerous Simples; from whose juycie birth
Night gathers sleep, and sheds it on the Earth.
No doores here on their creaking hinges jarr'd:
Throughout this court there was no doore, nor guard.
Amid the Heben cave a downy bed
High mounted stands, with sable coverings spred.
Here lay the lazie God, dissolv'd in rest.
Fantastick Dreames, who various formes exprest,
About him lay: then Autumn's ears far more;
Or leaves of trees, or sands on Neptune's shore.

THOMAS MAY

(1595-1650)

Educated at Sidney Sussex College, Cambridge, May went on to Gray's Inn,
but did not enter the law, probably because of a speech impediment. Instead
he turned his hand to the pen, of which the first product was a comedy, *The
Heir.* He then translated Lucan's *Pharsalia*, and the work was published in
1627. It went through eight editions, was praised by Ben Jonson and won him
the favour of Charles I, who commissioned him to write historical poems on
Henry II and Edward III. His successes made him a candidate for Poet
Laureate to succeed Ben Jonson in 1637, but the honour went to D'Avenant.
Contemporaries attributed to this disappointment his espousal of the
paliamentarian cause thereafter: he became secretary to the Long Parliament,
and afterwards its historian. Besides Lucan, he translated Vergil's *Georgics* and
a selection from Martial; his other works – plays, poetry, and prose – are
numerous.

Soil-testing
(Vergil, *Georgics* 2.226-58)

How to discerne each soile Ile teach thee now,
Which mould is thick and which is loose to know.
(For one Lyaeus, tother Ceres loves:
Vines love loose grounds, corne best in thickest proves).
Choose with thine eie that piece that is most plain;
There digge a pit, and then throw in againe
The clods and earth, and tread them strongly in;
If they'le not fill the pit, the soile is thin,
And best for vineyards, and for pasture grasse;

But if the clods do more than fill the place,
The earth is thick and solid; try that soile,
And plow it well, though hard and full of toile.
That earth that's salt, or bitter, bad for sowing,
(For that will never be made good by plowing,
Nor wines, nor apples planted there, abide
In their first generous tast) may thus be tride;
Take a thick-woven osiar colander
Through which the pressed wines are strained clear,
And put a piece of that bad earth into it
Well mixt with water, and then strain them through it,
You shall perceive the struggling water slow,
And in great drops will through the osiars goe.
But by the tast you may discerne it plaine;
The bitterness will make the taster straine
His countenance awry. So you may know
By handling, whether ground be fat or no;
Leane earth will crumble into dust: but thicke
Like pitch fat earth will to your fingers sticke.
Moist land brings forth tall grasse, and oft is found
Too rich; oh give me not so rank a ground,
Nor let it corns yong husks too richly raise.
Earth that is heavy her own weight betrayes,
And so of light; our eyes do judge aright
The collour of the land or blacke or white.
But to finde out that cursed quality
Of cold in grounds, of all, will hardest be;
Yet that the trees, which prosper there, will shew,
Pitch trees, black ivie, and the balefull yew.

                          Vanity
                 (Martial, *Epigrams* 3.43)

Thou dy'st thy haire to seeme a younger man,
And turn'st a crow, that lately wert a swan.
All are not cousen'd; hels queene knows thee grey.
She'll take the vizor from thy head away.

                  SIR JOHN BEAUMONT

                      (1583-1627)

After his education at Oxford, Beaumont won the patronage of the Duke of
Buckingham, and distinguished himself as a royalist and cavalier. His poems
were first collected and published by his son; besides the translations they

include a considerable amount of religious poetry. His largest work, the
'Crown of Thorns' in eight books, is lost. Religious themes are also apparent in
the texts he chose for translation and in his treatment of them: Persius'
insistence that the gods are more interested in the state of a man's soul than in
gifts, and Vergil's Messianic *Eclogue* 4.

The town and the country mouse
(Horace, *Satires* 2.6.79-117)

> 'Long since a countrey mouse
> Receav'd into his low and homely house
> A citty mouse, his friend and guest before;
> The hoste was sharpe and sparing of his store,
> Yet much to hospitality inclin'd:
> For such occasions could dilate his mind.
> He chiches gives for winter layd aside,
> Nor are the long and slender otes deny'd:
> Dry grapes he in his lib'rall mouth doth beare,
> And bits of bacon, which halfe eaten were:
> With various meates to please the stranger's pride,
> Whose dainty teeth through all the dishes slide.
> The father of the family in straw
> Lies stretcht along, disdaigning not to gnaw
> Base corne or darnell, and reserves the best,
> To make a perfect banquet for his guest.
> To him at last the citizen thus spake:
> "My friend, I muse what pleasure thou canst take,
> Or how thou canst endure to spend thy time
> In shady groves and up steep hills to clime.
> In savage forrests build no more thy den:
> Goe to the city, there to dwell with men.
> Begin this happy journey; trust to me,
> I will thee guide, thou shalt my fellow be.
> Since earthly things are ty'd to mortall lives,
> And ev'ry great and little creature strives,
> In vaine, the certaine stroke of death to flie,
> Stay not till moments past thy joy denie.
> Live in rich plenty and perpetuall sport:
> Live ever mindfull, that thy life is short."
> The ravisht field mouse holds these words so sweet,
> That from his home he leapes with nimble feet.
> They to the citie travaile with delight,
> And underneath the walles they creepe at night.
> Now darknesse had possest Heav'n's middle space,
> When these two friends their weary steps did place
> Within a wealthy palace, where was spred
> A scarlet cov'ring on an iv'ry bed:

The baskets (set farre off aside) contain'd
The meates, which after plenteous meales remain'd:
The citie mouse with courtly phrase intreates
His country friend to rest in purple seates;
With ready care the master of the feast
Runnes up and down to see the store increast:
He all the duties of a servant showes,
And tastes of ev'ry dish that he bestowes.
The poore plaine mouse, exalted thus in state,
Glad of the change, his former life doth hate,
And strive in lookes and gesture to declare
With what contentment he receives this fare.
But straight the sudden creaking of a doore
Shakes both these mice from beds into the floore.
They run about the room halfe dead with feare,
Through all the house the noise of dogs they heare.
The stranger now counts not the place so good,
He bids farewell, and saith, "The silent wood
Shall me hereafter from these dangers save,
Well pleas'd with simple vetches in my cave." '

The gods love a pure heart best
(Persius, *Satires* 2.55-75)

Hence comes it, that with gold in triumph borne,
Thou do'st the faces of the gods adorne:
Among the brazen brethren they that send
Those dreames, where evill humours least extend,
The highest place in men's affections hold,
And for their care receive a beard of gold:
The glorious name of gold hath put away
The use of Saturne's brass, and Numae's clay.
The glitt'ring pride to richer substance turnes
The Tuscan earthen pots and vestall urnes.
O crooked soules, declining to the earth,
Whose empty thoughts forget their heav'nly birth:
What end, what profit, have we, when we strive
Our manners to the temples to derive?
Can we suppose, that to the gods we bring
Some pleasing good for this corrupted spring?
This flesh, which casia doth dissolve and spoyle,
And with that mixture taints the native oyle:
This boyles the fish with purple liquor full,
And staines the whitenesse of Calabrian wooll.
This from the shell scrapes out the pearle, and straines
From raw rude earth the fervent metal's veines.
This sinnes, it sinnes, yet makes some use of vice:

But tell me, ye great flamins, can the price
Raise gold to more account in holy things,
Than babies, which the maide to Venus brings?
Nay, rather let us yeeld the gods such gifts,
As great Messallae's offspring never lifts,
In costly chargers stretcht to ample space,
Because degenerate from his noble race:
A soul, where just and pious thoughts are chain'd;
A mind, whose secret corners are unstain'd;
A brest, in which all gen'rous vertues lie,
And paint it with a never-fading die.
Thus to the temples let me come with zeale,
The gods will hear me, though I offer meale.

WYE SALTONSTALL

(fl. 1630-1640)

Educated at Queen's College, Oxford, Saltonstall proceeded to Gray's Inn, but seems to have returned to Oxford, where he apparently taught for a while before ending his life in poverty, some time before 1672. Besides his translations of Ovid's *Tristia, Heroicall Epistles* and *Ex Ponto*, he translated Eusebius, an index to Comenius' *Porta Linguarum*, and Jodocus Hondius' Latin *Historia Mundi, or Mercator's Atlas* – all of them works of an educational bent – and wrote funeral elegies on the death of his father.

Paris writes to Helen
(Ovid, *Heroides* 16.121-72)

My sister Cassandra with loosen'd haire,
When as my ships even weighing anchor were,
Said, whither goest thou? thou shalt bring againe,
By crossing the seas, a destroying flame.
The truth she said, for I have found a fire,
Love hath enflam'd my soft breast with desire.
A faire wind from the port my sails did drive,
And I in Hellen's countrey did arrive.
Where thy husband did me much kindnesse show,
And sure the gods decreed it should be so.
He shew'd me all that worthy was of sight
In Lacedemon, to breed me delight.
But there was nothing that my fancy tooke,
But only thee, and thy sweet beautious looke:
For when I saw thee, I was ev'n amaz'd,
My heart was wounded while on thee I gaz'd.

For I remember Venus was like thee,
When she would have her beauty judg'd by me.
And if thou hadst contended with her, I
Had surely given thee the victorie.
For the report of thee abroad was blowne,
Thy beauty was in every countrey knowne.
For through all nations where the sun doth rise,
Thy beauty only bore away the prize,
Beleeve me, fame did not report so much
As thou deserv'st, thy beauty seemeth such,
That Theseus did not thy love disdaine,
And to steale thee away did think't no shame;
When suiting to the Lacedemonian fashion,
Thou didst sport with the young men of thy nation.
In stealing thee, I like his just desire,
But how he could restore thee, I admire.
For such a beauteous prey had sure deserv'd,
To have been kept, and constantly preserv'd.
For before thou should'st be tooke from my bed,
Before I would lose thee, I would lose my head.
Alas! could I have ever so forgone thee,
Or while I liv'd have let thee beene tooke from me?
Yet if I must restore thee needs at last,
I would have yet presum'd to touch, and taste
The golden apples of thy virgin tree;
And not sent thee backe with virginity.
Or if that I had spar'd thy virgin treasures,
I would have rifled some other pleasures.
Then grant thy love to Paris, who will be,
While I doe live, most constant unto thee.
I will be constant to your owne desire,
My love, and life shall both at once expire.
Before great kingdomes I preferred thee,
Which royall Juno promis'd unto me.
And learning, Pallas gift, I did refuse,
And to enjoy thy sweet selfe I did chuse.
When Juno, Venus, and faire Pallas too,
Their naked beauties unto me did shew;
And in the Idean vallies did not grudge,
In case of beauty to make me their judge,
Yet I doe not repent of my election,
My mind is constant to my first affection.
I beseech thee let not my hope prove vaine.
Who spar'd no labour in hope thee to gaine.

RICHARD CRASHAW

(1613?-1649)

Crashaw was educated at Charterhouse and at Pembroke Hall, Cambridge, where he is said to have excelled in five languages. The bulk of his religious poetry was composed in long sessions of meditation in St Mary's Church. He never became a priest, because of his lack of sympathy with the growth of puritanism. On the outbreak of the Civil War he retired to Paris, and by the time Cowley met him there he had become a Roman Catholic.

The poetry of England's most baroque poet poses something of a bibliographical problem: much of his work survives only in manuscript, or has been lost altogether. Martin's Oxford edition of 1957 includes several translations from Latin authors; Crashaw's own very visual style is an excellent mirror for the sometimes startling imagery of Horace.

A narrow escape
(Horace, *Odes* 2.13)

Shame of thy mother soyle! ill-natur'd tree!
Sett to the mischiefe of posteritie!
That hand, (what e're it were) that was thy nurse,
Was sacrilegious, (sure) or somewhat worse.
Black, as the day was dismall; in whose sight
Thy rising topp first stained the bashfull light.
That man (I thinke) wrested the feeble life
From his old father. That man's barbarous knife
Conspir'd with darkness 'gainst the strangers throate;
(Whereof the blushing walles tooke bloody note)
Huge high-floune poysons, ev'n of Colchos breed,
And whatsoe're wild sinnes black thoughtes doe feed,
His hands have padled in; his hands, that found
Thy traiterous root a dwelling in my ground.
Perfidious totterer! longing for the staines
Of thy kind master's well-deserving braines.
Mans daintiest care, and caution cannot spy
The subtile point of his coy destiny,
Which way it threats. With feare the merchants mind
Is plough'd as deepe, as is the sea with wind,
(Rouz'd in an angry tempest); oh the sea!
Oh! that's his feare; there flotes his destiny:
While from another (unseene) corner blowes
The storme of fate, to which his life he owes.
By Parthians bow the soldier looks to die,
(Whose hands are fighting, while their feet doe flie).
The Parthian starts at Rome's imperiall name,
Fledg'd with her eagles wing; the very chaine

Of his captivity rings in his eares.
Thus, ô thus fondly doe wee pitch our feares
Far distant from our fates. Our fates, that mocke
Our giddy feares with an unlookt for shocke.
   A little more, and I had surely seene
Thy greisly majesty, Hells blackest queene;
And Aeacus on his tribunall too,
Sifting the soules of guilt; and you (oh you!)
You ever-blushing meads, where doe the blest
Far from darke horrors home appeale to rest.
There amorous Sappho plaines upon her lute
Her loves cross fortune, that the sad dispute
Runnes murmuring on the strings. Alcaeus there
In high-built numbers wakes his golden lyre,
To tell the world, how hard the matter went
How hard by sea, by warre, by banishment.
There these brave soules deale to each wondring eare
Such words, soe precious, as they may not weare
Without religious silence; above all
Warres rattling tumults, or some tyrants fall,
The thronging clotted multitude doth feast.
What wonder? when the hundred-headed beast
Hangs his black lugges, stroakt with those heavenly lines;
The Furies curl'd snakes meet in gentle twines,
And stretch their cold limbes in a pleasing fire.
Prometheus selfe, and Pelops sterved sire
Are cheated of their paines; Orion thinkes
Of lions now noe more, or spotted linx.

Let us live and love
(Catullus 5)

Come and let us live my Deare,
Let us love and never feare,
What the sowrest fathers say:
Brightest Sol that dyes to day
Lives again as blith to morrow,
But if we darke sons of sorrow
Set; o then, how long a night
Shuts the eyes of our short light!
Then let amorous kisses dwell
On our lips, begin and tell
A thousand, and a hundred, score
An hundred, and a thousand more,
Till another thousand smother
That, and that wipe of another.
Thus at last when we have numbred

Many a thousand, many a hundred;
Wee'l confound the reckoning quite,
And lose our selves in wild delight:
While our joyes so multiply,
As shall mocke the envious eye.

HENRY VAUGHAN

(1622-1695)

Vaughan and his twin brother Thomas were born in Newton-by-Usk in Llansantffread, South Wales. They attended Oxford, but only Thomas graduated. Henry returned to Llansantffread and it remained his home all his life. He may have fought for the King in the Civil War. From about 1645 he practised as a doctor in Brecknock and in his own town. All his poetry dates from 1646-57 except for *Thalia Rediviva* (1678), marking his return to secular poetry. The translations, accordingly, come from the earliest and latest collections: they include besides the classical versions translations from Casimir Sarbiewski, 'the Polish Horace'. His translations are on the whole in a more conventional vein than his most famous poems, which however endured almost total neglect until the time of Wordsworth.

The Phoenix
(Claudian, *Phoenix* 129-42)

O happy bird! sole heir to thy own dust!
Death, to whose force all other creatures must
Submit, saves thee. Thy ashes make thee rise;
'Tis not thy nature, but thy age that dies.
Thou hast seen all! and to the times that run
Thou art as great a witness, as the sun.
Thou saw'st the deluge, when the sea outvied
The land, and drown'd the mountains with the tide.
What year the straggling Phaeton did fire
The world, thou know'st. And no plagues can conspire
Against thy life; alone thou do'st arise
Above mortality; the destinies
Spin not thy days out with their fatal clue;
They have no law, to which thy life is due.

The Elysian fields
(Ausonius, *Idyll* 6 (*Cupido*) 1-24)

In those blest fields of everlasting aire
(Where to a myrtle-grove the soules repaire

Of deceas'd lovers,) the sad, thoughtfull ghosts
Of injur'd ladyes meet, where each accoasts
The other with a sigh, whose very breath
Would break a heart, and (kind soules!) love in death.
A thick wood clouds their walks, where day scarse peeps,
And on each hand cypresse and poppey sleepes,
The drowsie rivers slumber, and springs there
Blab not, but softly melt into a teare,
A sickly dull aire fans them, which can have
When most in force scarce breath to build a wave.
On either bank through the still shades appear
A scene of pensive flowres, whose bosomes wear
Drops of a lover's bloud, the emblem'd truths
Of deep despair, and love-slain kings and youths.
The hyacinth, and self-enamour'd boy
Narcissus flourish there, with Venus joy
The spruce Adonis, and that prince whose flowre
Hath sorrow languag'd on him to this houre;
All sad with love they hang their heads, and grieve
As if their passions in each leafe did live;
And here (alas!) these soft-soul'd ladies stray,
And (oh! too late!) treason in love betray.

THOMAS STANLEY

(1625-1678)

Stanley was the nephew of William Hammond and a second cousin of Richard
Lovelace. He was educated at Pembroke Hall, Cambridge, and practised law.
His poems, which include a number of translations, were published in 1647,
and in expanded form in 1651. He turned his attention to a *History of Philosophy*,
starting from the earliest Greek philosophers, which includes a rather poor
translation of part of Aristophanes' *Clouds* as a document of the life of Socrates!
He also edited Aeschylus, a work of much value; and many of his learned notes
and MSS are preserved in the University Library at Cambridge.

'The Hostesse'
(Ps.-Vergil, *Copa* (*Hostess*))

The Syrian hostesse, with a Greek wreath crown'd,
Shaking her wither'd side to th' bagpipes sound,
Drunk, 'fore the tavern a loose measure leads,
And with her elbow blows the squeaking reeds.
    Who would the summers dusty labour ply,
That might on a soft couch carowsing ly?
Here's musick, wine, cups, and an arbour made

Of cooling flags, that cast a grateful shade:
A pipe whereon a shepherd sweetly playes,
Whilst the Maenalian cave resounds his layes:
A hogshead of brisk wine new pierc'd: a spring
Of pleasant water ever murmuring:
Wreaths twisted with the purple violet;
White garlands with the blushing rose beset;
And osier baskets with fair lillies fraught
From the bank-side by Achelois brought:
Fresh cheese in rushy cradles layd to dry:
Soft plums, by autumn ripened leisurely:
Chessenuts, and apples sweetly streakt with red;
Neat Ceres by young love and Bacchus led:
Black mulberries, an overcharged vine;
Green cowcombers, that on their stalks decline:
The gardens Guardian, with no dreadful look,
Nor other weapon than a pruning hook.
Tabor and pipe come hither: see, alasse,
Thy tir'd beast sweats; spare him; our well-lov'd asse.
The grassehopper chirps on her green seat,
The lizard peeps out of his cold retreat;
Come, in this shade thy weary limbs repose,
And crown thy drowsie temples with the rose.
A maids lip safely maist thou rifle here;
Away with such whose foreheads are severe.
Flowers why reserv'st thou for unthankful dust?
To thy cold tomb wilt thou these garlands trust?
Bring wine and dice; hang them the morrow weigh:
Death warns, *I come* (saith he) *live while you may.*

The lover
(*Anacreontea* 12 Bergk)

Now will I a lover be,
Love himself commanded me.
Full at first of stubborn pride,
To submit, my soul denide:
He his quiver takes and bow,
Bids defiance, forth I go,
Arm'd with spear and shield; we meet:
On he charges, I retreat:
Till perceiving in the fight
He had wasted every flight,
Into me, with fury hot,
Like a dart himself he shot,
And my cold heart melts: my shield

Uselesse, no defence could yield;
For what boots an outward skreen
When (alas) the fights within?

Pan's music 'From Plato'
(*Greek Anthology* 9.823)

Dwell, awful silence, on the shady hills
Among the bleating flocks, and purling rills,
When Pan the reed doth to his lips apply,
Inspiring it with sacred harmony.
Hydriads, and Hamadryads at that sound
In a well order'd measure beat the ground.

SIR EDWARD SHERBURNE

(1618-1702)

Sherburne was born and educated in London, spent 1640 travelling in France, and was employed as a clerk of ordnance until 1642. He fought on the side of the King in the Civil War, and was seized in Oxford on the fall of that city in 1646, when he lost his library and was reduced to indigence. In 1648 he published his version of Seneca's *Medea*, and a translation into verse of one of Seneca's letters, 'Why Good Men suffer Misfortune', which he dedicated to Charles I. For a time he served Sir George Savile, who became Marquis of Halifax, and on the Restoration he was reappointed to his post of clerk of ordnance, and knighted in 1682. He retired at the time of the Glorious Revolution.

Besides the other tragedies of Seneca, his numerous translations include Colluthus, Theocritus and Manilius, as well as MS versions of parts of Lucretius, Pindar and Vergil. His Preface to the Seneca defends the principle of close translation, rather passé at this period, and Samuel Johnson's judgment was that 'his learning was greater than his powers of poetry'.

'Various opinions concerning the galaxies'
(Manilius, *Astronomica* 1.723-65)

The sacred causes human breasts enquire,
Whether the heavenly segments there retire
(The whole mass shrinking) and the parting frame
Through clearing chinks admits the stranger flame?
Astonishment must sore their senses reach
To see the worlds wounds, and Heavens gaping breach!
Or meets Heaven here? and the white cloud appears
The cement of the close-wedg'd hemispheres?
Or seems that old opinion of more sway

That the sun's horses here once ran astray,
And a new path mark'd in their straggling flight
Of scorched skies, and stars adjusted lights,
Changing to paler white Heavens azure face,
And with the burnt worlds ashes strew'd the place?
Fame likewise from old time to us succeeds
How Phaeton driving his fathers steeds
Through radiant signs, and with a wondring eye
Viewing th' approached beauties of the sky,
(Whilst in his chariot proud he childlike plays,
And things yet greater than his sire essays)
Left the known path, and a rough tract imprest
In the smooth skies, whilst wand'ring flames infest
Th' affrighted signs, not brooking the loose course
Of th' erring chariot and ill-guided horse.
Hence the whole world became a fiery spoyl,
And burning cities made earths funeral pile;
When from the hurried chariot lightning fled;
And scatterd blazes all the sky o're spred;
By whose approach new stars enkindled were,
Which still as marks of that sad chance appear.
Nor must that gentler murmur be supprest,
How Milk once flowing from fair Juno's breast,
Stain'd the coelestial pavement; from whence came
This milky path, its cause shown in its name.
Or is' t a crowd of stars crowning the night?
A candid diadem of condens'd light?
Or radiant souls freed from corporeal gives
Thither repair and lead aetherial lives?
There the Atrides, there th' Aeacides,
Fierce Diomede; he, who through lands and seas
His triumphs over conquer'd nature rear'd,
Subtle Ulysses, we believe inspher'd.
There Nestor's thron'd among the Grecian peers,
Crown'd with a triple century of years.

A marriage
(Martial, *Epigrams* 8.34)

Since both of you so like in manners be,
Thou the worst husband, and the worst wife she,
I wonder, you no better should agree.

Procrastination
(Martial, *Epigrams* 5.58)

Still, still thou cry'st, 'To morrow I'll live well':

But when will this to morrow come? canst tell?
How far is't hence? or where's it to be found?
Or upon Parthian or Armenian ground?
Priam's or Nestor's years by this't has got;
I wonder for how much it might be bought?
Thou'lt live tomorrow? – 'Tis too late today:
He's wise who yesterday, 'I liv'd,' can say.

'Epitaph on an old drunken crone'
(*Greek Anthology* 7.353)

This tomb Maronis holds, o'er which doth stand
A bowl, carv'd out of flint, by Mentor's hand:
The tipling crone while living, death of friends
Ne'er touch'd, nor husband's, nor dear children's ends.
This only troubles her, now dead, to think,
The monumental bowl should have no drink.

ROBERT HERRICK

(1591-1674)

Herrick was educated at St John's College, Cambridge, and on his ordination provided by Charles I with the living of Dean Prior in Devonshire, where the ennui he suffered is well known, though it encouraged some of his finest poetry. He was ousted by Cromwell in 1647, whereupon he moved to London and mingled in the circle of Ben Jonson. On the Restoration he returned to Dean Prior. His translations are not many, but the classical inspiration of his original poetry is very evident: the influences of Martial and Anacreon are particularly strong.

Life is fleeting: from 'His age, dedicated to his peculiar friend, Master
John Wickes, under the name of Posthumus'
(Horace, *Odes* 2.14, with other allusions)

Ah Posthumus! our years hence fly,
And leave no sound; nor piety,
   Or prayers, or vow
Can keep the wrinkle from the brow:
   But we must on,
As Fate does lead or draw us; none,
None, Posthumus, could ere decline
The doom of cruel Proserpine.

The pleasing wife, the house, the ground
Must all be left, no one plant found
   To follow thee,
Save only the curst cypress tree:
   A merry mind
Looks forward, scorns what's left behind;
Let's live, my Wickes, then, while we may,
And here enjoy our holiday.

W'ave seen the past-best times, and these
Will ne'er return; we see the seas
   And moons to wane,
But they fill up their ebbs again;
   But vanished man,
Like to a lily lost, ne'er can,
Ne'er can repullulate, or bring
His days to see a second spring.

But on we must, and thither tend,
Where Anchus and rich Tullus blend
   Their sacred seed;
Thus has infernal Jove decreed;
   We must be made,
Ere long, a song, ere long, a shade.
Why then, since life to us is short,
Let's make it full up by our sport.

RICHARD FANSHAWE

(1608-1666)

Fanshawe was educated at Jesus College, Cambridge. In the Civil War he took the royalist side; in September 1651 he was imprisoned in Whitehall following the battle of Worcester, and in the following year his translations from Horace were published. (His Vergil and *Pastor Fido* had appeared in 1647, and he also translated the *Lusiads* of Camoens.) On the Restoration he was made ambassador to Portugal and Spain and was knighted for his services. The Memoirs of his wife, Lady Ann, give a vivid picture of a man who consciously modelled his behaviour on Horatian principles.

Dido's curse on Aeneas
(Vergil, *Aeneid* 4.365-87)

Nor Goddesse was thy Mother, nor the source
   Of thy high blood renowned Dardanus,
     But some Hyrcanian Tigresse was thy Nource,

Out of the stony Loynes of Caucasus
Descended, cruell and perfidious.
For with what hopes should I thy hopes yet cover,
Did my teares make thee sigh? Or bend, but thus,
Thine Eyes? Or sadness for my griefe discover?
Or if thou couldst not Love, to pity yet a Lover?

Whom first accuse I since these Loves began?
 Jove is unjust, Juno her charge gives or'e,
 Whom may a Woman trust? I tooke this man
 Homelesse, a desp'rate wrack upon my shoare,
 And fondly gave him half the Crowne I wore:
 His Ships rebuilt, t'his men new lives I lent.
 And now the Fates, the Oracles, what more?
 (It makes me mad) Joves sonne on purpose sent
Brings him forsooth a menace through the Firmament.

As if the Gods their blissefull rest did breake
 With thinking on thy Voyages. But I
 Nor stop you, nor confute the words you speake.
 Goe, chase on rowling billowes Realmes that fly,
 With ficle windes uncertaine Italy.
 Some courteous Rock (if Heav'n just curses heare)
 Will be Revenger of my injury:
 When thou perceiving the sad Fate drew neere,
Shalt Dido, Dido, call; who surely will be there.

For when cold death shall part with dreary swoone
 My Soule and Flesh; my ghost, where ere thou bee,
 Shall haunt thee with dim Torch, and light thee downe
 To thy darke conscience: I'll be Hell to thee,
 And this glad newes will make Hell Heav'n to mee.

Conversion
(Horace, *Odes* 1.34)

I, that have seldom worshipt Heaven,
As to a mad sect too much given,
 My former waies am forc'd to balk,
 And after the old light to walk.
For cloud-dividing-lightning Jove
Through a clear firmament late drove
 His thundring horses, and swift wheels:
 With which, supporting Atlas reels:
With which Earth, seas, the Stygian lake,
And Hell, with all her furies, quake.
 It shook me too. God puls the proud
 From his high seat, and from their cloud

Draws the obscure: Levels the hills,
And with their earth the valleys fills:
  'Tis all he does, he does it all:
  Yet this, blind mortals fortune call.

Contentment
(Horace, *Satires* 1. 6.112-31)

  Where e're I list I go,
Alone, the price of broath, and barley know;
Crowd in at every sight, walk late in Rome:
Visit the temple with a prayer: then home
To my leek-pottage and chich-pease. Three boyes
Serve in my supper: whom to counterpoyse
One bowle, two beakers on a broad white slate,
A pitcher with two ears (Campanian plate).
Then do I go to sleep: securely do't,
Being next morning to attend no suite
In the great-hall (where Marsya doth look
As if lowd Numio's face he could not brooke)
I lie till four. Then walk, or read a while;
Or write, to please my self. Noint me with oil:
(Not such as Natta pawes himself withall,
Robbing the lamps). When neer his vertical
The hotter sun invites us to a bath
For our tir'd limbs, I fly the dog-stars wrath,
Having din'd onely so much as may stay
My appetite: loiter at home all day.
These are my solaces: this is the life
Of men that shun ambition, run from strife.
Lighter, then if I soar'd on glorie's wing,
The nephew, son, and grand-son to a king.

The benefits of study
(Horace, *Epistles* 1.2)

Unless to studies, and to honest things
Thou bend thy mind; with love's or envy's stings
Thou'lt lie awake tormented. If a fly
Get in thy eye, 'tis puld out instantly:
But if thy Mindes ey's hurt, day after day
That cure's deferr'd. Set forth, thou'rt half the way.
Dare to be wise: begin. He that to rule
And square his life, prolongs, is like the foole
Who staid to have the river first pass by:
Which rowles and rowles to all eternity.
Money is sought, and a rich wife for brood,

And a sharp culter tames the savage wood.
Let him that has enough, desire no more.
Not house and land, nor gold and silver oare,
The body's sickness, or the mind's dispell.
To rellish wealth, the palat must be well.
Who fears, or covets: house to him and ground,
Are pictures to blind men, Incentives bound
About a gouty limb, musick t'an eare
Dam'd up with filth. A vessell not sincere
Sowres whatsoere you pour into't. Abstain
From pleasures: pleasure hurts, that's bought with pain.
The cov'tous always want: your pray'rs designe
To some fixt mark. The envious man doth pine
To see another fat: envy's a rack:
Worse, no Sicilian tyrant ere did make.
Who cannot temper wrath, will wish undone
What, in his haste, he may have done to one,
To whom he (possibly) would be most kind.
Anger is a short madnesse: rule thy mind.
Which reignes, if it obeyes not: fetter it
With chains, restrain it with an iron bit.
The quiry moulds the horses tender mouth
T'his riders will. The beagle from his youth
Is train'd up to the woods, being taught to ball
(A whelp) at the bucks heads naild in the hall.
Now boy, in the white paper of thy breast
Write vertue: now suck precepts from the best.
A pot, well season'd holds the primitive tast
A long time after. If thou make no hast
Or spur to over-run me, I am one
For none will stay, and will contend with none.

'A Happy Life out of Martiall'
(Martial, *Epigrams* 10.47)

The things that make a life to please
(Sweetest Martiall) they are these:
Estate inherited, not got:
A thankfull Field, Hearth alwayes hot:
City seldome, Law-suits never:
Equall Friends agreeing ever:
Health of Body, Peace of Minde:
Sleepes that till the Morning binde:
Wise Simplicitie, Plaine Fare:
Not drunken Nights, yet loos'd from Care:
A Sober, not a sullen Spouse:
Cleane Strength, not such as his that Plowes:

Wish onely what thou art, to bee;
Death neither wish, nor feare to see.

JOHN OGILBY
(1600-1676)

Ogilby was born in Scotland, and served under the Earl of Strafford in Ireland.
In 1648 he returned to England, where he began work on his translation of
Vergil, which was published in 1653. He then learnt Greek and translated the
Iliad (1660). Thereafter he set up as a publisher, producing fine engraved
books, bibles and atlases, including his famous road maps of Britain. His
Odyssey appeared in 1665.

The power of lust
(Vergil, *Georgics* 3.242-63)

All men on earth, and beasts both wilde and tame,
Sea-monsters, gaudy fowle, runs to this flame:
The same love works in all, which love ingag'd.
The lioness mindlesse of her whelps, inrag'd
Wanders the fields; nor foul bears oftner take
So many lives, nor greater slaughter make;
Nor cruel tygers, nor the raging boar:
Ah! 'tis ill wandering then dry Lybias shore.
Seest thou how horses will all over shake,
When in their nostrils the known sent they take?
Nor they with curbs, nor stripes can be debar'd,
Nor rocks, nor rivers can their course retard,
Though down they sweep whole mountains with their waves.
The sabel boar whetting his tusks, then raves
Rubbing against a tree, and tears the ground,
Hard'ning his shoulders 'gainst th' insuing wound.
   How was that young man took, when fierce desire
In his hot blood kindled so great a fire!
For he, when all the elements did fight,
Through seas turn'd mountains swam in hideous night,
When at him heavens artillery thund'red round,
And broken billows 'gainst the rocks resound:
Nor could his woful parents him recal,
Nor she whose fate attends his funeral.

CHRISTOPHER WASE

(?1625-1690)

Wase, a fellow of King's College, Cambridge, dedicated his unusually early translation of a Greek play to Princess Elizabeth, the daughter of Charles I, and published it in the Hague in 1649, shortly after the execution of the King and the effective imprisonment of Elizabeth in Sion House. The parallel of the situations of Elizabeth and of Electra in the tragedy is obvious and deliberate; but no Orestes came for Elizabeth and she died the following year.

Wase was subsequently deprived of his fellowship, and caught and imprisoned while trying to flee to the continent. However, he escaped, and after fighting abroad, returned to England, held several headmasterships including that of Tonbridge School (1662-8), and ended his life as printer to the University of Oxford (from 1671).

The doom of the Atridae
(Sophocles, *Electra* 1058-97)

Why mark we the wise fowl, above,
In countrey and in nat'rall love;
Where the dam looks to be fed,
Of those she hath born and bred;
Nor do like tribute pay.
But if Jove thunder hath,
And heavenly Themis wrath;
They carry't not away.
Fame downward spring,
And this dolefull message ring:
In the dead Atrida's hearings
Of these cruell interferings,

Their house-affairs have long been weak,
Their children now in quarrels break:
Nor doth long converse as yet
Their divisions umpire set.
Electra still doth float:
Poore she betrayd alone,
Always her sire doth moan,
I' th nightingals sad note;
But provides to morgage breath,
While she those twin imps destroyeth.
In such life what lady joyeth?

None low of means, and high of place,
Endure their honours to debase
With scorn. Great lady, thus
You hard afflictions chuse

Companions of your age.
Opposing treasons rage.
At once with double honour crownd,
A child both wise and vertuous found.

O mayst thou live in wealth and strength
Above thine enemies at length,
More then thou dost below!
I thee entirely know;
Afflicted thou heldst forth
High principles of worth:
Thou alwayes didst for pilot own
Unmoveable religion.

RICHARD LOVELACE

(1618-1658)

Lovelace was educated at Charterhouse and at Gloucester Hall, Oxford, where his good looks ensured him the reputation of a gallant cavalier that has remained with him. He then entered the service of the King, and in 1642 he delivered to Parliament a petition on the King's behalf, which resulted in his imprisonment for seven weeks. He joined the King at Oxford, and then fought in France (1646), and was imprisoned again on his return in 1648, on which occasion he revised his poems, of which the most famous reflects his times of imprisonment. His brother Francis, to whom his imitation of Horace is addressed, also served the King, in Wales, until he was captured in 1645. Besides the dignified Epicureanism of *To my Best Brother*, classical influence is also strong in Lovelace's other works, notably *The Grasshopper*, which makes of Anacreon's slight poem a work of considerable force. Lovelace spent his substance in support of the King and ended his life in poverty.

'Catullus: to Fabullus'
(Catullus 13)

Fabullus, I will treat you handsomely
Shortly, if the kind gods will favour thee.
If thou dost bring with thee a del'cate mess,
An olio or so, a pretty lass,
Brisk wine, sharp tales, all sorts of drollery.
These if thou bring'st, I say, along with thee,
You shall feed highly, friend; for know, the ebbs
Of my lank purse are full of spiders' webs.
But then again you shall receive clear love,
Or what more grateful or more sweet may prove:

For with an ointment I will favour thee,
My Venuses and Cupids gave to me,
Of which once smelt, the gods thou wilt implore,
Fabullus, that they'd make thee nose all o'er.

'Catullus: of his love'
(Catullus 85)

I hate and love: wouldst thou the reason know?
I know not; but I burn, and feel it so.

'Catullus: to Quintius'
(Catullus 96)

Quintius, if you'll endear Catullus' eyes,
Or what he dearer than his eyes doth prize,
Ravish not what is dearer than his eyes,
Or what he dearer than his eyes doth prize.

'Advice to my best Brother, Coll. Francis Lovelace'
(Horace, *Odes* 2.10, adapted)

Frank wil't live handsomely? trust not too far
Thy self to waving seas, for what thy star
Calculated by sure event must be,
Look in the glassy-epithite and see.

   Yet settle here your rest, and take your state,
And in calm halcyon's nest ev'n build your Fate;
Prethee lye down securely, Frank, and keep
With as much no noyse the inconstant deep
As its inhabitants; nay steadfast stand,
As if discover'd were a New-found-land
Fir for plantation here; dream, dream still,
Lull'd in Dione's cradle, dream, untill
Horrour awake your sense, and you now find
Your self a bubled pastime for the wind;
And in loose Thetis blankets torn and tost,
Frank to undo thy self why art at cost?

   Nor be too confident, fix'd on the shore,
For even that too borrows from the store
Of her rich neighbour, since now wisest know,
(And this to Galileo's judgement ow)
The palsie earth it self is every jot
As frail, inconstant, waveing as that blot
We lay upon the deep, that sometimes lies
Chang'd, you would think, with 's botoms properties.

But this eternal, strange Ixions wheel
Of giddy earth, ne'r whirling leaves to reel
Till all things are inverted, till they are
Turn'd to that antick confus'd state they were.

   Who loves the golden mean, doth safely want
A cobwebb'd cot, and wrongs entail'd upon't;
He richly needs a pallace for to breed
Vipers and moths, that on their feeder feed.
The toy that we (too true) a mistress call,
Whose looking-glass and feather weighs up all;
And cloaths which larks would play with, in the sun,
That mock him in the night when's course is run.

   To rear an edifice by art so high
That envy should not reach it with her eye,
Nay with a thought come neer it, wouldst thou know
How such a structure should be raisd? build low.
The blust'ring winds invisible rough stroak,
More often shakes the stubborn'st, prop'rest oak,
And in proud turrets we behold withal,
'Tis the Imperial top declines to fall.
Nor does Heav'ns lightning strike the humble vales
But high aspiring mounts batters and scales.

   A breast of proof defies all shocks of Fate,
Fears in the best, hopes in the worser state;
Heaven forbid that, as of old, Time ever
Flourish'd in spring, so contrary, now never:
That mighty breath which blew foul winter hither,
Can eas'ly puff it to a fairer weather.
Why dost despair then, Franck? Aeolus has
A Zephyrus as well as Boreas.

   'Tis a false sequel, soloecisme, 'gainst those
Precepts by fortune giv'n us, to suppose
That cause it is now ill, 't will ere be so;
Apollo doth not always bend his bow;
But oft uncrowned of his beams divine,
With his soft harp awakes the sleeping Nine.

   In strictest things magnanimous appear,
Greater in hope, howere thy fate, then fear:
Draw all your sails in quickly, though no storm
Threaten your ruine with a sad alarm;
For tell me how they differ, tell me pray,
A cloudy tempest, and a too fair day.

THOMAS RANDOLPH

(1605-1635)

Educated at Westminister and at Trinity College, Cambridge, Randolph soon made himself known to Ben Jonson, and became one of the most loved of the 'Sons of Ben'. He lived mostly in Cambridge, writing verse in Latin and in English, and studying Aristotle. The extent of his part in *Hey for Honesty* has been disputed, as it contains much that is clearly of later date and is stated on the title page to have been augmented by one F. J.; it seems however that the bulk of the work can be safely attributed to Randolph (see C. L. Day, *PMLA* 41 (1926), 325-34). He died young and badly in debt, of smallpox.

If wealth should attend desert
(Aristophanes, *Wealth* 489-506) from *Hey for Honesty*

Dicaeus: If it be fit that good and honest men,
Whose souls are fraught with virtue, should possess
Riches and wealth, which heaven did mean should be
The just reward of goodness, while proud vice,
Stripp'd of her borrow'd and usurped robes,
Should have her loath'd deformities unmask'd;
And vicious men, that spread their peacocks' trains,
Have carcases as naked as their souls –
But if once Plutus should receive his eyes,
And but discern 'twixt men, the world were chang'd:
Then goodness and full coffers, wealth and honesty,
Might meet, embrace, and thrive and kiss together;
While vice with all her partners starves and pines,
Rotting to dirt and filth, leaving to hell
Black souls. Who better counsel can devise?
Ergo, 'tis fit Plutus receive his eyes.

Clodpole: That argo has netteld her, I warrant. Thou shalt be Plutus
his professor for this. What hast thou my she-Bellarmine now to answer?

Dicaeus: As the mad world goes now, who could believe
But purblind fate and chance did hold the sceptre
Of human actions? Who beholds the miseries
Of honest mortals, and compares their fortunes
With the unsatiable pleasures of gross epicures,
Whose bursting bags are glutted with the spoils
Of wretched orphans – who (I say) sees this,
But would almost turn atheist, and forswear
All heaven, all gods, all divine providence?
But if to Plutus we his eyes restore,
Good men shall grow in wealth, and knaves grow poor.

WILLIAM HAMMOND

(b. 1614)

Little is known of Hammond other than that he married a niece of George
Sandys, the translator of Ovid, and that his sister was the mother of Thomas
Stanley, to whom several of his poems, including the following, were
addressed. His *Poems* were published in 1655.

'To the Same [Thomas Stanley], being sick of a fever'
(Horace, *Odes* 2.17)

Am I not in thy fever sacrifiz'd?
That you alone by Fate should be surpriz'd,
You, my sole sunshine, my soul's wealth and pride,
Is both by me and by the Gods denied:
If hasty death take thee, my soul, away,
Can I, a loath'd imperfect carcass, stay?
No, no; our twisted lives must be cut both
Together; this I dare confirm by oath,
Whene'er thou leap'st into the fatal boat
I'll leap in, glad with thee in death to float:
Nor shall that dubious monster, breathing fire,
Nor Gyges' hundred hands, did he respire,
Pluck me from this resolve, approved so
By fate and justice: whither Scorpio
Fierce in my horoscope, or Capricorn
Oppressing Latium with his wat'ry horn,
Or Libra brooded my nativity,
'Tis sure our mutual stars strangely agree.

JOHN EVELYN

(1620-1706)

The translation of the first book of Lucretius was one of the many occupations
of Evelyn's busy leisure, which persisted, broken only by brief forays into
service for Charles I, until he was employed in the public service on the
Restoration. Richard Fanshawe greeted it: 'It puts me in minde of the two
Amphitruo's in Plautus; where the translation was taken for the original by her
that should best have known . . . I injure it with the name of a translation; it is
Lucretius himself.' Another friend, Jeremy Taylor, was sterner: 'I will not say
to you that your Lucretius is as far distant from the severity of a Christian, as
the fair Ethiopian was from the duty of Bp. Heliodorus . . . But, Sir, if you will
give me leave, I will impose such a penance upon you for your publication of

Lucretius as shall neither displease God nor you . . . I desire you to lend it me
for a week' (Letter of 16 April 1656).

The evils of religion
(Lucretius, *On the Nature of Things* 1.62-101)

Whilst sometimes human life dejected lay
On earth, under gross Superstitions sway,
Whose head aloft from heaven seem'd t'appear
And mankind with its horrid shape did scare,
With mortal eyes to look on her that durst
Or contradict; a Grecian was the first:
Him nor the fame of gods, nor lightnings flash,
Nor threatning burst of thundring skies could dash
But rather did his courage elevate,
Natures remotest doors to penetrate;
Thus did he with his vigorous wit transpierce
The flaming limits of the universe.
All that was great his generous soul had view'd,
Whence what could be produc'd, what not be shew'd
And how each finite thing hath bounds, nor may
By any means from her first limits stray:
Wherefore fond Superstition trampled lies
Beneath; we rear our trophies to the skies.
   Yet fear I least thou think my arguments
Should lead you into impious rudiments,
When as religion it self, oft times
Hath perpetrated foul and bloody crimes.
Thus when the Grecian chiefs of prime repute
The unwed Trivian altar did pollute
With Iphigenias blood at Aulis, where,
When as the chaplet round her virgin-hair
Dischevel'd down her cheeks on either side,
She near the altar, her sad father spy'd,
And from his eyes the priests the knife to keep,
Whil'st all the people round about her weep:
She mute with fear, kneeling, the earth doth press,
Nor did her birth avail in that distress,
Or that the king first she a father made,
But to the altar, trembling was convey'd;
Not so, as when in Hymen's solemn rites
The bride is led to nuptial delights,
But ripe for marriage the pure sacrifice,
By her sad sires consent, impurely dies,
That a safe expedition might be made,
To so much ill could foolish zeal perswade!

LUCY HUTCHINSON

(b. 1620)

Lucy Hutchinson was married to Colonel John Hutchinson who was among those who signed the sentence of death on Charles I. It is curious that a woman of so strong a Protestant background should translate the whole of the atheist Lucretius; but she absolves her conscience by her annotations to the text, such as her comment on the end of Book 3, 'Poor deluded bewitched mad wretch', and the frequent use of the word 'impious'. The translation has never been published.

    Her husband was arrested on the Restoration and imprisoned in Sandown Castle, where she visited him daily. In later years she appears to have become ashamed of her translation of Lucretius, and devoted her time to the composition of moral and religious works, as well as a biography of her husband. She died some time after 1675.

Pleasure in tranquillity
(Lucretius, *On the Nature of Things* 2.1-19)

Pleasant it is, when rough winds seas deforme,
On shore to see men labour in the storme;
Not that our pleasure springs from their distresse,
But from the safetie we ourselves possesse.
Pleasant, when without danger 'tis beheld,
To see engag'd armies in the feild;
But nothing more a pleasant prospect yeilds,
Then that high tower which wise mens learning builds,
Where well secur'd, we wandring troopes survey,
Who in a maze of error search their way,
For witt and glorie earnestly contend,
Both day and night in vain endeavours spend,
To hord up wealth, and swim in full delights,
O wretched soules whom ignorance benights!
To what vast perills are your lives expos'd,
With what darke mists is your whole age enclos'd:
See you not nature only seeks to find,
Within a body free from payne, a mind
Full of content, exempt from feare or care,
Learne then from hence, that human natures are
With little pleas'd, and best themselves enjoy,
When payne doth not torment, nor pleasure cloy.

JAMES HARRINGTON

(1611-1677)

'His genius lay chiefly towards the politiques and democraticall government.

'Anno 1647, if not 6, he was by order of Parliament made one of his Majestie's Bedchamber. Mr Harrington and the King often disputed about Government. The King loved his company; only he would not endure to heare of a Commonwealth: and Mr Harrington passionately loved his Majestie. He was on the scaffold with the King when he was beheaded; and I have oftentimes heard him speake of King Charles I with the greatest zeale and passion imaginable, and that his death gave him so great a griefe that he contracted a disease by it; that never any thing did goe so neer to him' (John Aubrey).

Harrington retired from public life after the King's execution and in the years 1656-60 composed, besides his translations of Vergil (1658-9) a very considerable quantity of works of political theory, chief among them the *Commonwealth of Oceana*. On the Restoration he was committed to the Tower (November 1661), after which his health and his wits never fully recovered.

Aubrey describes his Muse as 'rough', but if the felicities and vividnesses of his translation are far from Vergil, they are not infrequent. There is an original spirit in them that befits the eccentric career of the man.

Mercury visits Aeneas
(Vergil, *Aeneid* 4.239-80)

His wand he takes, his winged spurs puts on,
And mounting Zephyrus in post is gone
For his first stay unto the cloudy down
Of marble Atlas with his piny crown.
Atlas, whose beard is snow, whose eyes are streams,
Whose neck sustains the roof with starry beams.
Hence, for the second stage, himself he flings,
Like some king-fisher with inamel'd wings,
Plying his oares along the shoaly strand,
Until his feather'd navigation land
Him on the walls of Carthage; where he finds
The castles in the air Aeneas minds,
The founder of an Empire on the heads
Of kings to sit, intent on building sheds,
The monarch by the world to be ador'd
With Dido's jewels chaining up his sword,
The sacrifice design'd to mighty Rome,
Flaming in Tyrian purple; unto whom
Heav'n's oratour his message thus explains:
To you the Dardan prince, from him that raigns
In azure tow'rs, and wheels the studded sphere,

I come to ask, what is your business here.
Your fairest mother, when she thrice from Greece
Obtain'd your rescue, spake no word of this;
But of the pregnant Italy, whose womb
Unto reviving Troy should bear great Rome.
If you have lost these thoughts, all sense be gone
Of such a glory, think upon your son,
On past, on future fates, that make it known
The person you sustain, is not your own,
Nor in your pow're to alienate; a board
With speed, for so you must if Jove be Lord.
This said, the cruel Hermes dis-appears,
And leaves Aeneas bathing in his tears.

Palinurus drowned at sea
(Vergil, *Aeneid* 5.816-71)

Thus having eas'd the Goddess of her cares,
Neptune his horses yoaks by foamy pairs,
And, giving to his eager team the rein,
With nimble wheels skirs through the azure plain.
Unto his thundring axle-tree submit
The billows prostrate at his awful feet,
The Heav'ns with all their curtains open drawn,
Behold the triumph of the sea-green lawn.
Next to his own, comes up the chrystal car
Of Thetis, then of Panopea fair,
Whom Doris in her coral bowres succeeds,
Nisaea with the canopy of reeds,
Cymodoce upon her sedgy deck,
Spio and Melite on floats of wreck:
The van of dolphins with their silver shields
Commanded by Palaemon, beats the fields,
Phocus with all his troops, and Glaucus bring
Sea-cavalry, that march in either wing,
Where Tritons blazon with imprison'd gales
On writhen shells; and hundred thousand whales
Under their soveraign immediately
Brandish their spouts unto the threatned sky.
Thoughtful Aeneas, smooth'd again with hope,
Braces the sail, and gives his canvas scope;
Upon the nimble tack his sea-men lye,
And catch the gale which way so ere she flye.
Thus after Palinure their admiral
Till noon of night they rode, when slackned all
Both sails and limbs, their intermitted ranks
Lay snoring underneath their sweaty banks.

Here Somnus stooping from the starry sky
To vindicate his injur'd deity
On Palinure, whose eyes alone refuse
To trust the calmy seas, or drink his dews,
But fixt upon the planets hold them so
As if they never more would let them go,
With branches dipt in the Lethaean brook,
The pilot on his bowing temples strook;
Whose eyes forsake the stars, while at the gasp
His hands the steerage but the harder clasp.
At this the god in fury takes him up
And throws him stern and steersman from the poup,
The fleet perceiving nothing for a while,
First found her loss upon the sounding isle
Where Sirens with their charming ayres invite
To rocks which with the bones of men are white:
The danger of the fleet discovering here
How it betide, Aeneas took the stere,
And said, to shores unknown, ah! too secure
Of calmy seas, goes naked Palinure.

SIR JOHN DENHAM

(1615-1668)

Born in Dublin, Denham went to Oxford in 1631, where, according to Wood,
'being looked upon as a slow and dreaming young man by his seniors and
contemporaries, and given more to cards and dice, than to his study, they
could never in the least imagine, that he could ever inrich the world with his
fancy, or issue of his brain, as he afterwards did'. He proceeded to Lincoln's
Inn, wrote his Essay on Gaming, and in 1636 his translation of Vergil, *Aeneid 2*,
which however was not published until 1656. In 1648 he accompanied James
Duke of York to France, and published a translation into verse of Cicero's *Cato*
or *De Senectute*. The Restoration at last brought him prosperity.

   Johnson writes of his translations: 'He appears to have been one of the first
that understood the necessity of emancipating translation from the drudgery
of counting lines and interpreting single words . . . Denham saw the better
way, but has not pursued it with great success. His versions of Virgil are not
pleasing; but they taught Dryden to please better.' This estimate of Denham's
importance in the 'mid-century revolution' in translation remains an accurate
one.

Hector's ghost
(Vergil, *Aeneid* 2.268-97)

'Twas then, when the first sweets of sleep repair
Our bodies spent with toil, our minds with care;

(The gods' best gift) when, bath'd in tears and blood,
Before my face lamenting Hector stood,
His aspect such when, soil'd with bloody dust,
Dragg'd by the cords which through his feet were thrust
By his insulting foe; O how transform'd,
How much unlike that Hector, who return'd
Clad in Achilles' spoils; when he, among
A thousand ships, (like Jove) his lightning flung!
His horrid beard and knotted tresses stood
Stiff with his gore, and all his wounds ran blood:
Intranc'd I lay, then (weeping) said, the joy,
The hope and stay of thy declining Troy;
What region held thee, whence, so much desir'd,
Art thou restor'd to us consum'd and tir'd
With toils and deaths; but what sad cause confounds
Thy once fair looks, or why appear those wounds?
Regardless of my words, he no reply
Returns, but with a dreadful groan doth cry,
Fly from the flame, O goddess-born, our walls
The Greeks possess, and Troy confounded falls
From all her glories; if it might have stood
By any power, by this right hand it should.
What man could do, by me for Troy was done,
Take here her reliques and her gods, to run
With them thy fate, with them new walls expect,
Which, tost on seas, thou shalt at last erect:
Then brings old Vesta from the sacred quire,
Her holy wreaths, and her eternal fire.

Sarpedon encourages Glaucus
(Homer, *Iliad* 12.307-28)

Thus to Glaucus spake
Divine Sarpedon, since he did not find
Others as great in place, as great in mind.
Above the rest, why is our pomp, our power?
Our flocks, our herds and our possessions more?
Why all the tributes land and sea affords,
Heap'd in great chargers, load our sumptuous boards?
Our chearful guests carowse the sparkling tears
Of the rich grape, whilst musick charms their ears.
Why as we pass do those on Xanthus shore,
As Gods behold us, and as Gods adore?
But that as well in danger, as degree,
We stand the first; that when our Lycians see
Our brave examples, they admiring say,
Behold our gallant leaders! These are they

Deserve the greatness; and un-envied stand:
Since what they act, transcends what they command.
Could the declining of this fate (oh friend)
Our date to immortality extend?
Or if death sought not them, who seek not death,
Would I advance? Or should my vainer breath
With such a glorious folly thee inspire?
But since with Fortune Nature doth conspire,
Since age, disease, or some less noble end,
Though not less certain doth our days attend;
Since 'tis decreed, and to this period lead,
A thousand ways, the noblest path we'll tread;
And bravely on, till they, or we, or all,
A common sacrifice to honour fall.

ABRAHAM COWLEY

(1618-1667)

Educated at Westminster School, Cambridge and Oxford, he remained in Oxford until the surrender to Parliament, when he followed the Queen to Paris. Returning for a while to England, he returned to France on the death of Cromwell and remained there till the Restoration. He received a doctorate at Oxford in 1657, and became prolific in botanical poetry. He subsequently obtained the lease of a property in Surrey and passed the remainder of his life in retirement.

Johnson's judgment is severe: 'Not enquiring by what means the ancients have continued to delight through all the changes of human manners, he contented himself with a deciduous laurel, of which the verdure in its spring was bright and gay, but which time has been continually stealing from his brows.' Thomas Sprat, in his *Life*, is more flattering, referring to his translations as 'wonderfully happy'. His description of the origin of the Imitations of Pindar is noteworthy: 'The occasion of his falling on the Pindaric way of writing was his accidental meeting with Pindars works in a place where he had no other books to direct him. Having then considered at leisure the height of his invention and the majesty of his style, he try'd immediately to imitate it in English. And he perform'd it without the danger that Horace presag'd to the man who should dare to attempt it.'

Praise of Theron, tyrant of Acragas
(Pindar, *Olympian* 2, abridged)

Greatness of mind and Fortune too
    The' Olympique trophies shew.
Both their several parts must do
    In the noble chase of fame,

This without that is blind, that without this is lame.
Nor is fair virtues picture seen aright
    But in Fortunes golden light.
Riches alone are of uncertain date,
    And on short-man long cannot wait.
    The vertuous make of them the best,
And put them out to fame for interest.
    With a frail good they wisely buy
The solid purchase of eternity.
They whilst lifes air they breath, consider well and know
Th' account they must hereafter give below.
Whereas th' unjust and covetous above,
    In deep unlovely vaults,
   By the just decrees of Jove
   Unrelenting torments prove,
The heavy necessary effects of voluntary faults.

Whilst in the lands of unexhausted light
O'er which the God-like suns unwearied sight,
   Ne're winks in clouds, or sleeps in night,
And endless spring of age the good enjoy,
Where neither want does pinch, nor plenty cloy.
   There neither earth nor sea they plow,
    Nor ought to labour ow
For food, that whil'st it nourishes does decay,
And in the lamp of life consumes away.
Thrice had these men through mortal bodies past,
   Did thrice the trial undergo,
Till all their little dross were purged at last,
    The furnace had no more to do.
    Then in rich Saturns peaceful state
    Were they for sacred treasures plac'ed,
The Muse-discovered world of Islands Fortunate.

Soft-footed winds with tuneful voyces there
    Dance through the perfum'd air.
There silver meadows through enamell'd meadows glide,
    And golden trees enrich their side.
Th' illustrious leaves no dropping autumn fear,
    And jewels for their fruit they bear.
    Which by the blest are gathered
For bracelets to the arm, and garlands to the head.
Here all the hero's, and their poets live,
Wise Rhadamanthus did the sentence give,
    Who for his justice was thought fit
With soveraign Saturn on the bench to sit.
    Peleus here, and Cadmus reign,

Here great Achilles wrathful now no more,
   Since his blest mother (who before
   Had try'd it on his body' in vain)
  Dipt now his soul in Stygian lake,
Which did from thence a divine hardness take,
That does from passion and from vice invulnerable make.

Love duet
(Catullus 45)

Whilst on Septimius' panting brest
(Meaning nothing less than rest)
Acme lean'd her loving head
Thus the pleas'd Septimius said:

My dearest Acme, if I be
Once alive, and love not thee
With a passion far above
All that e're was called love,
In a Lybian desert may
I become some lion's prey,
Let him, Acme, let him tear
My brest, when Acme is not there.

The God of Love who stood to hear him,
(The God of Love was always near him)
Pleas'd and tickl'd with the sound,
Sneez'd aloud, and all around
The little Loves that waited by,
Bow'd and blest the augurie.

Acme, enflam'd with what he said,
Rear'd her gently-bending head,
And her purple mouth with joy
Stretching to the delicious boy
Twice (and twice would scarce suffice)
She kist his drunken, rowling eyes.

My little life, my all (said she)
So may we ever servants be
To this best god, and n'er retain
Our hated liberty again,
So may thy passion last for me,
As I a passion have for thee
Greater and fiercer much then can
Be conceiv'd by thee a man.
Into my marrow it is gone,
Fixt and settled in the bone,

It reigns not only in my heart,
But runs, like life, through ev'ry part.

She spoke; the God of Love aloud,
Sneez'd again, and all the crowd
Of little Loves that waited by
Bow'd and blest the augurie.

This good omen thus from heaven
Like a happy signal given,
Their loves and lives (all four) embrace,
And hand in hand run all the race.
To poor Septimius (who did now
Nothing else but Acme grow)
Acme's bosome was alone
The whole world's imperial throne,
And to faithful Acme's mind
Septimius was all human kind.

If the Gods would please to be
But advis'd for once by me,
I'de advise 'em when they spie
Any illustrious piety,
To reward her, if it be she
To reward him, if it be he;
With such a husband, such a wife,
With Acme's and Septimius' life.

Procrastination
(Martial, *Epigrams* 5.58)

To-morrow you will live, you always cry;
In what far country does this morrow lie,
That 'tis so mighty long ere it arrive?
Beyond the Indies does this morrow live?

'Tis so far fetch'd this morrow, that I fear
'Twill be both very old and very dear.
To-morrow I will live, the fool does say;
To-day itself's too late, the wise liv'd yesterday.

3. The Restoration: Dryden and the *Miscellanies*

SIR WILLIAM TEMPLE

(1628-1699)

Born in London, Temple studied at Cambridge before going abroad, where, during their seven-year separation, he and Dorothy Osborne exchanged their famous series of letters. They were married in 1655. Thereafter he pursued a diplomatic career in the Low Countries until forced to return in 1670; he finally retired in 1680. Most of his essays stem from this period, including the *Essay upon the Ancient and Modern Learning* (1690) which provided the starting point for the quarrel of the Ancients and Moderns in his generation in England. His verses are few and insignificant compared with his prose works, but the translations show how he put his preference for the ancients into practice.

Spring
(Horace, *Odes* 4.7)

The snows are melted all away,
The fields grow flow'ry green, and gay,
The trees put on their tender leaves;
And all the streams, that went astray,
The brook again into her bed receives.

See! the whole earth has made a change:
The nymphs and graces naked range
About the fields, who shrunk before
Into their caves. The empty grange
Prepares its room for a new summer's store.

Lest thou shouldst hope immortal things,
The changing year instruction brings,
The fleeting hour, that steals away
The beggar's time, and life of Kings,
But ne'er returns them, as it does the day.

The cold grows soft with western gales,
The Summer over Spring prevails,

But yields to Autumn's fruitful rain,
As this to Winter storms and hails;
Each loss the hasting moons repair again.

But we, when once our race is done,
With Tullus, and Anchises' son,
(Though rich like one, like t'other good)
To dust and shades, without a sun,
Descend, and sink in deep oblivion's flood.

Who knows, if the kind gods will give
Another day to men that live
In hope of many distant years;
Or if one night more shall retrieve
The joys thou losest by thy idle fears?

The pleasant hours thou spend'st in health,
The use thou mak'st of youth and wealth,
As what thou giv'st among thy friends
Escapes thy heirs, so those the stealth
Of time and death, where good and evil ends.

For when that comes, nor birth, nor fame,
Nor piety, nor honest name,
Can e'er restore thee. Theseus bold,
Nor chaste Hippolitus could tame
Devouring fate, that spares nor young nor old.

JOHN MILTON

(1608-1674)

England's greatest poet after Shakespeare was educated at St Paul's and at Christ's College, Cambridge, and the greater part of his earlier life was spent in schooling his genius for the works of his maturity, though the time taken by, and importance attached by Milton to, his pamphleteering in the revolutionary cause should not be underestimated. Milton's style owes more to the Latin poets than any other English poet's, and his Latinate style is particularly conspicuous in his translation from Horace which, though not published until 1673, after the great epics, must belong to an earlier period. It has not lacked for detractors as impossibly artificial; it nevertheless represents a serious attempt to reproduce the effect and pace of the original, perhaps the most translated poem of antiquity (R. Storrs, *Ad Pyrrham* (1959), gives a fascinating sampling of the innumerable translations into English and other languages).

Pyrrha
(Horace, *Odes* 1.5)

What slender youth, bedewed with liquid odours,
Courts thee on roses in some pleasant cave,
 Pyrrha? For whom bindst thou
 In wreaths thy golden hair,

Plain in thy neatness? O, how oft shall he
On faith and changed gods complain, and seas
 Rough with black winds and storms,
 Unwonted shall admire!

Who now enjoys thee, credulous, all gold,
Who, always vacant, always amiable,
 Hopes thee, of flattering gales
 Unmindful! Hapless they

To whom thou, untried, seemst fair. Me in my vowed
Picture, the sacred wall declares to have hung
 My dank and dripping weeds
 To the stern god of sea.

JOHN WILMOT, EARL OF ROCHESTER

(1647-1680)

Born at Ditchley, near Woodstock in Oxfordshire, and educated at Wadham
College, Oxford, Rochester remains notorious for his dissolute and rakish life
as a courtier, for savage satirical and obscene poetry as well as some of the
finest English lyrics, and for his deathbed conversion which inclines one to see
in his earlier life a conscious nihilism, fuelled by his inability to live up to the
felt virtue of his patient wife.

> Huddled in dirt the reasoning engine lies,
> Who was so proud, so witty and so wise,

he wrote, echoing this contempt for (his own) life with the painfully beautiful
'Absent from thee I languish still', as well as with his translation of the chorus
from Seneca's *Troades* which rejects the idea of an afterlife. His two short
translations from Lucretius present the same atheistic outlook; the hedonism
that follows therefrom is perfectly presented in his version from Ovid which
could read as an original poem, so well are the stances of the two poets attuned.

To Love
(Ovid, *Amores* 2.9)

O Love! how cold and slow to take my part,
Thou idle wanderer about my heart.

Why thy old faithful soldier wilt thou see
Oppressed in my own tents? They murder me.
Thy flames consume, thy arrows pierce thy friends;
Rather, on foes pursue more noble ends.
   Achilles' sword would generously bestow
A cure as certain as it gave the blow.
Hunters who follow flying game give o'er
When the prey's caught; hope still leads on before.
We thine own slaves feel thy tyrannic blows,
Whilst thy tame hand's unmov'd against thy foes.
On men disarm'd how can you gallant prove?
And I was long ago disarm'd by love.
Millions of dull men live, and scornful maids:
We'll own Love valiant when he these invades.
Rome from each corner of the wide world snatch'd
A laurel; else 't had been to this day thatch'd.
   But the old soldier has his resting place,
And the good batter'd horse is turn'd to grass.
The harassed whore, who liv'd a wretch to please,
Has leave to be a bawd and take her ease.
For me, then, who have freely spent my blood,
Love, in thy service, and so boldly stood
In Celia's trenches, were 't not wisely done
E'en to retire, and live at peace at home?

No! Might I gain a godhead to disclaim
My glorious title to my endless flame,
Divinity with scorn I would forswear,
Such sweet, dear, tempting mischiefs women are.
Whene'er those flames grow faint, I quickly find
A fierce black storm pour down upon my mind.
Headlong I'm hurl'd, like horsemen who in vain
Their fury-foaming coursers would restrain.
As ships, just when the harbour they attain,
By sudden blasts are snatch'd to sea again,
So Love's fantastic storms reduce my heart
Half-rescued, and the god resumes his dart.
   Strike here, this undefended bosom wound,
And for so brave a conquest be renowned.
Shafts fly so fast to me from every part,
You'll scarce discern your quiver from my heart.
What wretch can bear a livelong night's dull rest,
Or think himself in lazy slumbers blessed?
Fool! Is not sleep the pale image of death?
There's time for rest when fate has stopped your breath.
Me may my soft deluding dear deceive:
I'm happy in my hopes whilst I believe.
Now let her flatter, then as fondly chide:

Often may I enjoy, oft be denied.
  With doubtful steps the god of war does move
By thy example led, ambiguous Love.
Blown to and fro like down from thy own wing,
Who knows when joy or anguish thou wilt bring?
Yet at thy mother's and thy slave's request,
Fix an eternal empire in my breast;
  And let th' inconstant charming sex,
Whose wilful scorn does lovers vex,
Submit their hearts before thy throne:
  The vassal world is then thy own.

WENTWORTH DILLON, EARL OF ROSCOMMON

(1633?-1685)

As a boy Roscommon was sent to Caen on the disgrace of his uncle, the Earl of Strafford. From there he continued to Italy where he remained until the Restoration.

He 'formed the plan of a society for refining our language, and fixing its standard; in imitation, says Fenton, of those learned and polite societies with which he had been acquainted abroad. In this design his friend Dryden is said to have assisted him' (Johnson). The project came to nothing, but it is this interest which lies behind Roscommon's most important work, the *Essay upon Translated Verse*, as well as his version of Horace's *Ars Poetica*. His other works merely share in the general elegance of his generation.

The duties of a poet
(Horace, *Ars Poetica* 323-60)

Greece had a genius, Greece had eloquence,
For her ambition and her end was fame.
Our Roman youth is bred another way,
And taught no arts but those of usury;
And the glad father glories in his child,
When he can subdivide a fraction:
Can souls, who by their parents from their birth
Have been devoted thus to rust and gain,
Be capable of high and gen'rous thoughts?
Can verses writ by such an author live?
But you (brave youth) wise Numa's worthy heir,
Remember of what weight your judgment is,
And never venture to commend a book,
That has not pass'd all judges and all tests.

A poet should instruct, or please, or both;
Let all your precepts be succinct and clear,
That ready wits may comprehend them soon,
And faithful memories retain them long;
For superfluities are soon forgot.
Never be so conceited of your parts,
To think you may persuade us what you please,
Or venture to bring in a child-alive,
That cannibals have murder'd and devour'd.
Old age explodes all but morality;
Austerity offends aspiring youths;
But he that joins instructions with delight,
Profit with pleasure, carries all the votes:
These are the volumes that enrich the shops,
These pass with admiration through the world,
And bring their author an eternal fame.

Be not too rigidly censorious,
A string may jar in the best master's hand,
And the most skilful archer miss his aim;
But in a poem elegantly writ,
I will not quarrel with a slight mistake,
Such as our nature's frailty may excuse;
But he that hath been often told his fault,
And still persists, is as impertinent,
As a musician that will always play,
And yet is always out at the same note;
When such a positive abandoned fop
(Among his numerous absurdities)
Stumbles upon some tolerable line,
I fret to see them in such company,
And wonder by what magic they came there.
But in long works sleep will sometimes surprise,
Homer himself hath been observ'd to nod.

THOMAS HOBBES

(1588-1679)

Hobbes translated Euripides' *Medea* into Latin verse before going to Magdalen College, Oxford, at the age of fourteen. He only returned to translation from the classics in the eve of his life, when his philosophical work was completed and, as it seemed, unesteemed. Aubrey notes: 'he had very few bookes . . . Homer and Virgil were commonly on his table.' Besides his versions of the *Iliad* and *Odyssey*, the works of his old age include an autobiography in Latin elegiacs. He writes in his Preface: 'But howsoever I defend Homer, I aim not thereby at any reflection upon the following translation. Why then did I write it? Because I had nothing else to do. Why publish it? Because I thought it might take off my adversaries from showing their folly upon my more serious writings, and set them upon my verses to show their wisdom. But why without annotations? Because I had no hope to do it better than it is already done by Mr Ogilby.'

Jove's promise to Thetis
(Homer, *Iliad* 1.517-32)

Then Jove much grieved, spake to her, and said,
    'Twixt me and Juno 'twill a quarrel make.
For she before the Gods will me upbraid,
    When she shall know the Trojans' part I take.
But go, lest she observe what you do here.
    I'll give a nod to all that you have spoken,
That you may safely trust to and not fear.
    A nod from me is an unfailing token.
This said, with his black brows he to her nodded,
    Wherewith displayed were his locks divine;
Olympus shook at stirring of his Godhead;
    And Thetis from it jump'd into the brine.

Demodocus' song
(Homer, *Odyssey* 8.62-92)

Came in the singer, whom the muses kind
Had taught to sing divinely; but, could not
    Or would not him preserve from being blind.
Pontonous the squire then led him in,
    And set him by a pillar in the hall,
And hung his fiddle o'er him on a pin,
    And how to reach it showed him withal:
Sets him a table and a basket by,
    And a great bowl of wine before him plac'd,
To drink as often as he should be dry.
    And when their thirst and hunger was displac'd,
The singer sung the song in most request,
    How once Ulysses and Achilles great
In high and bitter language did contest,
    When at a sacred feast they sate at meat;
And how king Agamemnon pleased was,
    To see the two best of the Greeks fall out.
For Phoebus told him so 'twould come to pass,
    When he at Pythos asked him about
The issue of the fleet design'd for Troy.
    This song Demodocus sung to them then;

Which to Ulysses was of little joy;
  But he his tears to hide before those men,
Before his eyes his cloak of purple drew,
  And when the singer ceas'd, his eyes he dried,
And from before his face his cloak withdrew,
  And of the wine perform'd the sacrifice.

JOHN OLDHAM

(1653-1683)

Oldham was educated at St Edmund Hall, Oxford. His verses were admired
by Rochester and Sedley, with the result that he became known to the Wits,
and to Dryden, whose elegy on his death is among the most perfect English
poems of mourning. He supported himself until 1681 as a private tutor. He
died of smallpox in 1683.

His satires on the Jesuits reflect the consternation of the period of the Popish
Plot, which is also alluded to in the imitation of Horace, *Satires* 1.9. The model
of Horace is very apparent in his original works as well as providing this
superb imitation.

Mad poets
(Horace, *Ars Poetica* 453-69)

Not those with 'Lord have mercy!' on their doors,
Venom of adders, or infected whores,
Are dreaded worse by men of sense and wit,
Than a mad scribbler in his raving fit;
Like dog, whose tail is pegged into a bone,
The hooting rabble all about the town
Pursue the cur, and pelt him up and down.
Should this poor frantic, as he passed along,
Intent on's rhyming work amidst the throng,
Into Fleet-ditch, or some deep cellar fall,
And till he rent his throat for succour bawl,
No one would lend an helping hand at call;
For who, the plague! could guess at his design,
Whether he did not for the nonce drop in?
I'd tell you, sir, but questionless you've heard
Of the odd end of a Sicilian bard;
Fond to be deemed a god, this fool, it seems,
In's fit leapt headlong into Etna's flames.
Troth, I could be content an act might pass,
Such poets should have leave, whene'er they please,
To die, and rid us of our grievances.

A God's name let 'em hang, or drown, or choose
What other way they will themselves dispose;
Why should we life against their wills impose?
Might that same fool I mentioned now revive,
He would not be reclaimed, I dare believe,
But soon be playing his odd freaks again,
And still the same capricious hopes retain.

The Pest: 'An Imitation of Horace'
(Horace, *Satires* 1.9, abbreviated)

As I was walking in the Mall of late,
Alone, and musing on I know not what;
Comes a familiar fop, whom hardly I
Knew by his name, and rudely seizes me:
'Dear sir, I'm mighty glad to meet with you:
And pray, how have you done this age, or two?
'Well, I thank God,' said I, 'as times are now:
I wish the same to you.' And so passed on,
Hoping with this, the coxcomb would be gone.
But when I saw I could not thus get free,
I asked, what business else he had of me?
'Sir,' answered he, if learning, parts, or sense
Merit your friendship, I have just pretence.'
'I honour you,' said I, 'upon that score,
And shall be glad to serve you to my power.'
Meantime, wild to get loose, I try all ways
To shake him off; sometimes I walk apace,
Sometimes stand still; I frown, I chafe, I fret,
Shrug, turn my back, as in the Bagnio, sweat;
And show all kinds of signs to make him guess
At my impatience and uneasiness.
'Happy the folk in Newgate!' whispered I,
'Who, though in chains, are from this torment free;
Would I were like rough Manly in the play,
To send impertinents with kicks away!'
   He all the while baits me with tedious chat,
Speaks much about the drought, and how the rate
Of hay is raised, and what it now goes at;
Tells me of a new comet at the Hague,
Portending God knows what, a dearth, or plague;
Names every wench that passes through the park,
How much she is allowed, and who the spark;
Who had ill-hap at the groom-porter's board,
Three nights ago, in play with such a lord; . . .

   While at this savage rate he worried me,

By chance a doctor, my dear friend, came by,
That knew the fellow's humour passing well;
Glad of the sight I join him; we stand still:
'Whence came you, sir? and whither go you now?'
And such like questions passed betwixt us two.
Straight I began to pull him by the sleeve,
Nod, wink upon him, touch my nose, and give
A thousand hints, to let him know that I
Needed his help for my delivery;
He, naughty wag, with an arch fleering smile,
Seems ignorant of what I mean the while;
I grow stark wild with rage. 'Sir, said not you,
You'd somewhat to discourse, not long ago,
With me in private?' 'I remember 't well.
Some other time be sure, I will not fail;
Now I am in great haste upon my word;
A messenger came for me from a lord
That's in a bad condition, like to die.'
'Oh! sir, he can't be in a worse than I;
Therefore for God's sake do not stir from hence.'
'Sweet sir! your pardon; 'tis of consequence;
I hope you're kinder than to press my stay,
Which may be heaven knows what out of my way.'
This said, he left me to my murderer.
Seeing no hopes of my relief appear,
'Confounded be the stars,' said I, 'that swayed
This fatal day! would I had kept my bed
With sickness, rather than be visited
With this worse plague! What ill have I e're done,
To pull this curse, this heavy judgment down?'
    While I was thus lamenting my ill hap,
Comes aid at length; a brace of bailiffs clap
The rascal on the back: 'Here take your fees,
Kind gentlemen,' said I, 'for my release.'
He would have had me bail. 'Excuse me, sir,
I've made a vow ne'er to be surety more;
My father was undone by 't heretofore.'
Thus I got off, and blessed the fates that he
Was prisoner made, I set at liberty.

NAHUM TATE

(1652-1715)

Born in Co. Cavan, and educated at Trinity College, Dublin, Tate embarked
early on a literary career. His first play, *Brutus of Alba*, was staged in 1678;

subsequent works included adaptations of *Richard II* (*The Sicilian Usurper*: suppressed) and *King Lear*. He contributed to Part 2 of Dryden's *Absalom and Achitophel*, and in 1692 was made Poet Laureate on the death of Shadwell (Southey, from his glass house, called Tate the lowest of the laureates). Almost all his work consists of translation, or editions, or collaborations with other writers.

How to dispel infatuation
(Ovid, *Remedia Amoris* 311-56)

A certain nymph did once my heart encline,
Whose humour wholly disagreed with mine.
(I, your physician, my disease confess)
I from my own prescriptions found redress.
Her still I represented to my mind,
With what defects I could suppose or find.
Oh how ill-shap'd her legs, how thick and short!
(Tho' neater limbs did never nymph support.)
Her arms, said I, how tawny brown they are!
(Tho' never ivory statue had so fair.)
How low of stature! (yet the nymph was tall)
Oh for what costly presents will she call!
What change of lovers! – And, of all the rest,
I found this thought strike deepest in my breast.
Such thin partitions Good and Ill divide,
That one for t'other may be misapply'd.
Ev'n truth, and your own judgment, you must strain,
Those blemishes you cannot find, to feign:
Call her blackmoor, if she's but lovely brown;
Monster, if plump; if slender, skeleton.
Censure her free discourse as confidence;
Her silence, want of breeding and good sense.
Discover her blind side, and put her still
Upon the task which she performs but ill.
Court her to sing, if she wants voice and ear;
To dance, if she has neither shape nor air:
If talking misbecomes her, make her talk;
If walking, then in malice make her walk.
Commend her skill when on the lute she plays,
'Till vanity her want of skill betrays.
Take care, if her large breasts offend your eyes,
No dress do that deformity disguise.
Ply her with merry tales of what you will,
To keep her laughing, if her teeth are ill.
Or if blear-ey'd, some tragic story find,
'Till she has read and wept her self quite blind.
But one effectual method you may take:

Enter her chamber, ere she's well awake:
Her beauty's art, gems, gold, and rich attire,
Make up the pageant you so much admire;
In all that specious figure which you see
The least, least part of her own self is she.
In vain for her you love, amidst such cost,
You search; the mistress in the dress is lost.
Take her disrob'd, her real self surprize,
I'll trust you then, for cure, to your own eyes.
(Yet have I known this very rule to fail,
And beauty most, when stript of art, prevail.)
Steal to her closet, her close tiring place,
Whil she makes up her artificial face.
All colours of the rainbow you'll discern,
Washes and paints, and what you're sick to learn.

APHRA BEHN

(1640-1689)

Brought up in Surinam, Behn returned to England in 1683. After an episode as a spy in Antwerp, she turned her hand to poetry and plays, earning the ridicule of Matthew Prior, who spoke of writers who

> know what Roman authors mean
> No more than does our blind translatress Behn.

Her translations are few: the *Oenone to Paris* is her contribution to the joint translation of Ovid's *Heroides* or *Epistles* (1680) made by Dryden, Tate and many others.

Oenone's first sight of Paris
(Ovid, *Heroides* 5.61-74, expanded)

A rock there is, from whence I cou'd survey
From far the blewish shore, and distant sea,
Whose hanging top with toyl I climb'd each day.
With greedy view the prospect I ran o'er,
To see what wish'd for ships approach'd our shore.
One day all hopeless on its point I stood,
And saw a vessel bounding o'er the flood,
And as it nearer drew, I cou'd discern
Rich purple sails, silk cords, and golden stern;
Upon the deck a canopy was spread
Of antique work in gold and silver made,

Which mix'd with sun-beams dazling light display'd.
But oh! beneath this glorious scene of state
(Curst be the sight) a fatal beauty sate,
And fondly you were on her bosome lay'd,
Whilst with your perjur'd lips her fingers play'd;
Wantonly curl'd and dally'd with that hair,
Of which, as sacred charms, I bracelets wear.
   Oh! hadst thou seen me then in that mad state,
So ruin'd, so design'd for death and fate,
Fix'd on a rock, whose horrid precipice
In hollow murmurs wars with angry seas;
Whilst the bleak winds aloft my garments bear,
Ruffling my careless and dishevel'd hair,
I look'd like the sad statue of despair.
With out-strech'd voice I cry'd, and all around
The rocks and hills my dire complaints resound.
I rent my garments, tore my flattering face,
Whose false deluding charms my ruine was.
Mad as the seas in storms, I breathe despair,
Or winds let loose in unresisting air.
Raging and frantick through the woods I fly,
And Paris! lovely, faithless Paris cry.

THOMAS CREECH

(1659-1700)

Born and educated in Dorset, Creech continued to Wadham College, Oxford, of which he became a Fellow. Apart from two years as head of Sherborne, he spent all his life at Wadham, where he became increasingly inactive. In 1700 he hanged himself, apparently through frustrated love.

His Lucretius was as popular in its day as the great translations of Dryden and Pope; he is said to have composed it during his daily walks around the University Parks. He later edited the poet as well. This translation was followed by versions of Horace, Theocritus and Manilius; and parts of Vergil and Juvenal.

Pope's comment on his Lucretius is apt:

> Plain truth, dear Murray, needs no flowers of speech,
> So take it in the very words of Creech.

His excellence lies indeed in the more scientific passages of Lucretius, where vigour and precision are more important than elegance, and which in any case fall well into the idiom of an age still accustomed to the writing of scientific works in verse.

Echoes
(Lucretius, *On the Nature of Things* 4.568-94)

But some parts of the voice, that miss the ear,
Fly thro' the air diffus'd, and perish there:
Some strike on solid buildings, and, restor'd,
Bring back again the image of the word,
This shews thee why, whilst men, thro' caves and groves,
Call their lost friends, or mourn unhappy loves,
The pitying rocks, the groaning caves return
Their sad complaints again, and seem to mourn:
This all observe, and I myself have known
Both rocks and hills return six words for one:
The dancing words from hill to hill rebound,
They all receive, and all restore the sound:
The vulgar, and the neighbours think, and tell,
That there the nymphs, and fauns, and satyrs dwell:
And that their wanton sport, their loud delight
Breaks thro' the quiet silence of the night:
Their musick's softest airs fill all the plains,
And mighty Pan delights the list'ning swains:
The goat-fac'd Pan, whose flocks securely feed;
With long-hung lip he blows his oaten reed:
The horn'd, the half-beast god, when brisk and gay,
With pine-leafs crown'd, provokes the swains to play.
Ten thousand such romants the vulgar tell,
Perhaps, lest men should think the gods will dwell
In towns alone, and scorn their plains and cell:
Or somewhat: for man, credulous and vain,
Delights to hear strange things, delights to feign.

Archytas' grave
(Horace, *Odes* 1.28)

A Narrow Grave by the Matinian Shore
Confines thee now, and thou canst have no more:
Ah learn'd Architas, ah how small for thee
Whose wondrous Mind could measure Earth and Sea!
What Sands make up the Shore minutely teach,
And count as far as Number's self could reach!
What did it profit that thy nimble Soul
Had travell'd Heaven, and oft ran round the Pole,
Pursu'd the Motions of the rowling Light,
When Death came on, and spread a gloomy Night!
Wise Tantalus, the Guest of Gods, is dead,
And on strange Wings the chang'd Tithonus fled:
Jove's Friend, just Minos, hath resign'd his Breath,

And wise Pythagoras felt a second Death;
Altho' his Trojan Shield, and former State
Did prove his Soul above the Force of Fate;
Withdrew the Mind from Death's black conquering hand,
And left but Skin and Bones at Fate's Command;
In thy Opinion he did most excel,
Discover'd Truth, and follow'd Nature well:
But once o'er all long Night her Shades will spread,
And all must walk the Vallies of the Dead:
Some Rage spurs on, and Death attends in Wars;
The Sea destroys the greedy Mariners:
The Young and Old confus'd by numbers fall,
And Death with equal hand doth strike at all:
A boyst'rous Storm my feeble Tackling tore,
And left me naked on th' Illyrian Shore:
But, Seaman, pray be just, put near the Land,
Bestow a Grave, and hide my Limbs in Sand:
So may the threat'ning East Winds spare the Floods,
And idly spend their Rage on Hills and Woods,
Whilst you ride safely; so from every Shore
May Gain flow in, and feed thy growing Store:
May Jove and Neptune, soft Tarentum's Guard,
Conspire to bless, and join in one Reward.
Perhaps you scorn, and are design'dly base,
Thy Crime shall damn thy undeserving Race;
Thy Pride, vain Man, shall on thy self return,
Thou naked lie, and be the Publick Scorn:
My Prayers shall mount, and pull just Vengeance down.
No Offerings shall release, no Vows attone.
Tho' hasty now, driv'n by a prosperous Gale,
('Tis quickly done) thrice strew the Sand, and Sail.

PHILIP AYRES

(1638-1712)

Educated at Westminster and St John's College, Oxford, Ayres spent all his subsequent life as a tutor in the Drake family in Buckinghamshire. His translations show an unusual range of interest for the period, including as they do several of the lesser known Greek lyric poets, Bacchylides and Hybrias, as well as favourites like Theocritus and Anacreon.

Peace
(Bacchylides, *Paean* 4.61-80)

Great Goddess Peace does wealth on us bestow,
From her our sciences and learning flow,
Our arts improve, and we the artists prize,
Our altars fume with richest sacrifice:

Youths mind their active sports – they often meet,
Revel, and dance with maidens in the street;
The useless shield serves to adorn the hall,
Whence spiders weave their nets against the wall;

Gauntlets and spears lie cover'd o'er with dust,
And slighted swords half eaten up with rust;
No trumpets sound, no rattling drums we hear,
No frightful clamours pierce the tim'rous ear;

Our weary eyes enjoying natural rest,
Refresh the heart when 'tis with cares opprest;
Days steal away in feasting and delight,
And lovers spend in serenades the night.

CHARLES COTTON

(1630-1687)

Cotton is best remembered for his translation of the *Essais* of Montaigne, and
his contribution to Izaak Walton's *Compleat Angler*. He also translated many
other French works, and French influence is strong in his own works, for
example the *Scarronides; or le Virgile travesty*, which went through six editions,
each grosser than the last. The introspective humanism of Montaigne might
naturally lead him to Horace, but his translations from Horace, one of which
appeared in Alexander Brome's anthology (1666) are few: the best of them is
his version of *Epode* 2, a favourite poem especially chosen for translation by Ben
Jonson, Cowley, Dryden, Sir John Beaumont and numerous other poets.

A bald lady
(Martial, *Epigrams* 12.7)

If by her hairs Ligeia's age be told,
'Tis soon cast up, that she is three years old.

Happy is the countryman
(Horace, *Epode* 2)

Happy's that man that is from city care
Sequester'd, as the ancients were;

That with his own ox ploughs his father's lands,
    Untainted with usurious bands:
That from alarms of war in quiet sleeps;
    Nor's frighted with the raging deeps:
That shuns litigious law, and the proud state
    Of his more potent neighbour's gate.
Therefore, he either is employ'd to join
    The poplar to the sprouting vine,
Pruning luxurious branches, grafting some
    More hopeful offspring in their room:
Or else his sight in humble vallies feasts,
    With scatter'd troops of lowing beasts:
Of refin'd honey in fine vessels keeps;
    Or shears his snowy tender sheep:
Or, when Autumnus shows his fruitful head
    I'th' mellow fields with apples covered,
How he delights to pluck the grafted pear,
    And grapes, whose cheeks do purple wear!
Of which to thee, Priapus, tithes abound,
    And Silvan patron of his ground.
Now, where the aged oak his green arms spreads,
    He lies; now in the flow'ry meads:
Whilst through their deep-worn banks the murmuring floods
    Do glide, and birds chant in the woods:
And bubbling fountains flowing streams do weep,
    A gentle summons unto sleep.
But when cold Winter does the storms prepare,
    And snow of thund'ring Jupiter;
Then with his dogs the furious boar he foils,
    Compell'd into objected toils:
Or, on the forks extends his mashy net,
    For greedy thrushes a deceit.
The fearful hare too, and the stranger crane
    With gins he takes, a pleasant gain.
Who but with such diversions would remove
    All the malignant cares of love?
But, if to these he have a modest spouse,
    To nurse his children, keep his house,
Such, as the Sabine women, or the tann'd
    Wife o' th' painful Apulian,
To make a good fire of dry wood, when come
    From his hard labour weary home;
The wanton cattle in their booths to tie,
    Stripping their stradling udders dry,
Drawing the must from forth the cleanly vats,
    To wash down their unpurchas'd cates;
Mullet or thornback cannot please me more,

Nor oysters from the Lucrine shore,
When by an eastern tempest they are tost,
    Into the sea, that sweeps this coast.
The turkey fair of Afric shall not come,
    Within the confines of my womb:
As olives from the fruitfull'st branches got,
    Ionian suites so sweet are not;
Or sorrel growing in the meadow ground,
    Or mallow for the body sound;
The lamb kill'd for the Terminalia;
    Or kid redeem'd from the wolf's prey.
Whilst thus we feed, what joy 'tis to behold
    The pastur'd sheep haste to their fold!
And th' wearied ox with drooping neck to come
    Haling th' inverted culture home;
And swarms of servants from their labour quit
    About the shining fire sit!
Thus when the usurer Alphius had said,
    Now purposing this life to lead,
I' th' Ides call'd in his money; but for gain
    I' th' Kalends put it forth again.

JOHN DRYDEN

(1631-1700)

Born in Northamptonshire, and educated at Westminster and at Trinity College, Cambridge, Dryden began his literary career as a dramatist, and the opening years of his career show him as the author of no less than twenty-eight plays. Among them are one or two with classical subjects – the *Oedipus*, composed with Lee and based on an amalgam of Sophocles, Seneca and Corneille (1679) and the *Amphytrion* of 1690. But his most important works of these years are the Satires of 1681-2, *Absalom and Achitophel*, *The Medal*, and *MacFlecknoe*. He had been made Poet Laureate in 1668. The Glorious Revolution of 1688 both reduced Dryden's hopes of patronage from the King and made it prudent to refrain from satire. Thereafter he returned to writing for the stage, and also to translation. His first translations had appeared in 1680, in the joint version of Ovid's *Epistles*, in which Johnson is already able to commend him for breaking loose from the rigidity and literalness of Jonson, Sandys and Holyday. In the Preface to this work Dryden expounds his theory of the three types of translation (see above, Introduction), to which no writer since has been able to add very much. The translations of the 1690s are numerous, and include the Lucretius, Juvenal and Persius as well as the complete Vergil. He also translated the *Lives* of Plutarch, and edited the first volumes of the *Miscellanies* which were devoted in no small measure to translations from classical poets. The importance of Dryden in refining English poetic diction is to a considerable extent due to his constant exercise with translation, and to his incisive and ever fresh criticism.

Against the fear of death
(Lucretius, *On the Nature of Things* 3.830-51, 888-943)

What has this bugbear death to frighten man,
If souls can die, as well as bodies can?
For, as before our birth we felt no pain,
When Punic arms infested land and main,
When heaven and earth were in confusion hurled
For the debated empire of the world,
Which awed with dreadful expectation lay,
Sure to be slaves, uncertain who should sway:
So, when our mortal frame shall be disjoin'd,
The lifeless lump uncoupled from the mind,
From sense of grief and pain we shall be free;
We shall not feel, because we shall not be.
Though earth in seas, and seas in heaven were lost,
We should not move, we only should be tost.
Nay, e'en suppose, when we have suffer'd fate,
The soul could feel in her divided state,
What's that to us? for we are only we
While souls and bodies in one frame agree.
Nay, though our atoms should revolve by chance,
And matter leap into the former dance;
Though time our life and motion could restore,
And make our bodies what they were before,
What gain to us would all this bustle bring?
The new-made man would be another thing.
When once an interrupting pause is made,
That individual being is decay'd.
We, who are dead and gone, shall bear no part
In all the pleasures, nor shall feel the smart,
Which to that other mortal shall accrue,
Whom of our matter time shall mould anew . . .

If after death 'tis painful to be torn
By birds, and beasts, then why not so to burn,
Or drench'd in floods of honey to be soak'd,
Imbalm'd at once to be preserv'd and chok'd;
Or on an airy mountain's top to lie,
Expos'd to cold and heaven's inclemency;
Or crowded in a tomb to be oppress'd
With monumental marble on thy breast?
But to be snatch'd from all thy household joys,

From thy chaste wife, and thy dear prattling boys,
Whose little arms about thy legs are cast,
And climbing for a kiss prevent their mother's haste,
Inspiring secret pleasure through thy breast;
Ah! these shall be no more: thy friends oppress'd
Thy care and courage now no more shall free;
Ah! wretch, thou criest, ah! miserable me!
One woful day sweeps children, friends, and wife,
And all the brittle blessing of thy life!
Add one thing more, and all thou say'st is true;
Thy want and wish of them is vanish'd too:
Which, well consider'd, were a quick relief
To all thy vain imaginary grief.
For thou shalt sleep, and never wake again,
And, quitting life, shalt quit thy living pain.
But we, thy friends, shall all those sorrows find,
Which in forgetful death thou leav'st behind;
No time shall dry our tears, nor drive thee from our mind.
The worst that can befall thee, measur'd right,
Is a sound slumber, and a long good night.
Yet thus the fools, that would be thought the wits,
Disturb their mirth with melancholy fits;
When healths go round, and kindly brimmers flow,
Till the fresh garlands on their foreheads glow,
They whine, and cry, Let us make haste to live,
Short are the joys that human life can give.
Eternal preachers, that corrupt the draught,
And pall the god, that never thinks, with thought;
Idiots with all that thought, to whom the worst
Of death is want of drink, and endless thirst,
Or any fond desire vain as these.
For, e'en in sleep, the body, wrapt in ease,
Supinely lies, as in the peaceful grave;
And, wanting nothing, nothing can it crave.
Were that sound sleep eternal, it were death;
Yet the first atoms then, the seeds of breath,
Are moving near to sense; we do but shake
And rouse that sense, and straight we are awake.
Then death to us, and death's anxiety,
Is less than nothing, if a less could be.
For then our atoms, which in order lay,
Are scatter'd from their heap, and puff'd away,
And never can return into their place,
When once the pause of life has left an empty space.
And last, suppose great Nature's voice should call
To thee, or me, or any of us all,
'What do'st thou mean, ungrateful wretch, thou vain,

Thou mortal thing, thus idly to complain,
And sigh and sob, that thou shalt be no more?
For if thy life were pleasant heretofore,
If all the bounteous blessings, I could give,
Thou hast enjoy'd, if thou hast known to live,
And pleasure not leak'd through thee like a sieve;
Why dost thou not give thanks as at a plenteous feast,
Cramm'd to the throat with life, and rise and take thy rest?
But if my blessing thou hast thrown away,
If indigested joys pass'd thro', and would not stay,
Why dost thou wish for more to squander still?
If life be grown a load, a real ill,
And I would all thy cares and labours end,
Lay down thy burden, fool, and know thy friend.'

Portents of civil war
(Vergil, *Georgics* 1.463-97)

The sun reveals the secrets of the sky;
And who dares give the source of light the lie?
The change of empires often he declares,
Fierce tumults, hidden treasons, open wars.
He first the fate of Caesar did foretell,
And pitied Rome, when Rome in Caesar fell;
In iron clouds conceal'd the public light;
And impious mortals fear'd eternal night.
  Nor was the fact foretold by him alone:
Nature herself stood forth, and seconded the sun.
Earth, air, and seas, with prodigies were signed;
And birds obscene, and howling dogs, divined.
What rocks did Aetna's bellowing mouth expire
From her torn entrails! and what floods of fire!
What clanks were heard, in German skies afar.
Of arms and armies, rushing to the war!
Dire earthquakes rent the solid Alps below,
And from their summits shook the eternal snow;
Pale spectres in the close of night were seen,
And voices heard, of more than mortal men,
In silent groves; dumb sheep and oxen spoke;
And streams ran backward, and their beds forsook;
The yawning earth disclosed the abyss of hell;
The weeping statues did the wars foretell;
And holy sweat from brazen idols fell.
Then, rising in his might, the king of floods
Rushed through the forests, tore the lofty woods,
And, rolling onward, with a sweepy sway,
Bore houses, herds, and labouring hinds away.

Blood sprang from wells; wolves howled in towns by night,
And boding victims did the priests affright.
Such peals of thunder never poured from high,
Nor forky lightnings flashed from such a sullen sky.
Red meteors ran across the ethereal space;
Stars disappeared, and comets took their place.
For this, the Emathian plains once more were strew'd
With Roman bodies, and just heaven thought good
To fatten twice those fields with Roman blood.
Then, after length of time, the labouring swains
Who turn the turfs of those unhappy plains,
Shall rusty piles from the ploughed furrows take,
And over empty helmets pass the rake –
Amazed at antique titles on the stones,
And mighty relics of gigantic bones.

Happy is the countryman
(Vergil, *Georgics* 2.495-502)

Happy the man, who, studying nature's laws,
Through known effects can trace the secret cause –
His mind possessing in a quiet state,
Fearless of Fortune, and resigned to Fate!
And happy too is he, who decks the bowers
Of sylvans, and adores the rural powers –
Whose mind, unmoved, the bribes of courts can see,
Their glittering baits, and purple slavery –
Nor hopes the people's praise, nor fears their frown,
Nor, when contending kindred tear the crown,
Will set up one, or pull another down.
Without concern he hears, but hears from far,
Of tumults, and descents, and distant war;
Nor with a superstitious fear is awed,
For what befalls at home, or what abroad.
Nor his own peace disturbs with pity for the poor.
Nor envies he the rich their happy store.
He feeds on fruits, which, of their own accord,
The willing ground and laden trees afford.

Fame
(Vergil, *Aeneid* 4.173-90)

The loud report through Libyan cities goes.
Fame, the great ill, from small beginnings grows –
Swift from the first; and every moment brings
New vigour to her flights, new pinions to her wings.
Soon grows the pigmy to gigantic size;

Her feet on earth, her forehead in the skies.
Enraged against the gods, revengeful Earth
Produced her, last of the Titanian birth:
Swift is her walk, more swift her winged haste:
A monstrous phantom, horrible and vast.
As many plumes as raise her lofty flight;
So many piercing eyes enlarge her sight;
Millions of opening mouths to Fame belong,
And every mouth is furnished with a tongue;
And round, with listening ears the flying plague is hung.
She fills the peaceful universe with cries:
No slumbers ever close her wakeful eyes:
By day, from lofty towers her head she shows,
And spreads through trembling crowds disastrous news;
With court-informers, haunts, and royal spies;
Things done, relates; not done, she feigns, and mingles truth with lies.
Talk is her business; and her chief delight
To tell of prodigies, and cause affright.

Aeneas sees Dido in the Underworld
(Vergil, *Aeneid* 4.440-74)

Not far from thence, the Mournful Fields appear,
So called from lovers that inhabit there.
The souls whom that unhappy flame invades,
In secret solitude and myrtle shades
Make endless moans, and, pining with desire,
Lament too late their unextinguished fire.
Here Procris, Eriphyle here he found
Baring her breast, yet bleeding with the wound
Made by her son. He saw Pasiphae there,
With Phaedra's ghost; a foul incestuous pair.
There Laodamia, with Evadne, moves:
Unhappy both, but loyal in their loves:
Caeneus, a woman once, and once a man,
But ending in the sex she first began.
Not far from these Phoenician Dido stood,
Fresh from her wound, her bosom bathed in blood;
Whom when the Trojan hero hardly knew,
Obscure in shades, and with a doubtful view
(Doubtful as he who sees, through dusky night,
Or thinks he sees, the moon's uncertain light),
With tears he first approached the sullen shade;
And as his love inspired him, thus he said:
'Unhappy queen! then is the common breath
Of rumour true, in your reported death,
Am I, alas! the cause? – By Heaven, I vow,

And all the powers that rule the realms below,
Unwilling I forsook your friendly state,
Commanded by the gods, and forced by Fate!
Those gods, that Fate, whose unresisted might
Have sent me to these regions void of light,
Through the vast empire of eternal night!
Nor dared I to presume, that, pressed with grief,
My flight should urge you to this dire relief.
Stay, stay your steps, and listen to my vows!
'Tis the last interview that Fate allows!'
In vain he thus attempts her mind to move
With tears and prayers, and late repenting love.
Disdainfully she looked; then turning round,
She fixed her eyes unmoved upon the ground;
And, what he says and swears, regards no more
Than the deaf rocks, when the loud billows roar:
But whirled away, to shun his hateful sight,
Hid in the forest, and the shades of night:
Then sought Sichaeus through the shady grove,
Who answered all her cares, and equalled all her love.

Praise of Maecenas
(Horace, *Odes* 3.29)

Descended of an ancient line,
    That long the Tuscan sceptre sway'd,
Make haste to meet the generous wine,
    Whose piercing is for thee delay'd:
The rosy wreath is ready made;
    And artful hands prepare
The fragrant Syrian oil, that shall perfume thy hair.

When the wine sparkles from afar,
    And the well-natur'd friend cries, Come away;
Make haste, and leave thy business and thy care:
    No mortal interest can be worth thy stay.

Leave for a while thy costly country seat;
    And, to be great indeed, forget
The nauseous pleasures of the great:
    Make haste and come:
Come, and forsake thy cloying store;
    Thy turret that surveys, from high,
The smoke, and wealth, and noise of Rome;
    And all the busy pageantry
That wise men scorn, and fools adore:
Come, give thy soul a loose, and taste the pleasures of the poor.

Sometimes 'tis grateful to the rich to try
A short vicissitude, and fit of poverty:
  A savoury dish, a homely treat,
  Where all is plain, where all is neat,
  Without the stately spacious room,
The Persian carpet, or the Tyrian loom,
Clear up the cloudy foreheads of the great.

  The sun is in the Lion mounted high;
     The Syrian star
     Barks from afar,
  And with his sultry breath infects the sky;
The ground below is parch'd, the heavens above us fry.
  The shepherd drives his fainting flock
  Beneath the covert of a rock,
  And seeks refreshing rivulets nigh:
  The Sylvans to their shades retire,
Those very shades and streams new shades and streams require,
  And want a cooling breeze to fan the raging fire.

  Thou, what befits the new Lord Mayor,
  And what the city factions dare,
  And what the Gallic arms will do,
  And what the quiver-bearing foe,
  Art anxiously inquisitive to know:
But God has, wisely, hid from human sight
  The dark decrees of future fate,
  And sown their seeds in depth of night;
He laughs at all the giddy turns of state;
When mortals search too soon, and fear too late.

  Enjoy the present smiling hour;
  And put it out of fortune's power:
The tide of business, like the running stream,
  Is sometimes high, and sometimes low,
A quiet ebb, or a tempestuous flow,
    And always in extreme.
  Now with a noiseless gentle course
  It keeps within the middle bed;
  Anon it lifts aloft the head,
And bears down all before it with impetuous force;
  And trunks of trees come rolling down,
  Sheep and their folds together drown:
  Both house and homestead into seas are borne;
  And rocks are from their firm foundations torn,
And woods, made thin with winds, their scatter'd honours mourn.

  Happy the man, and happy he alone,
    He, who can call to-day his own:

He who, secure within, can say,
To-morrow do thy worst, for I have liv'd today.
Be fair or foul, or rain, or shine,
The joys I have possess'd, in spite of fate, are mine.
Not heaven itself upon the past has power;
But what has been, has been, and I have had my hour.
Fortune, that with malicious joy
Does man her slave oppress,
Proud of her office to destroy,
Is seldom pleas'd to bless:
Still various, and unconstant still,
But with an inclination to be ill,
Promotes, degrades, delights in strife,
And makes a lottery of life.
I can enjoy her while she's kind;
But when she dances in the wind,
And shakes the wings, and will not stay,
I puff the prostitute away:
The little or the much she gave is quietly resign'd:
Content with poverty, my soul I arm;
And virtue, though in rags, will keep me warm.

What is't to me,
Who never sail in her unfaithful sea,
If storms arise, and clouds grow black;
If the mast split, and threaten wreck?
Then let the greedy merchant fear
For his ill-gotten gain;
And pray to gods that will not hear,
While the debating winds and billows bear
His wealth into the main.
For me, secure from Fortune's blows,
Secure of what I cannot lose,
In my small pinnace I can sail,
Contemning all the blustering roar;
And running with a merry gale,
With friendly stars my safety seek,
Within some little winding creek;
And see the storm ashore.

Apollo and Daphne
(Ovid, *Metamorphoses* 1.502-67)

Swift as the wind, the damsel fled away,
Nor did for these alluring speeches stay:
Stay, nymph, he cried, I follow, not a foe:
Thus from the Lion trips the trembling Doe:
Thus from the Wolf the frighten'd Lamb removes,

And from pursuing Falcons fearful Doves;
Thou shunn'st a god, and shunn'st a god that loves.
Ah lest some thorn should pierce thy tender foot,
Or thou shouldst fall in flying my pursuit!
To sharp uneven ways thy steps decline;
Abate thy speed, and I will bate of mine.
Yet think from whom thou dost so rashly fly;
Nor basely born, nor shepherd's swain am I.
Perhaps thou know'st not my superior state;
And from that ignorance proceeds thy hate.
Me Claros, Delphos, Tenedos obey;
These hands the Patareian sceptre sway.
The king of Gods begot me: what shall be,
Or is, or ever was, in fate, I see.
Mine is the invention of the charming lyre;
Sweet notes, and heavenly numbers I inspire.
Sure is my bow, unerring is my dart;
But ah! more deadly his, who pierc'd my heart.
Med'cine is mine, what herbs and simples grow
In fields and forests, all their powers I know;
And am the great physician call'd below.
Alas, that fields and forests can afford
No remedies to heal their love-sick lord!
To cure the pains of love no plant avails;
And his own physic the physician fails.
　She heard not half, so furiously she flies,
And on her ear the imperfect accent dies.
Fear gave her wings; and as she fled, the wind
Increasing spread her flowing hair behind;
And left her legs and thighs expos'd to view;
Which made the god more eager to pursue . . .

He gathers ground upon her in the chase:
Now breathes upon her hair, with nearer pace;
And just is fastening on the wish'd embrace.
The nymph grew pale, and in a mortal fright,
Spent with the labour of so long a flight;
And now despairing, cast a mournful look,
Upon the streams of her paternal brook:
Oh help, she cried, in this extremest need,
If water-gods are deities indeed:
Gape, Earth, and this unhappy wretch intomb:
Or change my form whence all my sorrows come.
Scarce had she finish'd, when her feet she found
Benumb'd with cold, and fasten'd to the ground:
A filmy rind about her body grows,
Her hair to leaves, her arms extend to boughs:

The nymph is all into a laurel gone,
The smoothness of her skin remains alone.
Yet Phoebus loves her still, and, casting round
Her bole his arms, some little warmth he found.
The tree still panted in the unfinish'd part,
Not wholly vegetive, and heav'd her heart.
He fix'd his lips upon the trembling rind;
It swerv'd aside, and his embrace declin'd.
To whom the god: Because thou canst not be
My mistress, I espouse thee for my tree:
Be thou the prize of honour and renown;
The deathless poet, and the poem, crown.
Thou shalt the Roman festivals adorn,
And, after poets, be by victors worn.
Thou shalt returning Caesar's triumph grace;
When pomps shall in a long procession pass:
Wreath'd on the post before his palace wait;
And be the sacred guardian of the gate:
Secure from thunder, and unharm'd by Jove,
Unfading as the immortal powers above:
And as the locks of Phoebus are unshorn,
So shall perpetual green thy boughs adorn.
The grateful tree was pleas'd with what he said,
And shook the shady honours of her head.

The adulterer's code
(Ovid, *Amores* 1.4)

Your husband will be with us at the treat;
May that be the last supper he shall eat.
And am I a poor guest invited there,
Only to see, while he may touch the fair?
To see you kiss and hug your nauseous lord,
While his lewd hand descends below the board?
Now wonder not that Hippodamia's charms,
At such a sight, the Centaurs urg'd to arms;
That in a rage they threw their cups aside,
Assail'd the bridegroom, and would force the bride.
I am not half a horse, (I would I were)
Yet hardly can from you my hands forbear.
Take then my counsel; which observ'd, may be
Of some importance both to you and me.
Be sure to come before your man be there;
There's nothing can be done; but come howe'er.
Sit next him (that belongs to decency)
But tread upon my foot in passing by.
Read in my looks what silently they speak,

And slily, with your eyes, your answer make.
My lifted eyebrow shall declare my pain;
My right-hand to his fellow shall complain;
And on the back a letter shall design;
Besides a note that shall be writ in wine.
Whene'er you think upon our last embrace,
With your fore-finger gently touch your face.
If any word of mine offend my dear,
Pull, with your hand, the velvet of your ear.
If you are pleas'd with what I do or say,
Handle your rings, or with your fingers play.
As suppliants use at altars, hold the board,
Whene'er you wish the de'il may take your lord.
When he fills for you, never touch the cup,
But bid th' officious cuckold drink it up.
The waiter on those services employ:
Drink you, and I will snatch it from the boy;
Watching the part where your sweet mouth hath been,
And thence with eager lips will suck it in.
If he, with clownish manners, thinks it fit
To taste, and offer you the nasty bit,
Reject his greasy kindness, and restore
Th' unsav'ry morsel he had chew'd before.
Nor let his arms embrace your neck, nor rest
Your tender cheek upon his hairy breast.
Let not his hand within your bosom stray,
And rudely with your pretty bubbies play.
But above all, let him no kiss receive;
That's an offence I never can forgive.
Do not, O do not that sweet mouth resign,
Lest I rise up in arms, and cry, 'Tis mine.
I shall thrust in betwixt, and void of fear
The manifest adulterer will appear.
These things are plain to sight; but more I doubt
What you conceal beneath your petticoat.
Take not his leg between your tender thighs,
Nor with your hand, provoke my foe to rise.
How many love-inventions I deplore,
Which I myself have practis'd all before?
How oft have I been forc'd the robe to lift
In company; to make a homely shift
For a bare bout, ill huddled o'er in haste,
While o'er my side the fair her mantle cast.
You to your husband shall not be so kind;
But, lest you should, your mantle leave behind.
Encourage him to tope; but kiss him not,
Nor mix one drop of water in his pot.

If he be fuddled well, and snores apace,
Then we may take advice from time and place.
When all depart, when compliments are loud,
Be sure to mix among the thickest crowd:
There I will be, and there we cannot miss,
Perhaps to grubble, or at least to kiss.
Alas! what length of labour I employ,
Just to secure a short and transient joy!
For night must part us: and when night is come,
Tuck'd underneath his arm he leads you home.
He locks you in; I follow to the door,
His fortune envy, and my own deplore.
He kisses you, he more than kisses too;
Th' outrageous cuckold thinks it all his due.
But add not to his joy by your consent,
And let it not be given, but only lent.
Return no kiss, nor move in any sort;
Make it a dull and a malignant sport.
Had I my wish, he should no pleasure take,
But slubber o'er your business for my sake.
And whate'er fortune shall this night befall,
Coax me to-morrow, by forswearing all.

WILLIAM CONGREVE

(1670-1729)

Born near Leeds, Congreve was educated in Ireland, at Kilkenny and at
Trinity College, Dublin, where he was a contemporary of Swift. He then
entered the Middle Temple, and embarked upon his career as a playwright.
After 1700 he produced no more plays and lived a life of ease. His translation of
Juvenal, *Satire* 11 dates from early in his life; his other translations are mostly
from Ovid and Horace. The Ovid versions appear as contributions to Garth's
joint *Metamorphoses* of 1717 and to the *Art of Love* of 1725. Pope dedicated his
Iliad to him.

Enjoy the moment
(Horace, *Odes* 1.9)

Bless me, 'tis cold! how chill the air!
How naked does the world appear!
But see (big with the offspring of the North)
    The teeming clouds bring forth:
    A shower of soft and fleecy rain
Falls, to new-clothe the earth again.

Behold the mountain-tops around,
As if with fur of ermine crown'd;
    And lo! how by degrees
The universal mantle hides the trees
    In hoary flakes, which downward fly,
As if it were the autumn of the sky:
Trembling, the groves sustain their weight, and bow
    Like aged limbs, which feebly go
Beneath a venerable head of snow.

Diffusive cold does the whole earth invade,
Like a disease, through all its veins 'tis spread,
And each late living stream is numb'd and dead.
Let's melt the frozen hours, make warm the air;
Let cheerful fires Sol's feeble beams repair;
    Fill the large bowl with sparkling wine;
Let's drink till our own faces shine,
        Till we like suns appear,
    To light and warm the hemisphere.
Wine can dispense to all both light and heat,
    They are with wine incorporate;
That powerful juice, with which no cold dares mix,
Which still is fluid, and no frost can fix:
    Let that but in abundance flow,
And let it storm and thunder, hail and snow,
'Tis Heaven's concern; and let it be
    The care of Heaven still for me:
Those winds which rend the oaks and plough the seas,
    Great Jove can, if he please,
    With one commanding nod appease.
    Seek not to know to morrow's doom;
    That is not ours, which is to come:
    The present moment's all our store;
        The next should Heaven allow,
        Then this will be no more:
So all our life is but one instant now.
        Look on each day you've past
    To be a mighty treasure won;
And lay each moment out in haste;
        We're sure to live too fast,
        And cannot live too soon.
    Youth doth a thousand pleasures bring,
    Which from decrepit age will fly;
The flowers that flourish in the spring,
    In winter's cold embraces die.

Now Love, that everlasting boy, invites
To revel, while you may, in soft delights:

Now the kind nymph yields all her charms,
Nor yields in vain to youthful arms.
Slowly she promises at night to meet,
But eagerly prevents the hour with swifter feet.
To gloomy groves and shades obscure she flies,
There veils the bright confession of her eyes,
    Unwillingly she stays,
  Would more unwillingly depart,
    And in soft sighs conveys
    The whispers of her heart.
  Still she invites and still denies,
And vows she'll leave you if you're rude;
Then from her ravisher she flies,
    But flies to be pursu'd;
If from his sight she does herself convey,
With a feign'd laugh she will herself betray,
And cunningly instruct him in the way.

New love
(Horace, *Odes* 1.19)

The tyrant Queen of soft desires,
With the resistless aid of sprightly wine,
And wanton ease, conspires
To make my heart its peace resign,
And readmit Love's long rejected fires.
For beauteous Glycera I burn,
The flames so long repelled, with double force return;
Matchless her face appears and shines more bright
Than polished marble, when reflecting light;
Her very coyness warms,
And with a look of graceful sullenness she charms;
Each look darts forth a thousand rays,
Whose lustre an unwary sight betrays;
My eyeballs swim, and I grow giddy while I gaze.
She comes! she comes! she rushes in my veins;
At once all Venus enters, and at large she reigns;
Cyprus no more with her abode is blest:
I am her palace and her throne my breast.
Of savage Scythian arms no more I write
Or Parthian archers, who in flying fight,
And make rough war their idle sport;
Such idle themes no more can move,
Nor anything but what's of high import;
And what of high import but love?
Vervain and gums and the green turf prepare;
With wine of two years old your cups be filled:

After our sacrifice and prayer,
The goddess may incline her heart to yield.

Orpheus' plea to the gods of the Underworld
(Ovid, *Metamorphoses* 10.17-44)

'Ye powers, who under earth your realms extend,
To whom all mortals must one day descend;
If here 'tis granted sacred truth to tell;
I come not, curious, to explore your hell;
Nor come to boast (by vain ambition fir'd)
How Cerberus at my approach retir'd.
My wife alone I seek; for her lov'd sake
These terrors I support, this journey take.
She luckless wandering, or by fate misled,
Chanc'd on a lurking viper's crest to tread;
The vengeful beast inflam'd with fury starts,
And through her heel his deathful venom darts.
Thus was she snatch'd untimely to her tomb;
Her growing years cut short, and springing bloom.
Long I my loss endeavour'd to sustain,
And strongly strove, but strove, alas! in vain:
At length I yielded, won by mighty love:
Well known is that omnipotence above!
But here, I doubt, his unfelt influence fails;
And yet a hope within my heart prevails,
That here, ev'n here, he has been known of old;
At least if truth be by tradition told;
If fame of former rapes belief may find,
You both by love, and love alone, were join'd.
Now by the horrors which these realms surround;
By the vast chaos of these depths profound;
By the sad silence which eternal reigns
O'er all the waste of these wide-stretching plains;
Let me again Eurydice receive,
Let fate her quickspun thread of life re-weave.
All our possessions are but loans from you,
And soon or late you must be paid your due:
Hither we haste to human-kind's last seat,
Your endless empire, and our sure retreat.
She too, when ripen'd years she shall attain,
Must, of avoidless right, be yours again:
I, but the transient use of that require,
Which soon, too soon, I must resign entire.
But if the destinies refuse my vow,
And no remission of her doom allow;
Know, I'm determin'd to return no more;

So both retain, or both to life restore.'
   Thus, while the bard melodiously complains,
And to his lyre accords his vocal strains,
The very bloodless shades attention keep,
And, silent, seem compassionate to weep;
Ev'n Tantalus his flood unthirsty views,
Nor flies the stream, nor he the stream pursues;
Ixion's wandering wheel its whirl suspends,
And the voracious vulture, charm'd, attends;
No more the Belides their toil bemoan,
And Sisyphus, reclin'd, sits listening on his stone.

THOMAS OTWAY

(1652-1685)

Otway left Christ Church, Oxford, without taking his degree, and entered on a
playwright's career. His plays include translations from Racine and Molière.
His poems were collected after his early death.

Desire for tranquillity
(Horace, *Odes* 2.16)

In storms when clouds the moon do hide,
And no kind stars the pilot guide,
Shew me at sea the boldest there,
Who does not wish for quiet here.
For quiet, friend, the soldier fights,
Bears weary marches, sleepless nights,
For this feeds hard, and lodges cold;
Which can't be bought with hills of gold.
Since wealth and power too weak we find,
To quell the tumults of the mind;
Or from the monarch's roofs of state
Drive thence the cares that round him wait;
Happy the man with little blest,
Of what his father left possest;
No base desires corrupt his head,
No fears disturb him in his bed.
What then in life, which soon must end,
Can all our vain designs intend?
From shore to shore why should we run,
When none his tiresome self can shun?
For baneful care will still prevail,
And overtake us under sail,

'Twill dodge, the great man's train behind,
Out-run the foe, out-fly the wind.
If then thy soul rejoice today,
Drive far to-morrow's cares away.
In laughter let them all be drown'd:
No perfect good is to be found.
One mortal feels Fate's sudden blow,
Another's lingering death comes slow;
And what of life they take from thee,
The gods may give to punish me.
Thy portion is a wealthy stock,
A fertile glebe, a fruitful flock,
Horses and chariots for thy ease,
Rich robes to deck and make thee please.
For me, a little cell I chuse,
Fit for my mind, fit for my Muse,
Which content does best adorn,
Shunning the knaves and fools I scorn.

RICHARD DUKE

(1658-1711)

Fellow of Trinity College, Cambridge, and chaplain to Queen Anne, Johnson
wrote of Duke: 'with the wits he shared the dissoluteness of the times.'
Nevertheless, a volume of sermons was published, as well as his poetical works,
which include a satire on Titus Oates besides the handful of translations from
classical poetry.

The Cyclops to Galatea
(Theocritus, *Idyll* 11.50-64) from Dryden's *Miscellany* 1

But if you fear that I, o'ergrown with hair,
Without a fire defy the winter air,
Know I have mighty stores of wood, and know
Perpetual fires on my bright hearth do glow.
My soul, my life itself should burn for thee,
And this one eye, as dear as life to me.
Why was I not with fins, like fishes, made,
That I, like them might in the deep have play'd?
Then would I dive beneath the yielding tide,
And kiss your hand, if you your lips deny'd.
To thee I'd lilies and red poppies bear,
And flowers that crown each season of the year.
But I'm resolv'd I'll learn to swim and dive

Of the next stranger that does here arrive,
That th' undiscover'd pleasures I may know
Which you enjoy in the deep flood below.
Come forth, O nymph! and coming forth forget,
Like me that on this rock unmindful sit
(Of all things else unmindful but of thee),
Home to return forget, and live with me.

WILLIAM WALSH

(1663-1708)

Walsh was educated at Wadham College, Oxford, but left without taking his degree. He subsequently shone not only as a critic but as a man of fashion. Though 'a friend of the revolution' he kept the friendship of Dryden, and later of Pope who called him 'knowing Walsh'. Johnson writes of him 'he seldom rises higher than to be pretty'; his versions of Catullus, however, have the merit of accuracy as well as the expected elegance.

A faithless mistress
(Catullus 76)

Is there a pious pleasure that proceeds
From contemplation of our virtuous deeds?
That all mean sordid action we despise,
And scorn to gain a throne by cheats and lies?
Thyrsis, thou hast sure blessings laid in store
From thy just dealing in this curst amour.
What honour can in words or deeds be shown
Which to the fair thou hast not said or done?
On her false heart they all are thrown away:
She only swears more easily to betray.
Ye powers that know the many vows she broke,
Free my just soul from this unequal yoke.
My love boils up, and like a raging flood
Runs through my veins and taints my vital blood.
I do not vainly beg she may grow chaste,
Or with an equal passion burn at last –
The one she cannot practise, though she would,
And I contemn the other, though she should – :
Nor ask I vengeance on the perjured jilt;
'Tis punishment enough to have her guilt.
I beg but balsam for my bleeding breast,
Cure for my wounds and from my labours rest.

JOSEPH ADDISON

(1672-1719)

Addison was educated at Charterhouse, where he made the acquaintance of Steele, his later partnership with whom was to be so significant. His first poetical works were in Latin; but in his early twenties he published his translation of Vergil's fourth *Georgic*, on seeing which Dryden remarked that 'my latter swarm is hardly worth the hiving'. He thus began to establish his literary reputation, but turned down an offer for a translation of Herodotus. In 1699 he went abroad, and visited Boileau in Paris, before going on to Italy, the landscape of which he appreciated by having the works of Vergil and Horace constantly at his side. He returned to England in 1702, and his other translations date from the first decade of the century. The climax of his career was his production of the *Spectator* (1711-12), which 'adjusted the unsettled practice of daily intercourse by propriety and politeness' (Johnson). His literary eminence made him patron of a number of writers, particularly Tickell to whom he entrusted the publication of his works. It also resulted in tension between him and Pope which produced satire on the one side and envy on the other; Addison had, for at least part of his life, his political career to increase his self-esteem, though it does not afford him the posthumous reputation that, but for Pope, he would have deserved.

The story of Phaethon
(Ovid, *Metamorphoses* 2.122-324, selected)

Th' unhappy youth then, bending down his head,
Saw earth and ocean far beneath him spread:
His colour chang'd, he startled at the sight,
And his eyes darken'd by too great a light.
Now could he with the fiery steeds untry'd,
His birth obscure, and his request deny'd:
Now would he Merops for his father own,
And quit his boasted kindred to the Sun . . .

Now all the horrors of the heavens he spies,
And monstrous shadows of prodigious size,
That, deck'd with stars, lie scatter'd o'er the skies.
There is a place above, where Scorpio bent
In tail and arms surrounds a vast extent;
In a wide circuit of the heavens he shines,
And fills the space of two celestial signs.
Soon as the youth beheld him, vex'd with heat,
Brandish his sting, and in his poison sweat,
Half dead with sudden fear he dropt the reins;
The horses felt 'em loose upon their mains,
And, flying out through all the plains above,

Ran uncontroul'd where-e'er their fury drove;
Rush'd on the stars, and through a pathless way
Of unknown regions hurry'd on the day.
And now above, and now below they flew,
And near the earth the burning chariot drew.
   The clouds disperse in fumes, the wond'ring moon
Beholds her brother's steeds beneath her own;
The highlands smoak, cleft by the piercing rays,
Or, clad with woods, in their own fewel blaze.
Next o'er the plains, where ripen'd harvests grow,
The running conflagration spreads below.
But these are trivial ills: whole cities burn,
And peopled kingdoms into ashes turn . . .

   Th'astonisht youth, where-e'er his eyes cou'd turn,
Beheld the Universe around him burn:
The world was in a blaze; nor could he bear
The sultry vapours and the scorching air,
Which from below, as from a furnace, flow'd;
And now the axle-tree beneath him glow'd:
Lost in the whirling clouds, that round him broke,
And white with ashes, hov'ring in the smoke,
He flew where-e'er the horses drove, nor knew
Whither the horses drove, or where he flew . . .

Jove call'd to witness every power above,
And even the god, whose son the chariot drove,
That what he acts he is compell'd to do,
Or universal ruine must ensue.
Strait he ascends the high ethereal throne,
From whence he us'd to dart his thunder down,
From whence his showers and storms he us'd to pour,
But now could meet with neither storm nor shower.
Then, aiming at the youth, with lifted hand,
Full at his head he hurl'd the forky brand,
In dreadful thund'rings. Thus th' Almighty Sire
Suppress'd the raging of the fires with fire.
   At once from life, and from the chariot driven,
Th' ambitious boy fell thunder-struck from heaven.
The horses started with a sudden bound,
And flung the reins and chariot to the ground:
The studded harness from their necks they broke,
Here fell a wheel, and here a silver spoke,
Here were the beam and axle torn away;
And, scatter'd o'er the earth, the shining fragments lay.
The breathless Phaeton, with flaming hair,
Shot from the chariot, like a falling star,

That in a summer's evening from the top
Of heaven drops down, or seems at least to drop;
'Till on the Po his blasted corps was hurl'd,
Far from his country, in the western world.

Bees at battle
(Vergil, *Georgics* 4.67-87)

If once two rival Kings their right debate,
And factions and cabals embroil the state,
The people's actions will their thoughts declare;
All their hearts tremble, and beat thick with war;
Hoarse broken sounds, like trumpets' harsh alarms,
Run thro' the hive, and call them to their arms;
All in a hurry spread their shiv'ring wings,
And fit their claws, and point their angry stings;
In crowds before the king's pavilion meet,
And boldly challenge out the foe to fight!
At last, when all the heavens are warm and fair,
They rush together out, and join; the air
Swarms thick, and echoes with the humming war.
All in a firm round clustre mix, and strow
With heaps of little corps the earth below
As thick as hailstones from the floor rebound,
Or shaken acorns rattle on the ground.
No sense of danger can their kings control,
Their little bodies lodge a mighty soul;
Each obstinate in arms pursues his blow,
Till shameful flight secures the routed foe:
This hot dispute, and all this mighty fray,
A little dust flung upward will allay.

ANON.

These anonymous translations of Martial and some other epigrams are attributed by the British Library catalogue to Henry Killigrew. There seems to be no very good evidence to support this attribution, which is perhaps somewhat unlikely as Killigrew (1613-1700) is otherwise known as a writer of plays and sermons.

Ideal beauty
(Martial, *Epigrams* 4.42, of a boy in the original)

If I could such obtain, as I desire,
Hear then what beauty, Flaccus, I admire.

One born in Egypt, i' th' first place, I'd choose,
Such artificial charms none else do use:
I'd have her skin white as the driven snow, –
From that swarth clime the fair do fairest show;
Her eyes with stars should vie, her flowing hair
Fall on her neck, which I to curls prefer;
Her forehead should be smooth, well shaped her nose,
Her lovely lips a rosy red disclose;
Sometimes I'd have her kind, and sometimes coy,
In no man's courtship, but mine own, to joy;
Young men to hate, ev'n her own sex to fear;
To others ice, to me a maid appear.
Now, Flaccus, I foreknow what thou wilt say.
Caelia, my Caelia, thou dost here display.

Self-preservation
(Martial, *Epigrams* 6.31)

Oft with thy wife does the physician lie,
Thou knowing, Charidem, and standing by.
I see, thou wilt not of a fever die.

Brevity
(Martial, *Epigrams* 8.29)

Who distichs writes to brevity does look:
But where's the brevity, if 't fills a book?

Window-shopping
(Martial, *Epigrams* 9.59)

Mamurra many hours does vagrant tell
I' th' shops, where Rome her richest ware does sell.
Beholds fair boys, devours them with his eyes,
Not those of common note, one first espies;
But which in inner rooms they closely mew,
Remov'd from mine, and from the people's view.
Glutted with these, choice tables he uncases,
Others of ivory, set high, displaces.
Rich tortoise beds he measures four times o'er.
Sighs, they fit not, and leaves them on that score.
Consults the statues of Corinthian brass
By the scent; and not without blame lets pass
Thy pieces, Polyclet. He next complains
Of crystals mix'd with glass, and them disdains.
Marks porcelain cups, sets ten of them apart:
Weighs antique plate (of Mentor's noble art

If any be); counts, i' th' enamell'd gold,
The gems that stand. Rich pendants does behold:
For the sardonyx makes a search most nice,
And of the biggest jaspers beats the price.
Tir'd now, at last, after eleven hours' stay,
Two farthing pots he bought, and himself bore away.

Ausonius' Echo
(Ausonius, *Epigrams* 10)

Fond painter, why to me a face do'st lend?
To make me subject to the eye contend?
None my mysterious deity ere saw,
Much less my figure durst attempt to draw.
Daughter of tongue and aire, a voice, I am
Speeches that utter, from no mind that come
But other words I catch, as they decline,
And mocking them reherse with like of mine.
My sole existence in the ear is found,
Who will my likeness paint, must paint the sound.

ANON.
(From a seventeenth-century MS)

Epitaph
(Martial, *Epigrams* 1.88)

Snatch'd from thy lord in thy youth's verdant bloome,
Whose earth nought but earth-turfes gently entombe:
Accept no vague vast marble piles, which must
Instead of keeping thine, themselves bee dust:
Butt this frail boxe and palme-trees' gloomy shade,
And greene sodds, with my dewy teares so made:
Accept, deare boy, these griefs pour'd on thy hearse,
Thus shall thy name live ever in my verse.
When Fates my life's last thredd shall cutt in twaine,
May I no other grave, than such, obtayne.

SIR CHARLES SEDLEY
(1639-1701)

Probably born in London, and notorious at court for his debauchery and his
wit, Sedley prospered under James II, but joined William III at the

Revolution. Charles II said of him that Nature had given him a patent to be Apollo's viceroy, and there is an easy charm in all his writings, though his songs and even his translations are better remembered than his plays.

A faithless mistress
(Horace, *Odes* 2.8)

Did any punishment attend
   Thy former perjuries,
I should believe a second time,
   Thy charming flatteries:
Did but one wrinkle mark this face,
Or hadst thou lost one single grace.

No sooner hast thou, with false vows,
   Provk'd the powers above;
But thou art fairer than before,
   And we are more in love,
Thus Heaven and Earth seem to declare,
They pardon falsehood in the fair.

Sure 'tis no crime vainly to swear,
   By every power on high,
And call our bury'd mother's ghost
   A witness to the lye:
Heaven at such perjury connives,
And Venus with a smile forgives.

The Nymphs and cruel Cupid too,
   Sharp'ning his pointed dart
On an old hone, besmear'd with blood,
   Forbear thy perjur'd heart.
Fresh youth grows up, to wear thy chains,
And the old slave no freedom gains.

Thee, mothers for their eldest sons,
   Thee, wretched misers fear,
Lest thy prevailing beauty should
   Seduce the hopeful heir:
New-marry'd virgins fear thy charms
Should keep their bridegroom from their arms.

Town virtues
(Martial, *Epigrams* 3.38)

What business, or what hope brings thee to town,
   Who canst not pimp, nor cheat, nor swear, nor lye?

This place will nourish no such idle drone;
    Hence, in remoter parts thy fortune try.
But thou hast courage, honesty and wit,
    And one, or all these three, will give thee bread:
The malice of this town thou knowst not yet,
    Wit is a good diversion, but base trade;
Cowards will, for thy courage, call thee bully,
    Till all, like Thraso's, thy acquaintance shun!
Rogues call thee for thy honesty a cully;
    Yet this is all thou hast to live upon:
Friend, three such vertues, Audley had undone;
    Be wise, and e're th' art in a jayl, be gone,
Of all that starving crew we saw today
None but had killed his man, or writ his play.

An exiled tenant farmer is entertained by Tityrus at his farm
(Vergil, *Eclogues* 1.46-83)

Meliboeus: Oh bless'd old man! thy lands shall then endure,
And all possessions still to thee secure;
And large enough shall for thyself be found,
Tho' stones and reeds o'erspread the nearest ground:
Thy flocks from beasts of prey no harm shall find
Nor catch infection from their neighbouring kind.
Oh fortunate old man! who may abide
Thus sweetly by this noted river's side,
Here with delight thy leisure time employ,
And of these sacred springs the cool enjoy.
Here from the bord'ring hedge the passing bees,
Thy ears shall with continual murmurs please,
Soft sleep invite, and give thy labours ease.
The pruner from the lofty mountain there,
With chearful songs shall chace intruding care:
Here thy lov'd pidgeons shall delight thy view,
There on sweet elms the turtles sweetly coo.

Tityrus: Therefore the stags shall mounting feed in air,
And oceans sinking, leave their fishes bare
On the dry sands, the Parthians from their home,
And hardy Germans shall be forc'd to roam,
And to each other's land in exile come,
Before the figure of this youth depart,
And quit possession of my grateful heart.

Meliboeus: But we must hence dispers'd and driven go
To sultry Africk, and to Scythia's snow,
Part must with speed repair to spacious Crete,

And near the swift Oaxis take their seat:
Part must on Britain's barbarous land be hurl'd,
Amongst a race divided from the world:
Yet when a long unhappy time is pass'd,
Oh! may I see my country's bounds at last,
And pleas'd, and wond'ring visit once again
My poor thatch'd dwelling where I us'd to reign!
Shall a vile soldier these neat fields command?
This harvest bless a wicked barbarous hand?
Oh fatal strife! from thee what sorrows flow?
From thee what ills we wretched people know?
See who the fruits of all our toil possess,
Now graft thy pears, fond swain! thy vineyards dress!
Hence ye she-goats! Once prosp'rous and my care,
Begone, henceforth stretch'd on the grass, I ne'er
Shall see ye hanging on a rock afar;
Henceforth no verses shall I sing, nor more
Protect and feed ye as I did before.

Tityrus: With me this night however chuse to stay,
Forgetting care yourself reposing lay
On the green leaf, and of our present fare,
(Curds, chessnuts, apples) take a welcome share,
For see the village tops begin to fume,
And vaster shadows from the mountains come.

ANON.

Pygmalion
(Ovid, *Metamorphoses* 10. 270-94) from Dryden's *Miscellany* 5

The festival of Venus now return'd,
When offer'd incense in the temple burn'd,
Where anxious lovers yearly did repair
With presents, and with more prevailing pray'r:
Amongst the supplicants Pygmalion came,
His, you'll acknowledge, was a hopeless flame;
Before the altar with his gift he stands,
Where with low voice, and with up-lifted hands,
Ye Pow'rs, (he said) if you can all things do,
As we are taught, and I wou'd think it true,
Grant that the wife you shall alot me, may
(Directly ivory he durst not say)
Be like some iv'ry statue that cou'd prove,
Of charms to make the carver fall in love.

Bright Venus, ever to Love's interest true,
The meaning of the dark petition knew;
Auspicious flashes thrice from th' altar broke,
And wreath'd the temple's roof with curling smoke.
Home (but desponding still) the lover hasts,
His arms about his iv'ry mistress casts,
Who more than ever now appear'd to charm,
At his first kiss he thinks her lips are warm;
The next salute does more than thought confirm.
Then, with his eager hand her breast he tries,
Her panting breast with ev'ry touch complies:
So handling does to pliantness reduce
Hymettian wax, and make it fit for use.
His hand withdrawn, his hand he does apply
Once more (for doubtful was his joy) to try
If that were flesh he felt, or ivory.
'Twas now a body, quick with vital heat,
He grasps her wrists, and feels her pulses beat.
In torrents of transported words he gives
The goddess thanks, that his carv'd mistress lives:
Kisses of real gust he now bestows,
Which that she felt the blushing virgin shows,
Whose new-enliven'd eyes at once discover,
Days chearful light, and a more chearful lover.

TOM BROWN

(1663-1704)

Born in Shropshire, Brown attended Christ Church, Oxford, where he produced his best remembered poem, addressed to the then Dean of the College, Dr Fell. On leaving the university he became usher in a school in Kingston. 'His life', says the *DNB*, 'was as licentious as his writings'; Addison referred to him as Tom Brown 'of facetious memory', and his jocularity is the keynote of his published writings.

Etiquette
(Horace, *Odes* 1.27)

To fight in your cups, and abuse the good creature,
Believe it, my friends, is a sin of the that nature,
That were you all damn'd for a tedious long year,
To nasty Mundungus, and heath'nish small beer,
Such as after debauches your sparks of the town,
For a penance next morning devoutly pour down,

It would not atone for so vile a transgression,
You're a scandal to all of the drinking profession.

What a pox do ye bellow, and make such a pother,
And throw candlesticks, bottles, and pipes, at each other?
Come keep the king's peace, leave your damning and sinking,
And gravely return to good Christian drinking.
He that flinches his glass, and to drink is not able,
Let him quarrel no more, but knock under the table.

Well, Faith, since you've rais'd my ill nature so high,
I'll drink on no other condition, not I,
Unless my old friend in the corner declares,
What mistress he courts, and whose colours he wears,
You may safely acquaint me, for I'm none of those
That use to divulge what's spoke under the rose.
Come part with't – What she! forbid it ye powers,
What unfortunate planet rul'd o'er thy amours!
Why man, she has lain (oh thy fate how I pity!)
With half the blue breeches and whigs in the city.
Go thank Mr Parson, give him thanks with a curse,
On those damnable words, *For better for worse!*
To regain your old freedom you vainly endeavour,
Your doxy and you no priest can dissever,
You must dance in the circle, you must dance in 't for ever.

Dr Fell
(Martial, *Epigrams* 1.32)

I do not love thee, Doctor Fell.
The reason why, I cannot tell;
But this I know, and know full well,
I do not love thee, Doctor Fell.

MATTHEW PRIOR

(1664-1721)

Educated at Westminster, Prior was early put to work in his uncle's house to
assist in keeping accounts. On being found there reading Horace by Lord
Dorset, the latter set him to translate an ode into English verse. The result was
so successful that it became a fashion with visitors to the house to make this
request of the boy; and his aptitude eventually enabled him to return to
Westminster to complete his schooling, and to continue to St John's College,
Cambridge. Thereafter he pursued a distinguished career as a diplomat in

Holland and elsewhere. His first published work was the *Town and Country
Mouse,* an answer to Dryden's *The Hind and the Panther,* in which his model is
Horace. His poetry was always an activity of his spare time and reflects the
usual concerns of the Tory literary coterie which included Harley, Bolingbroke
and Swift. 'Horace is always in his mind', said Thackeray of him – betraying
incidentally thereby his own limited appreciation of Horace as well as
illustrating the changed image of the Horatian persona in the Restoration.
Prior's works are elegant and competent, mostly occasional, verse.

Hymn to Apollo
(Callimachus, *Hymn 2,* abridged)

Hah! how the laurel, great Apollo's tree,
And all the cavern shakes! far off, far off,
The man that is unhallow'd: for the God,
The God approaches. Hark! he knocks: the gates
Feel the glad impulse: and the sever'd bars
Submissive clink against their brazen portals.
Why do the Delian palms incline their boughs,
Self-mov'd: and hov'ring swans, their throats releas'd
From native silence, carol sounds harmonious?
   Begin, young men, the hymn: let all your harps
Break their inglorious silence; and the dance,
In mystic numbers trod, explain the music.
But first by ardent pray'r, and clear lustration
Purge the contagious spots of human weakness:
Impure no mortal can behold Apollo.
So may ye flourish, favor'd by the God,
In youth with happy nuptials, and in age
With silver hairs, and fair descent of children;
So lay foundations for aspiring cities,
And bless your spreading colonies encrease. ...

Envy thy latest foe suggested thus:
Like thee I am a pow'r immortal; therefore
To thee dare speak. How can'st thou favour partial
Those poets who write little? Vast and great
Is what I love: the far extended ocean
To a small riv'let I prefer. Apollo
Spurn'd Envy with his foot; and thus the God:
Daemon, the head-long current of Euphrates,
Assyrian river, copious runs, but muddy;
And carries forward with his stupid force
Polluting dirt; his torrent still augmenting,
His wave still more defil'd: mean while the Nymphs
Melissan, sacred and recluse to Ceres
Studious to have their off'rings well receiv'd,

And fit for heav'nly use, from little urns
Pour streams select, and purity of waters.
  Io! Apollo, mighty king, let Envy
Ill-judging and verbose, from Lethe's lake
Draw tons unmeasurable; while thy favor
Administers to my ambitious thirst
The wholesome draught from Aganippe's spring
Genuine, and with soft murmers gently rilling
Adown the mountains, where thy daughters haunt.

4. The Augustans

AMBROSE PHILIPS
(1675?-1749)

Philips composed his Pastorals while still at St John's College, Cambridge, and they rapidly gained admiration when they were published in Tonson's *Miscellany*. However, they won him the enmity of Pope, whose own pastorals, modelled on Vergil rather than Spenser, were quite dissimilar, and the two engaged in a long controversy on the subject in the pages of the *Guardian*. Philips soon became a member of Addison's circle, and the latter praised his translations of Sappho in *Spectator* 223 and 229; of the second, 'Blest as the gods is he . . .', he writes: 'This translation is written in the very spirit of Sappho, and as near the Greek as our own language will possibly suffer', and of 'O Venus, beauty of the skies' he speaks of 'its genuine and natural beauty, without any foreign or affected ornaments'. Johnson's appraisal of the Pindar versions, and of Philips' works as a whole, is less fulsome.

'An Hymn to Venus, from the Greek of Sappho'
(Sappho 1 L-P) from *Spectator* 229

O Venus, beauty of the skies,
To whom a thousand temples rise,
Gayly false in gentle smiles,
Full of love-perplexing wiles,
O goddess! from my heart remove
The wasting cares and pains of love.

If ever thou hast kindly hear'd
A song in soft distress prefer'd,
Propitious to my tuneful vow,
O gentle goddess! hear me now.
Descend thou bright, immortal, guest,
In all thy radiant charms confess'd.

Thou once didst leave almighty Jove,
And all the golden roofs above:
The car thy wanton sparrows drew;

Hov'ring in air they lightly flew;
As to my bower they wing'd their way,
I saw their quiv'ring pinions play.

The birds dismiss'd (while you remain)
Bore back their empty car again:
Then you, with looks divinely mild,
In ev'ry heav'nly feature smil'd,
And ask'd, what new complaints I made,
And why I call'd you to my aid?

What frenzy in my bosom rag'd,
And by what care to be asswag'd?
What gentle youth I would allure,
Whom in my artful toils secure?
Who does thy tender heart subdue,
Tell me, my Sappho, tell me who?

Tho now he shuns thy longing arms,
He soon shall court thy slighted charms;
Tho now thy off'rings he despise,
He soon to thee shall sacrifice;
Tho now he freez, he soon shall burn,
And be thy victim in his turn.

Celestial visitant, once more
Thy needful presence I implore!
In pity come and ease my grief,
Bring my distemper'd soul relief:
Favour thy suppliant's hidden fires,
And give me all my heart desires.

Praise of Hieron's Olympic victory
(Pindar, *Olympian* 1.1-36, 111-16)

Strophe I

Each element to water yields;
And gold, like blazing fire by night,
Amidst the stores of wealth that builds
The mind aloft, is eminently bright:
But if, my soul, with fond desire
To sing of games thou dost aspire,
As thou by day can'st not descry,
Through all the liquid waste of sky,

One burnish'd star, that like the sun does glow,
And cherish every thing below,
So, my sweet soul, no toil divine,
In song, does like the Olympian shine:
Hence do the mighty poets raise
A hymn, of every tongue the praise,
The son of Saturn to resound,
When far, from every land, they come
To visit Hiero's regal dome,
Where peace, where plenty, is for ever found:

Antistrophe I

Lord of Sicilia's fleecy plains,
He governs, righteous in his power,
And, all excelling while he reigns,
From every lovely virtue crops the flower:
In musick, blossom of delight,
Divinely skill'd, he cheers the night,
As we are wont, when friends design
To feast and wanton o'er their wine:
But from the wall the Dorian harp take down,
If Pisa, city of renown,
And if the fleet victorious steed,
The boast of his unrival'd breed,
Heart-pleasing raptures did inspire,
And warm thy breast with sacred fire,
When late, on Alpheus' crouded shore,
Forth-springing quick, each nerve he strain'd,
The warning of the spur disdain'd,
And swift to victory his master bore.

Epode I

The lov'd Syracusian, the prince of the course,
The king, who delights in the speed of the horse:
Great his glory, great his fame,
Throughout the land where Lydian Pelops came
To plant his men, a chosen race,
A land the ocean does embrace,
Pelops, whom Neptune, ruler of the main,
Was known to love, when into life again,
From the reviving cauldron warm,
Clotho produc'd him whole, his shoulder-blade,
And its firm brawn, of shining ivory made.

But truth, unvarnish'd, oft neglected lies,
When fabled tales, invented to surprise,
In miracles mighty, have power to charm,
Where fictions, happily combin'd,
Deceive and captivate the mind:

Strophe II

Thus Poesy, harmonious spell,
The source of pleasures ever new,
With dignity does wonders tell;
And we, amaz'd, believe each wonder true.
Day, after day, brings truth to light,
Unveil'd, and manifest to sight:
But, of the bless'd, those lips, which name
Foul deeds alone, shall suffer blame. . . .

Epode IV

Even now the muse prepares to raise,
Her growth, the strongest dart of praise,
For me to wield. Approv'd in other things,
Do others rise, conspicuous: only Kings,
High mounting, on the summit fix:
There bound thy view, wide-spread, nor vainly try
Farther to stretch the prospect of thine eye:
Be, then, thy glorious lot to tread sublime,
With steady steps, the measur'd tract of time:
Be mine, with the prize-bearing worthies to mix,
In Greece, throughout the learned throng,
Proclaim'd unrival'd in my song.

JOHN GAY

(1685-1732)

Gay was born in Barnstaple, Devon, and was apprenticed to a silk-mercer.
However, he soon abandoned this trade for a literary career. His first poem
appeared in 1708, and was followed by several plays and the *Fables* of 1727.
The climax of his career came with the *Beggar's Opera* in 1728. He contributed
Book 9 to Sir Samuel Garth's composite translation of Ovid's *Metamorphoses*
(1717).

The story of Arachne
(Ovid, *Metamorphoses* 6.50-69, 129-45)

Desire of conquest sways the giddy maid,
To certain ruin by vain hope betray'd:
The goddess with her stubborn will comply'd,
And deign'd by trial to convince her pride.
Both took their stations, and the piece prepare,
And order every slender thread with care.
The web enwraps the beam; the reed divides,
While thro' the widening space the shuttle glides,
Which their swift hands receive; then, pois'd with lead,
The swinging weight strikes close th' inserted thread.
They gird their flowing garments round the waist,
And ply their feet and arms with dex'trous haste.
Here each inweaves the richest Tyrian dye,
There fainter shades in soften'd order lie;
Such various mixtures in the texture shine,
Set off the work, and brighten each design.
As when the sun his piercing rays extends,
When from thin clouds some drisling shower descends,
We see the spacious humid arch appear,
Whose transient colours paint the splendid air:
By such degrees the deepening shadows rise
As pleasingly deceive our dazzled eyes;
And though the same th' adjoining colour seems,
Yet hues of diff'rent natures dye th' extremes.
Here heightening gold they 'midst the woof dispose,
And in the web this antique story rose. . . .

Not Pallas, nor ev'n spleen itself, could blame
The wondrous work of the Maeonian dame;
With grief her vast success the goddess bore,
And of celestial crimes the story tore.
Her boxen shuttle now, enrag'd, she took,
And thrice the proud Idmonian artist struck:
Th' unhappy maid, to see her labours vain,
Grew resolute with pride, and shame, and pain:
Around her neck a fatal noose she ty'd,
And sought by sudden death her guilt to hide.
Pallas with pity saw the desperate deed,
And thus the virgin's milder fate decreed:
'Live, impious rival, mindful of thy crime,
Suspended thus to waste thy future time!
Thy punishment involves thy numerous race,
Who, for thy fault, shall share in thy disgrace.'
Her incantation magic juices aid,

With sprinkling drops she bath'd the pendent maid,
And thus the charm its noxious power display'd.
Like leaves in autumn drop her falling hairs,
With these her nose, and next her rising ears.
Her head to the minutest substance shrunk,
The potent juice contracts her changing trunk,
Close to her sides her slender fingers clung,
There, chang'd to nimble feet, in order hung;
Her bloated belly swells to larger size,
Which now with smallest threads her work supplies;
The virgin in the Spider still remains;
And in that shape her former art retains.

WILLIAM BROOME

(1689-1745)

Educated at Eton and at St John's College, Cambridge, Broome's earliest
poetry appeared in Lintott's miscellany of 1712. In 1714 was published his
joint translation, with Ozell and Oldisworth, of Mme Dacier's *Iliad* into blank
verse laid out as prose. He became an amanuensis to Pope in the work on his
own *Iliad*, condensing the voluminous commentaries of Eustathius for Pope's
use; and when Pope began his *Odyssey*, he together with Elijah Fenton under-
took a share of the translation.

> Pope came off clean with Homer; but they say
> Broome went before, and kindly swept the way (John Henley).

His later translations from Anacreon belong to a genre popular in that
generation, but were first collected by Francis Fawkes in his own translation of
Anacreon in 1760.

Spring
(*Anacreontea* 44 Bergk)

See! winter's past; the seasons bring
Soft breezes with returning spring;
At whose approach the Graces wear
Fresh honours in their flowing hair;
The raging seas forget to roar,
And, smiling, gently kiss the shore;
The sportive duck, in wanton play,
Now dives, now rises into day;
The cranes from freezing skies repair,
And sailing float to warmer air;
Th' enlivening suns in glory rise,

And gaily dance along the skies;
The clouds disperse, or, if in showers
They fall, it is to wake the flowers.

See! verdure clothes the teeming earth;
The olive struggles into birth;
The swelling grapes adorn the vine,
And kindly promise future wine:
Bless'd juice! already I in thought
Quaff an imaginary draught.

THOMAS TICKELL

(1686-1740)

Tickell was born in Cumberland and became a Fellow of Queen's College, Oxford, in 1710. He achieved the notice of Joseph Addison by his verses *To Rosamund*, and in 1715 Addison acclaimed his translation of *Iliad* 1 as superior even to Pope's. Pope responded with the assertion that Addison had in fact written Tickell's version, and alluded to him in the person of Atticus,

> Who when two wits on rival themes contest,
> Approves them both, but likes the worst the best.

In fact Addison clearly did no more than correct Tickell's version. Dr Johnson himself found it difficult to make a firm decision for Pope's version over Tickell's. Tickell's translation of Claudian's *Phoenix* appeared in the sixth *Miscellany*.

A description of the Phoenix
(Claudian, *Phoenix*, selected)

In utmost ocean lies a lovely isle,
Where spring still blooms and greens for ever smile
Which sees the sun put on his first array,
And hears his panting steeds bring on the day;
When, from the deep, they rush with rapid force,
And whirl aloft, to run their glorious course;
When first appear the ruddy streaks of light,
And glimmering beams dispel the parting night.
    In these soft shades, unprest by human feet,
The happy Phoenix keeps his balmy seat,
Far from the world disjoin'd; he reigns alone,
Alike the empire, and its king unknown.
A god-like bird! whose endless round of years
Out-lasts the stars, and tires the circling spheres;

Not us'd like vulgar birds to eat his fill,
Or drink the crystal of the murmuring rill;
But fed with warmth from Titan's purer ray,
And slak'd by streams which eastern seas convey;
Still he renews his life in these abodes,
Contemns the power of fate, and mates the gods.
His fiery eyes shoot forth a glittering ray,
And round his head ten thousand glories play;
High on his crest, a star celestial bright
Divides the darkness with its piercing light;
His legs are stain'd with purple's lively dye,
His azure wings the fleeting winds out-fly;
Soft plumes of cheerful blue his limbs infold,
Enrich'd with spangles, and bedropt with gold.

Begot by none himself, begetting none,
Sire of himself he is, and of himself the son;
His life in fruitful death renews his date,
And kind destruction but prolongs his fate:
Ev'n in the grave new strength his limbs receive,
And on the funeral pile begin to live. . . .

Thrice happy Phoenix! heaven's peculiar care
Has made thyself thyself's surviving heir;
By death thy deathless vigour is supply'd,
Which sinks to ruin all the world beside;
Thy age, not thee, afflicting Phoebus burns,
And vital flames light up thy funeral urns.
Whate'er events have been, thy eyes survey,
And thou art fixt, while ages roll away;
Thou saw'st when raging ocean burst his bed,
O'er-top'd the mountains, and the earth o'er-spread;
When the rash youth inflam'd the high abodes,
Scorch'd up the skies, and scar'd the deathless gods.
When nature ceases, thou shalt still remain,
Nor second Chaos bound thy endless reign;
Fate's tyrant laws thy happier lot shall brave,
Baffle destruction, and elude the grave.

ALEXANDER POPE

(1688-1744)

Pope claimed to have been fired with love of Homer when he first encountered
him in the translation of John Ogilby at the age of eight. His translation of the
Iliad was thus a homage to an early passion, as well as the culmination of an

apprenticeship in Statius, Ovid and Theocritus, when it appeared in 1715-20. Obliged to go on to translate the *Odyssey*, he enlisted the aid of two collaborators, William Broome (Books 2, 6, 8, 11, 12, 16, 18, 23) and Elijah Fenton (Books 1, 4, 19, 20), but so extensively revised their work that even Dr Johnson admits that the different hands are indiscernible.

Despite Bentley's remark, 'A very pretty poem, Mr Pope, but you must not call it Homer', Pope's version *was* the Homer of his generation, and an Augustan theodicy in the sense of order, of 'extension with coherence' (Maynard Mack) that his version excellently conveys.

These virtues of order, harmony and coherence are further exhibited in the *Imitations of Horace*, the acme of Augustan 'raillery'; though Lady Mary Wortley Montagu no doubt spoke for many of Pope's enemies when she attacked the

> two large columns, on thy motly page,
> Where Roman wit is striped with English rage;
> Where ribaldry to satire makes pretence;
> And modern scandal rolls with ancient sense:
> Whilst on one side we see how Horace thought;
> And on the other, how he never wrote.

(Works (Oxford 1977), pp. 265f.)

Pope's achievement is proof against the attacks of lesser writers.

The funeral of Patroclus
(Homer, *Iliad* 23.218-57)

All night Achilles hails Patroclus' soul,
With large libations from the golden bowl.
As a poor father, helpless and undone,
Mourns o'er the ashes of an only son,
Takes a sad pleasure the last bones to burn,
And pours in tears, ere yet they close the urn:
So stay'd Achilles, circling round the shore,
So watch'd the flames, till now they flame no more.
'Twas when, emerging through the shades of night,
The morning planet told the approach of light;
And, fast behind, Aurora's warmer ray
O'er the broad ocean pour'd the golden day:
Then sank the blaze, the pile no longer burn'd,
And to their caves the whistling winds return'd:
Across the Thracian seas their course they bore;
The ruffled seas beneath their passage roar.

 Then parting from the pile he ceas'd to weep,
And sank to quiet in the embrace of sleep,
Exhausted with his grief: meanwhile the crowd
Of thronging Grecians round Achilles stood;
The tumult waked him: from his eyes he shook
Unwilling slumber, and the chiefs bespoke:

'Ye kings and princes of the Achaian name!
First let us quench the yet remaining flame
With sable wine; then, as the rites direct,
The hero's bones with careful view select:
(Apart, and easy to be known they lie
Amidst the heap, and obvious to the eye:
The rest around the margin will be seen
Promiscuous, steeds and immolated men:)
These wrapp'd in double cauls of fat, prepare;
And in the golden vase dispose with care;
There let them rest with decent honour laid,
Till I shall follow to the infernal shade.
Meantime erect the tomb with pious hands,
A common structure on the humble sands:
Hereafter Greece some nobler work may raise,
And late posterity record our praise!'
    The Greeks obey; where yet the embers glow,
Wide o'er the pile the sable wine they throw,
And deep subsides the ashy heap below.
Next the white bones his sad companions place,
With tears collected, in the golden vase.
The sacred relics to the tent they bore;
The urn a veil of linen cover'd o'er.
That done, they bid the sepulchre aspire,
And cast the deep foundations round the pyre;
High on the midst they heap the swelling bed
Of rising earth, memorial of the dead.

Achilles recognises Priam's grief for Hector
(Homer, *Iliad* 24.513-58)

    Satiate at length with unavailing woes,
From the high throne divine Achilles rose;
The reverend monarch by the hand he raised;
On his white beard and form majestic gazed,
Not unrelenting; then serene began
With words to soothe the miserable man:
    'Alas, what weight of anguish hast thou known,
Unhappy prince! thus guardless and alone
To pass through foes, and thus undaunted face
The man whose fury has destroy'd thy race!
Heaven sure has arm'd thee with a heart of steel,
A strength proportion'd to the woes you feel.
Rise, then: let reason mitigate your care:
To mourn avails not: man is born to bear.
Such is, alas! the gods' severe decree:
They, only they are blest, and only free.

Two urns by Jove's high throne have ever stood,
The source of evil one, and one of good;
From thence the cup of mortal man he fills,
Blessings to these, to those distributes ills;
To most he mingles both: the wretch decreed
To taste the bad unmix'd, is cursed indeed;
Pursued by wrongs, by meagre famine driven,
He wanders, outcast both of earth and heaven.
The happiest taste not happiness sincere;
But find the cordial draught is dash'd with care.
Who more than Peleus shone in wealth and power
What stars concurring bless'd his natal hour!
A realm, a goddess, to his wishes given;
Graced by the gods with all the gifts of heaven.
One evil yet o'ertakes his latest day:
No race succeeding to imperial sway;
An only son; and he, alas! ordain'd
To fall untimely in a foreign land.
See him, in Troy, the pious care decline
Of his weak age, to live the curse of thine!
Thou too, old man, hast happier days beheld;
In riches once, in children once excell'd;
Extended Phrygia own'd thy ample reign,
And all fair Lesbos' blissful seats contain,
And all wide Hellespont's unmeasur'd main.
But since the god his hand has pleas'd to turn,
And fill thy measure from his bitter urn,
What sees the sun, but hapless heroes' falls?
War, and the blood of men, surround thy walls!
What must be, must be. Bear thy lot, nor shed
These unavailing sorrows o'er the dead;
Thou canst not call him from the Stygian shore,
But thou, alas! may'st live to suffer more!'
   To whom the king: 'O favour'd of the skies!
Here let me grow to earth! since Hector lies
On the bare beach depriv'd of obsequies.
O give me Hector! to my eyes restore
His corse, and take the gifts: I ask no more.
Thou, as thou may'st, these boundless stores enjoy;
Safe may'st thou sail, and turn thy wrath from Troy:
So shall thy pity and forbearance give
A weak old man to see the light and live!'

The amour of Mars and Venus
(Homer, *Odyssey* 8.256-369)

Meantime the bard, alternate to the strings,
The loves of Mars and Cytherea sings;
How the stern god, enamour'd with her charms,
Clasp'd the gay panting goddess in his arms,
By bribes seduced; and how the sun, whose eye
Views the broad heavens, disclosed the lawless joy.
Stung to the soul, indignant through the skies
To his black forge vindictive Vulcan flies:
Arrived, his sinewy arms incessant place
The eternal anvil on the massy base.
A wondrous net he labours, to betray
The wanton lovers, as entwined they lay,
Indissolubly strong! Then instant bears
To his immortal dome the finish'd snares:
Above, below, around, with art dispread,
The sure enclosure folds the genial bed:
Whose texture even the search of gods deceives,
Thin as the filmy threads the spider weaves.
Then, as withdrawing from the starry bowers,
He feigns a journey to the Lemnian shores,
His favourite isle: observant Mars descries
His wish'd recess, and to the goddess flies;
He glows, he burns, the fair-hair'd queen of love
Descends, smooth gliding from the courts of Jove,
Gay blooming in full charms: her hand he press'd
With eager joy, and with a sigh address'd:
    'Come, my beloved! and taste the soft delights:
Come, to repose the genial bed invites:
Thy absent spouse, neglectful of thy charms,
Prefers his barbarous Sintians to thy arms!'
    Then, nothing loth, the enamour'd fair he led,
And sunk transported on the conscious bed.
Down rush'd the toils, enwrapping as they lay
The careless lovers in their wanton play:
In vain they strive; the entangling snares deny
(Inextricably firm) the power to fly.
Warn'd by the god who sheds the golden day,
Stern Vulcan homeward treads the starry way:
Arrived, he sees, he grieves, with rage he burns:
Full horribly he roars, his voice all heaven returns.
    'O Jove, (he cried) O all ye powers above,
See the lewd dalliance of the queen of love!
Me, awkward me, she scorns; and yields her charms
To that fair lecher, the strong god of arms.

If I am lame, that stain my natal hour
By fate imposed; such me my parent bore.
Why was I born? See how the wanton lies!
Oh sight tormenting to a husband's eyes!
But yet, I trust, this once e'en Mars would fly
His fair-one's arms – he thinks her, once, too nigh.
But there remain, ye guilty, in my power,
Till Jove refunds his shameless daughter's dower.
Too dear I prized a fair enchanting face:
Beauty unchaste is beauty in disgrace.'
   Meanwhile the gods the dome of Vulcan throng;
Apollo comes, and Neptune comes along;
With these gay Hermes trod the starry plain;
But modesty witheld the goddess train.
All heaven beholds, imprison'd as they lie,
And unextinguish'd laughter shakes the sky.
Then mutual, thus they spoke: 'Behold on wrong
Swift vengeance waits; and art subdues the strong!
Dwells there a god on all the Olympian brow
More swift than Mars, and more than Vulcan slow?
Yet Vulcan conquers, and the god of arms
Must pay the penalty for lawless charms.'
   Thus serious they; but he who gilds the skies,
The gay Apollo, thus to Hermes cries:
'Wouldst thou enchain'd like Mars, O Hermes, lie,
And bear the shame like Mars to share the joy?)
   'O envied shame! (the smiling youth rejoin'd;)
And thrice the chains, and thrice more firmly bind;
Gaze all ye gods, and every goddess gaze,
Yet eager would I bless the sweet disgrace.'
   Loud laugh the rest, e'en Neptune laughs aloud,
Yet sues importunate to loose the god:
'And free, (he cries) O Vulcan! free from shame
Thy captives! I ensure the penal claim.'
   'Will Neptune (Vulcan then) the faithless trust?
He suffers who gives surety for the unjust:
But say, if that lewd scandal of the sky,
To liberty restored, perfidious fly;
Say, wilt thou bear the mulct?' He instant cries,
'The mulct I bear, if Mars perfidious flies.'
   To whom appeased: 'No more I urge delay;
When Neptune sues, my part is to obey.'
Then to the snares his force the god applies;
They burst; and Mars to Thrace indignant flies:
To the soft Cyprian shores the goddess moves,
To visit Paphos and her blooming groves,
Where to the Power an hundred altars rise,

And breathing odours scent the balmy skies;
Concealed she bathes in consecrated bowers,
The Graces unguents shed, ambrosial showers,
Unguents that charm the gods! she last assumes
Her wondrous robes; and full the goddess blooms.
   Thus sung the bard; Ulysses hears with joy,
And loud applauses rend the vaulted sky.

Circe's palace
(Homer, *Odyssey* 10.210-43)

   The palace in a woody vale they found,
High raised of stone; a shaded space around;
Where mountain wolves and brindled lions roam,
(By magic tamed,) familiar to the dome.
With gentle blandishment our men they meet,
And wag their tails, and fawning lick their feet.
As from some feast a man returning late,
His faithful dogs all meet him at the gate,
Rejoicing round, some morsel to receive,
(Such as the good man ever used to give,)
Domestic thus the grisly beasts drew near;
They gaze with wonder not unmix'd with fear.
Now on the threshold of the dome they stood,
And heard a voice resounding through the wood:
Placed at her loom within, the goddess sung;
The vaulted roofs and solid pavement rung.
O'er the fair web the rising figures shine,
Immortal labour! worthy hands divine.
Polites to the rest the question moved
(A gallant leader, and a man I loved):
   'What voice celestial, chanting to the loom
(Or nymph, or goddess), echoes from the room?
Say, shall we seek access?' With that they call;
And wide unfold the portals of the hall.
   The goddess, rising, asks her guests to stay,
Who blindly follow where she leads the way.
Eurylochus alone of all the band,
Suspecting fraud, more prudently remain'd.
On thrones around with downy coverings graced,
With semblance fair, the unhappy men she placed.
Milk newly press'd, the sacred flour of wheat,
And honey fresh, and Pramnian wines the treat:
But venom'd was the bread, and mix'd the bowl,
With drugs of force to darken all the soul:
Soon in the luscious feast themselves they lost,
And drank oblivion of their native coast.

Instant her circling wand the goddess waves,
To hogs transforms them, and the sty receives.
No more was seen the human form divine;
Head, face, and members, bristle into swine:
Still cursed with sense, their minds remain alone,
And their own voice affrights them when they groan.
Meanwhile the goddess in disdain bestows
The mast and acorn, brutal food! and strows
The fruits and cornel, as their feast, around;
Now prone and grovelling on unsavoury ground.

The Sirens
(Homer, *Odyssey* 12.166-200)

While yet I speak the winged galley flies,
And lo! the Siren shores like mists arise.
Sunk were at once the winds; the air above,
And waves below, at once forgot to move:
Some demon calm'd the air and smooth'd the deep,
Hush'd the loud winds, and charm'd the waves to sleep.
Now every sail we furl, each oar we ply:
Lash'd by the stroke, the frothy waters fly.
The ductile wax with busy hands I mould,
And cleft in fragments, and the fragments roll'd:
The aerial region now grew warm with day,
The wax dissolved beneath the burning ray;
Then every ear I barr'd against the strain,
And from access of frenzy lock'd the brain.
Now round the mast my mates the fetters roll'd,
And bound me limb by limb with fold on fold.
Then bending to the stroke, the active train
Plunge all at once their oars, and cleave the main.
While to the shore the rapid vessel flies,
Our swift approach the Siren choir descries;
Celestial music warbles from their tongue,
And thus the sweet deluders tune the song:
'Oh stay, O pride of Greece! Ulysses stay!
Oh cease thy course, and listen to our lay!
Blest is the man ordain'd our voice to hear,
The song instructs the soul, and charms the ear.
Approach! thy soul shall into raptures rise!
Approach! and learn new wisdom from the wise!
We know whate'er the kings of mighty name
Achieved at Ilion in the field of fame;
Whate'er beneath the sun's bright journey lies.
Oh stay, and learn new wisdom from the wise!'
Thus the sweet charmers warbled o'er the main;

My soul takes wing to meet the heavenly strain;
I give the sign, and struggle to be free:
Swift row my mates, and shoot along the sea;
New chains they add, and rapid urge the way,
Till, dying off, the distant sounds decay:
Then scudding swiftly from the dangerous ground,
The deafen'd ear unlock'd, the chains unbound.

Spurs to satire
(Horace, *Satires* 2.1.1-7, 39-78)

P: There are (I scarce think it, but am told)
There are to whom my satire seems too bold,
Scarce to wise Peter complaisant enough,
And something said of Chartres much too rough.
The lines are weak, another's pleas'd to say,
Lord Fanny spins a thousand such a day.
Tim'rous by Nature, of the rich in awe,
I come to council learned in the law.
You'll give me, like a friend both sage and free,
Advice; and (as you use) without a fee.
F: I'd write no more.
                    P: Not write? but then I *think*,
And for my soul I cannot sleep a wink.
I nod in company, I wake at night,
Fools rush into my head, and so I write . . .

What arm'd for virtue when I point the pen,
Brand the bold front of shameless, guilty men,
Dash the proud gamester in his gilded car,
Bare the mean heart that lurks beneath a star;
Can there be wanting to defend her cause,
Lights of the church, or guardians of the laws?
Could pension'd Boileau lash in honest strain
Flatt'rers and bigots e'en in Louis' reign?
Could laureate Dryden pimp and fry'r engage,
Yet neither Charles nor James be in a rage?
And I not strip the gilding off a knave,
Un-plac'd, un-pension'd, no man's heir, or slave?
I will, or perish in the gen'rous cause.
Hear this! and tremble, you who 'scape the laws.
Yes, while I live, no rich or noble knave
Shall walk the world, in credit, to his grave.
To virtue only and her friends, a friend
The world beside may murmur, or commend.
Know, all the distant din the world can keep
Rolls o'er my grotto, and but sooths my sleep.

There, my retreat the best companions grace,
Chiefs, out of war, and statesmen, out of place.
There St. John mingles with my friendly bowl,
The feast of reason and the flow of soul:
And he, whose lightning pierc'd th' Iberian lines,
Now, forms my quincunx, and now ranks my vines,
Or tames the genius of the stubborn plain,
Almost as quickly, as he conquer'd Spain.

Envy must own, I live among the great,
No pimp of pleasure, and no spy of state,
With eyes that pry not, tongue that ne'er repeats,
Fond to spread friendships, but to cover heats,
To help who want, to forward who excel;
This, all who know me, know; who love me, tell;
And who unknown defame me, let them be
Scriblers or peers, alike are mob to me.

In praise of George II
(Horace, *Epistles* 2.1.1-22, of Augustus in the original)

While you, great patron of mankind, sustain
The balanc'd world, and open all the main;
Your country, chief, in arms abroad defend,
At home, with morals, arts, and laws amend;
How shall the Muse, from such a monarch, steal
An hour, and not defraud the publick weal?

Edward and Henry, now the boast of fame,
And virtuous Alfred, a more sacred name,
After a life of gen'rous toils endur'd,
The Gaul subdu'd, or property secur'd,
Ambition humbled, mighty cities storm'd,
Or laws establish'd, and the world reform'd;
Clos'd their long glories with a sigh, to find
Th' unwilling gratitude of base mankind!
All human virtue to its latest breath
Finds envy never conquer'd, but by death.
The great Alcides, ev'ry labour past,
Had still this monster to subdue at last.
Sure fate of all, beneath whose rising ray
Each star of meaner merit fades away;
Oppress'd we feel the beam directly beat,
Those suns of glory please not till they set.

To thee, the world its present homage pays,
The harvest early, but mature the praise:
Great friend of liberty! in kings a name
Above all Greek, above all Roman fame:
Whose word is truth, as sacred and rever'd,

As Heav'n's own oracles from altars heard.
Wonder of kings! like whom, to mortal eyes
None e'er has risen, and none e'er shall rise.

Inconsistency
(Horace, *Epistles* 1.1.80-108)

But show me one, who has it in his pow'r
To act consistent with himself an hour.
Sir Job sail'd forth, the evening bright and still,
'No place on earth (he cry'd) like Greenwich hill!'
Up starts a palace, lo! th' obedient base
Slopes at its foot, the woods its sides embrace,
The silver Thames reflects its marble face.
Now let some whimzy, or that Dev'l within
Which guides all those who know not what they mean
But give the Knight (or give his Lady) spleen;
'Away, away! take all your scaffolds down,
For Snug's the word: My dear! we'll live in town.'
    At am'rous Flavio is the stocking thrown?
That very night he longs to live alone.
The fool whose wife elopes some thrice a quarter,
For matrimonial solace dies a martyr.
Did ever Proteus, Merlin, any witch,
Transform themselves so strangely as the rich?
'Well, but the poor' – the poor have the same itch:
They change their weekly barber, weekly news,
Prefer a new Japanner to their shoes,
Discharge their garrets, move their beds, and run
(They know not whither) in a chaise and one;
They hire their sculler, and when once aboard,
Grow sick, and damn the climate – like a lord.
    You laugh, half beau half sloven if I stand,
My wig all powder, and all snuff my band;
You laugh, if coat and breeches strangely vary,
White gloves, and linnen worthy Lady Mary!
But when no Prelate's lawn with hair-shirt lin'd,
Is half so incoherent as my mind,
When (each opinion with the next at strife,
One ebb and flow of follies all my life)
I plant, root up, I build, and then confound,
Turn round to square, and square again to round;
You never change one muscle of your face,
You think this madness but a common case,
Nor once to chanc'ry, nor to Hales apply;
Yet hang your lip, to see a seam awry!
Careless how ill I with myself agree;

Kind to my dress, my figure, not to me.
Is this my guide, philosopher, and friend?
This, he who loves me, and who ought to mend?
Who ought to make me (what he can, or none,)
That man divine whom wisdom calls her own,
Great without title, without fortune bless'd,
Rich ev'n when plunder'd, honour'd while oppress'd,
Lov'd without youth, and follow'd without power,
At home tho' exil'd, free, tho' in the Tower.
In short, that reas'ning, high, immortal thing,
Just less than Jove, and much above a king,
Nay half in Heav'n – except (what's mighty odd)
A fit of vapours clouds this demi-god.

NICHOLAS ROWE

(1673-1718)

Rowe succeeded Nahum Tate as Poet-Laureate under George I. His chief
employment was in the writing of tragedies; parts of the translation of Lucan
appeared in the *Miscellanies,* but the whole was not published until after his
death. Johnson calls the Lucan 'one of the greatest productions of English
poetry; for there is perhaps none that so completely exhibits the genius and
spirit of the original. . . . [it] deserves more notice than it obtains, and as it is
more read will be more esteemed.'

The apotheosis of Pompey
(Lucan, *Pharsalia* 9.1-18)

Nor in the dying embers of its pile
Slept the great soul upon the banks of Nile,
Nor longer, by the earthy parts restrain'd,
Amidst its wretched reliques was detain'd;
But, active and impatient of delay,
Shot from the mouldering heap, and upwards urg'd its way.
Far in those azure regions of the air
Which border on the rolling starry sphere,
Beyond our orb, and nearer to that height,
Where Cynthia drives around her silver light;
Their happy seats the demi-gods possess,
Refin'd by virtue, and prepar'd for bliss;
Of life unblam'd, a pure and pious race,
Worthy that lower heaven and stars to grace,
Divine, and equal to the glorious place.
There Pompey's soul, adorn'd with heavenly light,
Soon shone among the rest, and as the rest was bright.

New to the blest abode, with wonder fill'd,
The stars and moving planets he beheld;
Then looking down on the sun's feeble ray,
Survey'd our dusky, faint, imperfect day,
And under what a cloud of night we lay.
But when he saw, how on the shore forlorn
His headless trunk was cast for public scorn;
When he beheld, how envious fortune, still,
Took pains to use a senseless carcase ill,
He smil'd at the vain malice of his foe,
And pity'd impotent mankind below,
Then lightly passing o'er Emathia's plain,
His flying navy scatter'd on the main,
And cruel Caesar's tents; he fix'd at last
His residence in Brutus' sacred breast:
There brooding o'er his country's wrongs he sate,
The state's avenger, and the tyrant's fate;
There mournful Rome might still her Pompey find,
There, and in Cato's free unconquer'd mind.

ALLAN RAMSAY

(1686-1758)

Ramsay was born in Lanarkshire and apprenticed at 16 to an Edinburgh wig-maker. In due course he was able to set up a successful wig-making business of his own, but soon after 1716 he turned to bookselling, an activity more closely tied to his already evident literary penchant. He had issued occasional poems on individual sheets, and had entertained the members of the Jacobite 'Easy Club' (founded in 1712) with readings of his work. As members were obliged to adopt pseudonyms, he had used the name, significantly, of Gawin Douglas.

His *Scots Songs* were published in 1719, his *Collected Poems* in 1721. He also engaged in a verse correspondence with William Hamilton of Bangour. After this he turned more to drama, both his own plays and the contribution of prologues and epilogues to London plays; in 1736 he built a playhouse in Edinburgh, which however was closed down under the licensing act within a year. He ceased writing in 1730 and retired from business in 1755.

He was widely celebrated in Scots literary circles, and Sir Alexander Fraser-Tytler (the theorist of translation) dedicated to him a temple on his estate at Woodhouselee. Poor as an editor of classical texts, he successfully achieved in his own work a Horatian tone, in both Scots and English. In his aim of saving Scots from oblivion, he was a pioneer of the Scots poetry explosion of the next generations. His nationalism may seem provincialism, particularly due to his eclipse by Burns, but his work is of real significance for the Scottish literary Renaissance.

Enjoy the moment
(Horace, *Odes* 1.9)

Look up to Pentland's tow'ring taps,
    Buried beneath big wreaths o' snaw,
O'er ilka cleugh, ilk scar an' slap,
    As high as ony Roman wa'.

Driving their ba's frae whins or tee,
    There's no ae gowfer to be seen;
Nor douser fouk, wysing a – jee
    The byas bouls on Tamson's green.

Then fling on coals, an' ripe the ribs,
    An' beek the house baith butt an' ben;
That mutchkin-stoup it hauds but dribs,
    Then let's get in the tappit hen.

Guid claret best keeps out the cauld,
    An' drives awa' the winter soon;
It makes a man baith gash an' bauld,
    An' heaves his saul ayont the moon.

Leave to the gods your ilka care;
    If that they think us worth their while,
They can a rowth o' blessings spare,
    Which will our fashious fears beguile.

For what they hae a mind to do,
    That will they do, shou'd we gang wud;
If they command the storms to blaw,
    Then upo' sight the hailstanes thud.

But soon as e'er they cry, Be quiet,
    The blatt'ring winds daur nae mair move,
But cour into their caves, an' wait
    The high command o' supreme Jove.

Let neist day come as it thinks fit,
    The present minute's only ours;
On pleasure let's employ our wit,
    An' laugh at fortune's feckless pow'rs.

Be sure ye dinna quat the grip
    O' ilka joy when ye are young,
Before auld age your vitals nip,
    An' lay ye twafald o'er a rung.

Sweet youth's a blythe an' heartsome time;
    Then, lads an' lasses, while it's May,
Gae pou the gowan in its prime,
    Before it wither an' decay.

Watch the saft minutes o' delyte,
    Whan Jenny speaks beneath her breath,
An' kisses, laying a' the wyte
    On you, if she kepp ony skaith.

Haith ye're ill-bred, she'll smiling say,
    Ye'll worry me, ye greedy rook;
Syne frae your arms she'll rin away,
    An' hide hersell in some dark nook;

Her laugh will lead you to the place
    Where lies the happiness you want,
An' plainly tells you to your face,
    Nineteen nay-says are hauf a grant.

Now to her heaving bosom cling,
    An' sweetly toolie for a kiss,
Frae her finger whup a ring,
    As taiken o' a future bliss.

These bennisons, I'm very sure,
    Are o' the gods' indulgent grant;
Then, surly carles, whisht, forbear
    To plague us wi' your whining cant.

WILLIAM DIAPER

(1685-1717)

Born in Bridgwater and educated at Balliol College, Oxford, Diaper took orders and held a succession of livings both in Somerset and elsewhere. In 1712 he published the bulk of his poetry – *Nereides, Callipaedia* and *Dryades.* As a result he won the grudging patronage of Swift, who however regretted that he should squander his talent on translation as he thereafter did. But to Diaper Oppian becomes not a bridle but an inspiration, and his version is expansive and amusing. The translation of Oppian was unfinished at his death and was completed and published by John Jones (1722), who added a defence of Diaper's earlier piscatory eclogues against the ridicule of Tickell (*Guardian* 28).

Lobsters
(Oppian, *Halieutica* 1.259-79)

In shelly armour wrapt, the lobsters seek
Safe shelter in some bay, or winding creek;
To rocky chasms the dusky natives cleave,
Tenacious hold, nor will the dwelling leave.
Nought like their home the constant lobsters prize,
And forreign shores, and seas unknown despise.
Tho' cruel hand the banish'd wretch expell,
And force the captive from his native cell,
He will, if freed, return, with anxious care
Find the known rock, and to his home repair:
No novel customs learns in diff'rent seas,
But wonted food, and home-taught manners please.
His long-deserted house the lobster owns,
And with close ardent claw indents the fav'rite stones.
The love of country's not to man confin'd;
The same propensions sway the brutal mind.
Fishes their native caves with transport view;
They have their countries, and their fondness too.
No nation may with that blest clime compare,
That gave us first to breath the vital air.
How dear the first acquaintance of our eyes!
How rich the soil! how beautiful the skies!
The name of country fills the grateful mind
With all that's tender, generous and kind.
Ah! wretched those, who forc'd from what they love
Necessitous in vagrant exile rove;
Still restless must the killing grief renew,
Despis'd by all, or pity'd but by few.

THOMAS COOKE

(1703-1756)

Cooke's name is so associated with his translation of Hesoid that he was known
as Hesiod Cooke. According to Pope, his father was a Muggletonian, which
might explain the attraction of Hesiod, the underdog's and small man's poet,
for the translator. In 1722 he went to London to earn his living by his pen; he
joined the group of Whigs which included Tickell, Philips, and Steele. His
attacks on Pope and Swift in the *Battle of the Poets* earned him a place in the
Dunciad (2.138). The Hesiod translation of 1728 remained his chief source of
income, and he died a poor man.

The path to virtue
(Hesiod, *Works and Days* 286-313)

O! Perses, foolish Perses, bow thine ear
To the good counsels of a soul sincere.
To wickedness the road is quickly found,
Short is the way, and on an easy ground.
The paths of virtue must be reach'd by toil,
Arduous and long, and on a rugged soil,
Thorny the gate, but when the top you gain,
Fair is the future, and the prospect plain.
Far does the man all other men excel,
Who, from his wisdom, thinks in all things well,
Wisely consid'ring, to himself a friend,
All for the present best, and for the end.
Nor is the man without his share of praise,
Who well the dictates of the wise obeys;
But he that is not wise himself, nor can
Hearken to wisdom, is a useless man.
  Ever observe, Perses, of birth divine,
My precepts, and the profit shall be thine;
Then famine always shall avoid thy door,
And Ceres, fair-wreath'd goddess, bless thy store.
  The slothful wretch, who lives from labour free,
Like drones, the robbers of the painful bee,
Has always men, and gods, alike his foes;
Him famine follows with her trail of woes.
With cheerful zeal your mod'rate toils pursue,
That your full barns you may in season view.
The man industrious, stranger is to need,
A thousand flocks his fertile pastures feed;
As with the drone, with him it will not prove,
Him men and gods behold with eyes of love.
To care and labour think it no disgrace,
False pride! the portion of the sluggard race;
The slothful man, who never work'd before,
Shall gaze with envy on thy growing store;
Like thee to flourish, he will spare no pains;
For lo! the rich virtue and glory gains.

JAMES THOMSON

(1700-1748)

One of the most distinguished sons of the Scottish Englightment, Thomson's major work is *The Seasons*, one of the most often printed books of its time. J.

Chalker, *The English Georgic* (1969) traces its extensive debt to Vergil's poem – this was the period when Vergil was so widely admired that Jethro Tull had to devote a special chapter of his *Horse-hoeing Husbandry* (1731) to discrediting many of Vergil's prescriptions – but there are few passages close enough to be called translation. In the passage below Thomson romanticises and pastoralises Vergil's picture: *anni labor* and *armenta boum* are transformed into 'flowery solitudes'.

The happy countryman
(Vergil, *Georgics* 2.458-66, 503ff., adapted)

Oh, knew he but his happiness, of men
The happiest he! who far from public rage
Deep in the vale, with a choice few retired,
Drinks the pure pleasures of the rural life.
What though the dome be wanting, whose proud gate
Each morning vomits out the sneaking crowd
Of flatterers false, and in their turn abused?
Vile intercourse! What though the glittering robe,
Of every hue reflected light can give,
Or floating loose or stiff with mazy gold,
The pride and gaze of fools, oppress him not?...

Let others brave the flood in quest of gain,
And beat for joyless months the gloomy wave,
Let such as deem it glory to destroy
Rush into blood, the sack of cities seek –
Unpierced, exulting in the widow's wail,
The virgin's shriek, and infant's trembling cry.
Let some, far distant from their native soil,
Urged or by want or hardened avarice,
Find other lands beneath another sun.
Let this through cities work his eager way
By legal outrage and established guile,
The social sense extinct; and that ferment
Mad into tumult the seditious herd,
Or melt them down to slavery. Let these
Ensnare the wretched in the toils of law,
Fomenting discord, and perplexing right,
An iron race! and those of fairer front,
But equal inhumanity, in courts,
Delusive pomp, and dark cabals, delight;
Wreathe the deep bow, diffuse the lying smile,
And tread the weary labyrinth of state.
While he, from all the stormy passions free
That restless men involve, hears, and but hears,
At distance safe, the human tempest roar,

Wrapped close in conscious peace. The fall of kings,
The rage of nations, and the crush of states
Move not the man who, from the world escaped,
In still retreats and flowery solitudes
To Nature's voice attends from month to month,
And day to day, through the revolving year –
Admiring, sees her in her every shape;
Feels all her sweet emotions at his heart;
Takes what she liberal gives, nor thinks of more.

JONATHAN SWIFT

(1667-1745)

Born in Dublin, Swift was educated at Kilkenny and at Trinity College, Dublin. He began his career under the patronage of Sir William Temple, and his *Battle of the Books* is his contribution to the quarrel of the ancients and moderns occasioned by Temple's *Essay upon Ancient and Modern Learning,* memorable for its picture of Bentley drowning all his opponents with a bucket of ordure. Swift was, of course, on the side that was in error over the *Epistles of Phalaris.* His life in politics in London brought him among the Whigs, as a result of his association with Temple, but he gradually turned to Toryism. The Scriblerus Club in which he was the moving spirit folded in 1713, after which he returned to the Deanery in Dublin and made only two more trips to London. 'Though ambition pressed Swift into a life of bustle, the wish for a life of ease was always returning' (Samuel Johnson). This is exactly the attitude that shines through his imitation of Horace, given below.

Retreat from affairs
(Horace, *Satires* 2.6.1-5, 40-62)

I often wish'd, that I had clear
For life, six hundred pounds a year,
A handsome house to lodge a friend,
A river at my garden's end,
A terras walk, and half a rood
Of land set out to plant a wood.

Well, now I have all this and more,
I ask not to increase my store,
And should be perfectly content,
Could I but live on this side Trent;
Nor cross the channel twice a year,
To spend six months with statesmen here. . . .

'Tis (let me see) three years and more,
(October next, it will be four)
Since Harley bid me first attend,
And chose me for an humble friend;
Would take me in his coach to chat,
And question me of this and that;
As, 'What's a-clock?' and 'How's the wind?
Whose chariot's that we left behind?'
Or gravely try to read the lines
Writ underneath the country signs;
Or, 'Have you nothing new today
From Pope, from Parnel, or from Gay?'
Such tattle often entertains
My lord and me as far as Stains,
As once a week we travel down
To Windsor, and again to town,
Where all that passes, *inter nos,*
Might be proclaim'd at Charing Cross.

Yet some I know with envy swell,
Because they see me us'd so well:
'How think you of our friend the Dean?
I wonder what some people mean;
My lord and he are grown so great,
Always together, *tete a tete*:
What, they admire him for his jokes –
See but the fortune of some folks!'
There flies about a strange report
Of some express arriv'd at court;
I'm stopt by all the fools I meet,
And catechis'd in ev'ry street.
'You, Mr Dean, frequent the great;
Inform us, will the Emp'ror treat?
Or do the prints and papers lye?'
Faith Sir, you know as much as I.
'Ah Doctor, how you love to jest?
'Tis now no secret' – I protest
'Tis one to me. – 'Then, tell us, pray
When are the troops to have their pay?'
And, though I solemnly declare
I know no more than my Lord Mayor,
They stand amaz'd, and think me grown
The closest mortal ever known.

Thus in a sea of folly tost,
My choicest hours of life are lost:
Yet always wishing to retreat;

Oh, could I see my country seat.
There leaning near a gentle brook,
Sleep, or peruse some antient book;
And there in sweet oblivion drown
Those cares that haunt a court and town.

JOHN ADDISON
(fl. 1735)

Translator of Anacreon (1735) and Petronius (1736).

On the Grasshopper
(*Anacreontea* 32 Bergk)

On thy verdant Throne elate,
Lovely Insect! there in State,
Nectar'd Dew you sip, and sing,
Like a little happy King.
    All thou see'st so bloomy-fine,
Lovely Insect, all is thine!
Which the painted Fields produce,
Or the soft-wing'd Hours profuse.
    Swains adore thy guiltless Charms,
None thy blissful Revel harms.
Thee, sweet Prophet! all revere,
Thou foretell'st the ripen'd year.
    By the Muses thou'rt carest,
Thou'rt by golden *Phoebus* blest;
He indulg'd thy tuneful Voice,
Age ne'er interrupts thy Joys.
    Wisest Offspring of the Earth!
Thou for nothing car'st but Mirth;
Free from Pain, and Flesh, and Blood,
Thou'rt almost a little God.

Silence in death
(Sappho 55 L-P)

When Death shall close those Eyes, imperious Dame!
Silence shall seize on thy inglorious Name.
For thy unletter'd Hand ne'er pluck'd the Rose,
Which on Pieria's happy Summit glows.
To *Pluto's* Realms unhonour'd you shall go,
And herd among th'ignobler Ghosts below.
Whilst I on Wings of Fame shall rise elate,
And snatch a bright eternity from Fate.

SAMUEL JOHNSON
(1709-1784)

Born in Lichfield, and educated at Stourbridge and Pembroke College,
Oxford, Johnson's early life was characterised by indigence. The greatest
literary figure of the age once asserted that no man ever wrote except for
money. After leaving Oxford his career led him into education, and he founded
an academy with his wife's dowry. Coming eventually to London, his first
literary effort was *Irene*, produced in 1738 and praised by Pope. Soon after this
began the labour on the Dictionary, followed in 1749 by his first major poem,
The Vanity of Human Wishes, where the savagery of Juvenal is overlaid by the sol-
emnity and seriousness of the translator. It is one of the noblest poems of the
century. In 1750 he embarked on the series of *The Rambler*, and in 1758 *The
Idler*. His edition of Shakespeare at last made his fortune, and from 1766 some
comfort entered his life when he spent several months a year at the Thrales's
home in Streatham, until Mrs Thrale's remarriage in 1784. In this period he
produced his *Lives of the Poets*, perhaps his greatest memorial. After Mrs
Thrale's remarriage his decline was swift, and he died the same year.

Vanities
(Juvenal, *Satire* 10.33-55, 114-32, 188-245) from *The Vanity of Human Wishes*

> Once more, Democritus, arise on earth,
> With chearful wisdom and instructive mirth,
> See motley life in modern trappings dress'd,
> And feed with varied fools th' eternal jest:
> Thou who couldst laugh where want enchain'd caprice,
> Toil crush'd conceit, and man was of a piece;
> Where wealth unlov'd without a mourner dy'd;
> And scarce a sycophant was fed by pride;
> Where ne'er was known the form of mock debate,
> Or seen a new-made mayor's unwieldy state;
> Where change of fav'rites made no change of laws,
> And senates heard before they judg'd a cause;
> How wouldst thou shake at Britain's modish tribe,
> Dart the quick taunt, and edge the piercing jibe?
> Attentive truth and nature to descry,
> And pierce each scene with philosophic eye.
> To thee were solemn toys or empty shew,
> The robes of pleasure and the veils of woe:
> All aid the farce, and all thy mirth maintain,
> Whose joys are causeless, or whose griefs are vain.
>   Such was the scorn that fill'd the sage's mind,
> Renew'd at ev'ry glance on humankind;
> How just that scorn ere yet thy voice declare,
> Search ev'ry state, and canvass ev'ry pray'r. . . .

When first the college rolls receive his name,
The young enthusiast quits his ease for fame;
Through all his veins the fever of renown
Burns from the strong contagion of the gown;
O'er Bodley's dome his future labours spread,
And Bacon's mansion trembles o'er his head;
Are these thy views? proceed, illustrious youth,
And virtue guard thee to the throne of truth,
Yet should thy soul indulge the gen'rous heat,
Till captive science yields her last retreat;
Should reason guide thee with her brightest ray,
And pour on misty doubt resistless day;
Should no false kindness lure to loose delight,
Nor praise relax, nor difficulty fright;
Should tempting novelty the cell refrain,
And sloth effuse her opiate fumes in vain;
Should beauty blunt on fops her fatal dart,
Nor claim the triumph of a letter'd heart;
Should no disease thy torpid veins invade,
Nor melancholy's phantoms haunt thy shade;
Yet hope not life from grief or danger free,
Nor think the doom of man revers'd for thee:
Deign on the passing world to turn thine eyes,
And pause awhile from letters to be wise;
There mark what ills the scholar's life assail,
Toil, envy, want, the patron, and the jail.
See nations slowly wise, and meanly just,
To buried merit raise the tardy bust.
If dreams yet flatter, once again attend,
Hear Lydiat's life and Galileo's end. . . .

Enlarge my life with multitude of days,
In health, in sickness, thus the suppliant prays;
Hides from himself his state, and shuns to know,
That life protracted is protracted woe.
Time hovers o'er, impatient to destroy,
And shuts up all the passages of joy:
In vain their gifts the bounteous seasons pour,
The fruit autumnal, and the vernal flow'r,
With listless eye the dotard views the store,
He views, and wonders that they please no more;
Now pall the tasteless meats, and joyless wines,
And luxury with sighs her slave resigns.
Approach, ye minstrels, try the soothing strain,
Diffuse the tuneful lenitives of pain:
No sounds alas would touch th' impervious ear,
Though dancing mountains witness'd Orpheus near;

Nor lute nor lyre his feeble pow'rs attend,
Nor sweeter musick of a virtuous friend,
But everlasting dictates croud his tongue,
Perversely grave, or positively wrong.
The still returning tale, and ling'ring jest,
Perplex the fawning niece and pamper'd guest,
While growing hopes scarce awe the gath'ring sneer,
And scarce a legacy can bribe to hear;
The watchful guests still hint the last offence,
The daughter's petulance, the son's expence,
Improve his heady rage with treach'rous skill,
And mould his passions till they make his will.
  Unnumber'd maladies his joints invade,
Lay siege to life and press the dire blockade;
But unextinguish'd av'rice still remains,
And dreaded losses aggravate his pains;
He turns, with anxious heart and cripled hands,
His bonds of debt, and mortgages of lands;
Or views his coffers with suspicious eyes,
Unlocks his gold, and counts it till he dies.
  But grant, the virtues of a temp'rate prime,
Bless with an age exempt from scorn or crime;
An age that melts with unperceiv'd decay,
And glides in modest innocence away;
Whose peaceful day benevolence endears,
Whose night congratulating conscience cheers;
The gen'ral fav'rite as the gen'ral friend:
Such age there is, and who shall wish its end?
  Yet ev'n on this her load misfortune flings,
To press the weary minutes flagging wings:
New sorrow rises as the day returns,
A sister sickens, or a daughter mourns,
Now kindred merit fills the sable bier,
Now lacerated friendship claims a tear,
Year chases year, decay pursues decay,
Still drops some joy from with'ring life away;
New forms arise, and diff'rent views engage,
Superfluous lags the vet'ran on the stage,
Till pitying nature signs the last release,
And bids afflicted worth retire to peace.

Spring
(Horace, *Odes* 4.7)

The snow dissolv'd no more is seen,
The fields, and woods, behold, are green,
The changing year renews the plain

The rivers know their banks again
The spritely Nymph and naked Grace
The mazy dance together trace.
The changing year's successive plan
Proclaims mortality to man.
Rough winter's blasts to spring give way
Spring yields to summer's sovereign ray
Then summer sinks in autumn's reign
And winter chills the world again
Her losses soon the moon supplies
But wretched man, when once he lies
Where Priam and his sons are laid
Is nought but ashes and a shade.
Who knows if Jove who counts our score
Will toss us in a morning more?
What with your friend you nobly share
At least you rescue from your heir.
Not you, Torquatus, boast of Rome,
When Minos once has fix'd your doom,
Or eloquence, or splendid birth
Or virtue shall replace on earth.
Hyppolytus unjustly slain
Diana calls to life in vain,
Nor can the might of Theseus rend
The chains of hell that hold his friend.

PHILIP FRANCIS

(1708?-1773)

Educated at Trinity College, Dublin, Francis became the Rector of St Mary's
in Dublin, where he published his Horace, the two parts respectively in 1742
and 1746. He then moved to London, where for a while Edward Gibbon lived
with him. His career was marked by ambition and extravagence – Churchill
called him 'the atheist chaplain of the atheist lord' – and after obtaining
various livings he received a crown pension in 1764.

Samuel Johnson said of him 'The lyrical part of Horace never can be
perfectly translated. Francis has done it the best. I'll take his, five out of six,
against them all.'

Spring
(Horace, *Odes* 1.4)

West winds of spring speed winter frore,
Dry keels are rolled to seaward down the shore;
No more the ploughman loves his fire,

No more the lowing herds their stall desire,
　While Earth her richest verdure yields,
Nor hoary frosts now whiten all the fields.
　Now joyous through the verdant meads
Beneath the rising moon fair Venus leads
　Her various dance and with her train
Of Nymphs and modest Graces treads the plain,
　While Vulcan's glowing breath inspires
The toilsome forge and blows up all its fires.
　Now crowned with myrtle or the flowers
Which the glad Earth from her free bosom pours,
　We'll offer in the shady grove
Or lamb or kid, as Pan shall best approve.
　With equal pace impartial fate
Knocks at the palace as the cottage gate,
　Nor should our sum of life extend
Our growing hopes beyond their destined end.
　When sunk to Pluto's shadowy coasts,
Oppressed with darkness and the fabled ghosts,
　No more the dice shall there assign
To thee the jovial monarchy of wine,
　No more shall you the Fair admire,
The Virgin's envy and the youth's desire.

Equanimity
(Horace, *Odes* 2.3)

In adverse hours an equal mind maintain,
　Nor let your spirit rise too high,
Though Fortune kindly change the scene –
　Remember, Dellius, you were born to die.

Whether your life in sorrows pass,
　And sadly joyless glide away;
Whether, reclining on the grass,
　You bless with choicer wine the festal day,

Where the pale poplar and the pine
　Expel the sun's intemperate beam,
In hospitable shades their branches twine,
　And winds with toil, though swift, the tremulous stream.

Here pour your wines, your odours shed.
　Bring forth the rose's short-liv'd flower,
While Fate yet spins thy mortal thread,
　While youth and fortune give th'indulgent hour.

Your purchas'd woods, your house of state,
  Your villa, wash'd by Tiber's wave,
You must, my Dellius, yield to Fate,
  And to your heir these high-pil'd treasures leave.

Whether you boast a monarch's birth,
  While wealth unbounded round you flows,
Or poor, and sprung from vulgar earth,
  No pity for his victim Pluto knows.

We all must tread the paths of Fate;
  And ever shakes the mortal urn,
Whose lot embarks us, soon or late,
  On Charon's boat, ah! never to return.

'To Venus'
(Horace, *Odes* 3.26)

I lately was fit to be call'd upon duty,
And gallantly fought in the service of beauty:
But now crown'd with conquest I hang up my arms,
My harp, that campaign'd it in midnight alarms:
Here fix on this wall, here my ensigns of wars,
By the statue of Venus, my torches and bars,
And arrows, which threaten'd, by Cupid their liege,
War, war on all doors that dare hold out a siege.
  O goddess of Cyprus, and Memphis, that know
Nor the coldness or weight of love-chilling snow,
With a high-lifted stroke, yet gently severe,
Avenge me on Chloe, the proud and the fair.

Nil admirari
(Horace, *Epistles* 1.6)

Not to admire, is of all means the best,
The only means, to make, and keep us blest.
There are, untainted with the thoughts of fear,
Who see the certain changes of the year
Unerring roll; who see the glorious sun,
And the fix'd stars, their annual progress run:
But with what different eye do they behold
The gifts of earth; or diamonds or gold;
Old ocean's treasures, and the pearly stores,
Wafted to farthest India's wealthy shores?
Or with what sense, what language, should we gaze
On shows, employments, or the people's praise?
  Whoever dreads the opposite extreme

Of disappointment, poverty, or shame,
Is raptur'd with almost the same desires,
As he, who dotes on what the world admires;
Equal their terrors, equal their surprise
When accidental dangers round them rise:
Nor matters it, what passions fill his breast,
With joy or grief; desire or fear opprest,
With down-fix'd eyes, who views the varying scene,
Whose soul grows stiff, and stupified his brain.
Even Virtue when pursu'd with warmth extreme,
Turns into vice, and fools the sage's fame.
    Now go, Numicius, and with higher gust
Admire thy treasur'd gold; the marble bust,
Or bronze antique; the purple's various glow,
And lustred gem; those works which arts bestow
Let gazing crouds your eloquence admire;
At early morn to court, at night retire,
Lest Mutus wed a wife of large estate,
While deeper your dishonour to compleat,
The low-born wretch to you no honour pays,
Though you on him with admiration gaze.
    But time shall bring the latent birth to light,
And hide the present glorious race in night;
For though Agrippa's awful collonade,
Or Appian way, thy passing pomp survey'd,
It yet remains to tread the drear descent,
Where good Pompilius, and great Ancus went.
    Would you not wish to cure th'acuter pains.
That rack thy tortur'd side, or vex thy reins?
Would you, and who would not, with pleasure live?
If virtue can alone the blessing give,
With ardent spirit her alone pursue,
And with contempt all other pleasures view.
Yet if you think, that virtue's but a name;
That groves are groves, nor from religion claim
A sacred awe; fly to the distant coast,
Nor let the rich Bithynian trade be lost.
A thousand talents be the rounded sum,
You first design'd; then raise a second plumb;
A third successive be your earnest care,
And add a fourth to make the mass a square;
For gold, the sovereign queen of all below,
Friends, honour, birth and beauty can bestow:
The goddess of persuasion forms her train,
And Venus decks the well-bemoneyed swain.
    The Cappadocian king, though rich in slaves,
Yet wanting money, was but rich by halves.

Be not like him. Lucullus, as they say,
Once being ask'd, to furnish for a play
An hundred martial vests, in wonder cried,
Whence can so vast a number be supplied?
But yet, what'er my wardrobe can afford,
You shall command; then instant wrote him word,
Five thousand vests were ready at his call,
He might have part, or, if he pleas'd, take all.
Poor house! where no superfluous wealth's unknown
To its rich lord, that thieves may make their own.
    If fortune, then, alone our bliss insure,
Our first, our latest toil should wealth secure:
If pride, and public pomp the blessing claim,
Let's buy a slave, to tell each voter's name,
Dextrous to give the hint, and bid us greet,
And stretch the hand across the crouded street.
'The Fabian tribe his interest largely sways;
This the Velinian; there a third, with ease,
Can give or take the honours of the state,
The consul's fasces, and the praetor's seat.
According to their age adopt them all,
And brother, father, most facetious call'.
    If he lives well, who revels out the night,
Be gluttony our guide; away; 'tis light.
Let's fish, or hunt; and then, at early day,
Across the crouded Forum take our way,
Or to the Campus Martius change the scene,
And let our slaves display our hunting train,
That gazing crouds by one poor mule be taught,
At what a price the mighty boar was bought.
Then let us bathe, while th'indigested food
Lies in the swelling stomach raw and crude;
Forgetting all of decency and shame,
From the fair book of freedom strike our name,
And like th'abandon'd Ulyssean crew,
Our Ithaca forgot, forbidden joys pursue.
    If life's insipid without mirth and love,
Let love and mirth insipid life improve.
Farewel, and if a better system's thine,
Impart it frankly, or make use of mine.

WILLIAM HAMILTON OF BANGOUR

(1704-1754)

Hamilton was born into the period of Scotland's intellectual flowering which took its impetus from the English Augustans, and was acquainted in his youth with Allan Ramsay, Lord Kames, David Hume and Adam Smith. His first essay in verse was a translation of part of Vergil, *Aeneid* 10 (1719), and his subsequent works are competent enough. Boswell admired Hamilton's works but was unable to impart his enthusiasm to Johnson. Nevertheless the imitations of Horace are of interest, in particular that of *Epistles* 1. 18 (1737) which drifts into a very personal meditation. Hamilton's biographer writes 'in the light of Willie's future relations with Prince Charles Edward, and that young gentleman's latter end, a wry zest can be extracted from the prose speculations as to a poet's salutary influence on the character of the statesman he celebrates. In the concluding lines of verse the conventional ideal of rural peace and rational restraint is presented with a note of sincerity whose pathos is not dulled by our knowledge of the reckless decisions and dismal ordeals in store for the poet' (N. S. Bushnell, *William Hamilton of Bangour* (Aberdeen 1957), p. 43).

In 1740/1 Hamilton met Prince Charles Edward in Rome, enlisted under him and took part in the doomed 'Forty-Five', after which he escaped capture by a remarkable series of adventures, through all of which he continued to compose poetry. He became a distinguished figure in Edinburgh society, and died in Lyons while taking a cure.

A tranquil retirement
(Horace, *Epistles* 1.18.104-12, much expanded and elaborated)

What think'st thou, then, my friend, shall be my cares,
My daily studies, and my nightly prayers?
Of the propitious Pow'r this boon I crave,
Still to preserve the little that I have;
Nor yet repugnance at the lot express,
Should fate decree that little to be less,
That what remains of life to Heav'n I live,
If life indeed has any time to give:
Or if the fugitive will no longer stay,
To part as friends should do, and slip away:
Thankful to Heav'n, or for the good supply'd,
To Heav'n submissive for the good deny'd,
Renounce the household charm, a bliss divine!
Heav'n never meant for me, and I resign:
In other joys th' allotted hours improve,
And gain in friendship what was lost in love:
Some comfort snatch'd, as each vain year return'd,
When nature suffer'd, or when friendship mourn'd,

Of all that stock so fatally bereft,
Once youth's proud boast, alas! the little left;
These friends, in youth belov'd, in manhood tried,
Age must not change through avarice or pride:
For me let wisdom's sacred fountain flow,
The cordial draught that sweetens every woe;
Let fortune kind, the *just enough* provide,
Nor dubious float on hope's uncertain tide;
Add thoughts compos'd, affections ever even. –
Thus far suffices to have ask'd of Heaven,
Who in the dispensations of a day,
Grants life, grants death; now gives, now takes away;
To scaffolds oft the ribbon'd spoiler brings;
Takes power from statesmen, and their thrones from kings;
From the unthankful heart the bliss decreed –
But leaves the man of worth still bless'd indeed:
Be life Heaven's gift, be mine the care to find
Still equal to itself the balanc'd mind;
Fame, beauty, wealth forgot, each human toy,
With thoughtful quiet pleas'd, and virtuous joy;
In these, and these alone, supremely blest,
When fools and madmen scramble for the rest.

Tantalus
(Pindar, *Olympian* 1.54-66)

Yet certain, if the pow'r who wide surveys,
    From his watch-tow'r, the earth and seas,
E'er dignified the perishable race;
        Him, Tantalus they rais'd on high,
        Him, the chief favourite of the sky,
            Exalted to sublimest grace.
But his proud heart was lifted up and vain,
        Swell'd with his envy'd happiness,
            Weak and frail his mortal brain,
            The lot superior to sustain;
        He fell degraded from his bliss.
            For on his head th' Almighty Sire,
            Potent in his kindled ire,
                Hung a rock's monstrous weight:
            Too feeble to remove the load,
            Fix'd by the sanction of the god,
                He wander'd erring from delight.
The watchful synod of the skies decreed
        His wasted heart a prey to endless woes,
Condemn'd a weary pilgrimage to lead,
        On earth secure, a stranger to repose.

Because, by mad ambition driv'n,
He robb'd the sacred stores of Heav'n:
Th' ambrosial vintage of the skies
Became the daring spoiler's prize,
And brought to sons of mortal earth
The banquet of celestial birth,
 With endless blessing fraught,
And to his impious revellers pour'd the wine,
Whose precious sweets make blest the pow'rs divine,
 Gift of the rich immortal draught.
Foolish the man who hopes his crimes may lie
 Unseen by the supreme all-piercing eye;
He, high enthron'd above all Heaven's height,
 The works of men with broad survey,
 As in the blazing flame of day,
Beholds the secret deeds of night.
Therefore his son th' immortals back again
Sent to these death-obnoxious abodes,
 To taste his share of human pain,
 Exil'd from the celestial reign,
And sweet communion of the gods.

GILBERT WEST

(1703-1756)

Educated at Eton and Christ Church, Oxford, West continued his career by entering the army. In 1729 he became a clerk to the Privy Council, but soon afterwards retired to Kent, and devoted himself to learning, for which, in the view of Dr Johnson, he was as conspicuous as for his saintliness. Several of his works are of a religious character. His learning is evidenced in the lengthy *Dissertation on the Olympick Games* prefixed to his translation of Pindar. Though a free translation, and rather laboured in its sublimity, it has more life than most other English translations of Pindar.

Address to the Graces
(Pindar, *Olympian* 14)
Ye pow'rs o'er all the flowery meads,
Where deep Cephisus rolls his lucid tide,
 Allotted to preside,
And haunt the plains renown'd for beauteous steeds,
 Queens of Orchomenus the fair,
And sacred guardians of the ancient line
 Of Minyas divine,

Hear, O ye Graces, and regard my prayer!
  All that's sweet and pleasing here
   Mortals from your hands receive:
  Splendor ye and fame confer,
   Genius, wit, and beauty give.
  Nor, without your shining train
  Ever on the' ethereal plain
  In harmonious measures move
  The celestial choirs above:
  When the figur'd dance they lead,
  Or the nectar'd banquet spread.
  But with thrones immortal grac'd,
  And by Pythian Phoebus plac'd,
  Ordering through the bless'd abodes
  All the splendid works of gods,
  Sit the sisters in a ring,
  Round the golden-shafted king:
  And with reverential love
   Worshipping the' Olympian throne,
  The majestick brow of Jove
   With unfading honours crown.

  Aglaia, graceful virgin, hear!
  And thou, Euphrosyna, whose ear
Delighted listens to the warbled strain!
  Bright daughters of Olympian Jove,
  The best, the greatest pow'r above;
   With your illustrious presence deign
   To grace our choral song!
  Whose notes to victory's glad sound
  In wanton measures lightly bound.
   Thalia, come along!
  Come, tuneful maid! for lo! my string
  With meditated skill prepares
  In softly soothing Lydian airs
   Asopichus to sing;
Asopichus, whose speed by thee sustain'd
The wreath for his Orchomenus obtain'd.
   Go then, sportive Echo, go
   To the sable dome below,
   Proserpine's black dome, repair,
   There to Cleodemus bear
   Tidings of immortal fame:
   Tell, how in the rapid game
O'er Pisa's vale his son victorious fled;
   Tell, for thou saw'st him bear away
   The winged honours of the day;
And deck with wreaths of fame his youthful head.

'Triumphs of the Gout'
(Lucian, *Podagra* (The Gout))

Hear stubborn Virgin, fierce and strong,
    Impracticable maid!
O listen to our holy song!
    And grant thy servants aid!

Thy pow'r, imperious dame, dismays
    The monarch of the dead,
And strikes the ruler of the seas,
    And thund'ring Jove with dread.

Thee soft reposing beds delight
    And flannels warm embrace,
And bandag'd legs nor swift in flight,
    Nor victors in the race.

Thy flames the tumid ankles feel,
The finger maim'd, the burning heel,
    And toe that dreads the ground.
Thy pains unclos'd our eyelids keep,
Or grant at best tumultuous sleep,
    And slumbers never sound.

Thy cramps our limbs distort,
    Thy knots our joints invade:
Such is thy cruel sport!
    Inexorable maid!

THOMAS GRAY

(1716-1771)

Educated at Eton and Peterhouse, Cambridge, Gray spent some time
travelling in France and Italy, initially with Horace Walpole. His earlier
works, apart from some translations from Latin, include a good deal of Latin
poetry. His fame was established with the *Elegy written in a Country Churchyard* of
1750; but when the *Progress of Poesy* and the *Bard* were published in 1757,
Johnson attributes to contemporaries his own bafflement and displeasure at
the Pindaric rambling of Gray's style. Like so many translators, Gray had
learnt the wrong things from Pindar: his sublimity without his discipline and
his (admittedly obscure) structural devices. In 1768 he became Professor of
History at Cambridge, though his studies ranged widely over Greek authors as
well. Johnson quotes Temple's description of him as 'Perhaps the most learned
man in Europe'.

Music
(Pindar, *Pythian* 1.5-12, altered) from *The Progress of Poesy. A Pindaric Ode*

Oh! Sovereign of the willing soul,
Parent of sweet and solemn-breathing airs,
Enchanting shell! the sullen cares,
And frantic passions hear thy soft controul.
On Thracia's hills the lord of war,
Has curb'd the fury of his car,
And drop'd the thirsty lance at thy command.
Perching on the scept'red hand
Of Jove, thy magic lulls the feather'd king
With ruffled plumes, and flagging wing:
Quench'd in dark clouds of slumber lie
The terror of his beak, and lightnings of his eye.

FRANCIS FAWKES

(1720-1777)

Born near Doncaster, and educated at Jesus College, Cambridge, Fawkes was ordained, and became curate of Bramham and then Croydon, and then vicar of Orpington. His talents as a translator were regarded as the best since Pope, and his translations include two pieces from Gavin Douglas besides his wide range of classical versions: Anacreon, Sappho, Bion, Moschus and Musaeus (1760), Theocritus (1767), in the Preface to which he feels obliged to defend himself for undertaking a task already done by Creech, and to castigate those who 'having no ear for poetical numbers, are better pleased with the rough music of the last age than the refined harmony of this'; and in 1767 he contributed some Horatian versions to the joint translation put out by Duncombe. The last labour of his career was the translation of Apollonius Rhodius, on which he was working in 1772; it was not finished before his death, and was published in 1780.

Jealousy
(Sappho 31 L-P)

More happy than the gods is he,
Who, soft-reclining, sits by thee;
His ears thy pleasing tale beguiles,
His eyes thy sweetly-dimpled smiles.

This, this, alas! alarm'd my breast,
And robb'd me of my golden rest:
While gazing on thy charms I hung,
My voice died faltering on my tongue.

With subtle flames my bosom glows,
Quick through each vein the poison flows:
Dark, dimming mists my eyes surround;
My ears with hollow murmurs sound.

My limbs with dewy chillness freeze,
On my whole frame pale tremblings seize,
And, losing colour, sense, and breath,
I seem quite languishing in death.

Silence in death
(Sappho 55 L-P)

Whene'er the Fates resume thy breath,
    No bright reversion shalt thou gain,
Unnotic'd thou shalt sink in death,
    Nor even thy memory remain:
For thy rude hand ne'er pluck'd the lovely rose
Which on the mountain of Pieria blows.

To Pluto's mansions shalt thou go,
    The stern inexorable king,
Among th' ignoble shades below
    A vain, ignoble thing;
While honour'd Sappho's Muse-embellish'd name
Shall flourish in eternity of fame.

JOSEPH WARTON
(1722-1800)

The Reverend Joseph Warton was the elder son of Thomas Warton, and brother of Thomas Warton junior, both of them Professors of Poetry at Oxford. He was educated at Winchester, where he became a friend of William Collins, and at Oriel College, Oxford; his first publication was a volume entitled *Ode on reading West's Pindar*. He edited Vergil and translated the *Eclogues* and *Georgics*, which he issued with Pitt's translation of the *Aeneid*; but more important are the essays prefaced to the translation, on pastoral poetry. His major work, the essay *On the Genius and Writings of Pope*, gave a new direction and impetus to literary criticism; he later edited Pope and Dryden.

Shepherds' lives
(Vergil, *Georgics* 3.339-59)

Why should I sing of Lybia's artless swains;
Her scattered cottages, and trackless plains?

By day, by night, without a destin'd home,
For many a month their flocks all lonely roam;
So vast th' unbounded solitude appears.
While, with his flock, his all the shepherd bears:
His arms, his household gods, his homely shed,
His Cretan darts, and dogs of Sparta bred.
So Rome's brave sons, beneath th' oppressive load
Of arms and baggage, trace the destin'd road;
And while he ne'er suspects th' impending blow,
Sudden unfurl their standards on the foe.
Not so in Scythia shepherds tend their sheep;
Where sad Moeotis spreads his sable deep:
Thick yellow sands where Ister's torrents roll,
And Rhodope returns to meet the pole.
Their flocks they stall; for o'er th' unfruitful scene,
Nor fields, nor trees are cloath'd in lively green.
One waste of snow the joyless landscape lies,
Seven ells in height the ridgy drifts arise.
There still the bitter blasts of winter dwell;
Nor the sun's rays the paly shade dispel,
When first he climbs his noon-tide course, or laves
His headlong car in ocean's purple waves.

5. Grecians and Romantics

MARK AKENSIDE

(1721-1770)

Born in Newcastle into a Dissenting family, Akenside displayed his poetical talents early, and his first success after being sent to the University of Edinburgh was the publication of *The Pleasures of Imagination* in 1744, for which he received, on Pope's commendation, an exceptionally large advance from Robert Dodsley.

His interests had already turned from theology to medicine, in which he made a distinguished career, though that did not prevent him from acquiring a great deal of learning in other fields. His Croonian lectures of 1756 to the Royal College of Physicians were on the curiously inappropriate subject of The Revival of Learning. He is satirised in the person of the doctor in *Peregrine Pickle*, forever quoting snippets of Greek poetry. His learning however had remarkably little direct influence on his poetry, except the opulent *Hymn to the Naiads*.

Progressive and even anarchic in temperament, he is reported to have been conspicuously unpleasant to his poorer patients at Christ's and St Thomas' Hospitals, where he worked from 1759.

Music
(Pindar, *Pythian* 1.1-12, adapted) from *The Hymn to the Naiads*

>   . . . those powerful strings
> That charm the mind of gods, that fill the courts
> Of wide Olympus with oblivion sweet
> Of evils, with immortal rest from cares,
> Assuage the terrors of the throne of Jove,
> And quench the formidable thunderbolt
> Of unrelenting fire. With slacken'd wings,
> While now the solemn concert breathes around,
> Incumbent o'er the sceptre of his lord
> Sleeps the stern eagle, by the number'd notes
> Possess'd, and satiate with the melting tone,
> Sovereign of birds. The furious god of war
> His darts forgetting, and the winged wheels
> That bear him vengeful o'er th' embattled plain,

Relents, and soothes his own fierce heat to ease,
Most welcome ease. The sire of gods and men
In that great moment of divine delight,
Looks down on all that live; and whatsoe'er
He loves not, o'er the peopled earth and o'er
The interminated ocean, he beholds
Cursed with abhorrence by his doom severe,
And troubled at the sound.

CHRISTOPHER SMART

(1722-1771)

Born in Kent, Smart was educated at Pembroke Hall, Cambridge, of which he became a Fellow in 1745. Here he had a share with Thomas Warton and George Colman in *The Student, or the Oxford and Cambridge Monthly Miscellany*, and later on other magazines. He was also friendly with Bonnell Thornton and with other members of the Nonsense Club, and produced a fair quantity of light and occasional verse, much of it in elegant Latin. His prose version of Horace appeared in 1756, and was a great commercial success. His jaunty verse Horace appeared in 1767, two years after a translation of Phaedrus in the same mould. He died insane.

The vanity of acquisition
(Horace, *Odes* 2.18)

Gold or iv'ry's not intended
    For this little house of mine,
Nor Hymettian arches, bended
    On rich Afric pillars shine.
For a court I've no ambition,
    As not Attalus his heir,
Nor make damsels of condition
    Spin me purple for my wear.
But for truth and wit respected,
    I possess a copious vein,
So that rich men have affected
    To be number'd of my train.
With my Sabine field contented,
    Fortune shall be dunn'd no more;
Nor my gen'rous friend tormented
    To augment my little store.
One day by the next's abolish'd,
    Moons increase but to decay;
You place marbles to be polish'd
    Ev'n upon your dying day.

Death unheeding, though infirmer
   On the sea your buildings rise,
While the Baian billows murmur,
   That the land will not suffice.
What though more and more incroaching,
   On new boundaries you press,
And in avarice approaching,
   Your poor neighbour dispossess;
The griev'd hind his gods displaces,
   In his bosom to convey,
And with dirty ruddy faces
   Boys and wife are driven away.
Yet no palace ground and spacious
   Does more sure its lord receive,
Than the seat of death rapacious,
   Whence the rich have no reprieve.
Each alike to all is equal,
   Whither would your views extend?
Kings and peasants in the sequel
   To the destin'd grave descend.
There, though brib'd, the guard infernal
   Would not shrewd Prometheus free;
There are held in chains eternal
   Tantalus, and such as he.
There the poor have consolation
   For their hard laborious lot;
Death attends each rank and station,
   Whether he is call'd or not.

WILLIAM LEWIS

(fl. 1773)

The obscure William Lewis deserves a place here for the comments, highly characteristic of his period, which he makes on Statius to whom he devoted his energy as a translator: 'The characteristic of Statius, as an heroic poet, is an amazing boldness in imagery and diction. To say he always reaches the pure sublime, would be running counter to the opinion of the best critics, and consequently presumptuous and dogmatical. But to affirm he never does, would be equally unjust and unreasonable. The present passage is of the mixed kind, and, at the same time that it borders upon fustian, is not wholly destitute of sublimity. I will only add, that the most celebrated instance of this kind in Homer or Virgil, when reduced to the standard of reason, will seem a pleasing extravagance, and elaborate piece of nonsense.' The combination of deference to received opinion with an evident fondness for the untamed and wild epitomises the turning point from classicism to romanticism.

Mars
(Statius, *Thebaid* 3.420-39)

Meanwhile, involv'd in shades of deepest night,
The god of war renews his airy flight.
His rattling armour thunders o'er the sky,
The subject hills and vales in turn reply.
Where e'er he moves, he kindles vengeful fires,
And love of war, and thirst of blood inspires.
Stern wrath and rage adjust his coursers' manes,
And fear array'd in armour, guides the reins.
Commission'd by the god, before the car
Fame flies, and sounds aloud the charge of war;
And, by the breathing coursers wafted, springs
Aloft in air, and shakes her clatt'ring wings.
Oft premature the watchful goddess flies,
Feigns things undone, and mingles truth with lies.
For Mars, and his impatient charioteer
With goads provoke her, and the Scythian spear.
Thus when dismiss'd from their Aeolian caves,
The winds invade the calm Aegean waves,
The lord of ocean follows; while around
The tumult thickens, and the deeps resound.
Then storms and show'rs collected from afar,
Enclose the god, and rage around his car.
Scarce can the Cyclades the shock sustain,
And Delos, fearing lest she float again,
Invokes the pow'r, by whose auspicious smiles
She stands connected with her sister-isles.

WILLIAM HAY

(1695-1755)

Hay was educated at Christ Church, Oxford, and proceeded to the Middle
Temple. Thereafter he travelled abroad; he became a magistrate in the 1720s,
and MP for Seaford in 1734, in which post he remained. He is the author of
numerous moral and political works; the translation of Martial is the last of his
works, and was published in the year of his death. It captures peculiarly well
the man-about-townish quality of Martial's epigrams, giving them added bite
by updating all the characters and allusions.

Neighbourliness
(Martial, *Epigrams* 1.86)

Sir Formal's house adjoining stands:
We from our windows may shake hands.

Blest situation! you will say.
Do not you envy me, I pray,
Who may, at early hours and late,
Enjoy a friend so intimate?
Sir Formal is to me as near
As is the Consul at Algier.
So far from intimacy is it,
We seldom speak, we never visit.
In the whole town no soul can be
So near, and yet so far from me.
'Tis time for him or me to start;
We cannot meet, unless we part.
Would you Sir Formal keep aloof?
Take lodgings under the same roof.

Strange transactions
(Martial, *Epigrams* 5.61)

Who is that beau? pray tell me, for you know,
Still near your wife? pray tell me, who's that beau,
Still pouring nonsense in her glowing ear;
With his right elbow leaning on her chair;
Who on his hand the sparkling brilliant wears –
His hand almost as soft and white as hers?
'That man is, though he now so gay appears,
A lawyer who transacts my wife's affairs.'
A lawyer that! I vow, you make me stare!
Surely Lord Foppington's turn'd practiser.
A lawyer that! you are a precious 'squire,
Fit for a Gomez in the Spanish Fryar!
Your wife's affairs! believe me, one so fine
Transacts not her affairs, so much as thine.

The suitors
(Martial, *Epigrams* 6.8)

Welsh judges two, four military men,
Seven noisy lawyers, Oxford scholars ten,
Were of an old man's daughter in pursuit.
Soon the curmudgeon ended the dispute,
By giving her unto a thriving grocer.
What think you? did he play the fool, or no, sir?

Ostentation
(Martial, *Epigrams* 8.6)

In leathern jack to drink much less I hate,
Than in Sir William's antique set of plate.

He tells the gasconading pedigree,
Till the wine turns insipid too as he.
'This tumbler, in the world the oldest toy,'
Says he, 'was brought by Brute himself from Troy.
That handled cup, and which is larger far,
A present to my father from the Czar:
See how 'tis bruis'd, and the work broken off;
'T was when he flung it at Prince Menzikoff.
The other with the cover, which is less,
Was once the property of good Queen Bess:
In it she pledg'd duke d'Alençon, then gave it
To Drake, my wife's great-uncle: so we have it.
The bowl, the tankard, flagon, and the beaker,
Were my great-grandfather's, when he was Speaker.'
What pity 'tis, that plate so old and fine
Should correspond no better with the wine.

The expert
(Martial, *Epigrams* 9.35)

By these stale arts a dinner you pursue;
You trump up any tale and tell as true.
Know how the councils at the Hague incline;
What troops in Italy and on the Rhine.
A letter from the general produce,
Before the officers could have the news.
Know to an inch the rising of the Nile:
What ships are coming from each sugar isle:
What we expect from this year's preparation:
Who shall command the forces of the nation.
Leave off these tricks; and with me if you choose
To dine to-day, do so; but then, no news.

ROBERT POTTER

(1721-1804)

Born in Norfolk and educated at Emmanuel College, Cambridge, Potter took orders and returned to a curacy in Norfolk; in 1761 he became master of Scarning school, where he remained until 1789. His translation of Aeschylus – the first complete Aeschylus in English – was much admired by contemporaries, among them Beattie, though Samuel Johnson found little to praise in his work. The later Euripides is distinctly inferior; nevertheless, Potter deserves the recognition due to a pioneer and an index of changing taste.

Prometheus, chained to his rock, is visited by the daughters of Ocean
(Aeschylus, *Prometheus Vinctus* 115-92) from *Prometheus Chain'd*

Prometheus: Ah me! what sound, what softly-breathing odour
Steals on my sense? Be you immortal gods,
Or mortal men, or of th' heroic race,
Whoe'er have reach'd this wild rock's extreme cliff,
Spectators of my woes, or what your purpose,
Ye see me bound, a wretched god, abhorr'd
By Jove, and ev'ry god that treads his courts,
For my fond love to man. Ah me! again
I hear the sound of flutt'ring nigh; the air
Pants to the soft beat of light-moving wings:
All, that approaches now, is dreadful to me.

Chorus: Forbear thy fears: a friendly train
    On busy pennons flutt'ring light,
    We come, our sire not ask'd in vain,
    And reach this promontory's height.
    The clanging iron's horrid sound
    Re-echo'd through our cave profound;
And though my cheek glows with shame's crimson dye,
Thus with unsandal'd foot with winged speed I fly.

Prom: Ah me! ah me!
Ye virgin sisters, who derive your race
From fruitful Thetis, and th' embrace
Of old Oceanus, your sire, that rolls
Around the wide world his unquiet waves,
This way turn your eyes, behold
With what a chain fix'd to this rugged steep
Th' unenvied station of the rock I keep.

Cho: I see, I see; and o'er my eyes,
    Surcharg'd with sorrow's tearful rain,
    Dark'ning the misty clouds arise;
    I see thy adamantine chain;
    In its strong grasp thy limbs confin'd,
    And withering in the parching wind: •
Such the stern pow'r of heav'n's new-sceptred lord,
And law-controlling Jove's irrevocable word.

Prom: Beneath the earth,
Beneath the gulfs of Tartarus, that spread
Interminable o'er the dead,
Had his stern fury fix'd this rigid chain,
Nor gods nor men had triumph'd in my pain.

But pendent in th' ethereal air,
The pageant gratifies my ruthless foes,
That gaze, insult, and glory in my woes.

Cho: Is there a god, whose sullen soul
   Feels a stern joy in thy despair?
   Owns he not pity's soft control,
   And drops in sympathy the tear?
   All, all, save Jove; with fury driv'n
   Severe he tames the sons of heav'n;
And he will tame them, till some pow'r arise
To wrest from his strong hand the sceptre of the skies.

Prom: Yet he, e'en he,
That o'er the gods holds his despotic reign,
And fixes this disgraceful chain,
Shall need my aid, the counsels to disclose
Destructive to his honour and his throne.
But not the honied blandishment, that flows
From his alluring lips, shall aught avail;
His rigid menaces shall fail;
Nor will I make the fatal secret known,
Till his proud hands this galling chain unbind,
And his remorse sooths my indignant mind.

Cho: Bold and intrepid is thy soul,
   Fir'd with resentment's warmest glow;
   And thy free voice disdains control,
   Disdains the tort'ring curb of woe.
   My softer bosom, thrill'd with fear
   Lest heavier ills await thee here,
By milder counsels wishes thee repose:
For Jove's relentless age no tender pity knows.

Prom: Stern though he be,
And, in the pride of pow'r terrific drest,
Rears o'er insulted right his crest,
Yet gentler thoughts shall mitigate his soul,
When o'er his head this storm shall roll;
Then shall his stubborn indignation bend,
Submit to sue, and court me for a friend.

JAMES ELPHINSTON
(1721-1809)

Elphinston was born in Edinburgh, and one of his first works was an edition of the *Rambler* with the mottoes translated into English, which won him the regard of Samuel Johnson with whom he occasionally corresponded. Johnson may have admired him as an educationalist – at least for the sons of tradesmen, though not for a lettered upbringing – but he was wary of his 'inverted understanding' and had no time for his Martial, of which Burns later wrote

> O thou whom poesy abhors,
> Whom prose has turned out of doors!
> Heardst thou that groan? Proceed no further;
> 'Twas laurell'd Martial roaring murther.

It is indeed one of the aberrations of English translation, though even in 1914 H. G. Bohn could not avoid including much of it in his complete Martial because it was still accepted as *the* English Martial. Elphinston's later projects include a more or less demented attempt to reform English spelling on supposedly phonetic principles.

Farm produce
(Martial, *Epigrams* 3.47)

Where the Capenian gate her pool extends,
Where to the Phrygian parent Almo bends;
Where the Horatians verdure still the spot;
Where puny Hercules's fane is hot;
Poor Bassus drove his team, but sang no song;
Lugging the struggling stores of the blest land along.
　There coleworts might you see of noblest shoot;
There might admire each lettuce, leek, and root;
But, above all, the deobstructive beet;
Here a rich frail of fatted thrushes greet;
And here a hare, the cruel hounds could crunch;
With a sow's unwean'd babe, that bean could never munch.
　Before the car, behold no idler stray:
Yet one preceded, stuffing eggs in hay.
Was Bassus winding his glad way to town?
No; winding his glad way to his dear villa down.

Old lady
(Martial, *Epigrams* 3.93)

Alert Antiquilla, on thee
　Kind consuls three hundred have smiled:

What beauties remain, let us see,
  Of one but so lately a child.

Three hairs, and four teeth, are the dwindle
  Fell Chronus allows thy command:
Thy grasshopper-breast on a spindle
  As fine as an antling's can stand.

Thy forehead more furrows has made,
  Than any high dame in her stole:
Thy panters, unpropt, are decay'd
  To nets of Arachne's control.

Think not that I search for thy flaws;
  Too mean a pursuit to be mine!
But narrow the crocodile's jaws,
  Compared, Antiquilla, with thine.

Ravenna's brisk froglings becroke
  Less hoarse, my gruff crony, than thou;
And Adria's high hornets invoke
  A hum thou canst hardly avow.

Thine eyes are as clear as thy notes:
  Thou seest as the owl in the morn.
Thou smell'st like the lord of the goats:
  Compare of each kind is thy scorn.

But now, to descend to the stump:
  What gives an old cynic to rage,
Emaciate duck, is thy rump;
  And bony the war he must wage.

The bather will blow out his lamp,
  To thee ere he open his doors;
Then, careless of age, or of stamp,
  Admit all the bustuary whores.

Bland August thy winter we know:
  Insatiate must still be thy maw?
Ah! how can poor Hymen e'er glow,
  Where pestilence' self cannot thaw?

Thou only two hundred hast slain,
  And would'st the third century wed:
Would'st have a man, madding in vain,
  Attend thy cold ashes to bed?

Yet, wish'd he to harrow a stone,
   Who'd honour such mate as a wife?
Whom call'd Philomelus a crone,
   Who'd e'er call the love of his life?

But, scraped if thy carcase must be,
   Coricles the clinic shall strow
The couch: he alone can agree
   With thy hymenean to go.

The burner the torches shall bear,
   Before the desirable bride:
A torch can alone enter there;
   Where Pluto himself will preside.

WILLIAM COWPER

(1731-1800)

Educated at Westminster, Cowper was apprenticed to the law, but his morbidly retiring temperament unfitted him for work in a public capacity; his first attack of madness was precipitated by the prospect of employment as a clerk in the House of Lords. Thereafter he lived with the Unwin family, latterly at Olney in Buckinghamshire, where he turned to poetry at the late age of fifty. The prompting for his labours seems to have come in part from a widow, Lady Austen, who moved to the town: it was she who suggested *John Gilpin*, the Homer, and *The Task* to Cowper. He was forced to break off relations with her, due to the disapproval of Mrs Unwin, a deprivation which no doubt hastened his final collapse. The Homer went through two editions, in 1791 and 1799, the second radically altered from the first. Cowper said of his work,

> It is a maxim of much weight,
>   Worth conning o'er and o'er –
> He, who hath Homer to translate,
>   Had need do nothing more.

His other translations show something of the light-hearted and facetious quality of his contemporaries, Smart, Thornton, and Hay.

A salad
(Ps.-Vergil, *Salad* 61-118, abridged)

Close to his cottage lay a garden-ground,
With reeds and osiers sparely girt around:
Small was the spot, but lib'ral to produce;
Nor wanted aught that serves a peasant's use,

And sometimes ev'n the rich would borrow thence,
Although its tillage was his sole expense.
But oft, as from his toils abroad he ceas'd,
Home-bound by weather, or some stated feast,
His debt of culture here he duly paid,
And only left the plough to weild the spade.
He knew to give each plant the soil it needs,
To drill the ground, and cover close the seeds;
And could with ease compel the wanton rill
To turn, and wind, obedient to his will.
There flourish'd star-wort, and the branching beet,
The sorrel acid, and the mallow sweet,
The skirret, and the leek's aspiring kind,
The noxious poppy – quencher of the mind!
Salubrious sequel of a sumptuous board,
The lettuce, and the long huge-bellied gourd;
But these (for none his appetite controll'd
With stricter sway) the thrifty rustic sold
With broom-twigs neatly bound, each kind apart,
He bore them ever to the public mart:
Whence, laden still, but with a lighter load,
Of cash well-earn'd, he took his homeward road,
Expending seldom, ere he quitted Rome,
His gains, in flesh-meat for a feast at home.
There, at no cost, on onions rank and red,
Or the curl'd endive's bitter leaf, he fed:
On scallions slic'd, or with a sensual gust,
On rockets – foul provocatives of lust!
Nor even shunn'd with smarting gums to press
Nasturtium – pungent face-distorting mess!

Some such regale now also in his thought,
With hasty steps his garden-ground he sought,
There delving with his hands, he first displac'd
Four plants of garlick, large, and rooted fast;
The tender tops of parsley next he culls,
Then the old rue-bush shudders as he pulls,
And coriander last to these succeeds,
That hangs on slightest threads her trembling seeds.

Plac'd near his sprightly fire he now demands
The mortar at his sable servant's hands;
When stripping all his garlick first, he tore
Th' exterior coats, and cast them on the floor,
Then cast away with like contempt the skin,
Flimsier concealment of the cloves within.
These search'd, and perfect found, he one by one,

Rins'd, and dispos'd within the hollow stone.
Salt added, and a lump of salted cheese,
With his injected herbs he cover'd these,
And tucking with his left his tunic tight,
And seizing fast the pestle with his right,
The garlick bruising first he soon express'd,
And mixed the various juices of the rest.
He grinds, and by degrees his herbs below
Lost in each other their own pow'rs forego,
And with the cheese in compound, to the sight
Nor wholly green appear, nor wholly white.
His nostrils oft the forceful fume resent,
He curs'd full oft his dinner for its scent,
Or with wry faces, wiping as he spoke
The trickling tears, cried 'Vengeance on the smoke!'
The work proceeds: not roughly turns he now
The pestle, but in circles smooth and slow,
With cautious hand, that grudges what it spills,
Some drops of olive-oil he next instils.
Then vinegar with caution scarcely less,
And gathering to a ball the medley mess,
Last, with two fingers frugally applied,
Sweeps the small remnant from the mortar's side,
And thus complete in figure and in kind,
Obtains at length the Salad he design'd.

Journey to Brundisium
(Horace, *Satires* 1.5, abridged)

'Twas a long journey lay before us,
When I, and honest Heliodorus,
Who far in point of rhetoric
Surpasses ev'ry living Greek,
Each leaving our respective home
Together sallied forth from Rome. . . .

   Now o'er the spangled hemisphere
Diffus'd the starry train appear,
When there arose a desp'rate brawl;
The slaves and bargemen, one and all,
Rending their throats (have mercy on us)
As if they were resolv'd to stun us.
'Steer the barge this way to the shore;
I tell you we'll admit no more;
Plague! will you never be content?'
Thus a whole hour at least is spent,
While they receive the sev'ral fares,

And kick the mule into his gears.
Happy, these difficulties past,
Could we have fall'n asleep at last!
But, what with humming, croaking, biting,
Gnats, frogs, and all their plagues uniting,
These tuneful natives of the lake
Conspir'd to keep us broad awake.
Besides, to make the concert full,
Two maudlin wights, exceeding dull,
The bargeman and a passanger,
Each in his turn, essay'd an air
In honour of his absent fair.
At length the passenger, opprest
With wine, left off, and snor'd the rest.
The weary bargeman too gave o'er,
And hearing his companion snore,
Seiz'd the occasion, fix'd the barge,
Turn'd out his mule to graze at large,
And slept forgetful of his charge.
And now the sun o'er eastern hill,
Discover'd that our barge stood still;
When one, whose anger vex'd him sore,
With malice fraught, leaps quick on shore;
Plucks up a stake, with many a thwack
Assails the mule and driver's back. . . .

To Beneventum next we steer;
Where our good host by over care
In roasting thrushes lean as mice
Had almost fall'n a sacrifice.
The kitchen soon was all on fire,
And to the roof the flames aspire.
There might you see each man and master
Striving, amidst this sad disaster,
To save the supper. Then they came
With speed enough to quench the flame.
From hence we first at distance see
Th' Apulian hills, well known to me,
Parch'd by the sultry western blast;
And which we never should have past,
Had not Trivicius by the way
Receiv'd us at the close of day.
But each was forc'd at ent'ring here
To pay the tribute of a tear,
For more of smoke than fire was seen —
The hearth was pil'd with logs so green.
From hence in chaises we were carried

Miles twenty-four, and gladly tarried
At a small town, whose name my verse
(So barb'rous is it) can't rehearse,
Know it you may by many a sign,
Water is dearer far than wine. . . .

Brundusium last we reach: and there
Stop short the muse and traveller.

The Greek troops at Troy
(Homer, *Iliad* 2.453-73, 581-600, 738-600)

War won them now, war sweeter now to each
Than gales to waft them over ocean home.
As when devouring flames some forest seize
On the high mountains, splendid from afar
The blaze appears, so, moving on the plain,
The steel-clad host innumerous flash'd to heaven.
And as a multitude of fowls in flocks
Assembled various, geese, or cranes, or swans
Lithe-neck'd, long hovering o'er Cayster's banks
On wanton plumes, successive on the mead
Alight at last, and with a clang so loud
That all the hollow vale of Asius rings;
In number such from ships and tents effused,
They cover'd the Scamandrian plain; the earth
Rebellow'd to the feet of steeds and men.
They overspread Scamander's grassy vale,
Myriads, as leaves, or as the flowers of spring.
As in the hovel where the peasant milks
His kine in spring-time, when his pails are filled,
Thick clouds of humming insects on the wing
Swarm all around him, so the Greecians swarm'd
An unsumm'd multitude o'er all the plain,
Bright arm'd, high crested, and athirst for war. . . .

From hollow Lacedaemon's glen profound,
From Phare, Sparta, and from Messa, still
Resounding with the ring-dove's amorous moan,
From Brysia, from Augeia, from the rocks
Of Laas, from Amycla, Otilus,
And from the towers of Helos, at whose foot
The surf of Ocean falls, came sixty barks
With Menelaus. From the monarch's host
The royal brother ranged his own apart,
And panted for revenge of Helen's wrongs,
And of her sighs and tears. From rank to rank,

Conscious of dauntless might he pass'd, and sent
Into all hearts the fervour of his own.
    Gerenian Nestor in thrice thirty ships
Had brought his warriors; they from Pylus came,
From blythe Arene, and from Thryos, built
Fast by the fords of Alpheus, and from steep
And stately Aepy. Their confederate powers
Sent Amphigeneia, Cyparissa veiled
With broad redundance of funereal shades,
Pteleos and Helos, and of deathless fame
Dorion. In Dorion erst the Muses met
Threician Thamyris, on his return
From Eurytus, Oechalian chief, and hush'd
His song for ever; for he dared to vaunt
That he would pass in song even themselves
The Muses, daughters of Jove Aegis-arm'd.
They, therefore, by his boast incens'd, the bard
Struck blind, and from his memory dash'd severe
All traces of his once celestial strains. . . .

    Orthe, Gyrtone, Oloosson white,
Argissa and Helone; they their youth
Gave to control of Polypoetes, son
Undaunted of Pirithous, son of Jove.
Him, to Pirithous, (on the self-same day,
When he the Centaurs punish'd and pursued
Sheer to Aethicae driven from Pelion's heights
The shaggy race) Hippodamia bore.
Nor he alone them led. With him was join'd
Leonteus dauntless warrior, from the bold
Coronus sprung, who Caeneus call'd his sire.
Twice twenty ships awaited their command.
    Guneus from Cyphus twenty and two ships
Led forth; the Enienes him obey'd
And the robust Peroebi, warriors bold,
And dwellers on Dodona's wintry brow.
To these were join'd who till the pleasant fields
Where Titaresius winds; the gentle flood
Pours into Peneus all his limpid stores,
But with the silver-eddied Peneus flows
Unmixt as oil; for Stygian is his stream,
And Styx is the inviolable oath.
    Last with his forty ships, Tenthredon's son,
The active Prothous came. From the green banks
Of Peneus his Magnesians far and near
He gather'd, and from Pelion forest-crown'd.
    These were the princes and the chiefs of Greece.

The garden of Alcinous
(Homer, *Odyssey* 7.112-32)

Without the court, and to the gates adjoin'd
A spacious garden lay, fenced all around
Secure, four acres measuring complete.
There grew luxuriant many a lofty tree,
Pomegranate, pear, the apple blushing bright,
The honied fig, and unctuous olive smooth.
These fruits, nor winter's cold nor summer's heat
Fear ever, fail not, wither not, but hang
Perennial, whose unceasing zephyr breathes
Gently on all, enlarging these, and those
Maturing genial, in an endless course
Pears after pears to full dimensions swell,
Figs follow figs, grapes clust'ring grow again
Where clusters grew, and (ev'ry apple stript)
The boughs soon tempt the gath'rer as before.
There too, well-rooted, and of fruit profuse,
His vineyard grows; part, wide-extended, basks,
In the sun's beams; the arid level glows;
In part they gather, and in part they tread
The wine-press, while, before the eye, the grapes
Here put their blossom forth, there, gather fast
Their blackness. On the garden's verge extreme
Flow'rs of all hues smile all the year, arranged
With neatest art judicious, and amid
The lovely scene two fountains welling forth,
One visits, into ev'ry part diffus'd,
The garden-ground, the other soft beneath
The threshold steals into the palace-court,
Whence ev'ry citizen his vase supplies.
    Such were the ample blessings on the house
Of King Alcinous by the gods bestow'd.

WILLIAM WORDSWORTH

(1770-1850)

Wordsworth's translations are the work of his early years, and become increasingly free, through *Septimi Gades* of ?1790 to the Juvenal of *c*. 1796. The translation of the Harmodius song dates from the years between 1786 and 1791, and perhaps reflects that revolutionary enthusiasm which seized the young poet when

> 'Twas bliss in that first dawn to be alive
> But to be young was very heaven. . . .

They show little more than the early exercises of a poet finding his own way – which was to lead him to a very different kind of poetry from that of the classics.

The tyrannicides
(*Poetae Melici Graeci* 893 and 894)

–And I will bear my vengeful blade
With the myrtle boughs arrayed,
As Harmodius before,
As Aristogiton bore,
When the tyrant's breast they gored
With the myrtle-branded sword,
Gave to Triumph Freedom's cause
Gave to Athens equal laws.
Where, unnumbered with the dead,
Dear Harmodius, art thou fled?
Athens says 'tis thine to rest
In the islands of the blest,
Where Achilles swift of feet
And the brave Tydides meet.
I will bear my vengeful blade
With the myrtle boughs arrayed,
As Harmodius before,
As Aristogiton bore,
Towering mid the festal train
O'er the man Hipparchus slain,
Tyrant of his brother men;
Let thy name, Harmodius dear,
Live through heaven's eternal year;
Long as heaven and earth survive
Dear Aristogiton, live;
With the myrtle-branded sword
Ye the tyrant's bosom gored,
Gave to Triumph Freedom's cause,
Gave to Athens equal laws.

WALTER SAVAGE LANDOR

(1775-1864)

Landor was educated at Rugby School and at Trinity College, Oxford, but his ebullient disposition ensured his removal from both institutions. His first poems were published at the age of twenty; he then retired to South Wales on an allowance from his father. A bad marriage drove him abroad, and he lived abroad continuously from 1814-35. His translation from Vergil was written in 1794, though it was only published – like the Horace, in Leigh Hunt's *Examiner* – in 1841. His classical knowledge led him to compose works with a Grecian theme rather than direct imitations: his *Pericles and Aspasia* (1836) and *Hellenics* (1847) reflect the same preoccupations as the themes of the classicising painters of the generations following the rediscovery of Greek art.

The descent of Orpheus
(Vergil, *Georgics* 4.464-515)

The shell assuaged his sorrows: thee he sang,
Sweet wife! thee with him on the shore alone,
At rising dawn, at parting day, sang thee!
The mouth of Taenarus, the gates of Dis,
Groves dark with dread, he enter'd; he approacht
The Manes and their awful king, and hearts
That knew not pity yet for human prayer.
Rous'd at his song the shades of Erebus
Rose from their lowest, most remote abodes,
Faint Shades, and Spirits semblances of life;
Numberless as o'er woodland wilds the birds
That wintery evening drives or mountain storm;
Mothers and husbands, unsubstantial crests
Of high-soul'd heroes, boys, unmarried maids,
And youths on biers before their parents' eyes.
The deep black ooze and rank unsightly reed
Of slow Cocytuses unyielding pool,
And Styx confines them, flowing nine times round.
The halls and inmost Tartarus of Death
And (the blue adders twisting in their hair)
The Furies were astounded.
      On he stept,
And Cerberus held agape his triple jaws.
On stept the bard . . . Ixion's wheel stood still.
 Now past all peril, free was his return.
And now was following thro' upper air
Eurydice, when sudden madness seiz'd
The incautious lover: pardonable fault,
If those below could pardon: on the verge
Of light he stood, and on Eurydice,
Mindless of fate, alas, and soul-subdued,
Lookt back . . .
    There, Orpheus! Orpheus! there was all
Thy labor shed, there burst the dynast's bond,
And thrice arose that rumour from the lake.
 'Ah what,' she cried, 'what madness hath undone
Me, and (ah wretched!) thee, my Orpheus, too!

For lo! the cruel Fates recall me now,
Chill slumbers press my swimming eyes . . . adieu!
Night rolls intense around me as I spread
My helpless arms . . . thine, thine no more . . . to thee.'
   She spake, and (like a vapor) into air
Flew, nor beheld him as he claspt the void
And sought to speak, in vain: the ferry-guard
Now could not row him o'er the lake agen:
His wife twice lost, what could he? whither go?
What chaunt, what wailing, move the Powers of Hell?
Cold in the Stygian bark and lone was she!
   Beneath a rock o'er Strymon's flood on high
Seven months, seven long-continued months 'tis said
He breath'd his sorrows in a desart cave
And sooth'd the tiger, moved the oak, with song.
So Philomela mid the poplar shade
Bemoans her captive brood: the cruel hind
Saw them unplumed and took them; but all night
Grieves she, and sitting on the bough, runs o'er
Her wretched tale, and fills the woods with woe.

Paraphrase of Horace's Pyrrha
(Horace, *Odes* 1.5)

What slender youth perfused with fresh macassar
Wooes thee, O England, in St Stephen's bower?
For whom unlockest thou the chest that holds thy dower?

Simple as ever! Is there a deluder
Thou hast not listen'd to, thou hast not changed,
Laughing at one and all o'er whom thy fancy ranged?

The last that won thee was not overhappy,
And people found him wavering like thyself:
The little man looks less now laid upon the shelf.

While the big waves against the rock are breaking,
And small ones toss and tumble, fume and fret,
Along the sunny wall I have hung up my net.

THOMAS MOORE

(1779-1852)

Born in Dublin, Moore showed as a child his gifts for poetry and for music.
Under the new dispensation by which Catholics might attend the University,

he went to Trinity College, Dublin, where he was acquainted with the rebellious spirits in Ireland, and established the liberalism that he adhered to all his life; he also translated the poems of Anacreon, and was disappointed not to receive a prize for the production. On going to London he had more success; the work was dedicated to the Prince of Wales and published in 1800. Lord Erskine wrote:

> Oh! mourn not for Anacreon dead;
> Oh! weep not for Anacreon fled;
> The lyre still breathes he touch'd before,
> For we have one Anacreon Moore.

In 1803 he became Poet Laureate, but his *Irish Melodies* of 1807 established him as effectively the national poet of Ireland. His affection for Ireland is evident through the irony of his imitation of Horace, *Odes* 1.22. In 1819 he travelled to Venice where he met Byron; he is now perhaps best remembered for his burning of Byron's Memoirs, more than for composing his biography. His poetic reputation has not survived the competition of his contemporaries, but his range of classical interests is characteristic of the period.

The Grasshopper
(*Anacreontea* 32 Bergk)

Oh thou, of all creation blest,
Sweet insect, that delight'st to rest
Upon the wild wood's leafy tops,
To drink the dew that morning drops,
And chirp thy song with such a glee,
That happiest kings may envy thee.
Whatever decks the velvet field,
Whate'er the circling seasons yield,
Whatever buds, whatever blows,
For thee it buds, for thee it grows.
Nor yet art thou the peasant's fear,
To him thy friendly notes are dear;
For thou art mild as matin dew;
And still, when summer's flowery hue
Begins to paint the bloomy plain,
We hear thy sweet prophetic strain;
Thy sweet prophetic strain we hear,
And bless the notes and thee revere!
The Muses love thy shrilly tone;
Apollo calls thee all his own;
'Twas he who gave that voice to thee,
'Tis he who tunes thy minstrelsy.

Unworn by age's dim decline,
The fadeless blooms of youth are thine.

Melodious insect, child of earth,
In wisdom mirthful, wise in mirth;
Exempt from every weak decay,
That withers vulgar frames away;
With not a drop of blood to stain
The current of thy purer vein;
So blest an age is pass'd by thee,
Thou seem'st – a littel deity!

Why worry?
(Horace, *Odes* 2.11)

Come Y-rm-th, my boy, never trouble your brains,
    About what your old crony,
      The Emperor Boney,
Is doing or brewing on Muscovy's plains;

Nor tremble, my lad, at the state of our granaries:
    Should there come famine,
      Still plenty to cram in
You always shall have, my dear lord of the Stannaries.

Brisk let us revel, while revel we may;
For the gay bloom of fifty soon passes away,
    And then people get fat,
      And infirm, and – all that,
And a wig (I confess it) so clumsily sits,
That it frightens the little Loves out of their wits;

Thy whiskers, too, Y-rm-th! – alas, even they,
    Though so rosy they burn,
      Too quickly must turn
(What a heart-breaking change for thy whiskers!) to Grey.

Then why, my Lord Warden, oh! why should you fidget
    Your mind about matters you don't understand?
Or why should you write yourself down for an idiot,
    Because 'you', forsooth, 'have the pen in your hand!'
    Think, think how much better
    Than scribbling a letter,
    (Which both you and I
    Should avoid by the bye),
How much pleasanter 'tis to sit under the bust
    Of old Charley, my friend here, and drink like a new one;
While Charley looks sulky and frowns at me, just
    As the Ghost in the Pantomime does at Don Juan.
    To crown us, Lord Warden,
    In C-mb-rl-nd's garden

Grows plenty of monk's hood in venomous sprigs:
   While Otto of Roses
   Refreshing all noses
Shall sweetly exhale from our whiskers and wigs.

What youth of the Household will cool our Noyau
   In that streamlet delicious,
   That down 'midst the dishes,
   All full of gold fishes,
   Romantic doth flow?
   Or who will repair
   Unto M-ch-r Sq-e,
And see if the gentle Marchesa be there?
   Go – bid her haste hither,
   And let her bring with her
The newest No-Popery Sermon that's going –
Oh! let her come, with her dark tresses flowing,
All gentle and juvenile, curly and gay,
In the manner of – Ackermann's Dresses for May!

THOMAS CAMPBELL

(1777-1844)

Born and educated in Glasgow, Campbell travelled widely in Germany in
1800 and returned to London in 1801. His literary career in London is best
remembered for his edition of *Specimens of the British Poets* (1819), and for his
poem *The Pleasures of Hope*.

Evening
(Alcman fr. 89 Page)

The mountain summits sleep: glens, cliffs and caves,
   Are silent – all the black earth's reptile brood –
   The bees – the wild beasts of the mountain wood:
In depths beneath the dark red ocean's waves
   Its monsters rest, whilst wrapt in bower and spray
   Each bird is hushed that stretched its pinions to the day.

WILLIAM GIFFORD

(1756-1826)

Gifford graduated from Exeter College, Oxford, in 1782, and his first literary
productions were satirical poems, the *Baviad* (1794) and the *Maeviad* (1796); he

later became editor of the *Quarterly Review*. His gift of biting satire led him naturally to Juvenal and Persius, and he produced of the former a translation that lessens none of Juvenal's violence. His comment on Juvenal, *Satire* 10 marks him firmly as a man of his age: it 'is done with a boldness of imagery, an *awful and impressive sublimity* of style and manner, of which it would perhaps be difficult to find another example in any merely human composition'. He was an adviser of John Murray at the time when the latter took on Byron's *Childe Harold,* and Byron, despite Gifford's Tory politics, was ever eager for, and gratified by, his commendation.

Hypocrisy
(Juvenal, *Satire* 2.1-35)

O, for an eagle's wings! for I could fly
To the bleak regions of the polar sky,
Whene'er *they* make morality their theme
Who live like Bacchanals, yet Curii seem!
   Devoid of knowledge, as of worth, they thrust
In every nook some philosophic bust;
For he, amongst them, counts himself most wise,
Who most old sages of the sculptor buys
Sets most true Zenos', most Cleanthes' heads,
To guard the volumes which he – never reads.
   Trust not to outward show! In every street
Obscenity in formal garb, you meet.
And dost thou, hypocrite! our lusts arraign,
Thou! of Socratic pathics the mere drain!
Thy rough and shaggy limbs might seem design'd
The index of a fierce, and vigorous mind;
But all's so smooth below, the surgeon smiles,
'And scarcely can, for laughter, lance the piles.'
Gravely demure, in wisdom's solemn chair,
(His beetling eyebrows longer than his hair),
In silent state, the affected stoic sits,
And drops his maxims on the crowd by fits.
Yon tottering pathic, whose wan look betrays
His rank debaucheries, and more rank disease,
With patience I can bear; he braves disgrace,
Nor skulks behind a sanctimonious face:
Him may his folly, or his fate excuse –
But whip me those, who Virtue's name abuse,
And, soil'd with all the vices of the times,
Thunder damnation on their neighbours' crimes.

An inspiring master
(Persius, *Satire* 5.30-51)

When life's perplexing maze before me lay,
And error, heedless of the better way,
To straggling paths, far from the route of truth,
Woo'd, with blind confidence, my timorous youth,
I fled to you, Cornutus, pleased to rest
My hopes and fears on your Socratick breast;
Nor did you, gentle sage, the charge decline:
Then, dextrous to beguile, your steady line
Reclaim'd, I know not by what winning force,
My morals, warp'd from virtue's straighter course,
While reason press'd incumbent on my soul,
That struggled to receive the strong control,
And took, like wax, subdued by plastick skill,
The form your hand imposed – and bears it still!
  Can I forget, how many a summer's day,
Spent in your converse, stole, unmark'd away?
Or how, while listening with increased delight,
I snatch'd from feasts, the earlier hours of night?
– One time (for to your bosom still I grew)
One time of study, and of rest, we knew;
One frugal board, where, every care resign'd,
An hour of blameless mirth relax'd the mind.
  And sure our lives, which thus accordant move,
(Indulge me here, Cornutus,) clearly prove,
That both are subject to the self-same law,
And from one horoscope their fortunes draw:
And whether destiny's unerring doom,
In equal Libra, poised our days to come;
Or friendship's holy hour our fates combined,
And to the Twins, a sacred charge, assign'd;
Or Jove, benignant, broke the gloomy spell
By angry Saturn wove; – I know not well –
But sure some star there is, whose bland controul,
Subdues, to yours, the temper of my soul!

GEORGE GORDON, LORD BYRON

(1788-1824)

Bryon's first translations (from Catullus and from Euripides' *Medea*) date from
his early life. *Hints from Horace* was begun in Athens in 1811, partly in an
attempt to follow up the success of *English Bards and Scotch Reviewers*. He was at
the same time working on *Childe Harold*, which marked the turn of his interest

from classical literature *per se* to modern Greece in its diverse aspects, the inspiration of his greatest works.

Hints from Horace is the last notable attempt to reproduce the message of Horace's *Ars Poetica* until the twentieth century, and demonstrates clearly the classicist underpinning of the Romantic poet's genius. It was not published until after his death, in 1831.

Choice of words
(Horace, *Ars Poetica* 38-59) from *Hints from Horace*

Dear Authors! suit your topics to your strength,
And ponder well your subject, and its length;
Nor lift your load, before you're quite aware
What weight your shoulders will, or will not, bear.
But lucid Order, and Wit's siren voice,
Await the Poet, skilful in his choice;
With native eloquence he soars along,
Grace in his thoughts, and music in his song.
    Let Judgment teach him wisely to combine
With future parts the now omitted line:
This shall the author choose, or that reject,
Precise in style, and cautious to select;
Nor slight applause will candid pens afford
To him who furnishes a wanting word.
Then fear not, if 'tis needful, to produce
Some term unknown, or obsolete in use,
(As Pitt has furnished us a word or two,
Which Lexicographers declined to do;)
So you indeed, with care, – (but be content
To take this license rarely) – may invent.
New words find credit in these latter days,
If neatly grafted on a Gallic phrase;
What Chaucer, Spenser did, we scarce refuse
To Dryden's or to Pope's maturer Muse.
If you can add a little, say why not,
As well as William Pitt, and Walter Scott?
Since they, by force of rhyme and force of lungs,
Enriched our island's ill-united tongues;
'Tis then – and shall be – lawful to present
Reform in writing, as in Parliament.

Lesbia
(Catullus 51)

Equal to Jove that youth must be –
Greater than Jove he seems to me –
Who, free from Jealousy's alarms,

Securely views thy matchless charms.
That cheek, which ever dimpling glows,
That mouth, from whence such music flows,
To him, alike, are always known,
Reserved for him, and him alone.
Ah! Lesbia, though 'tis death to me,
I cannot choose but look on thee;
But, at the sight, my senses fly;
I needs must gaze, but, gazing, die;
Whilst trembling with a thousand fears,
Parched to the throat my tongue adheres,
My pulse beats quick, my breath heaves short,
My limbs deny their slight support,
Cold dews my pallid face o'erspread,
With deadly languor droops my head.
My ears with tingling echoes ring,
And life itself is on the wing;
My eyes refuse the cheering light,
Their orbs are veiled in starless night;
Such pangs my nature sinks beneath,
And feels a temporary death.

JOHN CAM HOBHOUSE, LORD BROUGHTON

(1786-1869)

Hobhouse was educated at Westminster and at Trinity College, Cambridge.
The translation from Horace given here was written shortly before his
departure with Lord Byron on the journey which he later recounted in his
Journey through Albania with Lord Byron (1813). He subsequently became a
radical politician, and his free translation of Juvenal provided a peg on which
to hang fierce and scurrilous pen-portraits of his contemporaries.

To Byron, on their departure for Greece
(Imitation of Horace, *Odes* 2.6)

Though we, my friend! prepare to roam
From happy Britain's native shore,
And leave the dear delights of home,
To hear the loud Atlantic roar:

Though to the distant lands we fly,
Where desolation widely reigns,
Where Tadmor's lonely ruins lie
On Syria's wild unpeopled plains:

This is my secret wish, to close
    My days in some secure retreat,
And from the toils of life repose,
    Content with my maternal seat.

Or if my follies or my fate
    Should that my own resort deny,
Then let me rent a small estate,
    Fast by the banks of lovely Wye.

Retir'd near Clongher's secret bowers,
    Oh! may that nook for life be mine,
Where honey drops from all the flowers,
    And orchard trees excel the vine!

Where lasting frosts and tempests wild
    Nor bind the earth, nor cloud the sky,
But summers long and winters mild
    The genial tepid airs supply.

Thou too, my B---n, shalt be near
    To sooth my life, my death attend;
And weep, for thou canst weep, one tear,
    To mourn the poet and the friend.

Gluttony
(Juvenal, *Satire* 11.38-55, expanded)

'In prime of manhood may I nobly die,
O'erpower'd by surfeits of my fav'rite pye;
Nor live and linger in old age, and curse
A tasteless palate or an empty purse.'
This on a full club night is Curties prayer,
Whilst waiters wonder, and the chaplains stare.
If you who saw the course which B---y ran,
Would see what other rogues and spendthrifts can,
Attend. – When empty stewards aid refuse,
They run to Britton, or some brother Jews;
Then live and eat, till all the thousands lent
On handsome premiums of twice ten per cent;
In Chalier's wines, or Jacquier's soups decay,
Or else in Simkin's sauces melt away.
At last, when frighten'd synagogues suspect,
And friends in city and at court reject,
These bankrupts bold (an honest name) repair
On Brighton Steyne to taste the country air.
There still too nice to live on boil'd and roast,

They crack live crabs and crayfish on the coast.
Depress'd and vex'd 'tis true: oblig'd to stay
One spring from town, from Opera, Park, and Play:
Nor need they blush; for shame from Britain flies
To seek the mansion of her native skies:
And Paull alone withstands Corruption's flood,
Content to be ridiculous and good.

JOHN HOOKHAM FRERE

(1769-1846)

Frere was a student and then Fellow of Caius College, Cambridge, and friend
of George Canning. He started a short-lived journal, the *Antijacobin*. His
translation of the *Frogs* seems to have been finished in 1827 but was not printed
until 1839; the other translations apparently appeared in the same year, but in
Malta. Coleridge called him one 'who of all men whom I have had the means of
knowing during my life appears to me eminently to deserve to be characterised
as *kalos kagathos*' (from Coleridge's Will). Frere's translations followed those of
T. Mitchell, which he castigated as artificial and high-flown, characterising
himself as a 'lawful and true translator'.

Cosmogony according to the birds
(Aristophanes, *Birds* 685-707)

Ye Children of Man! whose life is a span,
Protracted with sorrow from day to day,
Naked and featherless, feeble and querulous,
Sickly, calamitous creatures of clay!
Attend to the words of the Sovereign Birds
(Immortal, illustrious, lords of the air),
Who survey from on high, with a merciful eye,
Your struggles of misery, labour and care.
Whence you may learn and clearly discern
Such truths as attract your inquisitive turn;
Which is busied of late with a mighty debate,
A profound speculation about the creation,
And organical life, and chaotical strife,
With various notions of heavenly motions,
And rivers and oceans, and valleys and mountains,
And sources of fountains, and meteors on high,
And stars in the sky . . . We propose by and by
(If you'll listen and hear), to make it all clear.
And Prodicus henceforth shall pass for a dunce,
When his doubts are explain'd and expounded at once.

Before the creation of Aether and Light,
Chaos and Night together were plight,
In the dungeon of Erebus foully bedight.
Nor Ocean, or Air, or substance was there,
Or solid or rare, or figure or form,
But horrible Tartarus ruled in the storm:
    At length, in the dreary chaotical closet
Of Erebus old, was a privy deposit,
By Night the primeval in secrecy laid –
A Mystical Egg, that in silence and shade
Was brooded and hatch'd, till time came about,
And love, the delightful, in glory flew out,
In rapture and light, exulting and bright,
Sparkling and florid, with stars in his forehead,
His forehead and hair, with a flutter and flare,
As he rose in the air, triumphantly furnish'd
To range his dominions on glittering pinions,
All golden and azure, all blooming and burnish'd:
    He soon, in the murky Tartarean recesses,
With a hurricane's might, in his fiery caresses
Impregnated Chaos; and hastily snatched
To being and life, begotten and hatch'd
The primitive Birds; but the Deities all,
The celestial Lights, the terrestrial Ball,
Were later of birth, with the dwellers on earth
More tamely combined, of a temperate kind;
When chaotical mixture approach'd to a fixture.
    Our antiquity proved, it remains to be shown
That Love is our author, and master alone;
Like him we can ramble and gambol and fly
O'er ocean and earth, and aloft to the sky:
And, all the world over, we're friends to the lover,
And when other means fail, we are found to prevail,
When a Peacock or Pheasant is sent as a present.

The land of informers
(Aristophanes, *Birds* 1694-1705)

Along the Sycophantic shore,
And where the savage tribes adore
    The waters of the Clepsydra,
There dwells a nation, stern and strong,
Armed with an enormous tongue,
    Wherewith they smite and slay:

With their tongues, they reap and sow,
And gather all the fruits that grow,

The vintage and the grain;
Gorgias is their chief of pride,
And many more there be beside,
Of mickle might and main.

Good they never teach, nor show
But how to work men harm and woe,
Unrighteousness and wrong;
And hence, the custom doth arise,
When beasts are slain in sacrifice,
We sever out the tongue.

False friend
(Catullus 91)

Gellius, it never once was my design,
In all that wretched, tedious love of mine,
To treat you as a worthy man or just,
Alive to shame, susceptible of trust,
In word or act true, faithful or sincere;
But since that idol which my heart held dear
Was not your sister, niece, or near of kin,
The slight inducement of so small a sin
As broken faith to a confiding friend
Would scarce, methought, allure you to descend
From those proud heights of wickedness sublime –
Giant ambition that aspires to climb
The topmost pinnacles of human guilt:
To make the mistress of your friend a jilt
Appeared too poor a triumph. I was blind
To that perpetual relish which you find
In crimes of all degrees and every kind.

Hoist with his own petard
(Catullus 10)

Varus, whom I chanced to meet
The other evening in the street,
Engaged me there, upon the spot,
To see a mistress he had got.
She seemed, as far as I can gather,
Lively and smart, and handsome rather.
There, as we rested from our walk,
We entered into different talk –
As how much might Bithynia bring?
And had I found it a good thing?
I answered, as it was the fact,

The province had been stripped and sacked,
That there was nothing for the praetors,
And still less for us wretched creatures,
His poor companions and toad-eaters.
'At least,' says she, 'you bought some fellows
To bear your litter; for they tell us
Our only good ones come from there – '

I choose to give myself an air; –
'Why, truly with my poor estate,
The difference wasn't quite so great
Between a province, good or bad,
That where a purchase might be had,
Eight lusty fellows, straight and tall,
I shouldn't find the wherewithal
To buy them.' But it was a lie;
For not a single wretch had I:
No single cripple fit to bear
A broken bedstead or a chair.
She, like a strumpet, pert and knowing.
Said – 'Dear Catullus, I am going
To worship at Serapis' shrine:
Do lend me pray, those slaves of thine!'
I answered – 'It was idly said;
They were a purchase Cinna made
(Caius Cinna, my good friend) –
It was the same thing in the end,
Whether a purchase or a loan,
I always used them as my own;

Only the phrase was inexact;
He bought them for himself in fact.
But you have caught the general vice
Of being too correct and nice,
Over curious and precise;
And seizing with precipitation
The slight neglects of conversation.'

CHARLES BADHAM

(1780-1845)

After studying medicine in Edinburgh, Badham travelled for some time in Italy. In 1808 he published a treatise on bronchitis, and in 1812 his translation of Juvenal, which earned the censure of William Gifford. In 1827 he was appointed to the Chair of Physic at Glasgow.

A fit fate for a fool
(Catullus 17)

Colonia, dear,
That wouldst fain on thy pier
Be dancing,
And prancing,
And standest all ready,
But shrinkest through fear,
Lest the timbers unsteady
The crazy erection
Come down with a crash,
And a smash,
And a splash,
And repose in the wash,
Past all resurrection!
May Jupiter grant
Such a bridge as you want,
To stand e'en the motions
Of Jumper's devotions,
If from thence I may meet
With the exquisite treat
Of beholding a certain superlative ass,
Who's a man of my town,
Taken clean off his feet,
And like rubbish shot down,
To congenial ooze in the stinking morass.
The inanimate gaby
Knows less than a baby,
Sufficiently old
For its daddy to hold
In the utmost alarm
While it sleeps on his arm.
There's a bride
That is tied
To this nincompoop fellow;
A neat little thing
In her bloomiest spring,
As soft as a kid,
To be guarded and hid
Like grapes that are mellow.
But he's blind to the risk,
Lets her gambol and frisk,
And cares not a groat,
In his helplessness sunk,
Like a half-rotten trunk
Lying felled in a moat.
If she didn't exist,

She'd be just as much missed;
For the lout's deaf and blind,
Hasn't made up his mind
Who himself is, or what,
Or whether, in fact, he be or be not.

I should like from your bridge just to cant off the log,
For the chance that his rapid descent to the bog
   Might his lethargy jog,
   And the sloth of his mind,
   Being left there behind,
   In the quagmire should stay,
As the mule leaves his shoe in the glutinous clay.

LEIGH HUNT

(1784-1859)

Educated at Christ's Hospital, Hunt began to write poetry early, and from 1808 he spent thirteen years as editor of *The Examiner*, which became a focus of liberal opinion of the time, and in which many of Hunt's translations and poems appeared. In 1811 he was imprisoned for publishing an article insulting to the Prince Regent; his visitors included Tom Moore, Byron and Shelley. In 1821 he joined Byron and Shelley in Italy, in the hope of founding a new magazine. When Shelley was drowned, good relations between Byron and Hunt collapsed, partly under the strain of the importunities of the penniless Hunt. He returned to London to further literary journalism, including more translations, and to increasing ill-health. In 1847 a pension was secured for him by the intercession of Carlyle; other benefactors included Dickens. His importance as a catalyst of literary men is greater than his original works, which have been overshadowed by those of his greater contemporaries, notably his protégé Keats.

Drinking
(Anacreon, *Ode* 21 Bergk)

The tippling earth drinks up the dew,
The trees, O tippling earth, drink you;
Neptune drinks air at every motion,
And Sol drinks Neptune like a potion:
Till madam Luna, for a light,
Drinks up old Sol himself at night!
Why then d'ye hinder me from drinking,
When Heav'n itself's my way of thinking?

Hylas and the Water Nymphs
(Theocritus, *Idyll* 13.39-51)

And straight he was aware
Of water in a hollow place, low down,
Where the thick sward shone with blue celandine,
And bright green maiden-hair, still dry in dew,
And parsley rich. And at that hour it chanced
The nymphs unseen were dancing in the fount –
The sleepless nymphs, reverenced of housing men,
Winning Eunica; Malis, apple-cheeked;
And, like a night-bedewed rose, Nichea.
Down stepped the boy, in haste to give his urn
Its fill, and pushed it in the fount; when, lo!
Fair hands were on him – fair, and very fast;
For all the gentle souls that haunted there
Were drawn in love's sweet yearning tow'rds the boy;
And so he dropped within the darksome well –
Dropped like a star, that, on a summer eve,
Slides in ethereal beauty to the sea.

Attis
(Catullus 63)

Atys o'er the distant waters, driving in his rapid bark,
Soon with foot of wild impatience touched the Phrygian forest dark,
Where amid the awful shades possessed by mighty Cybele,
In his zealous frenzy blind,
And wand'ring in his hapless mind,
With flinty knife he gave to earth the weights that stamp virility.
Then as the widowed being saw its wretched limbs bereft of man,
And the unaccustomed blood that on the ground pollution ran,
With snowy hand it snatched in haste the timbrel's airy round on high
That opens with the trumpet's blast thy rites, Maternal Mystery;
And upon its whirling fingers, while the hollow parchment rung,
Thus in outcry tremulous to its wild companions sung:–

'Now come along, come along with me,
Worshippers of Cybele,
To the lofty groves of the deity!
Ye vagabond herds that bear the name
Of the Dindymenian dame!
Who seeking strange lands, like the banished of home,
With Atys, with Atys distractedly roam;
Who your limbs have unmanned in a desperate hour
With a frantic disdain of the Cyprian's power;
Who have carried my sect through the dreadful salt sea,
Rouse, rouse your wild spirits careeringly!

No delay, no delay,
But together away,
And follow me up to the dame all-compelling,
To her high Phrygian groves and her dark Phrygian dwelling,
Where the cymbals they clash, and the drums they resound,
And the Phrygian's curved pipe pours its moaning around,
Where the ivy-crowned priestesses toss with their brows,
And send their shrill howl through the deity's house,
Where they shriek, and they scour, and they madden about, –
'Tis there we go bounding in mystical rout.'

No sooner had spoken
This voice half-broken,
When suddenly from quivering tongues arose the universal cry,
The timbrels with a boom resound, the cymbals with a clash reply,
And up the verdant Ida with a quickened step the chorus flew,
While Atys with the timbrel's smite the terrible procession drew;
Raging, panting, wild, and witless, through the sullen shades it broke,
Like the fierce unconquered heifer bursting from her galling yoke;
And on pursue the sacred crew, till at the door of Cybele,
Faint and fasting, down they sink in pale immovability:
The heavy sleep, – the heavy sleep – grows o'er their failing eyes,
And locked in dead repose the rabid frenzy lies.

But when the Sun looked out with eyes of light
Round the firm earth, wild seas, and skies of morning white,
Scaring the lingering shades
With echo-footed steeds,
Sleep sped in flight from Atys, hurrying
To his Pasithea's arms on tremulous wing;
And the poor dreamer woke, oppressed with sadness,
To memory woke and to collected madness –
Struck with its loss, with what it was, and where,
Back trod the wretched being in despair
To the seashore, and stretching forth its eye
O'er the wide waste of waters and of sky
Thus to its country cried with tears of misery:–

'My country, oh my country, parent state,
Whom, like a very slave and runagate,
Wretch that I am, I left for wilds like these,
This wilderness of snow and matted trees,
To house with shivering beasts and learn their wants,
A fierce intruder on their sullen haunts –
Where shall I fancy thee? Where cheat mine eye
With tracking out thy quarter in the sky?
Fain, while my wits a little space are free,
Would my poor eye-balls strain their points on thee!
Am I then torn from home and far away?

Doomed through these woods to trample, day by day,
Far from my kindred, friends, and native soil,
The mall, the race, and wrestlers bright with oil?
Ah, wretch, bewail, bewail; and think for this
On all thy past variety of bliss!
I was the charm of life, the social spring,
First in the race and brightest in the ring;
Warm with the stir of welcome was my home,
And when I rose betimes my friends would come
Smiling and pressing in officious scores,
Thick as the flowers that hang at lovers' doors.
And shall I then a ministring madman be
To angry gods, a howling devotee,
A slave to bear what never senses can,
Half of myself, sexless, a sterile man?
And must I feel, with never-varied woes,
Th' o'erhanging winter of these mountain snows,
Skulking through ghastly woods for evermore,
Like the lean stag or the brute vagrant boar?
Ah me, ah me, already I repent;
E'en now, e'en now I feel my shame and punishment!'

As thus with rosy lips the wretch grew loud,
Startling the ears of heaven's imperial crowd,
The Mighty Mistress o'er her lion yoke
Bowed in her wrath; and loosening, as she spoke,
The left-hand savage, scatterer of herds,
Roused his fell nature with impetuous words:–
'Fly, ruffian, fly, indignant and amain,
And scare this being who resists my reign,
Back to the horror-breathing woods again.
Lash thee, and fly, and shake with sinewy might
Thine ireful hair, and as at dead of night
Fill the wide echoes with rebellowing fright.'

Threatening she spoke, and loosed the vengeance dire,
Who, gathering all his rage and glaring fire,
Starts with a roar and scours beneath her eyes,
Scattering the splintered bushes as he flies.
Down by the sea he spies the wretch at last
And springs precipitous:– the wretch as fast
Flies raving back into his living grave,
And there for ever dwells, a savage and a slave.

O Goddess! Mistress! Cybele! dread name!
O mighty power! O Dindymenian dame!
Far from my home thy visitations be:
Drive others mad, not me:
Drive others into impulse wild and fierce insanity!

THOMAS LOVE PEACOCK
(1785-1866)

Peacock was born at Weymouth and was, for the most part, privately educated, acquiring a knowledge of French and Italian as well as the classical languages. His first poems were published in 1804 and 1806. In 1812 he was introduced to Shelley, after which he turned his hand to the prose satirical romances for which he is best remembered. He continued to write verse, and the influence of Shelley on *Rhododaphne* is particularly apparent. In 1819 he entered the service of the East India Company, with whom he remained for most of his life. In his prose works he often quotes Aristophanes, clearly a favourite author, but his satirical bent is overlaid in his poetry by a sentimental melancholy quite at odds with it but perhaps necessary to him as a counterweight. His few classical translations cast the authors in the same mould.

Youth and Age
(Euripides, *Heracles Furens* 637ff.)

To me the hours of youth are dear,
In transient light that flow:
But age is heavy, cold, and drear,
As winters rocks of snow.
Already on my brows I feel
His grasp of ice and fangs of steel,
Dimming the visual radiance pale,
That soon eternal night shall veil.
Oh! not for all the gold that flings,
Through domes of Oriental kings,
Its mingled splendour, falsely bright,
Would I resign youth's lovelier light.
For whether wealth its path illume,
Or toil and poverty depress,
The days of youth are days of bloom,
And health, and hope, and loveliness.
Oh! were the ruthless demon, Age
Involved by Jove's tempestuous rage,
And fast and far to ruin driven,
Beyond the flaming bounds of heaven,
Or whelmed where arctic winter broods
O'er Ocean's frozen solitudes,
So never more to haunt again
The cities and the homes of men.

Yet, were the gods the friends of worth,
Of justice, and of truth,
The virtuous and the wise on earth

Should find a second youth.
Then would true glory shine unfurled,
A light to guide and guard the world,
If, not in vain with time at strife,
The good ran twice the race of life,
While vice, to one brief course confined,
Should wake no more to curse mankind.
Experience then might rightly trace
The lines that part the good and base,
As sailors read the stars of night,
Where shoreless billows murmuring roll,
And guide by their unerring light
The vessel to its distant goal.
But, since no signs from Jove declare
That earthly virtue claims his care;
Since folly, vice, and falsehood prove
As many marks of heavenly love;
The life of man in darkness flies;
The thirst of truth and wisdom dies;
And love and beauty bow the knee
To gold's supreme divinity.

GEORGE LAMB

(1784-1834)

Educated at Eton and Trinity College, Cambridge, Lamb contributed to the *Edinburgh Review*, and as a result was satirised by Byron – who later admitted the unfairness of the criticism – in *English Bards and Scotch Reviewers*. In 1815 he managed the Drury Lane Theatre with Byron and Douglas Kinnaird. Thomas Moore was also one of his circle. In 1819 he was elected to Parliament; and his translation of Catullus appeared in 1821, to be attacked in *Blackwood's Magazine* for its 'drivelling vapidity'. The criticism, which is confined to the romantic poems of Catullus, tells us as much about the sensibility of the reviewer and its limitations as about Lamb's translation, which is in fact at its best in the humorous poems.

Searching for a friend
(Catullus 55)

Oh! tell me, dear Friend, if it can be revealed,
In what dark abode you are lying concealed;
    For I vainly have traversed of late
The Campus, the Libraries all, and above
The Circus, the Temple of thundering Jove,
    And the Gardens of Pompey the great.

I questioned the damsels that roamed through the place,
Whenever I met any fair one whose face
   Was bedecked in contentment and smiles;
'Restore me, Camerius!' I confident cried, –
'Restore me, Camerius! nor venture to hide
   My friend with your profligate wiles.'

Then one of them laughing in wantonness said,
As she drew down her vest and her bosom displayed –
   'Hidden here in these roses he lies:
But ah! 'twere a labour Herculean to tear
Your friend from that nest; for while revelling there,
   He all friendship will proudly despise.'

Come, say where you are, whither going, I pray,
And boldly declare it in face of the day.
   If some snow-bosomed darling employs
Your moments in bliss, you by secrecy blight
The fruits of your love; for 'tis love's chief delight
   To converse and to boast of its joys.

Or secret be still, if your pleasure it be:
But yet, oh, preserve, I entreat you, for me
   As of old in your friendship a place.
For if I were Talus, the guardian of Crete,
Or rode I the winds upon Pegasus fleet,
   Or were Ladas, the first in the race,

Or could I the sandals of Perseus obtain,
The speed wherewith Rhesus rushed over the plain,
   When he urged on his horses of snow,
The force and the lightness of all living things
That gods ever gifted with swiftness or wings
   Of the hurricane winds when they blow,

All these might be joined in my body alone;
Yet wearied and faint in each sinew and bone,
   Every nerve, every limb, I should be;
And failing and sinking, exhausted and lame,
Would languor consume all the strength of my frame,
   O Camerius, in searching for thee.

PERCY BYSSHE SHELLEY

(1792-1822)

Shelley learnt his rebellious style from his sufferings at Eton, and from his
expulsion from Oxford for his pamphlet on *The Necessity of Atheism*. In 1816 he

met Byron while travelling in Switzerland, and in 1818 he and his wife Mary moved to Italy where he lived until his death. It was in these years that he produced his greatest works, including *Prometheus Unbound* but also his prose translation of Plato's *Symposium*, the first English translation of that work. His translations from classical and other poetry also date from the last five years of his life, and were written, as he tells us, in periods when he found himself incapable of original composition. His ability to immerse himself in another man's writings is an example of Keatsian 'negative capability'; these are not creative translations, though the *Hymn to Hermes* brings out all the latent humour of the original. The aim of the *Symposium* translation was rather different: Plato was to alter men's minds; but a kind of timidity kept Shelley from attempting to convey the message of the greater Greek poets in verse.

Mercury as a baby
(*Homeric Hymn* 4.17-62)

The babe was born at the first peep of day;
   He began playing on the lyre at noon,
And the same evening did he steal away
   Apollo's herds; – the fourth day of the moon
On which him bore the venerable May,
   From her immortal limbs he leaped full soon,
Nor long could in the sacred cradle keep,
But out to seek Apollo's herds would creep.

Out of the lofty cavern wandering
   He found a tortoise, and cried out – 'A treasure!'
(For Mercury first made the tortoise sing)
   The beast before the portal at his leisure
The flowery herbage was depasturing,
   Moving his feet in a deliberate measure
Over the turf. Jove's profitable son
Eying him laughed, and laughing thus begun:–

'A useful godsend are you to me now,
   King of the dance, companion of the feast,
Lovely in all your nature! Welcome, you
   Excellent plaything! Where, sweet mountain-beast,
Got you that speckled shell? Thus much I know,
   You must come home with me and be my guest;
You will give joy to me, and I will do
All that is in my power to honour you.

'Better to be at home than out of door,
   So come with me; and though it has been said
That you alive defend from magic power,
   I know you will sing sweetly when you're dead.'
Thus having spoken, the quaint infant bore,
   Lifting it from the grass on which it fed

And grasping it in his delighted hold,
His treasured prize into the cavern old.

Then scooping with a chisel of gray steel,
    He bored the life and soul out of the beast. –
Not swifter a swift thought of woe or weal
    Darts through the tumult of a human breast
Which thronging cares annoy – not swifter wheel
    The flashes of its torture and unrest
Out of the dizzy eyes – than Maia's son
All that he did devise hath featly done . . .

    And through the tortoise's hard stony skin
At proper distances small holes he made,
    And fastened the cut stems of reeds within,
And with a piece of leather overlaid
    The open space and fixed the cubits in,
Fitting the bridge to both, and stretched o'er all
Symphonious cords of sheep-gut rhythmical.

When he had wrought the lovely instrument,
    He tried the chords, and made division meet,
Preluding with the plectrum, and there went
    Up from beneath his hand a tumult sweet
Of mighty sounds, and from his lips he sent
    A strain of unpremeditated wit
Joyous and wild and wanton – such you may
Hear among revellers on a holiday.

He sung how Jove and May of the bright sandal
    Dallied in love not quite legitimate;
And his own birth, still scoffing at the scandal,
    And naming his own name, did celebrate;
His mother's cave and servant maids he planned all
    In plastic verse, her household stuff and state,
Perennial pot, trippet, and brazen pan, –
But singing, he conceived another plan . . .

Cyclopean philosophy
(Euripides, *Cyclops* 356-67)

Cyclops: Wealth, my good fellow, is the wise man's god,
All other things are a pretence and boast.
What are my father's ocean promontories,
The sacred rocks whereon he dwells, to me?
Stranger, I laugh to scorn Jove's thunderbolt,
I know not that his strength is more than mine.
As to the rest I care not. – When he pours

Rain from above, I have a close pavilion
Under this rock, in which I lie supine,
Feasting on a roast calf or some wild beast,
And drinking pans of milk, and gloriously
Emulating the thunder of high heaven.
And when the Thracian wind pours down the snow,
I wrap my body in the skins of beasts,
Kindle a fire, and bid the snow whirl on.
The earth, by force, whether it will or no,
Bringing forth grass, fattens my flocks and herds,
Which, to what other god but to myself
And this great belly, first of deities,
Should I be bound to sacrifice? I well know
The wise man's only Jupiter is this,
To eat and drink during his little day,
And give himself no care. And as for those
Who complicate with laws the life of man,
I freely give them tears for their reward.
I will not cheat my soul of its delight,
Or hesitate in dining upon you:–
And that I may be quit of all demands,
These are my hospitable gifts; – fierce fire
And yon ancestral cauldron, which o'er-bubbling
Shall finely cook your miserable flesh.
Creep in! –

Lament for Adonis
(Bion 1.1-35)

I mourn Adonis dead – loveliest Adonis –
Dead, dead Adonis – and the Loves lament.
Sleep no more, Venus, wrapped in purple woof –
Wake violet-stoled queen, and weave the crown
Of death, – 'tis Misery calls, – for he is dead.

The lovely one lies wounded in the mountains,
His white thigh struck with the white tooth; he scarce
Yet breathes; and Venus hangs in agony there.
The dark blood wanders o'er his snowy limbs,
His eyes beneath their lids are lustreless,
The rose has fled from his wan lips, and there
That kiss is dead, which Venus gathers yet.

A deep, deep wound Adonis . . .
A deeper Venus bears upon her heart.
See, his beloved dogs are gathering round –
The Oread nymphs are weeping – Aphrodite
With hair unbound is wandering through the woods,

'Wildered, ungirt, unsandalled – the thorns pierce
Her hastening feet and drink her sacred blood.
Bitterly screaming out, she is driven on
Through the long vales; and her Assyrian boy,
Her love, her husband, calls – the purple blood
From his struck thigh stains her white navel now,
Her bosom, and her neck before like snow.

Alas for Cytherea – the Loves mourn –
The lovely, the beloved is gone! – and now
Her sacred beauty vanishes away.
For Venus while Adonis lived was fair –
Alas! her loveliness is dead with him.
The oaks and mountains cry, Ai! ai! Adonis!
The springs their waters change to tears and weep –
The flowers are withered up with grief . . .

6. The Victorians

ELIZABETH BARRETT BROWNING
(1806-1861)

An infant prodigy, Elizabeth Barrett was reading Homer in the original at the age of eight, and she composed at the age of thirteen an epic on the Battle of Marathon which was published the following year. Her health was delicate but this did not prevent the spread of her fame. She met Robert Browning on his Italian tour in the 1840s, and they were married in 1846. Her major works were written in the Casa Guidi in Florence, including the revised version of her translation of Aeschylus' *Prometheus*, first published in 1833. Her essay on the Greek Christian poets, containing numerous translations, was not published until after her death, in 1863.

Love
(Euripides, *Trojan Women* 841-59)

Love, Love, who once didst pass the Dardan portals,
    Because of Heavenly passion!
Who once didst lift up Troy in exaltation,
To mingle in thy bond the high Immortals! –
    Love, turned from his own name
      To Zeus's shame,
    Can help no more at all.
And Eos' self, the fair, white-steeded Morning, –
Her light which blesses other lands, returning,
    Has changed to a gloomy pall!
She looked across the land with eyes of amber, –
    She saw the city's fall, –
    She, who, in pure embraces,
Had held there, in the hymeneal chamber,
Her children's father, bright Tithonus old,
Whom the four steeds with starry brows and paces
Bore on, snatched upward, on the car of gold,
And with him, all the land's full hope of joy!
The love-charms of the gods are vain for Troy.

The daughters of Pandarus
(Homer, *Odyssey* 20.66-78)

And so these daughters fair of Pandarus,
The whirlwinds took. The gods had slain their kin:
They were left orphans in their father's house.
And Aphrodite came to comfort them
With incense, luscious honey and fragrant wine;
And Heré gave them beauty of face and soul
Beyond all women; purest Artemis
Endowed them with her stature and white grace;
And Pallas taught their hands to flash along
Her famous looms. Then, bright with deity,
Toward far Olympus, Aphrodite went
To ask of Zeus (who has his thunder-joys
And his full knowledge of man's mingled fate)
How best to crown those other gifts with love
And worthy marriage: but, what time she went,
The ravishing Harpie snatched the maids away,
And gave them up, for all their loving eyes,
To serve the Furies who hate constantly.

Prometheus' gifts to man
(Aeschylus, *Prometheus Vinctus* 436-71)

Prometheus: Beseech you, think not I am silent thus
Through pride or scorn! I only gnaw my heart
With meditation, seeing myself so wronged.
For so – their honours to these new-made gods,
What other gave but I, – and dealt them out
With distributions? Aye – but here I am dumb!
For here, I should repeat your knowledge to you,
If I spake aught. List rather to the deeds
I did for mortals! – how, being fools before,
I made them wise and true in aim of soul.
And let me tell you – not as taunting men,
But teaching you the intention of my gifts,
How, first beholding, they beheld in vain,
And hearing, heard not, but, like shapes in dreams,
Mixed all things wildly down the tedious time,
Nor knew to build a house against the sun
With wicketed sides, nor any woodcraft knew,
But lived, like silly ants, beneath the ground
In hollow caves unsunned. There, came to them
No steadfast sign of winter, nor of spring
Flower-perfumed, nor of summer full of fruit,
But blindly and lawlessly they did all things,

Until I taught them how the stars do rise
And set in mystery, and devised for them
Number, the inducer of philosophies,
The synthesis of Letters, and, beside,
The artificer of all things, Memory,
That sweet Muse-mother. I was first to yoke
The servile beasts in couples, carrying
An heirdom of man's burdens on their backs.
I joined to chariots, steeds, that love the bit
They champ at – the chief pomp of golden ease!
And none but I originated ships,
The seaman's chariots, wandering on the brine
With linen wings. And I – oh, miserable! –
Who did devise for mortals all these arts,
Have no device left now to save myself
From the woe I suffer.

WILLIAM SEWELL

(1804-1874)

Educated at Winchester and Merton College, Oxford, Sewell became a fellow of Exeter, and then received a curacy – a sinecure – in the Isle of Wight. He was subsequently made Whyte's Professor of Moral Philosophy (1836-41). He moved in the circle of Newman, Pusey and Keble, and lectured on 'Christian Morals and Christian Politics'. He was one of the most prominent figures in Oxford University. His Horace, which Mark Pattison unaccountably preferred to Conington's, was published in 1850. In 1862 he emigrated to Deutz on the Rhine to avoid his creditors, and returned only in 1870. His published works include sermons, essays and novels; besides the Horace he published versions of Vergil's *Georgics* and Aeschylus' *Agamemnon*; translations of the *Iliad*, the *Odyssey* and the *Psalms* were left in manuscript at his death.

Infatuation
(Horace, *Odes* 3.12)

'Tis the lot of hapless maidens, – neither to indulge its play
To affection, nor in honied – wine their ills to wash away;
Or to be struck lifeless, dreading – scourges of an uncle's tongue.
From thee Cytherea's basket – does that winged stripling young, –
From thee all thy webs and study – of Minerva, labour's queen,
Now is taking, Neobule, – Liparaean Hebrus' sheen.
He, when once his oil-bathed shoulders – he was wash'd in Tiber's wave,
Than Bellerophon himself a – trooper more expert and brave,
Nor with cestus nor with slothful-foot o'ervanquish'd, – he the same,

At the harts in throng alarm'd scudding o'er the open plain
Dexterous to launch his arrows, – and as fleet in foot [or more],
Ambush'd in the deep-sunk thicket – to surprise and slay the boar.

FRANCIS NEWMAN

(1805-1897)

Brother of Cardinal Newman, Francis Newman travelled in the East after
leaving Oxford, and then held various university posts culminating in the
Chair of Latin at University College London. His fame rests on the attack
made on his translation of the *Iliad* by Matthew Arnold (see Introduction,
p.25). Though a lively lecturer, his translations of Horace as well as of Homer
are as misguided as Arnold's criticisms suggest, and severely misrepresent the
originals as well as being largely unreadable, though sometimes comic.

Jupiter's plan observed
(Iliad 1.551-67)

To him responded thereupon   the large-ey'd queenly Juno:
'O son of Saturn, grim and dire,   what saying hast thou blurted?
Naught in the past have I inquir'd;   in naught thy mind have fathom'd:
But troth! in much tranquillity,   whate'er thou wilt, thou plannest.
And now in soul I grimly dread,   lest silverfooted Thetis,
The daughter of the Ocean sire,   have haply won thee over.
For at thy side with early dawn   she sat, thy knees embracing.
Therefore, I guess, in promise sure   thou nodded hast, to honour
Achilles, and a carnage make   along the Achaian galleys.'
   Then cloud-collecting Jupiter,   addressing her, responded:
'O elf-possessed wight!   who aye suspectest, and discernest.
But naught wilt thou the more avail   to compass; yea, and rather
My heart from thee wilt separate;   which were to thee more painful.
If, as thou thinkest, so it is,   my will (be sure) decideth.
But dumb in silence sit thee down,   to my command submissive.
Lest near I draw, and cast my hands   inviolable on thee,
And all Olympus' habitants   to succour thee avail not.'

Clash of armies
(Iliad 13.795-807)

Then on rush'd they, with weight and mass   like to a troublous whirlwind
Which from the thundercloud of Jove   down on the champaign
   plumpeth,
And doth the briny flood bestir   with an unearthly uproar:
Then in the ever-brawling sea   full many a billow splasheth,

Hollow, and bald with hoary pate,   one racing after other:
So then the Trojans closely wedg'd,   one after other marching,
Sparkling in brazen panoply,   beside their leaders muster'd:
And Hector, Priam's son, a peer   for Ares, pest of mortals,
Led them; and forward held his shield,   which equal was on all sides,
Compact with bull-hides: over them   thick plates of brass were welded,
And his resplendent helmet's plume   around his temples nodded.
This way and that he tried, amid   the foeman's ranks advancing,
If, as beneath his shield he mov'd,   perchance they yield before him.

WILLIAM CORY

(1823-1892)

William Cory Johnson was a schoolmaster at Eton and author of the Eton Boating Song. He elevated the relationship of master and pupil into a romantic ideal modelled on Plato's portrayal of Socrates and his companions (see, for example, his Journal for February 1864). His famous *Heraclitus* exactly conveys the mood of these attachments. In 1872 he was compelled to leave Eton, for no very good reason. There is a life by F. Compton Mackenzie.

Heraclitus
(Callimachus *Epigram* 2)

They told me, Heraclitus, they told me you were dead;
They brought me bitter news to hear, and bitter tears to shed.
I wept, as I remember'd, how often you and I
Had tired the sun with talking and sent him down the sky.

And now that thou art lying, my dear old Carian guest,
A handful of grey ashes, long, long ago at rest,
Still are thy pleasant voices, thy nightingales, awake,
For Death, he taketh all away, but them he cannot take.

CHARLES STUART CALVERLEY

(1831-1884)

Educated at Harrow and Balliol College, Oxford, Calverley early distinguished himself in Latin verse composition, for which he won the Chancellor's Prize in 1851. After being expelled from the university, he went instead to Christ's, Cambridge, where he won more prizes despite his indolence and love of company. Many stories are told of his facetious wit, equally at home in Latin and in English. His power of pastiche and of parody is allied to his aptitude for verse composition, and is notable too in his parody of Browning. In 1865 he went to the Inner Temple, but in 1866/7 he fell on his head while skating and was incapacitated from serious work for the rest of his life, which he devoted instead to the exercise of his talent in verses and translations.

Carpe diem
(Horace, *Odes* 1.11)

Seek not, for thou shalt not find it, what my end, what thine shall be;
Ask not of Chaldaea's science what God wills, Leuconoe:
Better far, what comes, to bear it. Haply many a wintry blast
Waits thee still; and this, it may be, Jove ordains to be thy last,
Which flings now the flagging sea-wave on the obstinate sandstone-reef.
Be thou wise; fill up the wine-cup; shortening, since the time is brief,
Hopes that reach into the future. While I speak, hath stolen away
Jealous Time. Mistrust to-morrow, catch the blossom of To-day.

The sorceress
(Theocritus, *Idyll* 2.64-166)

Now, all alone, I'll weep a love whence sprung
When born? Who wrought my sorrow? Anaxo came,
Her basket in her hand, to Artemis' grove.
Bound for the festival, troops of forest beasts
Stood round, and in the midst a lioness.
  Bethink thee, mistress Moon, whence came my love.
Theucharidas' slave, my Thracian nurse now dead
Then my near neighbour, prayed me and implored
To see the pageant: I, the poor doomed thing,
Went with her, trailing a fine silken train,
And gathering round me Clearista's robe.
  Bethink thee, mistress Moon, whence came my love.
Now, the mid-highway reached by Lycon's farm,
Delphis and Eudamippus passed me by.
With beards as lustrous as the woodbine's gold
And breasts more sheeny than thyself, O Moon,
Fresh from the wrestler's glorious toil they came.
  Bethink thee, mistress Moon, whence came my love.
I saw, I raved, smit (weakling) to my heart.
My beauty withered, and I cared no more
For all that pomp; and how I gained my home
I know not: some strange fever wasted me.
Ten nights and days I lay upon my bed.
  Bethink thee, mistress Moon, whence came my love.
And wan became my flesh, as't had been dyed,

And all my hair streamed off, and there was left
But bones and skin. Whose threshold crossed I not,
Or missed what grandam's hut who dealt in charms?
For no light thing was this, and time sped on.
 Bethink thee, mistress Moon, whence came my love.
At last I spake the truth to that my maid:
'Seek, an thou canst, some cure for my sore pain.
Alas, I am all the Mindian's! But begone,
And watch by Timagetus' wrestling-school:
There doth he haunt, there smoothly take his rest.
 Bethink thee, mistress Moon, whence came my love.
'Find him alone: nod softly: say, "she waits";
And bring him.' So I spake: she went her way,
And brought the lustrous-limbed one to my roof.
And I, the instant I beheld him step
Lightfooted o'er the threshold of my door,
 (Bethink thee, mistress Moon, whence came my love)
Became all cold like snow, and from my brow
Brake the damp dewdrops: utterance had I none,
Not e'en such utterance as a babe may make
That babbles to its mother in its dreams;
But all my fair frame stiffened into wax.
 Bethink thee, mistress Moon, whence came my love.
He bent his pitiless eyes on me; looked down,
And sate him on my couch, and sitting, said:
'Thou hast gained on me, Simaetha, (e'en as I
Gaind once on young Philinus in the race,)
Bidding me hither ere I came unasked.
 Bethink thee, mistress Moon, whence came my love.
'For I had come, by Eros I had come,
This night, with comrades twain or may-be more,
The fruitage of the Wine-god in my robe,
And, wound about my brow with ribands red
The silver leaves so dear to Heracles.
 Bethink thee, mistress Moon, whence came my love.
'Had ye said "Enter," well: for 'mid my peers
High is my name for goodliness and speed:
I had kissed that sweet mouth once and gone my way.
But had the door been barred, and I thrust out,
With brand and axe would we have stormed ye them.
 Bethink thee, mistress Moon, whence came my love.
'Now be my thanks recorded, first to Love,
Next to thee, maiden, who didst pluck me out,
A half-burned helpless creature, from the flames,
And badst me hither. It is Love that lights
A fire more fierce than his of Lipara;
 (Bethink thee, mistress Moon, whence came my love.)

'Scares, mischief-mad, the maiden from her bower,
The bride from her warm couch.' He spake: and I,
A willing listener, sat, my hand in his,
Among the cushions, and his cheek touched mine,
Each hotter than its wont, and we discoursed
In soft low language. Need I prate to thee,
Sweet Moon, of all we said and all we did?
Till yesterday he found no fault with me,
Nor I with him. But lo, to-day there came
Philista's mother – hers who flutes to me –
With her Melampo's; just when up the sky
Gallop the mares that chariot rose-limbed Dawn:
And divers tales she brought me, with the rest
How Delphis loved, she knew not rightly whom:
But this she knew; that of the rich wine aye
He poured 'to Love'; and at the last had fled,
To line, she deemed, the fair one's hall with flowers.
Such was my visitor's tale, and it was true:
For thrice, nay four times, daily he would stroll
Hither, leave here full oft his Dorian flask:
Now – 'tis a fortnight since I saw his face.
Doth he then treasure something sweet elsewhere?
Am I forgot? I'll charm him now with charms.
But let him try me more, and by the Fates
He'll soon be knocking at the gates of hell.
Spells of such power are in this chest of mine,
Learned, lady, from mine host in Palestine.

Lady, farewell: turn ocean-ward thy steeds:
As I have purposed, so shall I fulfil.
Farewell, thou bright-faced Moon! Yet stars, farewell,
That wait upon the car of noiseless Night.

Mutability, from Ajax's speech
(Sophocles, *Ajax* 645-83)

All strangest things the multitudinous years
Bring forth, and shadow from us all we know.
Falter alike great oath and steeled resolve;
And none shall say of aught, 'This may not be'. . .

Do not all terrible and most puissant things
Yet bow to loftier majesties? The Winter,
Who walks forth scattering snows, gives place anon
To fruitage-laden Summer; and the orb
Of weary Night doth in her turn stand by,
And let shine out, with his white steeds, the Day.
Stern tempest-blasts at last sing lullaby

To groaning seas: even the archtyrant, Sleep,
Doth loose his slaves, not hold them chained for ever.
And shall not mankind too learn discipline?
I know, of late experience taught, that him
Who is my foe I must but hate as one
Whom I may yet call friend: and him who loves me
Will I but serve and cherish as a man
Whose love is not abiding. Few be they
Who, reaching Friendship's port, have there found rest.

ALFRED LORD TENNYSON

(1809-1892)

Tennyson's fame was established by 1842, twenty-one years before the
appearance of the translation below, with some experiments in classical
metres, in the *Cornhill Magazine* for December 1863. Throughout his life we
find him returning to classical themes, from the *Lotos-Eaters* and *Ulysses* to the
poem *To Vergil*. His admiration for Theocritus knew no bounds. But classical
writers served him better as inspiration than in the role of models.

Specimen of a translation of the *Iliad* in blank verse
(Homer, *Iliad* 8.542-61)

So Hector spake; the Trojans roar'd applause;
Then loosed their sweating horses from the yoke,
And each beside his chariot bound his own;
And oxen from the city, and goodly sheep
In haste they drove, and honey-hearted wine
And bread from out the houses brought, and heap'd
Their firewood, and the winds from off the plain
Roll'd the rich vapour far into the heaven.
And these all night upon the bridge of war
Sat glorying; many a fire before them blaz'd:
As when in heaven the stars about the moon
Look beautiful, when all the winds are laid,
And every height comes out, and jutting peak
And valley, and the immeasurable heavens
Break open to their highest, and all the stars
Shine, and the shepherd gladdens in his heart:
So many a fire between the ships and stream
Of Xanthus blazed before the towers of Troy,
A thousand on the plain; and close by each
Sat fifty in the blaze of burning fire;
And eating hoary grain and pulse the steeds,
Fixt by their cars, waited the golden dawn.

JOHN CONINGTON

(1825-69)

John Conington was the first incumbent of the Corpus Chair of Latin at Oxford when it was founded in 1854. His major works date from the 1860s, but he early revealed his interest in the problems of translation by a review, in the *Edinburgh Review*, of William Sewell's *Georgics* of Vergil, in which he at the same time enjoyed the opportunity of attacking one of the senior members of the University Establishment.

But he himself became converted to religion, to conservatism and to Pusey. This combined with his irritable temper aroused the animosity even of the liberals whose cause he had shared, among them his contemporary Mark Pattison, who wrote: 'He abandoned himself to the laziest of all occupations with the classics, that, namely, of translating them into English; he translated Horace, I daresay no worse and no better than the scores who have translated it before him; he translated Vergil, I think, more than once through, and it is remarkable that he who, as a young critic, found no expressions sufficiently depreciatory for William Sewell's Georgics, produced, on the whole, a translation of much less merit.' I do not know how common this opinion was at the time; certainly few would subscribe to it now.

Consolation
(Horace, *Odes* 2.9)

The rain, it rains not every day
    On the soak'd meads; the Caspian main
Not always feels the unequal sway
    Of storms, nor on Armenia's plain,
Dear Valgius, lies the cold dull snow
    Through all the year; not northwinds keen
Upon Garganian oakwoods blow,
    And strip the ashes of their green.
You still with tearful tones pursue
    Your lost, lost Mystes; Hesper sees
Your passion when he brings the dew,
    And when before the sun he flees.
Yet not for loved Antilochus
    Grey Nestor wasted all his years
In grief; nor o'er young Troilus
    His parents' and his sisters' tears
For ever flow'd. At length have done
    With these soft sorrows; rather tell
Of Caesar's trophies newly won,
    And hoar Niphates' icy fell,
And Medus' flood, 'mid conquer'd tribes
    Rolling a less presumptuous tide,

And Scythians taught, as Rome prescribes,
Henceforth o'er narrower steppes to ride.

The cynosure of girls' eyes
(Horace, <i>Odes</i> 3.12)</center>

How unhappy are the maidens who with Cupid may not play,
Who may never touch the wine-cup, but must tremble all the day
    At an uncle, and the scourging of his tongue!
Neobule, there's a robber takes your needle and your thread,
Lets the lessons of Minerva run no longer in your head;
    It is Hebrus, the athletic and the young!
O, to see him when anointed he is plunging in the flood!
What a seat he has on horseback! was Bellerophon's as good?
    As a boxer, as a runner, past compare!
When the deer are flying blindly all the open country o'er,
He can aim and he can hit them; he can steal upon the boar,
    As it couches in the thicket unaware.

All men are mad
(Horace, <i>Satires</i> 2.3.31-76)</center>

Damasippus: You're mad yourself, and so are all mankind,
If truth is in Stertinius, from whose speech
I learned the precious lessons that I teach,
What time he bade me grow a wise man's beard,
And sent me from the bridge, consoled and cheered.
For once, when, bankrupt and forlorn, I stood
With muffled head, just plunging in the flood,
'Don't do yourself a mischief,' so he cried
In friendly tones, appearing at my side:
"'tis all false shame: you fear to be thought mad,
Not knowing that the world are just as bad.
What constitutes a madman? if 'tis shown
The marks are found in you and you alone,
Trust me, I'll add no word to thwart your plan,
But leave you free to perish like a man.
The wight who drives through life with bandaged eyes,
Ignorant of truth and credulous of lies,
He in the judgment of Chrysippus' school
And the whole porch is tabled as a fool.
Monarchs and people, every rank and age,
That sweeping clause includes, – except the sage.
    'Now listen while I show you, how the rest
Who call you madman, are themselves possessed.
Just as in woods, when travellers step aside

From the true path for want of some good guide,
This to the right, that to the left hand strays,
And all are wrong, but wrong in different ways,
So, though you're mad, yet he who banters you
Is not more wise, but wears his pigtail too.
One class of fools sees reason for alarm
In trivial matters, innocent of harm:
Stroll in the open plain, you'll hear the talk
Of fires, rocks, torrents, that obstruct their walk:
Another, unlike these, but not more sane,
Takes fires and torrents for the open plain:
Let mother, sister, father, wife combined
Cry 'There's a pitfall! there's a rock! pray mind!'
They'll hear no more than drunken Fufius, he
Who slept the part of queen Ilione,
While Catienus, shouting in his ear,
Roared like a Stentor, "Hearken, mother dear!"
  'Well, now, I'll prove the mass of humankind
Have judgments just as jaundiced, just as blind.
That Damasippus shows himself insane
By buying ancient statues, all think plain:
But he that lends him money, is he free
From the same charge? "Oh, surely." Let us see.
I bid you take a sum you won't return:
You take it: is this madness, I would learn?
Were it not greater madness to renounce
The prey that Mercury puts within your pounce?
Secure him with ten bonds; a hundred; nay,
Clap on a thousand; still he'll slip away,
This Protean scoundrel: drag him into court,
You'll only find yourself the more his sport:
He'll laugh till scarce you'd think his jaws his own,
And turn to boar or bird, to tree or stone.
If prudence in affairs denotes men sane
And bungling argues a disordered brain,
The man who lends the cash is far more fond
Than you, who at his bidding sign the bond . . .'

The death of Patroclus
(*Iliad* 16.777-867)

Long as the sun was scaling heaven's high crest,
The darts took hold on both: they fell, they slew:
But when the sun 'gan slope toward the west,
The Achaians vantage got beyond their due:
Out from the darts brave Kebriones they drew
Despite the Trojans, and his harness pilled.

Infuriate on Troy's ranks Patroclus flew;
Thrice he rushed on, with Ares' spirit filled,
Shouting a terrible shout, and thrice nine men he killed.

When the fourth time he charged, a god in show,
Then fell death's shadow on Patroclus wight:
For Phoebus met him there, tremendous foe,
Walking in anger through the ranks of fight:
He knew not that dread presence: hid from sight
It moved, in covering mist enveloped dim:
Standing behind, his shoulders it did smite
With its flat hand, and made his eyes to swim,
And from his brow struck off the helm that frowned so grim.

Down with a clang among the horses' feet
Fell the high helmet, and the plume had stain
Of gore and dust: till now it was not meet
That crested cone should roll upon the plain:
But to Achilleus' brow the sweeping mane
Lent beauty, and the brass did death repel:
And now to Hector, who should soon be slain,
Zeus gave it for his own:– all shivered fell
The spear, grim, heavy, and strong, with steel y-pointed well.

Bursting its strap, from off his back the shield
Dropped down: his corslet Phoebus' hand derayed:
Confusion seized his sense: his faint knees reeled:
Quaking he stood: when with adventurous blade
To pierce his back a Dardan chief essayed,
Panthoides Euphorbus:– none more wight
In spearcraft, speed of foot, or horseman trade:
Full twenty chiefs he made the ground to bite,
First venturing with his car, a novice in the fight:–

He at Patroclus hurled his javelin first,
Nor slew him, but drew back, and joined the crowd,
Snatching the weapon forth: nor yet he durst
Meet whom he wounded, though disarmed and cowed.
Back to his friends, by stroke and spear-wound bowed,
Retired Patroclus, for his life in fear.
But soon as Hector saw that champion proud
Retiring, sorely wounded, he came near,
Threading the ranks of war, and with protended spear

Pierced deep his flank, and drove the steel outright:
He fell, and stung the Achaian host with pain.
As lion tames a sturdy boar in fight,
When on a mountain's top have striven the twain
For a scant stream, whence each to drink is fain,
And so at last subdues his panting prey;

So when Menoetius' son whole ranks had slain,
Hector advancing took his life away,
And, standing o'er him fallen, thus vauntingly did say:

'Patroclus! 'twas thy boast thou wouldst destroy
My city, and sweep off to slavery sheer
On shipboard to thy land the dames of Troy:
Fool! knowing not that Hector's steeds are near
With their fleet hoofs: their master with the spear
Each warrior doth excel, and from each maid
Keeps thraldom far: but thou shalt moulder here.
Ill served thee thy brave friend, who haply laid
His charge on thee, when forth thou wentest, and he staid:

' "Now, good Patroclus, come not home again
To him thou leav'st at the smooth ships behind
Without the tunic of grim Hector slain."
So haply spake he, swaying thy fond mind.'
And labouringly Patroclus thus rejoined:
'Ay, Hector, boast: Zeus gives thee victory now,
And Leto's son, who made me weak and blind,
And stripped my arms. Had twenty such as thou
Come near me in fair field, my lance had made them bow.

'But Fate and Phoebus slew me, and of men
Euphorbus: thou the third but kill'st the slain.
Yet one more truth I tell for thee to ken;
Not long shalt thou in triumph tread the plain,
For death and fate are rushing on amain,
And great Achilleus' hand shall deal thee doom.'
So closed his lips, that opened ne'er again:
And from the limbs the soul fled forth to gloom,
Lamenting its own lot, leaving its strength and bloom.

And Hector spoke, albeit to'a deaf ear:
'Why bode me death, Patroclus? who can say
That first Achilleus shall not taste my spear?'
And with his foot set on him as he lay
Wrenched out the dart, and thrust the corpse away.
Then on Automedon he turned the war,
Achilleus' godlike squire, intent to slay:
But the fleet steeds that drew Pelides' car,
Immortal, Heaven's own gift, whirled him from danger far.

EDWARD GEORGE GEOFFREY SMITH STANLEY, FOURTEENTH EARL OF DERBY

(1799-1869)

Educated at Eton and Christ Church, Stanley started his parliamentary career by being elected for Preston, despite the opposition of Cobbett. He immediately joined the supporters of Canning, and held a series of appointments including that of Chief Secretary for Ireland, and a post in the colonial office where he set himself against slavery. In 1833 he resigned from Parliament over the secularisation of Church property, and became Lord Derby in 1834. In 1841 he joined Peel's administration, and then entered the House of Lords. He became Chancellor of Oxford University in 1852, where he founded the scholarship that bears his name. In 1858 he formed an administration with Disraeli.

His translation of the *Iliad* appeared towards the end of this chequered career, published privately in 1862 and formally in 1864. For simple dignity it has no rival among English translations of Homer.

The laments over Hector
(Homer, *Iliad* 24.723-804)

White-arm'd Andromache the wail began,
The head of Hector clasping in her hands:
'My husband, thou art gone in pride of youth,
And in thine house hast left me desolate;
Thy child an infant still, thy child and mine,
Unhappy parents both! nor dare I hope
That he may reach the ripeness of his youth;
For ere that day shall Troy in ruin fall,
Since thou art gone, her guardian! thou whose arm
Defended her, her wives, and helpless babes!
They now shall shortly o'er the sea be borne,
And with them I shall go; thou too, my child,
Must follow me, to servile labour doom'd,
The suff'ring victim of a tyrant Lord;
Unless perchance some angry Greek may seize
And dash thee from the tow'r – a woful death!
Whose brother, or whose father, or whose son
By Hector hath been slain; for many a Greek
By Hector's hand hath bit the bloody dust;
Nor light in battle was thy father's hand!
Therefore for him the gen'ral city mourns;
Thou to thy parents bitter grief hast caus'd,
Hector! but bitt'rest grief of all hast left
To me! for not to me was giv'n to clasp
The hand extended from thy dying bed,

Nor words of wisdom catch, which night and day,
With tears, I might have treasur'd in my heart.'
　　Weeping she spoke – the women join'd the wail.
Then Hecuba took up the loud lament:
'Hector, of all my children dearest thou!
Dear to th' Immortals too in life wast thou,
And they in death have borne thee still in mind;
For other of my sons, his captives made,
Across the wat'ry waste, to Samos' isle
Or Imbros, or th' inhospitable shore
Of Lemnos, hath Achilles, swift of foot,
To slav'ry sold; thee, when his sharp-edg'd spear
Had robb'd thee of thy life, he dragg'd indeed
Around Patroclus' tomb, his comrade dear,
Whom thou hadst slain; yet so he rais'd not up
His dead to life again; now liest thou here,
All fresh and fair, as dew-besprent; like one
Whom bright Apollo, with his arrows keen,
God of the silver bow, hath newly slain.'
　　Weeping, she spoke; and rous'd the gen'ral grief.
Then Helen, third, the mournful strain renew'd:
'Hector, of all my brethren dearest thou!
True, godlike Paris claims me as his wife,
Who bore me hither – would I then had died!
But twenty years have pass'd since here I came,
And left my native land; yet ne'er from thee
I heard one scornful, one degrading word;
And when from others I have borne reproach,
Thy brothers, sisters, or thy brothers' wives,
Or mother, (for thy sire was ever kind
Ev'n as a father) thou hast check'd them still
With tender feeling, and with gentle words,
For thee I weep, and for myself no less;
For, through the breadth of Troy, none love me now,
None kindly look on me, but all abhor.'
　　Weeping she spoke, and with her wept the crowd.
At length the aged Priam gave command:
'Haste now, ye Trojans, to the city bring
Good store of fuel; fear no treach'rous wile;
For when he sent me from the dark-ribb'd ships,
Achilles promis'd that from hostile arms
Till the twelfth morn we should no harm sustain.'
　　He said; and they the oxen and the mules
Yok'd to the wains, and from the city throng'd:
Nine days they labour'd, and brought back to Troy
Good store of wood; but when the tenth day's light
Upon the earth appear'd, weeping, they bore

Brave Hector out; and on the fun'ral pile
Laying the glorious dead, applied the torch.
   While yet the rosy-finger'd morn was young
Round noble Hector's pyre the people press'd:
When all were gather'd round, and closely throng'd,
First on the burning mass, as far as spread
The range of fire, they pour'd the ruddy wine,
And quench'd the flames: his brethren then and friends
Weeping, the hot tears flowing down their cheeks,
Collected from the pile the whiten'd bones,
These in a golden casket they enclos'd,
And o'er it spread soft shawls of purple dye;
Then in a grave they laid it, and in haste
With stone in pond'rous masses cover'd o'er;
And rais'd a mound, and watch'd on ev'ry side,
From sudden inroad of the Greeks to guard.
The mound erected, back they turn'd; and all
Assembled duly, shar'd the solemn feast
In Priam's palace, Heav'n-descended King.
   Such were the rites to glorious Hector paid.

HENRY HART MILMAN

(1791-1868)

Educated at Eton and Brasenose College, Oxford, Milman won the English
Poetry Prize, and subsequently became Professor of Poetry at Oxford (1821),
to be succeeded by Keble in 1831. From 1818 he held a living at Reading, and
his first major poem dates from this year – an epic, *Samor*, on the Saxon
invasion of Britain. His translations from Sanskrit poetry (1835) were one of
the earliest manifestations of the increasing interest in Indian culture which
produced the work of Max Müller. His major works were his edition of the
works of Gibbon (1838) and his history of Latin Christianity (1855). From
1849 he was Dean of St Paul's; his Horace was published in that year and his
versions from Aeschylus, Euripides and others in 1865.

The boy and the dolphin
(Oppian, *Halieutica* 5.458-518)

Still on the Aeolian shore the tale is sung,
No ancient tale, but still in living memory young,
The island boy how once the dolphin loved,
Nor ever from these hallowed waters roved,
But dwelt a denizen of that smooth bay,
Basked on its waves, or in its cool depths lay.

Of youth, the fairest he, the island's grace:
The fish, the swiftest of the watery race.
   Day after day, along the crowded shore,
Still would the island's wondering thousands pour;
Light to his boat the boy would spring alone,
Call the familiar name, to both well known,
The name from childhood's earliest hours endeared.
Swift as an arrow, when that sound he heard,
The silver dolphin gleamed beneath the deck,
Fawned with his tail, and curled his glittering neck;
   Fain would he touch the boy, with motion bland
Who smoothed him down, and soft caressing hand.
Then leaped the boy within the yielding tide,
And lo! the loving dolphin by his side;
And cheek to cheek, and side to side, he prest.
And curled, and glanced, and wantoned round his breast;
He seemed as he would fondly kiss his face,
Or gently fold him in his cool embrace.
Soon as the shore they neared, the youth bestrode
His scaly back, and there in triumph rode.
Still where would guide the blithe and sportive boy,
The obedient fish went bounding in its joy;
Now where the deeper billows heave and roar,
Now smoothly glide along the quiet shore.
Nor e'er might skilful charioteer command
A steed more docile to his mastering hand,
Nor at the hunter's beck the well-trained hound
Track the fleet prey, and scent the tainted ground,
As this unbridled dolphin would obey
His self-chosen master's light and easy sway;
Nor him alone, all toil at his behest
Was pleasure, him to serve was to be blest.
So each in turn his blithe companions rode,
And light the dolphin bore th' unwonted load,
Such all his life the faithful love he bore.
   But the youth died – then all along the shore
Was sadly seen the mourning fish to roam;
At first seemed wondering that he did not come,
And searched each nook, each creviced rock in vain,
Ye almost heard a feeble voice complain.
Nought heeded he the crowds along the sands,
Nor took the offered food from strangers' hands;
Then far he fled to the great deep, nor more
Was seen to haunt that solitary shore,
Nor long survived his dear, his human mate,
But shared his living sports, and shared his fate.

EDWARD BULWER-LYTTON, LORD LYTTON

(1803-1873)

Privately educated, Lytton published his first poems precociously, in 1820. In 1822 he entered Trinity College, Cambridge. His first novel appeared in 1827, to be followed by many more, including *The Last Days of Pompeii* (1834). He belonged to J. S. Mill's debating society and admired Jeremy Bentham. In 1831 he entered Parliament. A history of Athens was left unfinished on the appearance of Grote's *History of Greece*. In the 1840s he travelled in Germany and made a translation of Schiller's poems. He was created a peer in 1866. The *Horace* was published in 1869.

The decline of Roman morals
(Horace, *Odes* 3.6)

Roman, the sins thy fathers have committed,
From thee, though guiltless, shall exact atonement,
    Till tottering fanes and temples be restored,
        And smoke-grimed statues of neglected gods.

Thou rul'st by being to the gods subjected,
To this each deed's conception and completion
    Refer; full many an ill the gods contemned
        Have showered upon this sorrowing Italy.

Twice have Monaeses and the Parthian riders
Of Pacorus crushed our evil-omened onslaught,
    And to their puny torques have smiled to add
        The spoils of armour stripped from Roman breasts.

Dacian and Aethiopian, dread-inspiring –
One with his archers, with his fleets the other –
    Well-nigh destroyed this very Rome herself,
        While all her thought was on her own fierce brawls.

This age, crime-bearing, first polluted wedlock,
Hence race adulterate, and hence homes dishallowed;
    And from this fountain flowed a poisoned stream,
        Pest-spreading through the people and the land.

The ripening virgin, blushless, learns, delighted
Ionian dances; in the art of wantons
    Studiously fashioned; even in the bud,
        Tingles within her meditated sin.

Later, a wife (her consort in his cups)
She courts some younger gallant, whom, no matter,
    Snatching the moment from the board to slip,
        And hide the lover from the tell-tale lights.

Prompt at her back (her venal spouse conniving)
Of some man-milliner or rude sea-captain
   Of trade-ship fresh from marts of pilfered Spain,
     Buying full dearly the disgrace she sells.

Not from such parents sprang that race undaunted,
Who reddened ocean with the gore of Carthage,
   Beat down stout Pyrrhus, great Antiochus,
     And broke the might of direful Hannibal.

That manly race was born of warriors rustic,
Tutored to cleave with Sabine spades the furrow,
   And at some rigid mother's bluff command,
     Shouldering the logs their lusty right hands hewed,

What time the sun reversed the mountain shadows,
And from the yoke released the wearied oxen,
   As his own chariot slowly passed away,
     Leaving on earth the kindly hour of rest.

What time does dwarf not and deform, corrupting!
Our father's age ignobler than our grandsires
   Bore us yet more depraved; and we in turn
     Shall leave a race more vicious than ourselves.

WILLIAM EWART GLADSTONE

(1809-1898)

Born in Liverpool, and educated at Eton and Christ Church, Oxford, Gladstone began his parliamentary career as a Conservative member in 1832, and it continued with interruptions until he became Prime Minister as a Liberal in 1868. His first translations appeared in 1861, in a volume published with Lord Lyttelton, with whom he had undertaken the miscellany of translations to console Lyttelton after the death of his wife. When Gladstone retired from politics in 1874 he devoted himself for much of the time to the study of Homer, on whom he wrote voluminously and excellently, besides making translations of some passages from the *Iliad*. These literary pursuits were ended by his resumption of the office of Prime Minister in 1880; he did not finally retire until 1894. His translations from Homer and Horace are important not for their own sake – their merit is not great – but as the product of the cultivated leisure of one of the last truly educated men of the world.

Jealousy
(Catullus 51)

Him rival to the gods I place,
Him loftier yet, if loftier be,

Who, Lesbia, sits before thy face,
  Who listens and who looks on thee;

Thee smiling soft. Yet this delight
  Doth all my sense consign to death;
For when thou dawnest on my sight,
  Ah, wretched! flits my labouring breath.

My tongue is palsied. Subtly hid
  Fire creeps me through from limb to limb:
My loud ears tingle all unbid:
  Twin clouds of night mine eyes bedim.

Ease is my plague: ease makes thee void,
  Catullus, with these vacant hours,
And wanton: ease that hath destroyed
  Great kings, and states with all their powers.

EDWARD FITZGERALD

(1809-1883)

Something of a recluse and far from prolific as a writer, Fitzgerald's fame rests on his *Rubaiyát*. Remarkably, he sometimes makes Aeschylus sound like Omar Khayyam, the greater achievement as his professed aim in his translations was to convey through free rendering some of the effect the works might be supposed to have had on their original hearers. But to condemn the *Agamemnon* translation as 'coy' (Peter Green, *Essays in Antiquity* (1960), 185-215) is to ignore the magnificence of his rendering of the Cassandra scene. His output of translations also includes, besides Calderón, the description of the retired pirate from Vergil's *Georgics*.

Cassandra's vision of the murder of Agamemnon
(Aeschylus, *Agamemnon* 1080-145)

Cassandra: Hither, whither, Phoebus? and with whom,
Leading me, lighting me –
Chorus: I can answer that –
Cass: Down to what slaughter-house!
Foh! the smell of carnage through the door
Scares me from it – drags me tow'rd it –
Phoebus! Apollo! Apollo!
Cho: One of the dismal prophet-pack, it seems,
That hunt the trail of blood. But here at fault –
This is no den of slaughter, but the house
Of Agamemnon.

Cass: Down upon the towers
Phantoms of two mangled children hover – and a famished man
At an empty table glaring, seizes and devours!
Cho: Thyestes and his children! strange enough
For any maiden from abroad to know,
Or, knowing –
Cass: And look! in the chamber below
The terrible Woman, listening, watching,
Under a mask, preparing the blow
In the fold of her robe –
Cho: Nay, but again at fault:
For in the tragic story of this house –
Unless, indeed, the fatal Helen –
No woman –
Cass: No woman – Tisiphone! Daughter
Of Tartarus – love-grinning Woman above,
Dragon-tail'd under – honey-tongu'd, Harpy-claw'd,
Into the glittering meshes of slaughter
She wheedles, entices, him into the poisonous
Fold of the serpent –
Cho: Peace, mad woman, peace!
Whose stony lips once open vomit out
Such uncouth horrors.
Cass: I tell you the lioness
Slaughters the lion asleep; and lifting
Her blood-dripping fangs buries deep in his mane,
Glaring about her insatiable, bellowing,
Bounds hither – Phoebus, Apollo, Apollo, Apollo!
Whither have you led me, under night alive with fire,
Through the trampled ashes of the city of my sire,
From my slaughtered kinsmen, fallen throne, insulted shrine,
Slave-like to be butcher'd, the daughter of a royal line.
Cho: And so returning, like a nightingale
Returning to the passionate note of woe
By which the silence first was broken!
Cass: Oh,
A nightingale, a nightingale, indeed,
That, as she 'Itys! Itys! Itys!' so
I 'Helen! Helen! Helen!' having sung
Amid my people, now to those who flung
And trampled on the nest, and slew the young,
Keep crying 'Blood! Blood! Blood!' and none will heed!
Now what for me is this prophetic creed,
And what for me is this immortal crown,
Who like a wild swan from Scamander's reed
Chaunting her death-song floats Cocytus-down?
There let the fatal leaves to perish lie!

To perish, or enrich some other brow
With that all-fatal gift of prophecy
They palpitate under Him who now,
Checking his flaming chariot in mid sky,
With divine irony sees disadorn
The wretch his love has made the people's scorn,
The raving quean, the mountebank, the scold,
Who, wrapt up in the ruin she foretold
With those who would not listen, now descends
To that dark kingdom where his empire ends.

MAURICE PURCELL FITZGERALD
(fl. 1867)

The volume containing this and other translations from the Greek (1867)
appears to be the only publication of this author.

The song of Lycidas
(Theocritus, *Idyll* 7.52-89)

'Fair be the voyage for Ageanax, I pray,
To Mitylene, though the rainy south
Press on the billows, when the Goats are low,
And old Orion rests his foot i' the sea,
If fate would snatch from Aphrodite's fires
The wasted Lycidas; fierce love for him
Consumes me; halcyons shall lay the waves,
Shall still the sea, the south-wind, and the east
That stirs the furthest sea-wrack – halcyons
Beyond all birds by grey-green Nereids
The best beloved, and peoples of the sea.
May all be fair and well for Ageanax,
And waft him sweetly to the wished-for port.
And I that day will wear upon my head
Wreath of anethum, or a garland-crown
Of roses or white violets, and quaff
From a deep flagon wine of Ptelea,
And by the fireside stretch myself to rest.
And one shall roast me beans amid the flame,
And one shall pile my bed a cubit high
With twining parsley and with asphodel
And flea-bane; I the while will drink at ease,
And toast Ageanax till to the cup
My lips cling fast and drain the very dregs.
And I will have two shepherds flute for me;

The one from Attica, Aeolian one;
And Tityrus shall stand beside, and sing
How Daphnis burned for Xenia long ago,
And how he roamed the mountain, and the oaks
Sighed dirges for him by the river-banks
Of Himera, what time he died away,
As dies a snow-flake upon Haemus' top,
Athos, or Rhodope, or on the steeps
Of extreme Caucasus. And he shall sing
How a wide cage received a shepherd once,
Yet living, through the vile scorn of his lord,
And how into the odorous cedarn wood
Came, with soft blossoms out of flowery fields,
The honey-hiving bees, and nourished him,
Because the Muse poured nectar from his tongue.
Happy Comatas! happy was thy lot,
Prisoned within a cage, to wile away
The summer months, and feed on honeycomb!
O, wert thou numbered with the living now!
How would I tend fair she-goats on the hills
For thee! how would I listen for thy voice!
And thou, divine Comatas, wouldst repose
In shade of oaks or pines, and sweetly sing.

BENJAMIN BICKLEY ROGERS

(1828-1919)

Born and educated in Somerset, Rogers attended Wadham College, Oxford, and Lincoln's Inn, and was called to the bar. His career was cut short by deafness at the age of fifty, after which he returned to the occupation he had begun as an undergraduate with his translation of Aristophanes' *Clouds* (1852). *Peace* and *Wasps* had already appeared when he retired. The remainder appeared in the years of his long retirement, and Oxford University created him a Doctor of Letters for the achievement. Rogers' chief mastery lies in his metrical adeptness, which has the lightness and incisiveness of Aristophanes himself. His version remains one of the most widely read of translations of Aristophanes, for all that his style and the things he chooses to omit or alter remove some of Aristophanes' acerbity and make him a Periclean W. S. Gilbert.

The chorus of clouds
(Aristophanes, *Clouds* 275-318)

Chorus: Clouds of all hue,
Rise we aloft with our garments of dew.
Come from old Ocean's unchangeable bed,
Come, till the mountain's green summits we tread,
Come to the peaks with their landscapes untold,
Gaze on the Earth with her harvests of gold,
Gaze on the rivers in majesty streaming,
  Gaze on the lordly, invincible Sea,
Come, for the Eye of the Ether is beaming,
  Come, for all Nature is flashing and free.
  Let us shake off this close-clinging dew
  From our members eternally new,
  And sail upwards the wide world to view.
        Come away! come away!

Socrates: O Goddesses mine, great Clouds and divine,
        ye have heeded and answered my prayer.
Heard ye their sound, and the thunder around,
        as it thrilled through the tremulous air?

Strepsiades: Yes, by Zeus, and I shake, and I'm all of a quake,
        and I fear I must sound a reply,
Their thunders have made my soul so afraid,
        and those terrible voices so nigh:
So if lawful or not, I must run to a pot,
        by Zeus, if I stop I shall die.

Socrates: Don't act in our schools like those Comedy-fools
        with their scurrilous scandalous ways.
Deep silence be thine: while this Cluster divine
        their soul-stirring melody raise.

Chorus: Come then with me,
Daughters of Mist, to the land of the free.
Come to the people whom Pallas hath blest,
Come to the soil where the Mysteries rest;
Come, where the glorified Temple invites
The pure to partake of its mystical rites:
Holy the gifts that are brought to the gods,
  Shrines with festoons and garlands are crowned,
Pilgrims resort to the sacred abodes,
  Gorgeous the festivals all the year round.
  And the Bromian rejoicings in Spring,
  When the flutes with their deep music ring,
  And the sweetly-toned Choruses sing
        Come away! Come away!

Strepsiades: O Socrates, pray, by all the Gods, say,
                        for I earnestly long to be told,
Who are these that recite with such grandeur and might?
                        are they glorified mortals of old?

Socrates: No mortals are there, but Clouds of the air,
                        great Gods who the indolent fill:
These grant us discourse, and logical force,
                        and the art of persuasion instil,
And periphrasis strange, and a power to arrange,
                        and a marvellous judgment and skill.

Aristophanes' defence
(Aristophanes, *Acharnians* 628-42)

Since first to exhibit his plays he began,
                        our chorus-instructor has never
Come forth to confess in this public address
                        how tactful he is and how clever.
But now that he knows he is slandered by foes
                        before Athens so quick to assent,
Pretending he jeers our City and sneers
                        at the people with evil intent,
He is ready and fain his cause to maintain
                        before Athens so quick to repent.
Let honour and praise be the guerdon, he says,
                        of the poet whose satire has stayed you
From believing the orators' novel conceits
                        wherewith they cajoled and betrayed you;
Who bids you despise adulation and lies
                        nor be citizens Vacant and Vain.
For before, when an embassy came from the states
                        intriguing your favour to gain,
And called you the town of the *violet crown*,
                        so grand and exalted ye grew,
That at once on your tiptails erect ye would sit,
                        those *crowns* were so pleasant to you.
And then, if they added the *shiny*, they got
                        whatever they asked for their praises,
Though apter, I ween, for an oily sardine
                        than for you and your City the phrase is,
By this he's a true benefactor to you,
                        and by showing with humour dramatic
The way that our wise democratic allies
                        are ruled by a state democratic.

ALGERNON CHARLES SWINBURNE

(1837-1909)

A delicate child, Swinburne was educated at Eton and Balliol, after which he made an extended tour of France. On his return he became acquainted with Rossetti, and later with William Morris. His third play, *Atalanta in Calydon* (1865) is the first to display the influence of Greek myth, apparent again in *Erectheus*. He has thoroughly absorbed the Greek cast of mind, even to the extent of including fragments of translation in his own compositions (see above, Introduction). His later works reflect the Pre-Raphaelite preoccupation with Arthurian legend and English history. His translations are few: that of a chorus from the *Birds* misses the humour brought out by Frere, but the Delphic Hymn to Apollo falls well into his style. Ezra Pound remarked that 'the Greeks were often rather Swinburnian'.

Delphic Hymn to Apollo
(*Collectanea Alexandrina*, p.141)

I

Thee, the son of God most high,
Famed for harping song, will I
Proclaim, and the deathless oracular word
From the snow-topped rock that we gaze on heard,
Counsels of thy glorious giving
Manifest for all men living,
How thou madest the tripod of prophecy thine
Which the wrath of the dragon kept guard on, a shrine
Voiceless till thy shafts could smite
All his live coiled glittering might.

II

Ye that hold of right alone
All deep woods on Helicon,
Fair daughters of thunder-girt God, with your bright
White arms uplift as to lighten the light,
Come to chant your brother's praise,
Gold-haired Phoebus, loud in lays,
Even his, who afar up the twin-topped seat
Of the rock Parnassian whereon we meet
Risen with glorious Delphic maids
Seeks the soft spring-sweetened shades
Castalian, fain of the Delphian peak
Prophetic, sublime as the feet that seek.

Glorious Athens, highest of state,
Come, with praise and prayer elate,
O thou that art queen of the plain unscarred
That the warrior Tritonis hath alway in guard,
Where on many a sacred shrine
Young bulls' thigh-bones burn and shine
As the god that is fire overtakes them, and fast
The smoke of Arabia to heavenward is cast,
Scattering wide its balm: and shrill
Now with nimble notes that thrill
The flute strikes up the song, and the harp of gold
Strikes up to the song sweet answer, and all behold,
All, aswarm as bees, give ear,
Who by birth hold Athens dear.

SAMUEL PALMER

(1805-1881)

Palmer was primarily a landscape painter, strongly influenced by William
Blake. The visionary style of his paintings in his Shoreham period gives place
to a more muted but still deeply charged realism in the engravings which
complement his translation of the *Eclogues*, his only essay into poetry. Though
substantially complete by 1872 (with the help of his friend Calvert), the
Eclogues was not published until two years after his death, in 1883.

Gallus
(Vergil, *Eclogue* 10)

Yield, Arethuse, to him this latest song,
It is for Gallus we our notes prolong,
Mournful and few, yet prompt if he but need
The verse: a verse Lycoris' self may read!
Euphorion's equal must not be denied;
So, under the Sicilian waters glide,
And never Doris taint thy glassy spring.
Begin: the anxious loves of Gallus sing,
While the goats, browsing, press the thymy ground;
We sing not to the deaf, the woods resound.
    What lawns detain'd you, Naiads, or what grove,
When he was perishing of slighted love?
From him indeed, no steeps of Pindus grey,
Or cleft Parnassus, very long might stay
Your ready feet, nor Aganippe's well:

'Twas thereabouts he loved to dream and dwell;
And him their laurels, him their myrtles mourn:
Him, stretch'd beside a desert rock forlorn,
Maenalian pines and cold Lycaeus wept.
Our very sheep, on yonder uplands kept,
Are coming round us; haply they divine
Something at fault, nor as they can, decline
To share our grief; nor thou the sheep disdain,
Sad poet, master of a nobler strain,
Nor let soft flutes nor reeds of Pan displease;
For oft, with crook and wallet, flocks like these,
To breezy down or shadowy fountain-head
Even the beautiful Adonis led.

    The shepherd came and the slow herdsmen, last
Menalcas, wet with gathering winter mast:
Their homely help was ready, if they knew
Alas! where balm for such a sorrow grew.
Apollo came: he said, 'Why rav'st thou thus
For false Lycoris? She, libidinous,
Hies her to a new paramour, and goes
Through bristling camps and ventures Alpine snows.'
Thither, as wont, with forest honours crown'd,
His way the tutelary Silvan found,
All weather-swarth'd, and with his flowering rod
And full-blown lilies shaking as he trod.
Pan came, Arcadian tetrarch ever good;
I myself saw him, glowing as he stood,
With wall-wort berries, crimson'd like the West.
'Is there no mean?' he said, 'and for the rest
Love cares not: cruel Love no tears can sate,
Nor rivulets the lust of meads abate,
Wild-thyme of bees, of goats the sapling-sprays.'

    At last the lover spoke: we saw him raise,
As waking from a dream, his languish'd head.
'Yet, henceforth in your mountains, you,' he said,
'Arcadians, will in verse her name prolong
With mine; you, ever excellent in song;
And O! how softly then these bones will rest,
Our story by your plaintive reeds express'd.

    Would, shepherds, that I had been bred with you,
To tend the roving flock, a gatherer too
Of the ripe vintages; for then whoe'er
Had been my passion, or Neaera fair,
Or sun-brown Phillis, (what if she be brown?
Hyacinths are dark, and shadowy violets blown
Refresh the glade); she had sat by my side
Beneath the willows, or o'ercanopied

With vine; Phillis had gather'd wreaths for me,
Neaera sung beneath a shady tree.
      Here are cool fountains and soft meads and bowers,
Lycoris: with but thee to crown the hours,
Delectably a life-time I could waste.
Now for the clash of iron, the triumpet-blast,
The grapple! love hath harness'd me for war.
But thou, alas! may I believe it? far
From thy forsaken home, see'st nought around
But Alps and snow, and like thy love, ice-bound,
The scarcely flowing Rhine:– careless and bold,
Without me and alone. May never cold
Distress thee, wandering, nor the stony sleet,
Nor rugged ice-tracks tear those dainty feet.
      Enough: why heed it? whither do I stray?
Hence, moping fantasies: Despair, be gay!
Better in listening ears to troll ere long
To the Sicilian shepherd's reed, that song
I made in verse of Chalcis. I am set;
Resolved; no fickleness will turn me yet;
Resolved the tangled forest to explore,
Among the dens of savage beasts, and score
My loves upon the bark of sapling groves:
Slowly they grow; as tardily my loves.
      Anon, methinks I hear the clamouring hounds:
With many a quiver'd Nymph I sweep the bounds
Of Maenalus, and chafe the startled boar.
Shall we be tether'd by the frost, the roar,
When Eurus drives the sleet, nor track the fawns
With packs uncoupled, o'er Parthenian lawns?
And now with racing winds the heights we sweep,
Now, plunge to the resounding hollows deep:
Cydonian arrows, if my mood be so,
I scatter from a horny Parthian bow.
Fool! as if these were medicines for love,
Or man's extremity its god could move.
      And now, nor light-foot Hamadryades,
Nor verse itself, nor you, soft woodlands, please.
Ye woods in turn, farewell! Will any cost
Or travail move him? In midwinter's frost
Even if we drink of Hebrus, or endure
Sithonian snows and numbing temperature:
Or when, upon the elm, the parching rind
Has shrunk, in Ethiopia if we bind
A sheep-cote, and each desert try by turns
For pasture, while the sun in Cancer burns,
Love will but tamper with the shaft he drove,

And we must yield to all-subduing Love.'
  Muses, let these suffice; your poet sung
Reclined all day the tender copse among,
And of lithe mallow-twigs a basket wove:
Weaving he sung, and bade the heifers rove.
Complete for him the sylvan rhyme and bear
In your own accents to Cornelius' ear.
Your graces that heroic name adorn
The more, with every moon that fills her horn;
With each my love is newly flourishing,
As alders bourgeon in the early spring.
  But let us rise, for never voice was made,
Nor verse, more tuneful by a chilling shade,
To man distasteful and the ripening field:
Such, even junipers at nightfall yield.
Now pales the latest crimson of the West:
Gather yon batten'd herd, I bring the rest;
And then wind homeward in the dying light;
Homeward my goats, for Hesperus is bright.

JOHN ADDINGTON SYMONDS

(1840-1893)

Born in Bristol, and educated at Harrow and Balliol College, Oxford, where he won the Newdigate Prize, Symonds became a fellow of Magdalen College in 1862. He wrote widely on Dante, Greek poetry and the Renaissance in Italy; but pulmonary disease kept him in Italy for much of his life. After 1878, the year of his translations from Michelangelo and Campanella, he lived almost entirely at Davos, where he counted Robert Louis Stevenson among his acquaintances, and composed his own verses as well as translations from medieval Latin poetry.

Hymn to Aphrodite
(Sappho 1 L-P)

Star-throned incorruptible Aphrodite,
Child of Zeus, wile-weaving, I supplicate thee,
Tame not me with pangs of the heart, dread mistress,
  Nay, nor with anguish.
But come thou, if erst in the days departed
Thou didst lend thine ear to my lamentation,
And from far the house of thy sire deserting,
  Camest with golden
Car yoked: thee thy beautiful sparrows hurried

Swift with multitudinous pinions fluttering
Round black earth, adown from the height of heaven
   Through middle ether:
Quickly journeyed they; and, O thou, blest Lady,
Smiling with those brows of undying lustre,
Asked me what new grief at my heart lay, wherefore
   Now I had called thee,
What I fain would have to assuage the torment
Of my frenzied soul; and whom now, to please thee,
Must persuasion lure to my love, and who now,
   Sappho, hath wronged thee?
Yea, for though she flies, she shall quickly chase thee;
Yea, though gifts she spurns, she shall bestow them;
Yea, though now she loves not, she soon shall love thee,
   Yea, though she will not!
Come, come now too! Come, and from heavy heart-ache
Free my soul, and all that my longing yearns to
Have done, do thou; be thou for me thyself too
   Help in the battle.

WILLIAM MORRIS

(1834-1896)

This multi-faceted genius – poet, designer, printer, craftsman and political
activist – expended the poetic energies of his early life, as did his
contemporaries, on Arthurian and other northern legendary themes. The
Scenes from the Fall of Troy and the *Life and Death of Jason* (both of the 1860s) mark
his first interest in classical legend. In 1874 he produced an illuminated *Horace*,
and in 1875, four years after his move to Kelmscott, he published his
translation of the *Aeneid*, medieval and courtly in diction but vigorous.
Metrically too it harks back several centuries, being composed in fourteeners.
His *Odyssey*, a recreation from political work, which he began in 1886 and
published the following year, cannot be regarded with much admiration (a
short passage is quoted above, in the Introduction). This marks more or less
the end of Morris's literary efforts; from 1880 he had been increasingly taken
up with political work and the Kelmscott Press. In view of his attack on Vergil
and other classical authors in the *Pall Mall Gazette* in 1886 it is rather
surprising that he still continued to occupy himself with the ancient authors at
all.

The death of Turnus
(Vergil, *Aeneid* 12.887-952)

But forth Aeneas goes, and high his spear he brandisheth,
A mighty tree, and from his heart grown fell a word he saith:

'And wherewith wilt thou tarry me? hangs Turnus back again?
No foot-strife but the armèd hand must doom betwixt us twain.
Yea, turn thyself to every shape, and, gathering everything
Wherewith thine heart, thy craft is strong, go soaring on the wing,
And chase the stars; or deep adown in hollow earth lie stored.'
But Turnus shakes his head and saith: "Tis not thy bitter word
That frights me, fierce one; but the Gods, but Jove my foeman grown.'
No more he said, but, looking round, espied a weighty stone,
An ancient mighty rock indeed, that lay upon the lea,
Set for a landmark, judge and end of acre-strife to be,
Which scarce twice six of chosen men upon their backs might raise,
Of bodies such as earth brings forth amid the latter days:
But this in hurrying hand he caught, and rising to the cast,
He hurled it forth against the foe, and followed on it fast;
Yet while he raised the mighty stone, and flung it to its fall,
Knew nought that he was running there, or that he moved at all:
Totter his knees, his chilly blood freezes with deadly frost,
And e'en the hero-gathered stone, through desert distance tost,
O'ercame not all the space betwixt, nor home its blow might bring:
E'en as in dreaming-tide of night, when sleep, the heavy thing,
Weighs on the eyes, and all for nought we seem so helpless-fain
Of eager speed, and faint and fail amidmost of the strain;
The tongue avails not; all our limbs of their familiar skill
Are cheated; neither voice nor words may follow from our will:
So Turnus, by whatever might he strives to win a way,
The Dread One bans his hope; strange thoughts about his heart-strings
     play.
He stareth on his Rutuli, and on the Latin town
Lingering for dread, trembling to meet the spear this instant thrown:
No road he hath to flee, no might against the foe to bear;
Nowhither may he see his car, or sister charioteer.

Aeneas, as he lingereth there, shaketh the fateful shaft,
And, following up its fate with eyes, afar the steel doth waft
With all the might his body hath: no stone the wall-sling bears
E'er roars so loud: no thunderclap with such a crashing tears
Amid the heaven: on flew the spear, huge as the whirlwind black,
And speeding on the dreadful death: it brings to utter wrack
The hauberk's skirt and outer rim of that seven-folded shield,
And goeth grating through the thigh: then falleth unto field
Huge Turnus, with his hampered knee twifolded with the wound:
Then with a groan the Rutuli rise up, and all around
Roar back the hill-sides, and afar the groves cast back the cry:
But he, downcast and suppliant saith, with praying hand and eye:

'Due doom it is; I pray no ruth; use what hath chanced to fall.
Yet, if a wretched father's woe may touch thine heart at all,
I pray thee – since Anchises once was even such to thee, –

Pity my father Daunus' eld, and send me, or, maybe,
My body stripped of light and life, back to my kin and land.
Thou, thou hast conquered: Italy has seen my craven hand
Stretched forth to pray a grace of thee; Lavinia is thy wife:
Strain not thine hatred further now!'
              Fierce in the gear of strife
Aeneas stood with rolling eyes, and held back hand and sword,
And more and more his wavering heart was softening 'neath the word –
When lo! upon the shoulder showed that hapless thong of war!
Lo, glittering with familiar boss the belt child Pallas bore,
Whom Turnus with a wound o'ercame and laid on earth alow,
And on his body bore henceforth those ensigns of his foe.

But he, when he awhile had glared upon that spoil of fight,
That monument of bitter grief, with utter wrath alight,
Cried terrible:
        'And shalt thou, clad in my beloved one's prey,
Be snatched from me? – 'Tis Pallas yet, 'tis Pallas thus doth slay,
And taketh of thy guilty blood atonement for his death!'

Deep in that breast he driveth sword e'en as the word he saith:
But Turnus, – waxen cold and spent, the body of him lies,
And with a groan through dusk and dark the scornful spirit flies.

ROBERT BROWNING

(1812-1889)

Browning was privately educated, though in 1829-30 he attended the Greek class of Professor George Long at University College, London. His first major work was *Sordello* of 1840, and his most famous works date from the years immediately following. He travelled in Italy in the 1840s, where he met Elizabeth Barrett, already famous for her poetry, and they were married in 1846. They lived in Italy until 1851. After the blow of her death in 1861 Browning worked on the *Ring and the Book* and made a study of Euripides which resulted in the translations incorporated in *Balaustion's Adventure* of 1871 and *Aristophanes' Apology* of 1875. This was followed two years later by his version of Aeschylus' *Agememnon*, which has never lacked for critics to condemn it as unreadable. It represents a serious attempt to come to terms with the strangeness of Aeschylus, and sometimes conveys more of a sense of Aeschylean power than any other version, even though some of its phrases went almost unaltered into A. E. Housman's 'Fragment of a Greek Tragedy'. As Reuben Brower says in his study of 'Seven Agamemnons' (bibliography), 'Browning was never more Browning than when he was most trying to be Greek'.

The beacons signal Troy's fall
(Aeschylus, *Agamemnon* 278-316)

Choros: Well, at what time was – even sacked, the city?
Klutaimnestra: Of this same mother Night – the dawn, I tell thee.
Cho: And who of messengers could reach this swiftness?
Klut: Hephaistos – sending a bright blaze from Ide.
Beacon did beacon send, from the fire the poster,
Hitherward: Ide to the rock Hermaian
Of Lemnos: and a third great torch o' the island
Zeus' seat received in turn, the Athoan summit.
And, – so upsoaring as to stride sea over,
The strong lamp-voyager, and all for joyance –
Did the gold-glorious splendour, any sun like,
Pass on – the pine-tree – to Makistos' watch-place;
Who did not, – tardy, – caught, no wits about him,
By sleep, – decline his portion of the missive.
And far the beacon's light, on stream Euripos
Arriving, made aware Messapios' warders,
And up they lit in turn, played herald onwards,
Kindling with flame a heap of grey old heather.
And, strengthening still the lamp, decaying nowise,
Springing o'er Plain Asopos, – full-moon-fashion
Effulgent, – toward the crag of Mount Kithairon,
Roused a new rendering-up of fire the escort –
And light, far escort, lacked no recognition
O' the guard – as burning more than burnings told you.
And over Lake Gorgopis light went leaping,
And, at Mount Aigiplanktos safe arriving,
Enforced the law – 'to never stint the firestuff'.
And they send, lighting up with ungrudged vigour,
Of flame a huge beard, ay, the very foreland
So as to strike above, in burning onward,
The look-out which commands the Strait Saronic.
Then did it dart until it reached the outpost
Mount Arachnaios here, the city's neighbour;
And then darts to this roof of the Atreidai
This light of Ide's fire not unforefathered!
Such are the rules prescribed the flambeau-bearers:
He beats that's first and also least in running.
Such is the proof and token I declare thee,
My husband having sent me news from Troia.

The doom of the Atridae
(Aeschylus, *Agamemnon* 355-84)

Choros:
O Zeus the king, and friendly Night
Of these brave boons bestower –
Thou who didst fling on Troia's every tower
The o'er-roofing snare, that neither great thing might,
Nor any of the young ones, overpass
Captivity's great sweep-net – one and all
Of Ate held in thrall!
Ay, Zeus I fear – the guest's friend great – who was
The doer of this, and long since bent
The bow on Alexandros with intent
That neither wide o' the white
Nor o'er the stars the foolish dart should light.
The stroke of Zeus – they have it, as men say!
This, at least, from the source track forth we may!
As he ordained, so has he done.
'No' – said someone –
'The gods think fit to care
Nowise for mortals, such
As those by whom the good and fair
Of things denied their touch
Is trampled!' but he was profane.
That they do care, has been made plain
To offspring of the over-bold,
Outbreathing 'Ares' greater than is just –
Houses that spill with more than they can hold,
More than is best for man. Be man's what must
Keep harm off, so that in himself he find
Sufficiency – the well-endowed of mind!
For there's no bulwark in man's wealth to him
Who, through a surfeit, kicks – into the dim
And disappearing – Right's great altar.

Lament for Alcestis
(Euripides, *Alcestis* 435-59) from *Balaustion's Adventure*
Daughter of Pelias, with farewell from me,
I' th' house of Hades have thy unsunned home!
Let Hades know, the dark-haired deity, –
And he who sits to row and steer alike,
Old corpse-conductor, let him know he bears
Over the Acherontian lake, this time,
I' the two-oared boat, the best – oh, best by far
Of womankind! For thee, Alkestis Queen!
Many a time those haunters of the Muse

Shall sing thee to the seven-stringed mountain-shell,
And glorify in hymns that need no harp,
At Sparta when the cycle comes about,
And that Karneian month wherein the moon
Rises and never sets the whole night through.
So too at splendid and magnificent
Athenai. Such the spread of thy renown,
And such the lay that, dying, thou hast left
Singer and sayer. O that I availed
Of my own might to send thee once again
From Hades' hall, Kokutos' stream, by help
O' the oar that dips the river, back to day!

OSCAR WILDE

(1856-1900)

The most flamboyant personality of the nineties, Wilde's fame rests on other supports than this translation, made while an undergraduate at Magdalen College, Oxford, of a chorus from Aristophanes' *Clouds*.

The chorus of clouds
(Aristophanes, *Clouds* 275-90, 298-313)

Cloud-maidens that float on for ever,
  Dew-sprinkled, fleet bodies, and fair,
Let us rise from our Sire's loud river,
  Great Ocean, and soar through the air
To the peaks of the pine-covered mountains where the pines hang as
      tresses of hair
Let us seek the watchtowers undaunted,
  Where the well-watered cornfields abound,
And through murmurs of rivers nymph-haunted
  The songs of the sea-waves resound;
And the sun in the sky never wearies of spreading his radiance around.
    Let us cast off the haze
      Of the mists from our band,
    Till with far-seeing gaze
      We may look on the land.

Cloud-maidens that bring the rain-shower,
  To the Pallas-loved land let us wing,
To the land of stout heroes and Power,
  Where Kekrops was hero and king,
Where honour and silence is given

To the mysteries that none may declare,
Where are gifts to the gods in high heaven
    When the house of the gods is laid bare,
Where are lofty roofed temples, and statues well carven and fair;
    Where are feasts to the happy immortals
When the sacred procession draws near,
    Where garlands make bright the bright portals
At all seasons and months in the year;
    And when spring days are here,
Then we tread to the wine-god a measure,
    In Bacchanal dance and in pleasure,
'Mid the contests of sweet singing choirs,
    And the crash of loud lyres.

ROBERT LOUIS STEVENSON

(1850-1894)

Born and educated in Edinburgh, Stevenson was called to the bar but never practised due to bronchial weakness. He devoted his time to essays, and *Virginibus Puerisque* was published in 1881. From 1880 his health was very poor and he spent his winters at Davos. In 1883 came the success of *Treasure Island*, and after travelling for some time in the Pacific he bought a home in Samoa in 1888. It is from these last years that his translations apparently date – the leisure occupation of a sick but already famous man.

Freedom
(Martial, *Epigrams* 5.20)

God knows, my Martial, if we two could be
To enjoy our days set wholly free;
To the true life together bend our mind,
And take a furlough from the falser kind,
No rich saloon, no palace of the great,
Nor suit at law should trouble our estate;
On no vainglorious statues should we look,
But of a walk, a talk, a little book,
Baths, wells, a mead, and the verandah shade,
Let all our travels and our toils be made.
Now neither lives unto himself, alas!
And the good suns we see, that flash and pass
And perish; and the bell that knells them cries,
'Another gone: O when will ye arise?'

A. E. HOUSMAN

(1859-1936)

The most brilliant classical scholar of his generation, Housman performed
dismally in his final examinations at Oxford, and went to work in the Patent
Office. He continued however to publish on classical authors, and was elected
Professor of Latin at University College, London, in 1892, and at Cambridge
in 1911. Better known for his marvellous parody in *Fragment of a Greek Tragedy*,
Housman's two serious translations from Greek drama echo the themes of his
own poetry with the same plangent sentimentality that contrasts so
remarkably with the acerbic and devastating lash of his criticism. Like many
scholars, he saw criticism and scholarship as unrelated; his test of poetry, as
described in *The Name and Nature of Poetry*, was whether it makes the bristles on
the back of one's neck stand on end. It was this very limited conception of
poetry which practically compelled him to devote his life to a scholarship free
of all values other than exactitude, exercised on a poet so second-rate that his
scholarly judgment was not likely to be disturbed by his passionate response to ˏ
the poetry.

'Diffugere Nives'
(Horace, *Odes* 4.7)

The snows are fled away, leaves on the shaws
  And grasses in the mead renew their birth,
The river to the river-bed withdraws,
  And altered is the fashion of the earth.

The Nymphs and Graces three put off their fear
  And unapparelled in the woodland play.
The swift hour and the brief prime of the year
  Say to the soul, *Thou wast not born for aye.*

Thaw follows frost; hard on the heel of spring
  Treads summer sure to die, for hard on hers
Comes autumn, with his apples scattering;
  Then back to wintertide, when nothing stirs.

But oh, whate'er the sky-led seasons mar,
  Moon upon moon rebuilds it with her beams:
Come *we* where Tullus and where Ancus are,
  And good Aeneas, we are dust and dreams.

underworld

Torquatus, if the gods in heaven shall add
  The morrow to the day, what tongue has told?
Feast then thy heart, for what thy heart has had
  The fingers of no heir will ever hold.

When thou descendest once the shades among,
  The stern assize and equal judgment o'er,

Not thy long lineage nor thy golden tongue,
  No, nor thy righteousness, shall friend thee more.

Night holds Hipploytus the pure of stain,
  Diana steads him nothing, he must stay;
And Theseus leaves Pirithous in the chain
  The love of comrades cannot take away.

didn't let Phaedra seduce him

Life's woe
(Sophocles, *Oedipus at Colonus* 1211-48)

What man is he that yearneth
  For length unmeasured of days?
Folly mine eye discerneth
  Encompassing all his ways.
For years over-running the measure
  Shall change thee in evil wise:
Grief draweth nigh thee; and pleasure,
  Behold, it is hid from thine eyes.
  This to their wage have they
  Which overlive their day.
And he that looseth from labour
  Doth one with other befriend,
  Whom bride nor bridesmen attend,
Song, nor sound of the tabor,
  Death, that maketh an end.

Thy portion esteem I highest,
  Who wast not ever begot;
Thine next, being born who diest
  And straightway again art not.
With follies light as the feather
  Doth Youth to man befall;
Then evils gather together,
  There wants not one of them all –
  Wrath, envy, discord, strife,
  The sword that seeketh life.
And sealing the sum of trouble
  Doth tottering Age draw nigh,
  Whom friends and kinsfolk fly,
Age, upon whom redouble
  All sorrows under the sky.

This man, as me, even so,
Have the evil days overtaken;
And like as a cape sea-shaken
With tempest at earth's last verges
And shock of all winds that blow,
His head the seas of woe,

The thunders of awful surges
Ruining overflow;
Blown from the fall of even,
  Blown from the dayspring forth,
Blown from the noon in heaven,
  Blown from night and the North.

SIR RICHARD BURTON

(1829-1890)

Burton served for some time in India, and joined Speke on the expedition
which resulted in the discovery of Tanganyika. Most of his literary output is
oriental in provenance – translations of the Arabian Nights, the Kama Sutra,
etc. – and the Catullus is his last work, begun in 1890 at Hamman R'irha and
incomplete at his death. In his Preface he writes 'Our youngers, in most
respects our seniors, now expect the translation not only to interpret the sense
of the original but also, when the text lends itself to such treatment, to render it
verbatim et literatim, nothing being increased or diminished, curtailed or
expanded.' The wheel has come full circle from the seventeenth-century
preoccupation with freedom and naturalness of rendering, and Burton's
Catullus shows all the oddness that characterises his Arabian Nights.

Spring journey
(Catullus 46)

Now Spring his cooly mildness brings us back,
Now th' equinoctial heaven's rage and wrack
Hushes at hest of Zephyr's bonny breeze.
Far left (Catullus!) be the Phrygian leas
And summery Nicaea's fertile downs:
Fly we to Asia's fame-illumined towns.
Now lust my fluttering thoughts for wayfare long,
Now my glad eager feet grow steady, strong,
O fare ye well, my comrades, pleasant throng,
Ye who together far from homesteads flying,
By many various ways come homewards hieing.

AUBREY BEARDSLEY

(1872-1898)

Known chiefly for his drawings illustrating the *Morte D'Arthur*, *Salome*, the *Rape
of the Lock*, and *Volpone*, Beardsley was editor of the *Yellow Book* begun in 1894 as
well as of the *Savoy*, in which this version from Catullus appeared in 1896.

Last farewell to a brother
(Catullus 101)

By ways remote and distant waters sped,
Brother, to thy sad grave-side am I come,
That I may give the last gifts to the dead,
And vainly parley with thine ashes dumb:
Since she who now bestows and now denies
Hath ta'en thee, hapless brother, from mine eyes.
But lo! these gifts, the heirlooms of past years,
Are made sad things to grace thy coffin shell;
Take them, all drenched with a brother's tears,
And, brother, for all time, hail and farewell!

EDWIN ARLINGTON ROBINSON

(1869-1935)

Robinson published his first book of poetry at his own expense in 1896, and a year later it reappeared in augmented form as *Children of the Night*. From there he went on to become one of the most admired poets of his generation in America.

The singer
(Nicarchus, in *Greek Anthology* 11.186)

The gloom of death is on the raven's wing,
    The song of death is in the raven's cries:
But when Demophilus begins to sing,
    The raven dies.

Doricha
(Posidippus 17 G-P)

So now the very bones of you are gone
Where they were dust and ashes long ago;
And there was the last ribbon you tied on
To bind your hair, and that is dust also;
And somewhere there is dust that was of old
A soft and scented garment that you wore –
The same that once till dawn did closely fold
You in with fair Charaxus, fair no more.

But Sappho, and the white leaves of her song
Will make your name a word for all to learn,
And all to love thereafter, even while

It's but a name; and this will be as long
As there are distant ships that will return
Again to Naucratis and to the Nile.

THOMAS HARDY

(1840-1928)

Hardy's output consisted entirely of verse until he began the series of novels set in his native Wessex with *Under the Greenwood Tree* (1872). The series concluded with *Jude the Obscure* in 1896. He then turned back to poetry, and his *Wessex Poems and Other Verses* of 1898 includes a number of poems from his early years, among which these translations are to be counted. The fatalism of Greek tragedy was a pronounced influence on his novels, and finds its fullest expression in the drama *The Dynasts*, though *Tess* also concludes with an (unsignalled) quotation from Aeschylus. The translation from Catullus was prompted by his passing the spot it celebrates.

'After passing Sirmione, April 1887'
(Catullus 31)

Sirmio, thou dearest dear of strands
That Neptune strokes in land and sea,
With what high joy from stranger lands
Doth thy old friend set foot on thee!
Yea, barely seems it true to me
That no Bithynia holds me now,
But calmly and assuringly
Around me stretchest homely Thou.
Is there a scene more sweet than when
Our clinging cares are undercast,
And, worn by alien moils and men,
The long untrodden sill repassed,
We press the kindly couch at last,
And find a full repayment there?
Then hail, sweet Sirmio; thou that wast,
And art, mine own unrivalled Fair!

7.   The Twentieth Century

GILBERT MURRAY

(1866-1957)

Murray was Regius Professor of Greek at Oxford, and one of the most influential classical scholars of his generation. He translated a prodigious number of Greek dramas. He also wrote books on most major Greek authors, and on Greek religion. T. S. Eliot did him the dubious honour of an essay on his translations in which he attacks them as symptomatic of a generation's failure to understand either Greek literature or poetry. They have worn better than most contemporary translations.

The chorus react to Phaedra's suicide
(Euripides, *Hippolytus* 732-75)

Could I but take me to some cavern for mine hiding,
In the hill-tops where the Sun scarce hath trod;
Or a cloud make the home of mine abiding.
As a bird among the bird-droves of God!
Could I wing me to my rest amid the roar
Of the deep Adriatic on the shore,
Where the waters of Eridanus are clear,
And Phaethon's sad sisters by his grave
Weep into the river, and each tear
Gleams, a drop of amber, in the wave.

To the strand of the Daughters of the Sunset,
The Apple-tree, the singing and the gold;
Where the mariner must stay him from his onset,
And the red wave is tranquil as of old;
Yea, beyond the Pillar of the End
That Atlas guardeth, would I wend;
Where a voice of living waters never ceaseth
In God's quiet garden by the sea,
And Earth, the ancient life-giver, increaseth
Joy among the meadows, like a tree.

O shallop of Crete, whose milk-white wing
Through the swell and the storm-beating,

Bore us thy Prince's daughter,
Was it well she came from a joyous home
To a far King's bridal across the foam?
What joy hath her bridal brought her?
Sure some spell upon either hand
Flew with thee from the Cretan strand,
Seeking Athena's tower divine;
And there, where Munychus fronts the brine,
Crept by the shore-flung cables' line,
The curse from the Cretan water!

And, for that dark spell that about her clings,
Sick desires of forbidden things
The soul of her rend and sever;
The bitter tide of calamity
Hath risen above her lips; and she,
Where bends she her last endeavour?
She will hie her alone to her bridal room,
And a rope swing slow in the rafters' gloom;
And a fair white neck shall creep to the noose,
A-shudder with dread, yet firm to choose
The one way strait for fame, and lose
The Love and the pain for ever.

JAMES ELROY FLECKER

(1884-1915)

Born in Lewisham, educated at Uppingham, and Trinity College, Oxford,
Flecker entered the consular service in 1908, and was posted to Cairo, and
subsequently to Constantinople from 1911 to 1913. These locations provided
the inspiration for most of his verse, notably *Hassan* and the *Golden Journey to
Samarkand*, though Greek themes also occur. He died of consumption at Davos.

His boat
(Catullus 4)

Proud is Phaselus here, my friends, to tell
That once she was the swiftest craft afloat:
No vessel, were she winged with blade or sail,
Could ever pass my boat.
Phaselus shunned to shun grim Adria's shore,
Or Cyclades, or Rhodes the wide renowned,
Or Bosphorus, where Thracian waters roar,
Or Pontus' eddying sound.

It was in Pontus once, unwrought, she stood,
And conversed, sighing, with her sister trees,
Amastris born, or where Cytorus' wood
Answers the mountain breeze.
Pontic Amastris, boxwood-clad Cytorus! –
You, says Phaselus, are her closest kin:
Yours were the forests where she stood inglorious:
The waters yours wherein
She dipped her virgin blades; and from your strand
She bore her master through the cringing straits,
Nought caring were the wind on either hand,
Or whether kindly fates
Filled both the straining sheets. Never a prayer
For her was offered to the gods of haven,
Till last she left the sea, hither to fare,
And to be lightly laven
By the cool ripple of the clear lagoon
     . . . . . .

This too is past; at length she is allowed
Long slumber through her life's long afternoon,
To Castor and the twin of Castor vowed.

RICHARD ALDINGTON

(1892-1962)

Aldington attended London University, and in 1913 became the editor of *The Egoist*, the Imagist periodical. His translation from Sappho is a homage to one of the triad of Imagist gods, Sappho, Catullus and Villon; it was rejected by Harriet Monroe for publication in *Poetry* on the advice of Paul Shorey, but was printed by Ezra Pound in his anthology *Des Imagistes* (1914). It introduced Pound to Sappho, and her influence is discernible in some of the poems of *Lustra* and especially in *Canto* 5. Aldington subsequently translated Anyte of Tegea (1915), medieval Latin poets (1916) and Meleager and the Anacreontica (1919) into prose. His *Images* of 1915 show frequent traces of hellenising, and hellenic allusions are apparent in his later works too.

'To Atthis'
(Sappho 96 L-P)

Atthis, far from me and dear Mnasidika,
Dwells in Sardis;
Many times she was near us
So that we lived life well
Like the far-famed goddess
Whom above all things music delighted.

And now she is first among the Lydian women
As the mighty sun, the rose-fingered moon,
Beside the great stars.

And the light fades from the bitter sea
And in like manner from the rich-blossoming earth;
And the dew is shed upon the flowers,
Rose and soft meadow-sweet
And many-coloured melilote.
Many things told are remembered of sterile Atthis.

I yearn to behold thy delicate soul
To satiate my desire . . .

ROBERT BRIDGES

(1844-1930)

Bridges was educated at Eton and Christ Church, Oxford, and studied
medicine, which he practised until his early retirement in 1882. In this period
he published several volumes of lyrics; these were followed by several plays
and the narrative poem *Eros and Psyche*, the story taken from Apuleius. His
interest in metric was encouraged by W. J. Stone's *Classical Metres in English
Verse* (1899) which he reprinted in the second edition of his own *Milton's
Prosody*. This interest found further outlet in *Ibant Obscuri*, an anthology of
earlier translations of Homer and Vergil with Bridges' own versions of some
passages in English hexameters. His enthusiasm for the poems of his friend
Gerard Manley Hopkins evinces the same interest in prosody.

Hermes to Priam
(Homer, *Iliad* 24.410ff.) from *Ibant Obscuri*

Then bespake him again God's angel, slayer of Argus.
'O good sire, not yet hath foul dog nor ravening bird
Made their prey of him: ev'n as he was, so lies he neglected
Hard by Achilles' ship i' the camp: and already twelve days
There hath lain, nor doth his flesh rot nor the corrupt worms
Touch him, that fatten on mankind nor spare the illustrious.
But when morning appears Achilles cometh and draggeth him forth
Trailing around the barrow builded to his old companyon.
Nor yet is injury done: thou mightest go thither, and see
How dew-fresh he lieth, how free from death's blemish or stain:
His blood bath'd away, and heal'd those heavy wounds all
Where many coward spears had pierc'd his fair body fallen.
Such care take the blessed gods for thy dearly belov'd son,
Yea, though he live no more; since they full heartily lov'd him.'

HILDA DOOLITTLE

(1886-1961)

Born in Pennsylvania; she edited the *Egoist*, in succession to her husband, Richard Aldington, from 1916-17. Her poetry blends an intense feeling for Greek light and landscape with an adherence to the tenets of Imagism, so that a romantic hellenism is tempered by a classic concreteness of diction, with the limitations as well as the virtues that concreteness entails.

The cause of the Trojan war
(Euripides, *Iphigeneia in Aulis* 573-89)

Paris came to Ida.
He grew to slim height
Among the silver-hoofed beasts.
Strange notes made his flute
A Phrygian pipe.
He caught all Olympos
In his bent reeds.
While his great beasts
Cropped the grass,
The goddesses held the contest
Which sent him among the Greeks.

He came before Helen's house.
He stood on the ivory steps.
He looked upon Helen and brought
Desire to the eyes
That looked back –

The Greeks have snatched up their spears.
They have pointed the helms of their ships
Toward the bulwarks of Troy.

EZRA POUND

(1885-1972)

Pound was born in Idaho; he taught for a while at Wabash College, then travelled in Europe. From 1914-15 he was editor of *Blast*, and from 1917-19 London editor of the *Little Review*. Pound deserves his reputation as the driving force behind modern poetry, and the Imagist movement of his early days expressed its principles (as do most real innovations) in terms of a return to the principles of classical writing, clarity and succinctness. Hand in hand with the cleansing of poetic diction goes a radically new attitude to classical poetry.

Homage to *Sextus Propertius* is seminal in its revaluation of a little read classic author: equally important is Pound's preoccupation throughout his life with the importance of translation – blood brought to ghosts (Hugh Kenner, *The Pound Era* (1972), p. 150). It is significant that the first of the Cantos, that microcosm of modern chaos, is a translation of the sixteenth-century Latin version of Homer, *Odyssey* 11. Though in the twentieth century classical authors have had to share their place with old authors of other cultures – notably French, Provençal, Italian and Chinese – the principle of 'What thou lov'st well is thy true heritage' has not been abandoned. Pound's politics might seem to show the increasing incompatibility of the aesthete's values with those of the humanist, but his poetry without doubt gives life to authors who in the hands of Wardour Street had become dangerously moribund.

Homage to Sextus Propertius
(Propertius, *Elegies* 2.13b & 3.5.13-16)

When, when, and whenever death closes our eyelids,

Moving naked over Acheron
Upon the one raft, victor and conquered together,
Marius and Jugurtha together,
  one tangle of shadows.
Caesar plots against India,
Tigris and Euphrates shall, from now on, flow at his bidding,
Tibet shall be full of Roman policemen,
The Parthians shall get used to our statuary
  and acquire a Roman religion;
One raft on the veiled flood of Acheron,
  Marius and Jugurtha together.

Nor at my funeral either will there be any long trail,
  bearing ancestral lares and images;
No trumpets filled with my emptiness,
Nor shall it be on an Atalic bed;
  The perfumed cloths shall be absent.
A small plebeian procession.
  Enough, enough and in plenty
There will be three books at my obsequies
ᐧWhich I take, my not unworthy gift, to Persephone.

You will follow the bare scarified breast
Nor will you be weary of calling my name, nor too weary
  To place the last kiss on my lips
When the Syrian onyx is broken.
    'He who is now vacant dust
    'Was once the slave of one passion':
Give that much inscription
    'Death why tardily come?'

You, sometimes, will lament a lost friend,
　　For it is a custom:
This care for past men,
Since Adonis was gored in Idalia, and the Cytherean
Ran crying with out-spread hair,
　　In vain, you call back the shade,
In vain, Cynthia. Vain call to unanswering shadow.
　　Small talk comes from small bones.

To Formianus' young lady friend
(Catullus 43)

All Hail; young lady with a nose
　　by no means too small,
With a foot unbeautiful,
　　and with eyes that are not black,
With fingers that are not long, and with a mouth undry,
And with a tongue by no means too elegant,
You are the friend of Formianus, the vendor of cosmetics,
And they call you beautiful in the province,
And you are even compared to Lesbia.

O most unfortunate age!

Odysseus summons the ghosts
(Homer, *Odyssey* 11. 26-78) from *Canto* 1

Poured we libations unto each the dead,
First mead and then sweet wine, water mixed with white flour.
Then prayed I many a prayer to the sickly death's-heads;
As set in Ithaca, sterile bulls of the best
For sacrifice, heaping the pyre with goods,
A sheep to Tiresias only, black and a bell-sheep.
Dark blood flowed in the fosse,
Souls out of Erebus, cadaverous dead, of brides,
Of youths and of the old who had borne much;
Souls stained with recent tears, girls tender,
Men many, mauled with bronze lance-heads,
Battle spoil, bearing yet dreory arms,
These many crowded about me; with shouting,
Pallor upon me, cried to my men for more beasts;
Slaughtered the herds, sheep slain of bronze;
Poured ointment, cried to the gods,
To Pluto the strong, and praised Proserpine;
Unsheathed the narrow sword,
I sat to keep off the impetuous impotent dead,
Till I should hear Tiresias.

But first Elpenor came, our friend Elpenor,
Unburied, cast on the wide earth,
Limbs that we left in the house of Circe,
Unwept, unwrapped in sepulchre, since toils urged other.
Pitiful spirit. And I cried in hurried speech:
'Elpenor, how art thou come to this dark coast?
'Cam'st thou afoot, outstripping seamen?'
　　And he in heavy speech:
'Ill fate and abundant wine. I slept in Circe's ingle.
'Going down the long ladder unguarded,
'I fell against the buttress,
'Shattered the nape-nerve, the soul sought Avernus.
'But thou, O King, I bid remember me, unwept, unburied,
'Heap up mine arms, be tomb by sea-bord, and inscribed:
'*A man of no fortune, and with a name to come.*
'And set my oar up, that I swung amid fellows.'

ARTHUR SYMONS

(1865-1945)

Apart from his own polished but superficial poetry, Symons' best known works are his translations of D'Annunzio and Baudelaire. He also wrote extensively on English literature, and earns a place in the history of English letters above all for his *The Symbolist Movement in Poetry* which strongly influenced Yeats and Eliot.

On a dead wife
(Catullus 96)

If living sorrows any boon
Unto the silent grave can give,
When sad remembrances revive
Old loves and friendships fugitive,
She sorrows less she died so soon
Than joys your love is still alive.

Let us live and love
(Catullus 5)

Let us live, my Lesbia, and let us love:
Old men's sayings are for old men wise enough:
Give them a farthing for the price of the stuff.
Suns may set and suns upon earth arise:
As for us, when for us the brief light dies,

There is only one night, and an everlasting sleeping.
Give me a thousand kisses, then; be heaping
A hundred upon a thousand, then a second hundred
Upon another thousand, and another hundred;
Then, when the number has up to a myriad mounted,
Let us lose the reckoning, lest our love shall be counted,
And we or another envying us should guess
How many lives make up our happiness.

BASIL BUNTING

(b. 1900)

Much of Bunting's early work is very much in a Poundian mould, for he was closely associated with the leading literary figures of Pound's generation, especially in America. After a long silence, *Briggflats* of 1966 was written in an utterly distinctive tone. Several of his translations date from the 1920s and 30s, though the Postumus ode dates only from 1971.

Invocation to Venus
(Lucretius, *On the Nature of Things* 1.1-28)

Darling of Gods and Men, beneath the gliding stars
you fill rich earth and buoyant sea with your presence
for every living thing achieves its life through you,
rises and sees the sun. For you the sky is clear,
the tempests still. Deft earth scatters her gentle flowers,
the level ocean laughs, the softened heavens glow
with generous light for you. In the first days of spring
when the untrammelled allrenewing southwind blows
the birds exult in you and herald your coming.
Then the shy cattle leap and swim the brooks for love.
Everywhere, through all seas mountains and waterfalls,
love caresses all hearts and kindles all creatures
to overmastering lust and ordained renewals.
Therefore, since you alone control the sum of things
and nothing without you comes forth into the light
and nothing beautiful or glorious can be
without you, Alma Venus! trim my poetry
with your grace; and give peace to write and read and think.

'You can't grip years, Postume'
(Horace, *Odes* 2.14)

You can't grip years, Postume,
that ripple away nor hold back

wrinkles and, soon now, age,
nor can you tame death

not if you paid three hundred
bulls every day that goes by
to Pluto, who has no tears,
who has dyked up

giants where we'll go aboard,
we who feed on the soil,
to cross, kings some, some penniless plowmen.

For nothing we keep out of war
or from screaming spindrift
or wrap ourselves against autumn,
for nothing, seeing

we must stare at that dark, slow
drift and watch the damned
toil, while all they build
tumbles back on them.

We must let earth go and home,
wives too, and your trim trees,
yours for a moment, save one
sprig of black cypress.

Better men will empty
bottles we locked away,
wine puddle our table,
fit wine for a pope.

WILLIAM BUTLER YEATS

(1865-1939)

Born near Dublin, Yeats in most of his work echoes the aspirations of the Irish to national identity, even among the traditionally Unionist Anglo-Irish class he sprang from. Like the English Pre-Raphaelites, he turned for his themes to the resources of national legend rather than to the classical past or, like Joyce later, to an amalgam of the two. His translations from classical poetry are *parerga*; yet the second given here reflects the aristocratic and apocalyptic pessimism of some of his finest original poems, like *The Second Coming*.

Colonus' praise
(Sophocles, *Oedipus at Colonus* 668-719)

Chorus: Come praise Colonus' horses, and come praise
The wine-dark of the wood's intricacies,

The nightingale that deafens daylight there,
If daylight ever visit where,
Unvisited by tempest or by sun,
Immortal ladies tread the ground
Dizzy with harmonious sound,
Semele's lad a gay companion.

And yonder in the gymnasts' garden thrives
The self-sown, self-begotten shape that gives
Athenian intellect its mastery,
Even the grey-leaved olive-tree
Miracle-bred out of the living stone;
Nor accident of peace nor war
Shall wither that old marvel, for
The great grey-eyed Athene stares thereon.

Who comes into this country, and has come
Where golden crocus and narcissus bloom,
Where the Great Mother, mourning for her daughter
And beauty-drunken by the water
Glittering among the grey-leaved olive-trees,
Has plucked a flower and sung her loss;
Who finds abounding Cephisus
Has found the loveliest spectacle there is.

Because this country has a pious mind
And so remembers that when all mankind
But trod the road, or splashed about the shore,
Poseidon gave it bit and oar,
Every Colonus lad or lass discourses
Of that oar and of that bit;
Summer and winter, day and night,
Of horses and horses of the sea, white horses.

Life and death
(Sophocles, *Oedipus at Colonus*, 1211-48)

Endure what life God gives and ask no longer span;
Cease to remember the delights of youth, travel-wearied aged man;
Delight becomes death-longing if all longing else be vain.

Even from that delight memory treasures so,
Death, despair, division of families, all entanglements of mankind grow,
As that old wandering beggar and these God-hated children know.

In the long echoing street the laughing dancers throng,
The bride is carried to the bridegroom's chamber through torchlight and
    tumultuous song;
I celebrate the silent kiss that ends life short or long.

Never to have lived is best, ancient writers say;
Never to have drawn the breath of life, never to have looked into the eye
  of day;
The second best's a gay goodnight and quickly turn away.

FREDERICK ADAM WRIGHT

(1869-1946)

Wright was Professor of Classics at Birkbeck College, London, and the author
of numerous books on classical literature as well as of translations from Greek
and Latin authors.

The poet summons his verses
(Catullus 42)

Come, my verses, each and sundry, gather round me one and all;
There's a certain filthy strumpet and on you for aid I call.
If you let her, she will treat me like a common jumping-jack;
For she's got your writing-tablets and she will not give them back.
'Who's the girl?' you ask. Each evening you may see her strutting here,
Looking like a tenth-rate actress with her nasty foreign leer.
Raise your voices loud against her – 'We our writing tablets lack:
Give them back, you filthy strumpet, filthy strumpet, give them back.'
Brothel mud, she takes no notice! Come, my lads, another try.
Let us make her blush, the wanton, if we can. Now louder cry –
'You have got our writing tablets' – shout it till your jawbones crack –
'Give them back, you filthy strumpet, filthy strumpet, give them back.'
No, that does not move her either. If we would successful be,
We must try another method; that I very plainly see.
So, my lads, for our last effort we will take another tack –
'Paragon of virtuous maidens, give our writing tablets back.'

LOUIS MacNEICE

(1870-1963)

Born in Belfast, and one of the major poets of his generation, MacNeice
produced a number of verse plays as well as his translations of *Faust* and of
Aeschylus' *Agamemnon* which has often been acclaimed as one of the most
successful versions of that difficult author, combining a fidelity to the sense
with a style recognisable as real contemporary poetry. His other poetry, which
is voluminous, contains very little translation.

The war at Troy
(Aeschylus, *Agamemnon* 551-572)

Herald: These things have taken time.
Some of them we could say have fallen well,
While some we blame. Yet who except the gods
Is free from pain the whole duration of life?
If I were to tell of our labours, our hard lodging,
The sleeping on crowded decks, the scanty blankets,
Tossing and groaning, rations that never reached us –
And the land too gave matter for more disgust,
For our beds lay under the enemy's walls.
Continuous drizzle from the sky, dews from the marshes,
Rotting our clothes, filling our hair with lice.
And if one were to tell of the bird-destroying winter
Intolerable from the snows of Ida
Or of the heat when the sea slackens at noon
Waveless and dozing in a depressed calm –
But why make these complaints? The weariness is over;
Over indeed for some who never again
Need even trouble to rise.
Why make a computation of the lost?
Why need the living sorrow for the spites of fortune?
I wish to say a long goodbye to disasters.

Helen, Troy's doom
(Aeschylus, *Agamemnon* 738-71)

Chorus:
So I would say there came
To the city of Troy
A notion of windless calm
Delicate adornment of riches,
Soft shooting of the eyes and flower
Of desire that stings the fancy.
But swerving aside she achieved
A bitter end to her marriage,
Ill guest and ill companion,
Hurled upon Priam's sons, convoyed
By Zeus, patron of guest and host,
Dark angel dowered with tears.
Long current among men an old saying
Runs that a man's prosperity
When grown to greatness
Comes to the birth, does not die childless –
His good luck breeds for his house
Distress that shall not be appeased.

I only, apart from the others,
Hold that the unrighteous action
Breeds true to its kind,
Leaves its own children behind it.
But the lot of a righteous house
Is a fair offspring always.

Ancient self-glory is accustomed
To bear to light in the evil sort of men
A new self-glory and madness,
Which sometime or sometime finds
The appointed hour for its birth,
And born therewith is the Spirit, intractable, unholy, irresistible,
The reckless lust that brings black Doom upon the house,
A child that is like the parents.

The fortunes of men
(Aeschylus, *Agamemnon* 1327-30)

Cassandra:
Ah the fortunes of men! When they go well
A shadow sketch would match them, and in ill-fortune
The dab of a wet sponge destroys the drawing.
It is not myself but the life of man I pity.

L. A. S. JERMYN

(fl. 1940-47)

Jermyn's translation of Vergil's *Georgics*, 'The Singing Farmer', was written in an internment camp in Singapore, where the author had been a teacher, during the Second World War. In his Preface he writes: 'The translation of Book III was finished in July, 1945, just a month before our release. By that time there was such a spirit of confidence throughout the camp that I was able positively to enjoy Vergil's description of the cattle plagues, even though they reminded us so keenly of our own.'

Description of the plague
(Vergil, *Georgics* 3.548-66)

No remedy was found in change of food:
New arts availed not: physic was all vain,
Though learned of Chiron, son of Phillyra,
Or of Melampus, Amythaon's child.
Bursting from Stygian gloom to light of suns,
Raged the pale fury, and before her drove
Disease and Dread, and ever day by day

Surged loftier, raising her insatiate head.
Streams and dry banks and hills that seem to drowse
Echoed the bleat of sheep, the frequent groans
Of oxen; and within the very stalls
The plague brought death to multitudes, and heaped
The bodies rotting in corruption foul,
Until men learned to cover them with earth,
Burying them deep. For no use was the hide,
Nor could the stench be washed out of the flesh
Or overcome by roasting, nor the fleece
Be shorn, all eaten through with putrid filth.
And if 't were tried, the web set up would break
In pieces at a touch; and, worse than this,
Should any seek to don such tainted cloth,
The burning pustules and foul sweat ran o'er
His fetid limbs, and, biding for no time,
Th' accursed fire consumed his stricken joints.

J. B. LEISHMAN
(1902-1963)

Educated at St John's College, Oxford, Leishman was a lecturer in English at Southampton and then at Oxford University. Best known for his writings on the Metaphysical Poets, Leishman translated Hölderlin and Rilke as well as Horace.

Hymn to Fortune
(Horace, *Odes* 1.35)

O goddess ruling fortunate Antium,
now manifest in raising from low degree
　　our mortal clay, and now in turning
into a funeral the proudest triumph;

by toiling peasants courted with anxious prayer
as rural overruler, as ocean's queen
　　by one defying with some Bithynian
keel the tempestuous eastern waters;

by unprovided Dacian or roving Scyth,
by cities, nations, combative Latium,
　　by fell barbarian monarchs' mothers
dreaded, and feared by the purple tyrant,

lest your insulting foot shall unpediment
the columned state and gathering populace

with cries of 'arms, to arms', incite the   *civil war*
peaceably-minded and wreck dominion.

Before you marches savage Necessity,
conveying the binding wedges and mighty nails
   in brazen hand, nor leaves the stuborn
clamp or the mortaring lead behind her.

Hope tends your shrine, and rarest Fidelity
in candid raiment, ever-companioning
   when you in changed and hostile mood have
quitted the mansion of mourning greatness.

Then, though, the traitrous rabble and perjured whore
give ground, and, when they've tippled the cellar dry,
   friends vanish like those dregs they've drained and
leave us to shoulder the yoke without them.

Take care of Caesar, bound for the uttermost
Britannic islands, him and the youthful band
   of newly-mustered warriors bringing
fear to the East and the Red Sea borders.

Alas, our shameful scars and our crimes and all
our perished brethren! What has our hardenedness
   refrained from? What still uncommitted
evil remains? From what profanation

has fear of the gods kept youthful impiety?
What altar's scaped their outrage? Re-forge for us
   on better anvil these our blunted
swords to encounter the Scyths and Arabs!

            persians

CHRISTOPHER LOGUE

(b. 1926)

Logue's poetry is strongly influenced by Pound, especially in the 'concrete' style of his *Iliad* versions. He has also translated – or adapted – Pablo Neruda, and his original poetry tends to themes of social and political commitment.

When Patroclus killed Sarpedon
(Homer, *Iliad* 16.644-83) from *War Music*

It is true that men are clever.
But the least of gods is cleverer than their best.
   And it was here, before God's hands
(Moons poised either side of the world's agate)

You overreached yourself, Patroclus.
    Yes, my darling,
Not only God was out that day but Lord Apollo.
'*You know he loves the Trojans, so,*
No Matter how, how much, how often, or how easily you win,
Once you have forced them back, you stop.'
    Remember it Patroclus? Or was it years ago
Achilles cautioned you outside his tent?
Remembering or not you stripped Sarpedon's gear,
That glittered like the sea's far edge at dawn
Ordered your borrowed Myrmidons to drag him off
And went for Troy alone.
    And God turned to Apollo, saying:
'Mousegod, take my Sarpedon out of range
And clarify his wounds with mountain water.
Moisten his body with tinctures of white myrrh
And the sleeping iodine; and when the chrysms dry,
Fold him in minivers that never wear
And lints that never fade,
And call my two blind footmen, Sleep and Death,
And let them carry him to Lycia by Taurus,
Where his tribe, playing stone chimes and tambourines,
Will consecrate his royal death as fits a man
Before whose memory even the stones shall fade.'
    And Apollo took Sarpedon out of range,
And clarified his wounds with mountain water.
Moistened his body with tinctures of white myrrh
And the sleeping iodine, and when the chrysms dried
The Mousegod folded him in minivers that never wear
And lint that never fades,
And fetched the two blind footmen, Sleep and Death,
And saw they carried him, as fits a man
Before whose memory even the stones shall fade,
To Lycia by Taurus.

TED HUGHES

(b. 1930)

Hughes won early acclaim for the violent and apocalyptic style that has characterised his poetry, and which is well suited to the violence of Seneca's imagination. He pares his original of his rhetoric and increases the vividness of his imagery particularly through the syntactical economy of his writing, creating an effect that conveys much of the quality of Seneca in a form more comprehensible than any closer rendition could achieve.

Oedipus recognises his doom
(Seneca, *Oedipus* 882-910)

Oedipus: birth birthbed blood take this open
the earth bury it bottom of the darkness
under everything I am not fit for the light
Thebans your stones now put a mountain on
me hack me to pieces pile the plague fires
on me make me ashes finish me put me
where I know nothing I am the plague I am
the monster Creon saw in hell I am the cancer
at the roots of this city and in your blood and in
the air I should have died in the womb
suffocated inside there drowned in my
mother's blood come out dead that first day
before anything Oedipus wait now I need
that strength something to fit this error drag
up the root of it and out something for me
alone first I shall go to the palace quickly to
seek out my mother and present her with her son
my mother

Chorus:
If only our fate were ours to choose you would see me on
quiet waters where the airs are gentle a full sail but a
light wind no more than a breath easy voyage that is
best no blast no smashed rigging no flogging downwind into
cliffs under surge nothing recovered no vanishing in
mid ocean

give me a quiet voyage neither under cliffs nor too far out
on the black water where the depth opens the middle course
is the safe one the only life easily on to a calm end
surrounded by gains

foolish Icarus he thought he could fly
it was a dream
tried to crawl across the stars
loaded with his crazy dream his crazy paraphernalia
the wings the wax and the feathers
up and up and up
saw eagles beneath him saw his enormous shadow on the clouds
  beneath him
met the sun face to face
fell

his father Daedalus was wiser he flew lower
he kept under clouds in the shadow of the clouds
the same crazy equipment but the dream different

till Icarus dropped past him   out of the belly of a cloud
past him
down
through emptiness
a cry   dwindling
a splash

tiny in the middle of the vast sea

ROBERT LOWELL

(1917-1977)

One of the most distinguished of modern American poets, Lowell's poetry has
reflected the stages of his personal development, from Catholicism, through
breakdown and political concern, to the looser discursive and reflective style of
History and his other later works. His first and finest translation of a classical
poet is *The Ghost*, from Propertius 2. 14, which it was unfortunately impossible
to include in this anthology. The later translations from *History* are fragments
from the tradition which Lowell shores against the ruin and the pain of his
experience of life.

'Achilles to the dying Lykaon'
(Homer, *Iliad* 21.122-35) from *History*

'Float with the fish, they'll clean your wounds, and lick
away your blood, and have no care of you;
nor will your mother walk beside your pyre
as you swirl down the Skamander to the sea,
but the dark shadows of the fish will shiver,
lunge and snap Lykaon's silver fat.
Trojans, you will perish till I reach Troy –
you'll run in front, I'll scythe you down behind;
nor will your Skamander, though whirling and silver, save you,
though you kill sheep and bulls, and drown a thousand
one-hoofed horse, still living. You must die
and die and die and die and die –
till the blood of my Patroklos is avenged,
killed by the wooden ships while I was gone.'

'Juvenal's Prayer'
(Juvenal, *Satire* 10.346-66) from *History*

What's best, what serves us . . . leave it to the gods.
We're dearer to the gods than to ourselves.

Harassed by impulse and diseased desire,
we ask for wives, and children by those wives –
what wives and children heaven only knows.
Still if you will ask for something, pray for
a healthy body and a healthy soul,
a mind that is not terrified of death,
thinks length of days the least of nature's gifts –
courage that drives out anger and longing . . . our hero,
Hercules, and the pain of his great labour . . .
Success is worshipped as a god; it's we
who set her up in palace and cathedral.
I give you simply what you have already.

ROBERT FITZGERALD

(b. 1910)

Fitzgerald is an American poet, whose poetry is less familiar only because of
the range of his translations, which include Greek tragedy as well as the *Iliad*,
besides translations from Dante, Valery and St John Perse.

Achilles to Lykaon
(Homer, *Iliad* 21.97-135)

In these terms Priam's son pled for his life,
but heard a voice of iron say:

'Young fool, don't talk to me of what you'll barter.
In days past, before Patroklos died
I had a mind to spare the Trojans, took them
alive in shoals, and shipped them out abroad.
But now there's not a chance – no man that heaven
puts in my hands will get away from death
here before Ilion – least of all a son
of Priam. Come, friend, face your death, you too.
And why are you so piteous about it?
Patroklos died, and he was a finer man
by far than you. You see, don't you, how large
I am, and how well-made? My father is noble,
a goddess bore me. Yet death waits for me,
for me as well, in all the power of fate.
A morning comes or evening or high noon
when someone takes my life away in war,
a spear-cast, or an arrow from a bow-string.'

At this the young man's knees failed, and his heart;

he lost his grip upon the spear
and sank down, opening his arms. Akhilleus
drew his sword and thrust between his neck
and collarbone, so the two-edged blade went in
up to the hilt. Now face down on the ground
he lay stretched out, as dark blood flowed from him,
soaking the earth. Akhilleus picked him up
by one foot, wheeled, and slung him in the river
to be swept off downstream. Then he exulted:

'Nose down there with fishes. In cold blood
they'll kiss your wound and nip your blood away.
Your mother cannot put you on your bed
to mourn you, but Skamander whirling down
will bear you to the sea's broad lap,
where any fish that jumps, breaking a wave,
may dart under the dark wind-shivered water
to nibble white fat of Lykaon. Trojans,
perish in this rout until you reach,
and I behind you slaughtering reach, the town!
The god-begotten river swiftly flowing
will not save you. Many a bull you've offered,
many a trim-hooved horse thrown in alive
to Xanthos' whirlpools. All the same, you'll die
in blood until I have avenged Patroklos,
paid you back for the death-wounds of Akhaians
cut down near the deep-sea-going ships
far from my eyes.'

C. H. SISSON

(b. 1914)

Sisson has drawn themes and inspiration from classical writers throughout his writing career, and justly regards the exercise of translating Horace as especially valuable 'not least because of his lack of sympathy with our most current prejudices'. The classic work is an occasion for rethinking one's relation to one's own world. His translations have included Heine as well as Horace, Catullus and Lucretius.

Hymn for the Secular Games
(Horace, *Carmen Saeculare*)

O sun, and moonlight shining in the woods,
The best things in heaven, always to be worshipped
As long as they give us exactly what we want

Now, at this season when selected girls
And the boys who are about to venture upon them,
Though still in bud, sing what will please London,

As you bring out one day and conceal another
Shine on the arms and legs and make them brown.
May all you see be greater than we are.

The time will come to open thighs in child-birth.
Gently, supervising god, look after the mothers.
Bringing to light is the true meaning of genitals.

Could you bring up these children without laws?
The statute-book is crowded, what wonder therefore
If all that interests them is an obscure kindness?

A hundred and ten years it may easily be
Before songs and game which come as speedily
As these three days, ah, and delicious nights.

You have sung truthfully enough, O fates.
Once it was ordained that everything should be stable
And will be again, but not now, or for ever.

Rich in apples, yes, and seething with cattle,
The succulent earth is dressed in barley whiskers.
And grow plump, embryo, from the natural gifts.

The sun will shine, as long as the boys are suppliant,
That will keep sickness away; and you girls,
Listen, for the moon will hear you if you do.

If you made London, as before it Engelland,
The Jutes coming over in ships, but only to be Romans,
Part of that remnant to join this one

The ways that have led here are multifarious,
Even Brutus from Troy, our ancestors believed,
But whatever they left they found better here.

You cannot credit the wish, that the young should be teachable
And old age quiet. Yet it is these wishes
Spring from the earth at last, when the country flowers.

Might you not even remember the old worship?
I could name ancestors, it is not done any more.
It remains true that, before you are king, you must win.

We have been through it all, victory on land and sea,
These things were necessary for your assurance.
The King of France. Once there was even India.

Can you remember the expression 'Honour'?
There was, at one time, even Modesty.

Nothing is so dead it does not come back.

There is God. There are no Muses without him.
He it is who raises the drug-laden limbs
Which were too heavy until he stood at Saint Martin's.

It is he who holds London from Wapping to Richmond,
May he hold it a little longer, Saint George's flag
Flap strenuously in the wind from the west country.

Have you heard the phrase: 'the only ruler of princes'?
Along the Thames, in the Tower, there is the crown.
I only wish God may hear my children's prayers.

He bends now over Trafalgar Square.
If there should be a whisper he would hear it.
Are not these drifting figures the chorus?

Bibliography

1. Translators

Short title list of first editions – and some modern editions – of the works represented in this anthology. For complete bibliographies of the translators, see the bibliographies listed in section 3. * denotes a work cited more fully in another part of the bibliography. The place of publication is London unless otherwise stated.

John Addison: *Works of Anacreon . . . and Sappho* (1735)

Joseph Addison: In Dryden's *Miscellanies* 4 (1694), 5 (1704), and 6 (1706). The translations occupy volume I of the *Works,* (ed. Thomas Tickell, 1721).

Mark Akenside: *Hymn to the Naiads* in Robert Dodsley's *Collection of Poems* (1763).

Anonymous: (1) in Tottel's *Miscellany* (1557)
(2) MS translations of Martial (a) sixteenth century, (b) seventeenth century. Selections from these works appear in H. G. Bohn's *Epigrams of Martial* (1914), and I have not been able to trace their provenance
(3) Translation of the story of Pygmalion from Ovid, *Miscellany* * 5 (1704)
(4) *Six Idillia chosen out of . . . Theocritus,* Oxford 1588. Reprinted in E. Arber, *An English Garner* (1877-96) vol. 8
(5) Martial 1695. Attributed to Henry Killigrew

Philip Ayres: *Lyric Poems* (1687). In *Poems of the Caroline Period,* (ed. G. Saintsbury; Oxford 1906) 2

Charles Badham: Catullus (1821). In F. A. Wright*. Juvenal (1814)

Aubrey Beardsley: Catullus, *Savoy* (1896). In Duckett*

Aphra Behn: *Ovid's Epistles translated* (1680). *Poems upon several occasions* (1684)

Sir John Beaumont: *Bosworth Field . . .* (ed. Sir John Beaumont the younger, 1629)

Francis Beaumont: *Salmacis and Hermaphroditus* (1602)

Robert Bridges: *Ibant Obscuri* * (Oxford 1916)

William Broome: Anacreon in *Gentleman's Magazine* (1739, 1740); collected by Fawkes in his own edition (1760). (Also *Iliad* with Ozell and Oldisworth (1714)

Thomas Brown: *A collection of dialogues . . . translations and imitations* (1704); and in *Miscellany Poems . . .* (1685)

Elizabeth Barrett Browning: *Prometheus Bound* (1833, revised 1850). *Early Poems* (first published 1888). *Some Account of the Greek Christian Poets* (1863)

Robert Browning: *Balaustion's Adventure* (1871). *Aristophanes' Apology* (1875). Aeschylus *Agamemnon* (1877)

Basil Bunting: Lucretius (1927) and Horace (1971) in *Collected Poems* (Oxford 1978)

Sir Richard F. Burton: *The Carmina of C. V. Catullus* (1894)

George Gordon Lord Byron: *Hours of Idleness* (1807). *Hints from Horace* (1831; MS dated 1811)

Charles Stuart Calverley: *Verses and Translations* (1862). Theocritus (1869)

Thomas Campbell: Alcman (*c.* 1800) in *Poems* (1803)

Thomas Campion: *A Booke of Ayres* (1601). *Two Bookes of Ayres* (1613)

George Chapman: *Seven bookes of Homers Iliades* (1598); *The Shield of Achilles* (1598); *Iliad* (1611). *Odyssey* (1615?). *The Divine Poem of Musaeus: Hero and Leander* (1616, but probably written before *Hero and Leander* of 1598). *Whole Workes of Homer* (1616). Hesiod (1618). Other translations (*c.* 1624). *Works* (ed. Allardyce Nicoll 1957). Musaeus in E. Story Donno, *Elizabethan Minor Epics* (1963)

Geoffrey Chaucer: *The Legend of Good Women* (written 1380-6); *Works* (ed. F. N. Robinson; Oxford 1966).

William Congreve: In Dryden's *Miscellany* 2* (1693). *Works* in 3 vols (1710). In *Ovid's Art of Love* (1725)*

John Conington: *Odes and Carmen Saeculare of Horace* (1863). Vergil *Aeneid* (1866). *Iliad* 13-24 (Edinburgh and London 1868). *Satires Epistles and Ars Poetica of Horace* (1870)

Thomas Cooke: Hesiod (1728). Also Moschus and Bion (1724), Terence (1734), Homer etc. in *Tales, Epistles, Odes, Fables* . . . (1729)

William (Johnson) Cory: *Ionica* (1858)

Charles Cotton: In A. Brome's *Horace** (1666). *Poems* (1689). Also *Scarronides, ou le Virgile travesty* (1664)

Abraham Cowley: *Poems* (1656; ed. Sprat, 1668). *Poems* (ed. A. R. Waller, Cambridge 1905)

William Cowper: *Poems* (1782; vol. 2 1785). Iliad and Odyssey (1791). *Poems* (three vols 1815)

Richard Crashaw: Horace: MS; in *Works* (ed. L. C. Martin, Oxford 1957). *The Delights of the Muses* (1646)

Thomas Creech: Lucretius (1682). Theocritus (1684). Horace (1688). Manilius (1697)

Sir John Denham: *Aeneid* 2 (1636; published 1656). *Poems and Translations* (1668). Translation from *Iliad* 12 in *Miscellany** 1, (1684)

Richard Maitland, Earl of Derby: *Iliad* (1864)

William Diaper: Oppian *Halieuticks* 1

posthumously published by John Jones, who added Book 2 (1722). *Complete Works* (ed. D. Broughton, 1951)

Leonard Digges: *The Rape of Proserpine. Translated out of Claudian* (1617; reprinted, ed. H. H. Huxley, Liverpool 1959)

Hilda Doolittle (H. D.): *Choruses from the Iphigenia in Aulis and the Hippolytus of Euripides* (1919)

Gavin Douglas: *Aeneid* (1553; but written by 1515, the date of the oldest MS). *Selections* (ed. D. F. C. Coldwell, Oxford 1964)

Thomas Drant: *A Medicinable Morall, that is, the two bookes of Horace his Satyres* (1566). Also *Horace his art of poetrie, pistles and satyrs* (1567)

John Dryden: In *Ovid's Epistles** (1680). Juvenal and Persius (1693). Vergil (1697, 1698). Other translations in *Miscellanies** 1-4; some reappear in *Fables* (1700)

Richard Duke: In *Ovid's Epistles** (1680). Theocritus 11 in *Miscellany* 1* (1684). Also in *Ovid's Amours** (1719)

James Elphinston: *Specimen of Martial* (1778). Martial (1782)

Sir Thomas Elyot: Claudian translation in *The Boke named the Governour* (1531)

John Evelyn: *First Book of Lucretius* (1656)

Sir Richard Fanshawe: Vergil *Aeneid* 4 (1648). *Selected Parts of Horace . . . with . . . Ausonius . . . and . . . Vergil* (1652; reprinted as *Shorter Poems and Translations* (ed. N. W. Bennett, Liverpool 1964). Also in Brome's *Horace** (1666)

Francis Fawkes: Anacreon, Sappho, Bion, Moschus and Musaeus (1760). *Original Poems and Translations* (1761). Theocritus (1767). In Duncombe etc. *Works of Horace** (1767). Apollonius Rhodius (1780)

Edward Fitzgerald: Agamemnon (1865, 1876). Oedipus (n.d. but 1880)

Maurice Purcell Fitzgerald: *Crowned Hippolytus of Euripides . . . (and) pastoral poets* (1867).

Robert Fitzgerald: Homer *Iliad* (1974).

James Elroy Flecker: *Thirty-Six Poems* (1910). *Forty-Two Poems* (1911)

Philip Francis: *Odes, Epodes and Carmen Saeculare* (1743). *Works of Horace* (1747; revised by H. Pye 1806)

John Hookham Frere: *Frogs* of Aristophanes (1839). 3 other plays (Malta 1839, Oxford 1840). *Four Plays* . . . (Oxford 1907). Catullus: poems first collected by W. E. Frere (1872)

John Gay: *Miscellaneous Poems and Translations* (1712) Translation from Ovid *Met.* 9 also in Garth* (1717)

William Gifford: Juvenal (1802). Persius (1821)

William Ewart Gladstone: Horace in *Quarterly Review* (1858; complete 1894). Catullus in *Translations by Lord Lyttelton and the Rt. Hon. W. E. Gladstone* (1861). Homer in *Contemporary Review*, (Feb. and May 1874)

Arthur Golding: Ovid *Metamorphoses* (Books 1-4, 1565; the whole 1567)

Thomas Gray: *The Progress of Poesy* (1757)

Arthur Hall: *Ten Bookes of Homers Iliades, translated out of French* (1581)

William Hamilton of Bangour: *Poems on several occasions* (pirate edition, 1748; first authorised edition posthumous, Edinburgh 1760)

William Hammond: *Poems* (1655)

Thomas Hardy: Imitations . . . in *Wessex Poems and Other Verses* (1898; many poems dating from the 1860s)

Sir James Harrington: Vergil *Aeneid* 1-2 and two *Eclogues* (1658). *Aeneid* 3-4 (1659)

William Hay: Martial (1775)

Robert Herrick: *Hesperides* (1648). MS translations: see *Works* (ed. L. C. Martin, Oxford 1956)

Jasper Heywood: Seneca *Thyestes* (1560; *Troas* 1559, *Hercules Furens* 1561), and in *Seneca his Tenne Tragedies* 1581)*. *Thyestes* also in *Five Elizabethan Tragedies* (ed. A. K. McIlwraith, Oxford 1938)

Thomas Hobbes: *Iliad* and *Odyssey* (1682)

John Cam Hobhouse, First Baron Broughton: *Imitations and Translations* (1809)

Barten Holyday: Juvenal and Persius (1673; posthumous)

A. E. Housman: Euripides translations in A. W. Pollard* (1890). Horace *Odes* 4.7 in *Collected Poems* (1939)

Ted Hughes: Seneca *Oedipus* (1969)

Leigh Hunt: Anacreon (1801). Catullus (1810). Theocritus (1844) etc: *Poetical Works* (ed. H. S. Milford, Oxford 1923)

Lucy Hutchinson: Lucretius: B. M. Add. MS 19333 (1657)

L. A. S. Jermyn: *The Singing Farmer* (1947)

Samuel Johnson: Horace et al. (*c.* 1726). *London* (1738). *The Vanity of Human Wishes* (1749, 1755 in Dodsley's Collection). Horace *Odes* 4.7 MS (1784). *Works* (1787-9)

Ben Jonson: *Poetaster* (1602). *Epigrammes* and *Forrest* (1616). *Underwoodes* and *Timber* (1640)

Timothe Kendall: *Floures of Epigrammes* (1577; reprinted as *Publications of the Spenser Society* 15 (1874))

Hon. George Lamb: Catullus (1821)

Walter Savage Landor: Vergil *Georgics* 4 (written 1794, published in *Examiner* 1841). Horace, Catullus *Examiner* (1852 et post)

J. B. Leishman: *Translating Horace* (1956)

William L. Lewis: Statius (1773)

Christopher Logue: *Patrokleia of Homer* (1963); revised, *War Music* (1981)

Richard Lovelace: *Lucasta* (1649). *Posthumous Poems* (1659)

Robert Lowell: *History* (1973)

Edward Bulwer, Lord Lytton: Horace *Odes* and *Epodes* (1869)

Louis MacNeice: Aeschylus *Agamemnon* (1936). Horace *Odes* 4.7 in *The Earth Compels* (1938)

Christopher Marlowe: *Epigrams and Elegies* (Middelburg 1590 ?). Lucan (1600, but entered in the Stationer's Register 1593)

Thomas May: Virgil's *Georgicks* (1628). Martial (1629). Also Lucan (1627)

Henry Hart Milman: *Aeschylus' Agamemnon and other translations* (1865)

John Milton: Horace *Odes* 1.5 (1673)

Thomas Moore: Anacreon (1800). *Works* (1841)

William Morris: Vergil *Aeneid* (1876). Also *Odyssey* (1887)

Gilbert Murray: Euripides *Hippolytus* etc. (1902). *Troades* (1905). Other translations of Greek drama (1902-1947)

Francis W. Newman: *Odes of Horace* (1853). *Iliad of Homer* (1856)

John Ogilby: Vergil (1649, 1654). *Iliad* (1660). *Odyssey* (1665)

John Oldham: *Poems and Translations* (anon.) (1683 translation of Horace *Serm.* 1.9 written 1681)

Thomas Otway: *Poems* (collected 1712)

Sir Thomas Overbury: Ovid *Remedia Amoris* (1620)

Samuel Palmer: Vergil *Eclogues* (1883; posthumous); substantially complete by 1872

Thomas Love Peacock: Translation from Euripides (1815)

Thomas Phäer: *Seven bookes of Aeneidos* (1558); *nine bookes* (1562); *twelve bookes* (1573); *thirteen bookes* (1584)

Ambrose Phillips: Sappho translations: *Spectator* 223 and 229 (1711). *Pastorals . . . with translations . . .* (1748)

Alexander Pope: Ovid translation (*c.* 1702; published in *Works* 1717). *Iliad* (1715-20). *Odyssey* (1725-6). *Imitations of Horace* in Works 2 (1738)

Robert Potter: Aeschylus (1777)

Ezra Pound: Translations in *Lustra* (1916). *Homage to Sextus Propertius* (1917). *Cantos* 1-54 (1954). Horace in *Collected Translations* (1953)

Matthew Prior: *Poems* (1707, 1709 enlarged, 1716, etc.)

Allan Ramsay: *Poems* (1720)

Thomas Randolph (with F. J.): *Ploutophthalmia ploutogamia . . . Hey for Honesty* (1651; after Randolph's death)

Edwin Arlington Robinson: *Children of the Night* (1897). Epigrams in *Collected Poems* New York 1927)

John Wilmot, Earl of Rochester: *Poems* (1680; posthumous)

Benjamin Bickley Rogers: Aristophanes *Peace* (1867, etc.) *Comedies of Aristophanes* (1904)

Wentworth Dillon, Earl of Roscommon:

Horace *Ars Poetica* (1680). Ovid *Ars Amatoria* (1692) Vergil *Eclogue* 6 in *Miscellany* 1 (1684)*

Nicholas Rowe: Lucan (1718)

Wye Saltonstall: *Ovids Heroicall Epistles* (1636). Also *Tristia* (1633); *De Ponto* (1639)

George Sandys: Ovid *Metamorphoses* (1626 etc.)

Sir Charles Sedley: *Miscellaneous Works* (1702). *Poetical Works* (1707)

William Sewell: Horace (1850). Also Aeschylus *Agamemnon* (1846); Vergil *Georgics* (1846); *Iliad* and *Odyssey* left in MS at death

Percy Bysshe Shelley: Translations written 1818-22; published posthumously

Sir Edward Sherburne: Colluthus, Theocritus etc. (1651). Manilius (1675). Seneca *Medea* (1648); other tragedies (1701). MS translations include Lucretius, Pindar, Vergil. *Poems and Translations* (ed. F. J. van Beeck, Assen 1961)

Sir Philip Sidney: Catullus in *Certain Sonnets* (before 1581). *Poems* (ed. W. A. Ringler, Oxford 1962)

C. H. Sisson: *In the Trojan Ditch* (1974)

Christopher Smart: Horace (1767). Also Phaedrus (1765)

Edmund Spenser: *Faerie Queene* (1590). Vergil's *Gnat* in *Complaints* (1591)

Thomas Stanley: *Poems and Translations* (1647-8). *Poems* (1651)

Richard Stanyhurst: Vergil *Aeneid* 1-4 (1582)

Robert Louis Stevenson: *Poems* (1880-1894)

John Studley: In *Seneca his Tenne Tragedies* (1581)*

Henry Howard, Earl of Surrey: Vergil (1557). Other translations in Tottel's *Miscellany** (1557)

Jonathan Swift: *Poems* (1735)

Algernon Charles Swinburne: *Poems and Ballads* (1866), etc.

John Addington Symonds: *Studies of Greek Poets, First Series,* (1873)

Arthur Symons: *From Catullus* (1924)

Nahum Tate: In Ovid's *Art of Love*

(1709)*. Also in Ovid's *Epistles* (1680)* and Ovid *Metamorphoses* (ed. Garth, 1717*)

Sir William Temple: *Poems* (1670)

Alfred Lord Tennyson: *Specimen of a translation from the Iliad* in *Cornhill Magazine* Dec, (1863); and in *Enoch Arden* (1864)

James Thomson: *Spring* (1727). *The Seasons* (1730), etc.

Bonnell Thornton: Plautus, completed by Richard Warner 1772

Thomas Tickell: *Iliad* 1 (1715). *Works* (1749)

Joseph Trapp: Vergil: *Aeneid* 1 (1718); 2 (1720); the whole (1731-5)

Thomas Underdowne: Ovid *Ibis* (1569)

Henry Vaughan: *Poems* and Juvenal *Satire* 10 (1646). *Olor Iscanus: Poems and Translations* (1651)

William Walsh: Catullus in *Miscellany* 4 (1694)*

Joseph Warton: *Eclogues* and *Georgics* in Pitt's Vergil (1763)

Christopher Wase: Sophocles *Electra* (The Hague 1649)

Gilbert West: *Odes of Pindar* . . . (1749; enlarged by R. Greene and H. Pye 1810)

Oscar Wilde: Translation from Aristophanes *Clouds* (Oxford 1874)

William Wordsworth: Translations (1786-1791?) Also Juvenal *Satire* 8 (1795-6?)

F. A. Wright: Catullus (1926)

W. B. Yeats: From *Oedipus at Colonus: The Tower* (1928)

2. Bibliographies

H. Brown, 'The Classical Tradition in English Literature', *Harv. Stud. and Notes in Phil. and Lit.* 18 (1935), 7-46

Bush, Douglas, 'English Translators of Homer', *PMLA* 41 (1926), 335-41

Foster, F. M. K., *English Translations from the Greek: A bibliographical survey* (Columbia U.P. 1918)

Green. A. M. W., *Classics in Translation: A Selective Bibliography 1930-1976* (Cardiff 1976)

Palmer, Henrietta R., *A list of English editions and translations of the Greek and Latin Classics printed before 1641* (1911)

Parks, G.B. and Temple, R. Z., *The Literatures of the World in English Translation. A Bibliography.* Vol. 1: *the Greek and Latin Literatures* (New York 1968)

Smith, F. Seymour, *The Classics in Translation* (1930)

Watson, G. (ed.), *The New Cambridge Bibliography of English Literature* (Cambridge 1974 et post)

3. Anthologies

(a) General

Classics in Translation. An Anthology (Wisconsin U.P. 1952). (I have not seen this work.)

Miscellany Poems 1-6 (1-4 edited by John Dryden): 1 (1684); 2 (*Sylvae*) (1685); 3 (*Examen Poeticum*) (1693); 4 *Annual Miscellany for 1694*; 5 *Poetical Miscellanies* (1704); 6 *Poetical Miscellanies* (1706)

Godolphin, F. R. B. (ed.), *The Latin Poets* (New York 1949)

Grant, Michael, *Greek Literature* (Harmondsworth 1973)

Grant, Michael, *Roman Readings* (Harmondsworth 1958), re-issued as *Latin Literature* (1978)

Davenport, Basil (ed.), *The Portable Roman Reader* (Viking Press 1951; Penguin

(Harmondsworth) 1977)

Lind, L. R. (ed.), *Latin Poetry in Verse Translation: from the beginnings to the Renaissance* (Boston 1957)

Steiner, George, *Poem into Poem* (Harmondsworth 1970)

Hamilton, Sir George Rostrevor, *The Greek Portrait. An Anthology of English Verse translations from the Greek Poets* (Nonsuch 1934)

Higham, T. F. and Bowra, C. M. (eds), *The Oxford Book of Greek Verse in Translation* (Oxford 1938)

Tottel's *Miscellany* (1557)

(b) Particular authors

Catullus

Duckett, E. S., *Catullus in English Poetry* (Northampton, Mass 1925)

Wright, F. A., *Catullus: the Complete Poems* (London n.d. but 1926)

Greek Drama

Pollard, A. W. (ed.), *Odes from the Greek Dramatists* (1890)

Homer and Vergil

Bridges, R. (ed.), *Ibant Obscuri* (Oxford 1916)

Horace

Brome, Alexander (ed.), *Poems of Horace* (1666)

Duncombe, William (ed.) (1767)

Storrs, Sir Ronald, *Ad Pyrrham* (1959)

Butler, H. E. (ed.), *The Odes of Horace in English Verse* (1929) *Odes and Satyrs of Horace ... by the most eminent hands* (1715)

Martial

H. G. B., *The Epigrams of Martial* (in Bohn's Classical Library; 1914)

Ovid

Ovid's *Amours* (1719)

Ovid's *Epistles* (1680)

Garth, Samuel (*et al.*), Ovid's *Metamorphoses* (1717)

Ovid's *Art of Love, together with his remedy of love ...* (1725)

Sappho

Tutin, J. R., *Sappho the Queen of Song* (Edinburgh n.d. but 1910)

Wharton, H. T., *Sappho: Memoir, Text, Selected Renderings* (1885)

Seneca

Thomas Newton (ed.), *Seneca his Tenne Tragedies* (1581)

4. Select bibliography of works consulted

Adams, R. M., *Proteus, his Lies, his Truth: discussions of literary translation* (New York, 1973)

Amos, F. R., *Early Theories of Translation* (New York 1920)

Arion, 'An Arion Questionnaire', *Arion* 3 (1964), 6-100

Arnold, Matthew, 'On Translating Homer' (1861-2); in *Essays* (Oxford 1914)

Attridge, Derek, *Well-weighed Syllables. Elizabethan verse in classical metres* (Cambridge 1974)

Bassnett-McGuire, Susan, *Translation Studies* (1980)

Baumann, Michael, *Die Anakreonteen in englischen Übersetzungen* (Heidelberg 1974)

Belloc, Hilaire, *On Translation* (1931)

Benjamin, Walter, 'The Task of the Translator', in *Illuminations* (1968), 69-82

Bennett, H. S., *English Books and Readers 1475-1557* (Cambridge 1969[2])

Bennett, H. S., *English Books and Readers 1558-1603* (Cambridge 1965)

Bennett, H. S., *English Books and Readers 1603-1640* (Cambridge 1970)

Bolgar, R.R., *The Classical Heritage and its Beneficiaries* (Cambridge 1954)

Braden, G., *The Classics and English Renaissance Poetry* (Yale U.P. 1978)

Brooks, Harold F., 'Contributors to Brome's Horace', *N&Q* 174 (1938), 200-1

Brower, Reuben A. (ed.), *On Translation* (New York 1966)

Buxton, John, *The Grecian Taste. Literature in the Age of Neo-Classicism 1740-1820* (1978)

Cameron, W. J., 'Brome's "Horace" 1666 and 1671', *N&Q* 202 (1957) 70-1

Carey, John, 'The Ovidian Love Elegy in England', unpublished Oxford D.Phil. thesis 1960

Cary, E., *Les Grands Traducteurs Français* (Geneva 1963)

Chalker, John, *The English Georgic* (1969)

Clarke, M. L., *Greek Studies in England 1700-1830* (Cambridge 1945)

Clarke, M. L., *Classical Education in Britain 1500-1900* (Cambridge 1959)

Cohen, J. M., *English Translators and Translations* (London 1962)

Conington, John, 'The English Translators of Vergil', *Quart. Rev.* 110 (1861), and in *Misc. Writings*, ed. J. A. Symonds (1872) vol. 1, pp. 137-97

Conley, C. H., *The First English Translators of the Classics* (Yale U.P. 1927)

Cunliffe, J. W., *The Influence of Seneca on Elizabethan Tragedy* (1893)

Dilke, O. A. W., 'Lucan and English Literature', in *Neronians and Flavians* ed. D. R. Dudley (1972), pp. 83-112

Dobree, Bonamy, *English Literature in the Early Eighteenth Century* (Oxford 1959)

Draper, J. W., 'The Theory of Translation in the Eighteenth Century', *Neophilologus* 6 (1921), 241-54

Eliot, T. S., 'Seneca in Elizabethan Translation' in *Selected Essays* (1932)

Emperor, J. B., *Catullan Influence in English Lyric Poetry, c. 1600-1650* (Missouri 1928)

Farrington, Benjamin, 'Shelley's Translations from the Greek', *Dublin Magazine* 3 (1928), 3-18

Finley, John H., Jnr., 'Milton and Horace', *Harv. Stud. Class. Phil.* 48 (1937), 29-74

Fleischmann, W. B., *Lucretius in English Literature 1680-1740* (Paris 1964)

Foerster, D. M., *Homer in English Criticism* (1947)

Frost, William, *Dryden and the Art of Translation* (New Haven 1955)

Fyler, John M., *Chaucer and Ovid* (Yale U.P. 1979)

(Gladstone) Bibliography: *N&Q* 8th ser. ii (1892) 461, 501; iii (1893) 1, 41

Goad, C., *Horace in the Literature of the Eighteenth Century* (New Haven 1918)

Green, Peter, 'Some Versions of Aeschylus. A study of tradition and method in translating classical poetry', in *Essays in Antiquity* (1960)

Harrison, Charles Trawick, 'The Ancient Atomists and English Literature of the Seventeenth Century', *Harv. Stud. Class. Phil.* 45 (1934), 1-79

Highet, Gilbert, *The Classical Tradition* (Oxford 1949)

Hoffman, Richard L., 'The Influence of the Classics on Chaucer' in B. Rowland (ed.), *Companion to Chaucer Studies* (Oxford 1968)

Hood, T. L., 'Browning's Ancient Classical Sources', *Harv. Stud. Class. Phil.* 33 (1922), 79-180

Humphreys, A. R., 'A Classical Education and Eighteenth Century Poetry', *Scrutiny* 8 (1939), 193-207

Jacobsen, Eric, *Translation a Traditional Craft* (Copenhagen 1958)

Jameson, Caroline, 'Ovid in the Sixteenth Century' in *Ovid*, ed. J. E. Binns (1973)

Johnson, Samuel, *Idler* 68 and 69 (Yale ed: vol. 2)

Keble, John, 'On Translation from Dead Languages' (1812), in *Oxford English Prize Essays* 3 (Oxford 1830)

Kelly, Louis, *The True Interpreter* (Oxford 1979)

Kerlin, Thomas, *Theocritus in English Literature* (Lynchburg 1910)

Knight, Douglas M., *Pope and the Heroic Tradition: A critical study of his Iliad* (Yale/Oxford 1951)

Knox, Ronald, *On English Translation*

(Oxford 1957)

Leishman, J. B., *Translating Horace* (Oxford 956)

Levi, Peter, *The English Bible* (1974)

Lord, George de F., *Homeric Renaissance: the Odyssey of George Chapman* (1956)

Lucas, F. L., *Seneca and Elizabethan Tragedy* (Cambridge 1922)

Macdonald, Hugh, *John Dryden. A bibliography of early editions and Drydeniana* (Oxford 1939)

McEuen, K. A., *Classical Influence on the Tribe of Ben* (1939)

Mack, Maynard, Introduction to the *Iliad of Homer*, The Poems of Alexander Pope (London/Yale 1961-7) vol. 7; and appendix to the *Odyssey*, op. cit., vol. 10, pp. 492-586

McPeek, J. F. S., *Catullus in Strange and Distant Britain* (Harvard 1939)

Martindale, Joanna, 'The Response to Horace in the Seventeenth Century: with special reference to the Odes and the period 1600-1660', unpublished Oxford D.Phil. thesis 1977

Mason, H.A., *To Homer Through Pope* (1972)

Mason, H. A., 'The *Women of Trachis* and creative translation', *Arion* 2 (1963); revised *Cambridge Quarterly* 4 (1969); and in *Ezra Pound* ed. J. P. Sullivan, Harmondsworth 1970, pp. 279-310

Matthiessen, F. O., *Translation: An Elizabethan Art* (Cambridge, Mass., 1931)

Mazon, Paul, *Mme Dacier et les Traductions d'Homère en France* (Oxford 1936)

Murray, Gilbert, *The Classical Tradition in English Poetry* (1927)

Musgrove, M. S., 'Critical and Literary Changes in the Seventeenth Century, as manifested in English verse translations from the Greek and Latin Classics', unpublished Oxford D.Phil. thesis 1944

Nitchie, E., *Vergil and the English Poets* (New York 1919)

Ogilvie, R. M., *Latin and Greek. A History of the influence of the classics on English life from 1600 to 1918* (1964)

Pfeiffer, R., *A History of Classical Scholarship 1300-1850* (Oxford 1976)

Phillimore, J. S., *Some Remarks on Translations and Translators* (1919)

Postgate, J. P., *Translation and Translations* (1922). Not recommended.

Pound, Ezra, *Literary Essays* (sel. T. S. Eliot, 1954)

Proudfoot, Leslie, *Dryden's Aeneid and its Seventeenth-Century Predecessors* (1960)

Rand, E. K., *Ovid and his Influence* (1925)

Robathan, Dorothy M., 'Ovid in the Middle Ages' in *Ovid*, ed. J. E. Binns (1973)

Saintsbury, George, *A History of English Prosody from the Twelfth Century to the Present Day* 3 vols, (1906-1910)

Sandys, J. E., A History of Classical Scholarship (Cambridge 1903-1908)

Shannon, E. F., *Chaucer and the Roman Poets* (Cambridge, Mass. 1929)

Simonsuuri, Kirsti, *Homer's Original Genius. Eighteenth Century Notions of the Early Greek Epic* (Cambridge 1979)

Smith, G. Gregory, *Elizabethan Critical Essays*, vols 1-3 (Oxford 1904)

Spearing, E. M., *The Elizabethan Translations of Seneca's Tragedies* (Cambridge 1912)

Spindler, Robert, *Robert Browning und die Antike* (Leipzig 1930)

Spingarn, J. E., *Critical Essays of the Seventeenth Century* (Oxford 1908)

Steiner, George, *After Babel* (Oxford 1975)

Störig, Hans Joachim, *Das Problem des Übersetzens* (Stuttgart 1963). Selections

Sullivan, J. P., 'Ezra Pound as a Latin Translator', *Arion* 3 (1964), 3, 100-11

Sullivan, J. P., *Ezra Pound and Sextus Propertius* (1964)

Sutherland, James, *English Literature of the Late Seventeenth Century* (Oxford 1969)

Thomson, J. A. K., *The Classical Background of English Literature* (1948)

Thomson, J. A. K., *Classical Influences on English Poetry* (1951)

Trickett, Rachel, *The Honest Muse, A study in Augustan verse* (Oxford 1967)

Tytler, Alexander Fraser, Lord Woodhouselee, *The Principles of*

Translation (1791)

Webb, Timothy, *The Violet in the Crucible: Shelley and Translation* (Oxford 1976)

Whipple, T. K., *Martial and the English Epigram from Sir Thomas Wyatt to Ben Jonson* (*Univ. Calif. Publ. in Mod. Philol.* 10.4, 1925)

Williams, R. D., 'Changing Attitudes to Virgil', in *Virgil*, ed. D. R. Dudley (1969)

Wilson, Penelope B., 'The Knowledge and Appreciation of Pindar in the Seventeenth and Eighteenth Centuries', unpublished Oxford D.Phil. thesis 1974

Wise, B. A., *Influence of Statius on Chaucer* (1911)

Index of classical authors

Aeschylus (Athens; 525-456 B.C.)
Agamemnon 278-316; 355-84: Robert
    Browning
    551-72; 738-71;
    1327-30: Louis MacNeice
    1080-1145: Edward Fitzgerald
Prometheus Vinctus 115-92: Robert Potter
    436-71: Elizabeth
    Barrett Browning

Alcman (Sparta; fl. 654-611 B.C. *or*
    631-628 B.C.)
Fragment 89 Page: Thomas Campbell

Anacreontea (poems in the style of
    Anacreon of Teos, b. *c.* 570 B.C., but of
    later date, and first collected about the
    sixth century A.D.)
No. 12 Bergk (14 vulg): Thomas Stanley
No. 21 Bergk (19 vulg): Leigh Hunt
No. 32 Bergk (43 vulg): John Addison,
    Thomas Moore
No. 44 Bergk (37 vulg): William Broome

Anonymous Greek Lyrics
Harmodius song (Athenian, fifth century
    B.C.; *Poetae Melici Graeci* nos 893 and
    894): William Wordsworth
Delphic Hymn to Apollo (Hellenistic;
    Collectanea Alexandrina ed. J. U. Powell
    (1925), p. 141): Algernon Charles
    Swinburne

Aristophanes (Athens; *c.* 450-385 B.C.)
Acharnians 628-42: Benjamin Bickley
    Rogers
Birds 685-707; 1694-705: John Hookham
    Frere
Clouds 275ff.: Benjamin Bickley Rogers,
    Oscar Wilde
Wealth 489ff.: Thomas Randolph

Ausonius, Decimus Magnus (Bordeaux;
    d. *c.* A.D. 395)
Cupido Idyll 6: Henry Vaughan
Epigram 10: Anon 1695

Bacchylides (Ceos, fifth century B.C.)
Paean 4.61-80: Philip Ayres

Bion (Phlossa near Smyrna; fl. *c.* 100
    B.C.)
Lament for Adonis: Percy Bysshe Shelley

Callimachus (Cyrene; *c.* 305-240 B.C.)
Hymn 2 (to Apollo): Matthew Prior
Epigram 2: William Cory

Catullus (Verona; ?84-54 B.C.)
Poem   4: James Elroy Flecker
        5: Richard Crashaw, Arthur
          Symons
        8: Thomas Campion
     10: John Hookham Frere
     13: Richard Lovelace
     17: Charles Badham
     31: Thomas Hardy
     42: F. A. Wright
     45: Abraham Cowley
     46: Sir Richard Burton
     51: Lord Byron, William
          Gladstone
     55: George Lamb
     63: Leigh Hunt
     70: Sir Philip Sidney
     76: William Walsh
     85: Richard Lovelace
     91: John Hookham Frere
     96: Richard Lovelace
    101: Aubrey Beardsley

Claudian (Claudius Claudianus, a native

Greek speaker from Alexandria; d. *c.* 404 A.D.)
Rape of Proserpine 1.89 ff.: Leonard Digges
On the fourth consulship of Honorius, 214-302 (selected): Sir Thomas Elyot
Phoenix 129-42: Henry Vaughan (selected): Thomas Tickell

Euripides (Athens; *c.* 485 – *c.* 406 B.C.)
Alcestis 435-59: Robert Browning
Cyclops 316-45: Percy Bysshe Shelley
Heracles Furens 637ff.: Thomas Love Peacock
Hippolytus 732-75: Gilbert Murray
Iphigeneia in Aulis 573-89: H. D.
Trojan Women 853ff.: Elizabeth Barrett Browning

The Greek Anthology (A collection of Greek epigrams was made by Cephalas before 900; this was absorbed into the Palatine Anthology of 980; around 1299 Planudes selected and added poems which appear in modern editions as the last book of the Anthology. The Anthology thus contains poems from the early classical period onwards. Planudes' anthology was first published in 1494, the Palatine anthology in 1606. The work was received as an entity though its sources are disparate.)
Cory
Book 7. 353 (Antipater; fl. *c.* 120 B.C.; = no. xxvii in Page *Epigrammata Graeca*): Sir Edward Sherburne
Book 9. 145 (anon.): Timothe Kendall
Book 9. 823 (Plato; *c.* 429-247 B.C.; = no. xvi in Page): Thomas Stanley
Book 9. 186 (Nicarchus; fl. second century B.C.): Edwin Arlington Robinson

Hesiod (Boeotia; ?fl. *c.* 700 B.C.)
Works and Days 286ff.: Thomas Cooke

Homer (The dates and provenance of Homer are not known, nor what his role was in the composition of *Iliad* and *Odyssey*. The poems contain much ancient material, but in their present

form may date from as late as the sixth century B.C.)
Iliad 1. 517-32: Thomas Hobbes
        551-67: Francis Newman
      2. 453-73; 581-600; 738-60: William Cowper
      6. 144-202: Arthur Hall
      8. 542-61: Alfred Lord Tennyson
     12. 299-328: George Chapman
        307-28: Sir John Denham
     13. 795-807: Francis Newman
     16. 777-867: John Conington
        644-83: Christopher Logue
     21. 97-135: Robert Fitzgerald
        122-35: Robert Lowell
     22. 261-72: George Chapman
     23. 218-57: Alexander Pope
     24. 410-23: Robert Bridges
        513-58: Alexander Pope
        513-51; 596-620: George Chapman
        723-804: Earl of Derby
Odyssey 5. 50-75: George Chapman
      7. 112-32: William Cowper
      8. 62-92: Thomas Hobbes
        256-369: Alexander Pope
     10. 210-43: Alexander Pope
     11. 26-78: Ezra Pound
     12. 166-200: Alexander Pope
        184-91: George Chapman
     20. 66-78: Elizabeth Barrett Browning

Homeric Hymns (eighth to sixth century B.C.)
To Hermes (4) 17-62: Percy Bysshe Shelley

Horace (Quintus Horatius Flaccus; b. at Venusia; 65-8 B.C.)
Odes 1. 4: Philip Francis
        5: John Milton, Walter Savage Landor
        9: William Congreve, Allan Ramsey
       11: Charles Stuart Calverley
       19: William Congreve
       27: Thomas Brown
       28: Thomas Creech
       31: Ezra Pound
       34: Sir Richard Fanshawe

Odes 1. 35: J. B. Leishman
2. 3: Philip Francis
6: John Cam Hobhouse
8: Sir Charles Sedley
9: John Conington
10: Richard Lovelace
11: Thomas Moore
13: Richard Crashaw
14: Robert Herrick, Samuel
Johnson, Basil Bunting
16: Thomas Otway
17: William Hammond
18: Christopher Smart
3. 9: Ben Jonson
12: William Sewell, John
Conington
13: Charles Stuart Calverley
26: Philip Francis
29: John Dryden
4. 1: Ben Jonson
7: Anon. in Tottel's
Miscellany, Sir William
Temple, Samuel Johnson,
A. E. Housman

Epodes 2: Charles Cotton
9: William Congreve
Carmen Saeculare: C. H. Sisson
Satires 1. 5: William Cowper
6. 112-31: Sir Richard
Fanshawe
9.1-13, 60-98: John Oldham
2. 1.1–7, 39-78: Alexander
Pope
3. 18-48: Thomas Drant
3. 31-76: John Conington
6. 1-5, 40-62: Jonathan
Swift
6. 79-117: Sir John
Beaumont
Epistles 1. 1. 80-108: Alexander Pope
2. 34-end: Sir Richard
Fanshawe
6: Philip Francis
18. 104-12: William Hamilton
of Bangour
2. 1. 1ff: Alexander Pope
Ars Poetica 24-37; 60-72: Ben
Jonson
38-59: Lord Byron

Ars Poetica 323-60: Earl of
Roscommon
453-69: John
Oldham

Hybrias the Cretan (? fifth century B.C.)
No. 909 in Page (ed.) *Poetae Melici
Graeci*: Philip Ayres

Juvenal (Decimus Junius Juvenalis)
(Aquinum; b. A.D. 65/50; d. after
A.D. 127)
Satires 2. 1-35: William Gifford
4. 37-44, 81-98, 105-18: Barten
Holyday
10. 33-55, 114-32, 188-245:
Samuel Johnson
346-66: Robert Lowell
11. 38-55 (expanded): John Cam
Hobhouse

Lucan (Marcus Annaeus Lucanus;
Corduba, Spain; A.D. 39-65;
committed suicide on losing the favour
of the Emperor Nero)
Pharsalia 1. 522-83: Christopher
Marlowe
9. 1-18: Nicholas Rowe

Lucian (Samosata; b. *c.* A.D. 120)
Podagra (The Gout): Gilbert West

Lucretius (T. Lucretius Carus; ?Rome;
?94-?55 B.C.)
De Rerum Natura (On the Nature of
Things)
1. 1-28: Edmund Spenser, Basil
Bunting
1. 62-101: John Evelyn
2. 1ff: Lucy Hutchinson
3. 830-51, 888-943: John Dryden
4. 568-94: Thomas Creech

Manilius, Marcus (fl. A.D. 10-20)
Astronomica 1. 723-65: Sir Edward
Sherburne

Martial (Marcus Valerius Martialis;
Bilbilis, Spain; *c.* A.D. 40-104)
Epigrams 1. 10: Timothe Kendall
32: Thomas Brown
86: William Hay